Get the eBooks FREE!

(PDF, ePub, Kindle, and liveBook all included)

We believe that once you buy a book from us, you should be able to read it in any format we have available. To get electronic versions of this book at no additional cost to you, purchase and then register this book at the Manning website.

Go to https://www.manning.com/freebook and follow the instructions to complete your pBook registration.

That's it!
Thanks from Manning!

The Joy of Kotlin

PIERRE-YVES SAUMONT

MANNING
SHELTER ISLAND

Manning Publications Co.
20 Baldwin Road
PO Box 761
Shelter Island, NY 11964

Development editor:	Marina Michaels and Kristen Waterson
Technical development editor:	Riccardo Terrell, Joshua White, and Joel Kotarski
Review editor:	Aleks Dragosavljević
Production editor:	Deirdre Hiam
Copy editor:	Frances Buran
Proofreader:	Keri Hales
Technical proofreader:	Alessandro Campeis
Typesetter:	Happenstance Type-O-Rama
Cover designer:	Marija Tudor

ISBN 9781617295362
Printed in the United States of America
1 2 3 4 5 6 7 8 9 10 – SP – 24 23 22 21 20 19

contents

preface

Although Kotlin appeared in 2011, it's one of the newest languages in the Java ecosystem. Since then, a version of Kotlin running on the JavaScript virtual machine as been released, as well as a version compiling to native code. This makes Kotlin a much more universal language than Java, although there are great differences between these versions because the Java version relies upon the Java standard library, which isn't available in the two others. JetBrains, the creator or Kotlin, is working hard to bring each version to an equivalent level, but this will take some time.

The JVM (Java Virtual Machine) version is by far the most used version, and this has seen a great boost when Google decided to adopt Kotlin as an official language for developing Android applications. One of the primary reasons for Google's adoption was that the version of Java available under Android is Java 6, whereas Kotlin offers most of the features of Java 11 and much more. Kotlin was also adopted by Gradle as the official language for writing build scripts to replace Groovy, which allows using the same language for the build and for what is built.

Kotlin is primarily targeted at Java programmers. There might come a time when programmers will learn Kotlin as their primary language. But for now, most programmers will only be transitioning from Java to Kotlin.

Each language has its own way, determined by some fundamental concepts. Java was created with several strong concepts in mind. It's supposed to run everywhere, meaning in any environment for which a JVM is available. The promise was, "Write once, run anywhere." Although some may argue otherwise, this promise was fulfilled. Not only can you run Java programs nearly everywhere, but you can also run programs written in other languages and compiled for the JVM. Kotlin is one of those languages.

Another of Java's promises was that no evolution would ever break existing code. Although this hasn't always been true, it has most often been respected. But this might not be a good thing. The main consequence is that many improvements in other languages couldn't be brought into Java because those improvements would have destroyed compatibility. Any program compiled with a previous version of Java must be able to run in the newer versions without being recompiled. Whether this is useful or not is a matter of opinion, but the result is that backward compatibility has constantly played against Java's evolution.

Java was also supposed to make programs safer by using checked exceptions, thus forcing programmers to take these exceptions into consideration. For many programmers, this has proven to be a burden, leading to the practice of constantly wrapping checked exceptions into unchecked ones.

Although Java is an object-oriented language, it's supposed to be as fast as most languages for crunching numbers. The language designers decided that besides objects representing numbers and Boolean values, Java would benefit from having corresponding non-object primitives, allowing for much faster computations. The consequence was that you couldn't (and still can't) put primitives into collections such as lists, sets, or maps. And when streams were added, the language designers decided to create specific versions for primitives—but not all primitives, only those most commonly used. If you're using some of the unsupported primitives, you're out of luck.

The same thing happened with functions. Generic functions were added to Java 8, but they only allowed manipulating objects, not primitives. So specialized functions were designed to handle integers, longs, doubles, and Booleans. (Again, unfortunately, not all primitives. There are no functions for byte, short, and float primitive types.) To make things even worse, additional functions were needed to convert from one primitive type to another or from primitives to objects and back.

Java was designed more than 20 years ago. Many things have changed since that time, but most of those changes couldn't be brought into Java. That's because it would have broken compatibility, or they were brought into Java in such a way that compatibility was preserved at the expense of usability.

Many new languages, such as Groovy, Scala, and Clojure, have since been released to address these limitations. These languages are compatible with Java to a certain extent, meaning that you can use existing Java libraries in projects written in these languages, and Java programmers can use libraries developed in these languages.

Kotlin is different. Kotlin is much more strongly integrated with Java, to the point that you can mix Kotlin and Java source code in the same project without any difficulties! Unlike other JVM languages, Kotlin doesn't look like a different language (although it's somewhat different). Instead, it looks like what Java should have become. Some even say that Kotlin is Java made right, meaning that it fixes most of the problems with the Java language. (Kotlin has yet to deal with the limitations of the JVM, however.)

But more importantly, Kotlin was designed to be much friendlier towards many techniques coming from functional programming. Kotlin has both mutable and immutable references, but it heavily promotes immutable ones. Kotlin also has a great part of the functional abstractions that let you avoid control structures (although it also has traditional control structures in order to smooth the transition from traditional languages).

Another great benefit of using Kotlin is that it reduces the need for boilerplate code, allowing for the bare minimum. With Kotlin, you can create a class with optional properties (plus equals, hashCode, toString, and copy functions) in a single line of code, where the same class written in Java would need about thirty lines (including getters, setters, and overloaded constructors).

Although other languages exist that were designed to overcome Java's limitations in the JVM environment, Kotlin is different because it integrates with Java programs at the project source level. You can mix Java and Kotlin source files in the same projects with a single build chain. This is a game changer, especially regarding team programming, where using Kotlin in a Java environment is no more a hassle than using any third-party library. This makes for the smoothest possible transition from Java to a new language, and that makes it possible for you to write programs that are:

- Safer
- Easier to write, test, and maintain
- More scalable

I suspect that many readers will be Java programmers looking for new solutions to their day-to-day problems. If this is you, you may be asking why you should use Kotlin. Aren't there already other languages in the Java ecosystem with which you can easily apply safe programming techniques?

Sure there are, and one of the most well-known is Scala. Scala is a very good alternative to Java, but Kotlin has something more. Scala can interact with Java at the library level, meaning that Java programs can use Scala libraries (objects and functions) and Scala libraries can use Java libraries (objects and methods). But Scala and Java programs have to be built as separate projects, or at least separate modules, whereas Kotlin and Java classes can be mixed inside the same module.

Read on to find out more about Kotlin.

acknowledgments

I would like to thank the many people who participated in making this book possible. First, a big thank you to my developmental editor, Marina Michaels. Besides your wonderful work on the manuscript, it's been a real pleasure to work with you. Also thank you to my review editor, Aleksandar Dragosavljević.

A big thank you, too, to Joel Kotarski, Joshua White, and Riccardo Terrell, my technical editors, and to Alessandro Campeis and Brent Watson, my technical proofreaders, all of whom helped me make this book much better than I could have done alone. To all the reviewers, MEAP readers, and everyone else who provided feedback and comments, thank you! This book would not be what it is today without your help. Specifically, I'd like to thank the following people who all took the time to review and comment on the book: Aleksei Slaikovskii, Alessandro Campeis, Andy Kirsch, Benjamin Goldberg, Bridger Howell, Conor Redmond, Dylan McNamee, Emmanuel Medina López, Fabio Falci Rodrigues, Federico Kircheis, Gergő Mihály Nagy, Gregor Raýman, Jason Lee, Jean-François Morin, Kent R. Spillner, Leanne Northrop, Mark Elston, Matthew Halverson, Matthew Proctor, Nuno Alexandre, Raffaella Ventaglio, Ronald Haring, Shiloh Morris, Vincent Theron, and William E. Wheeler.

I would also like to thank the staff at Manning: Deirdre Hiam, Frances Buran, Keri Hales, David Novak, Melody Dolab, and Nichole Beard.

about this book

Who should read this book

The goal of this book isn't simply to help you learn the Kotlin language, but also to teach you how you can write much safer programs using Kotlin. This doesn't mean that you should only use Kotlin if you want to write safer programs and, even less, that only Kotlin allows writing safer programs. This book uses Kotlin for all examples because Kotlin is one of the friendliest languages for writing safe programs in the JVM (Java Virtual Machine) ecosystem.

This book teaches techniques that were developed long ago in many different environments, although many of those come from functional programming. But this book isn't about fundamentalist functional programming. This book is about pragmatic safe programming.

All the techniques described have been put in production in the Java ecosystem for years and have proven to be effective in producing programs with much fewer implementation bugs than traditional imperative programming techniques. These safe techniques can be implemented in any language, and they've been used by some for many years in Java. But often, using these techniques has been accomplished through struggling to overcome Java limitations.

This book isn't about learning programming from level zero. It's aimed at programmers in professional environments who are looking for an easier and safer way to write bug-free programs.

What you'll learn

In this book, you'll learn specific techniques that might differ from what you've learned if you're a Java programmer. Most of these techniques will sound unfamiliar or will even contradict what programmers usually recognize as best practices. But many (though not all) best practices are from the days when computers had 640K of memory, 5 MB of disk storage, and a single-core processor. Things have changed. Nowadays, a simple smartphone is a computer with 3 GB or more RAM, 256 GB of solid-state disk storage, and an 8-core processor; likewise, computers have many gigabytes of memory, terabytes of storage, and multi-core processors.

The techniques I cover in this book include:

- Pushing abstraction further
- Favoring immutability
- Understanding referential transparency
- Encapsulating state mutation sharing
- Abstracting control flow and control structures
- Using the right types
- Working with laziness
- And more

Pushing abstraction further

One of the most important techniques you'll learn about is pushing abstraction much further (although traditional programmers consider premature abstraction to be as evil as premature optimization). But pushing abstraction further results in a much better understanding of the problem to solve, which, in turn, results in more often solving the right problem instead of a different one.

You might wonder what pushing abstraction further really means. Simply, it means recognizing common patterns in different computations and abstracting these patterns in order to avoid rewriting them again and again.

Immutability

Immutability is a technique that consists in using only non-modifiable data. Many traditional programmers have trouble imagining how it can be possible to write useful programs using only immutable data. Isn't programming primarily based upon modifying data? Well, this is like believing that accounting is primarily modifying values in an accounting book.

The transition from mutable to immutable accounting was made in the 15th century, and the principle of immutability has been recognized since then as the main element of safety for accounting. This principle also applies to programming, as you'll see in this book.

Referential transparency

Referential transparency is a technique that lets you write *deterministic* programs, meaning programs whose results you can predict and reason about. These programs always produce the same results when given the same input. This doesn't mean that they always produce the same results, but that variations in results only depend on variations in input and not on external conditions.

Not only are such programs safer (because you always know how they'll behave), but they're much easier to compose, to maintain, to update, and to test. And programs that are easier to test are generally tested better and, hence, are more reliable.

Encapsulated state mutation sharing

Immutable data is automatically protected against accidental sharing of state mutation, which causes many problems in concurrent and parallel processing, such as deadlock, livelock, thread starvation, and stale data. But making state mutation sharing impossible, because there's no state mutation, is a problem when state must be shared. This is the case in concurrent and parallel programming.

By removing state mutation, you make accidental sharing of state mutation impossible, so programs are safer. But parallel and concurrent programming implies sharing state mutation. Otherwise, there wouldn't be any cooperation between parallel or concurrent threads. This specific use case of shared state mutation can be abstracted and encapsulated so that it can be reused without risk because the single implementation will have been fully tested instead of reimplementing it each time it's used, as is the case in traditional programming.

In this book, you'll learn how to abstract and encapsulate state mutation sharing so that you'll only have to write it once. Then you can reuse it everywhere you need it.

Abstracting control flow and control structures

The second common source of bugs in programs, after sharing mutable state, is control structures. Traditional programs are composed of control structures such as loops and conditional testing. It's so easy to mess with these structures that language designers have tried to abstract the details as much as possible. One of the best examples is the for each loop that's now present in most languages (although in Java it's still simply called for).

Another common problem is the correct use of while and do while (or repeat until), and particularly determining where to test the condition. An additional problem is concurrent modification while looping on collections, where you encounter the problem of sharing mutable state although you're using a single thread! Abstracting control structures makes it possible to completely eliminate these kinds of problems.

Using the right types

In traditional programming, general types such as int and String are used to represent quantities without taking units into account. As a consequence, it's very easy to mess with these types, adding miles to gallons or dollars to minutes. Using value types can completely eliminate this kind of problem at a very low cost, even if the language you're using doesn't offer true value types.

Laziness

Most of the common languages are said to be *strict*, meaning that arguments passed to a method or function are evaluated first before being processed. This seems to make sense, although it often doesn't. On the contrary, laziness is a technique consisting in evaluating elements only if and when those are used. Programming is essentially based upon laziness.

For example, in an `if...else` structure, the condition is strictly evaluated, meaning that it's evaluated before being tested, but the branches are lazily evaluated, meaning that only the branch corresponding to the condition is executed. This laziness is totally implicit and the programmer doesn't control it. Making explicit use of laziness will help you write much more efficient programs.

Audience

This book is for readers with some previous programming experience in Java. Some understanding of parameterized types (generics) is also assumed. This book makes heavy use of such techniques, including parameterized function calls, or variance, which aren't often used in Java (although it's a powerful technique). Don't be afraid if you don't know these techniques already; I'll explain what they mean and why they're needed.

How this book is organized: A roadmap

This book is intended to be read sequentially because each chapter builds upon the concepts learned in the previous ones. I use the word *read*, but this book isn't intended to just be read. Very few sections contain theory only.

To get the most out of this book, read it at your computer, solving each exercise as you go. Each chapter includes a number of exercises with the necessary instructions and hints to help you arrive at the solution. Each exercise comes with a proposed solution and test that you can use to verify that your solution is correct.

> **NOTE** All the code is available as a separate free download from GitHub (http://github.com/pysaumont/fpinkotlin). The code comes with all the necessary elements for the project to be imported into IntelliJ (recommended) or to be compiled and run using Gradle 4. If you use Gradle, you can edit the code with any text editor. Kotlin is supposed to be usable with Eclipse, but I can't guarantee this. IntelliJ is a far superior IDE and is downloadable for free from the Jetbrains site (https://www.jetbrains.com/idea/download).

Completing the exercises

The exercises are essential to your learning and to understanding what this book teaches. Please note that you're not expected to understand most of the concepts presented in this book just by reading the text. Doing the exercises is probably the most important part of the learning process, so I encourage you not to skip any exercises.

Some exercises may seem quite difficult, and you might be tempted to look at the proposed solutions. It's perfectly okay to do so, but you should then go back to the exercise and do it without looking at the solution. If you only read the solution, you'll probably have trouble later trying to solve more advanced exercises.

This approach doesn't require much tedious typing because you've nearly nothing to copy. Most exercises consist in writing implementations for functions, for which you're given the environment and the function signature. No exercise solution is longer than a dozen lines of code; the majority are around four or five lines long. Once you finish an exercise (which means when your implementation compiles), just run the corresponding test to verify that it's correct.

One important thing to note is that each exercise is self-contained in regards to the rest of the chapter, so code created inside a chapter is duplicated from one exercise to the next. This is necessary because each exercise is often built upon the preceding one, so although the same class might be used, implementations differ. As a consequence, you shouldn't look at a later exercise before you complete the previous ones because you'd see the solutions to yet unsolved exercises.

Learning the techniques in this book

The techniques described in this book aren't more difficult to master than traditional ones. They are just different. You can solve the same problems with traditional techniques, but translating from one technique to the other can sometimes be inefficient.

Learning new techniques is like learning a foreign language. Just as you can't efficiently think in one language and translate to another, you can't think in traditional programming based upon state mutation and control flow and translate your code to functions handling immutable data. And, just as you have to learn to think in a new language, you have to learn to think differently. This doesn't come with reading alone; it comes with writing code. So you have to practice!

This is why I don't expect you to understand what's in this book just by reading it, and why I provide so many exercises; you *must* do the exercises to fully grasp the concepts. This isn't because each topic is so complex that it isn't possible to understand it through reading alone. If you could understand it just by reading without doing the exercises, you probably wouldn't need this book.

For all these reasons, the exercises are key to getting the most out of this book. I encourage you to try solving each exercise before you continue reading. If you don't find a solution, try again rather than going directly to the solution I provide.

If you've a hard time understanding something, ask questions on the forum (see the next section). Asking questions and getting answers on the forum will not only help you, it'll also help the person answering the question (along with others who have the same question). We all learn by answering questions (mostly our own questions, by the way) much more than by asking them.

About the code

This book contains many examples of source code both in numbered listings and in line with normal text. In both cases, source code is formatted in a `fixed-width font like this` to separate it from ordinary text.

In many cases, the original source code has been reformatted; we've added line breaks and reworked indentation to accommodate the available page space in the book. Code annotations accompany many of the listings, highlighting important concepts.

You can download the code as an archive, or you can clone it using Git. The code for the exercises is organized in modules with names that reflect the chapter titles rather than the chapter numbers. As a result, IntelliJ will sort them alphabetically rather than in the order in which they appear in the book.

To help you figure out which module corresponds to each chapter, I've provided a list of the chapters with the corresponding module names in the README file accompanying the code (http://github.com/pysaumont/fpinkotlin).

The source code for all listings in this book is also available for download from the Manning website at https://www.manning.com/books/the-joy-of-kotlin.

Book forum

Purchase of *The Joy of Kotlin* includes free access to a private web forum run by Manning Publications where you can make comments about the book, ask technical questions, and receive help from the author and from other users. To access the forum, go to https://forums.manning.com/forums/the-joy-of-kotlin. You can also learn more about Manning's forums and the rules of conduct at https://forums.manning.com/forums/about.

Manning's commitment to our readers is to provide a venue where a meaningful dialogue between individual readers and between readers and the author can take place. It is not a commitment to any specific amount of participation on the part of the author, whose contribution to the forum remains voluntary (and unpaid). We suggest you try asking the author some challenging questions lest his interest stray! The forum and the archives of previous discussions will be accessible from the publisher's website as long as the book is in print.

about the author

Pierre-Yves Saumont is a seasoned Java developer with three decades of experience designing and building enterprise software. He is an R&D engineer at ASN (Alcatel Submarine Networks).

about the cover illustration

The figure on the cover of *The Joy of Kotlin* is captioned "**Habit of a Lady in Chinese Tartary, 1700.**" The illustration is taken from Thomas Jefferys' *A Collection of the Dresses of Different Nations, Ancient and Modern* (four volumes), London, published between 1757 and 1772. The title page states that these are hand-colored copperplate engravings, heightened with gum arabic.

Thomas Jefferys (1719–1771) was called "Geographer to King George III." He was an English cartographer who was the leading map supplier of his day. He engraved and printed maps for government and other official bodies and produced a wide range of commercial maps and atlases, especially of North America. His work as a mapmaker sparked an interest in local dress customs of the lands he surveyed and mapped, which are brilliantly displayed in this collection. Fascination with faraway lands and travel for pleasure were relatively new phenomena in the late 18th century, and collections such as this one were popular, introducing both the tourist as well as the armchair traveler to the inhabitants of other countries.

The diversity of the drawings in Jefferys' volumes speaks vividly of the uniqueness and individuality of the world's nations some 200 years ago. Dress codes have changed since then, and the diversity by region and country, so rich at the time, has faded away. It's now often hard to tell the inhabitants of one continent from another. Perhaps, trying to view it optimistically, we've traded a cultural and visual diversity for a more varied personal life—or a more varied and interesting intellectual and technical life.

At a time when it's difficult to tell one computer book from another, Manning celebrates the inventiveness and initiative of the computer business with book covers based on the rich diversity of regional life of two centuries ago, brought back to life by Jeffreys' pictures.

Making programs safer

Programming is a dangerous activity. If you're a hobbyist programmer, you may be surprised to read this. You probably thought you were safe sitting in front of your screen and keyboard. You might think that you don't risk much more than some back pain from sitting too long, some vision problems from reading tiny characters onscreen, or even some wrist tendonitis if you happen to type too furiously. But if you're (or want to be) a professional programmer, the reality is much worse than this.

The main danger is the bugs that are lurking in your programs. Bugs can cost a lot if they manifest at the wrong time. Remember the Y2K bug? Many programs written between 1960 and 1990 used only two digits to represent the year in dates because the programmers didn't expect their programs would last until the next century. Many of these programs that were still in use in the 1990s would have handled the year 2000 as 1900. The estimated cost of that bug, actualized in 2017 US dollars, was $417 billion.[1]

But for bugs occurring in a single program, the cost can be much higher. On June 4, 1996, the first flight of the French Ariane 5 rocket ended after 36 seconds with a crash. It appears that the crash was due to a single bug in the navigation system. A single integer arithmetic overflow caused a $370 million loss.[2]

How would you feel if you were held responsible for such a disaster? How would you feel if you were writing this kind of program on a day-to-day basis, never sure that a program working today will still be working tomorrow? This is what most programmers do: write undeterministic programs that don't produce the same result each time they are run with the same input data. Users are aware of this, and when a program doesn't work as expected, they try again, as if the same cause could produce a different effect the next time. And it sometimes does because nobody knows what these programs depend on for their output.

With the development of artificial intelligence (AI), the problem of software reliability becomes more crucial. If programs are meant to make decisions that can jeopardize human life, such as flying planes or driving autonomous cars, we'd better be sure they work as intended.

What do we need to make safer programs? Some will answer that we need better programmers. But good programmers are like good drivers. Of the programmers, 90% agree that only 10% of all programmers are good enough, but at the same time, 90% of the programmers think they are part of the 10%!

The most needed quality for programmers is to acknowledge their own limitations. Let's face it: we are only, at best, average programmers. We spend 20% of our time writing buggy programs, and then we spend 40% of our time refactoring our code to obtain programs with no apparent bugs. And later, we spend another 40% debugging code that's already in production because bugs come in two categories: apparent and non-apparent. Rest assured, non-apparent bugs will become apparent—it's just a matter of time. The question remains: how long and how much damage will be done before the bugs become apparent.

What can we do about this problem? No programming tool, technique, or discipline will ever guarantee that our programs are completely bug-free. But many programming practices exist that can eliminate some categories of bugs and guarantee that the remaining bugs only appear in isolated (unsafe) areas of our programs. This makes a

---

[1]   Federal Reserve Bank of Minneapolis Community Development Project. "Consumer Price Index (estimate) 1800–" https://www.minneapolisfed.org/community/teaching-aids/cpi-calculator-information/consumer-price-index-1800.

[2]   Rapport de la commission d'enquête Ariane 501 Echec du vol Ariane 501 http://www.astrosurf.com/luxorion/astronautique-accident-ariane-v501.htm.

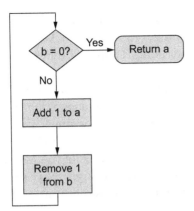

Figure 1.1 **A flow chart representing a program as a process that occurs in time. Various things are transformed and states are mutated until the result is obtained.**

huge difference because it makes bug hunting much easier and more efficient. Among such practices are writing programs that are so simple that they obviously have no bugs, rather than writing programs that are so complex that they have no obvious bugs.[3]

In the rest of this chapter, I briefly present concepts like immutability, referential transparency, and the substitution model, as well as other suggestions, which together you can use to make your programs much safer. You'll apply these concepts over and over in the upcoming chapters.

1.1 Programming traps

Programming is often seen as a way of describing how some process is to be carried out. Such a description generally includes actions that mutate a state in a program's model to solve a problem and decisions about the result of such mutations. This is something everyone understands and practices, even if they aren't programmers.

If you have some complex task to achieve, you divide it into steps. You then execute the first step and examine the result. Following the result of this examination, you continue with the next step or another. For example, a program for adding two positive values a and b might be represented by the following pseudocode:

- if b = 0, return a
- else increment a and decrement b
- start again with the new a and b

In this pseudocode, you can recognize the traditional instructions of most languages: testing conditions, mutating variables, branching, and returning a value. This code can be represented graphically by a flow chart like that shown in figure 1.1.

You can easily see how such a program could go wrong. Change any data on the flowchart, or change the origin or the destination of any arrow, and you get a potentially

---

[3] "...there are two ways of constructing a software design: One way is to make it so simple that there are obviously no deficiencies, and the other way is to make it so complicated that there are no obvious deficiencies. The first method is far more difficult." See C.A.R. Hoare, "The Emperor's Old Clothes," *Communications of the ACM* 24 (February 1981): 75–83.

buggy program. If you're lucky, you could get a program that doesn't run at all, or that runs forever and never stops. This could be considered as good luck because you'd immediately see that there's a problem that needs fixing. Figure 1.2 shows three examples of such problems.

The first example produces an erroneous result, and the second and the third never terminate. Note, however, that your programming language might not allow you to write some of these examples. None of these could be written in a language that doesn't allow mutating references, and none of them could be written in a language that doesn't allow branching or looping. You might think all you have to do is to use such a language. And, in fact, you could. But you'd be restricted to a small number of languages and probably none of them would be allowed in your professional environment.

Is there a solution? Yes, there is. What you can do is to avoid using mutable references, branching (if your language allows it), and looping. All you need to do is to program with discipline.

Don't use dangerous features like mutations and loops. It's as simple as that! And if you do find that you eventually need mutable references or loops, abstract them. Write some component that abstracts state mutation once and for all, and you'll never again have to deal with the problem. (Some more or less exotic languages offer this out of the box, but these too are probably not languages you can use in your environment.) The same applies to looping. In this case, most modern languages offer abstractions of looping alongside a more traditional usage of loops. Again, it's a question of discipline. Only use the good parts! More on this in chapters 4 and 5.

Another common source of bugs is the `null` reference. As you'll see in chapter 6, with Kotlin you can clearly separate code that allows null references from code that forbids these. But ultimately, it's up to you to completely eradicate the use of null references from your programs.

Many bugs are caused by programs depending on the outside world to execute correctly. But depending on the outside world is generally necessary in some way in all

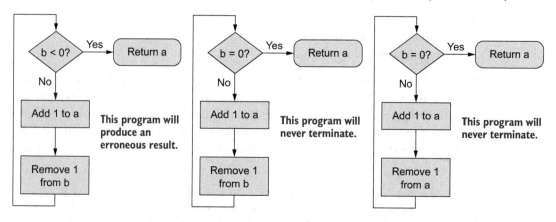

Figure 1.2   Three buggy versions of the same program

programs. Restricting this dependency to specific areas of your programs will make problems easier to spot and deal with, although it won't completely remove the possibility of these types of bugs.

In this book, you'll learn several techniques to make your programs much safer. Here's a list of these practices:

- Avoiding mutable references (variables) and abstracting the single case where mutation can't be avoided.
- Avoiding control structures.
- Restricting effects (interaction with the outside world) to specific areas in your code. This means no printing to the console or to any device, no writing to files, databases, networks, or whatever else that can happen outside of these restricted areas.
- No exception throwing. Throwing exceptions is the modern form of branching (GOTO), which leads to what's called *spaghetti code*, meaning that you know where it starts, but you can't follow where it goes. In chapter 7, you'll learn how to completely avoid throwing exceptions.

1.1.1 Safely handling effects

As I said, the word *effects* means all interactions with the outside world, such as writing to the console, to a file, to a database, or to a network, and also mutating any element outside the component's scope. Programs are generally written in small blocks that have scope. In some languages these blocks are called *procedures;* in others (like Java), they're called *methods.* In Kotlin they're called *functions,* although this doesn't have the same meaning as the mathematical concept of a function.

Kotlin functions are basically methods, as in Java and many other modern languages. These blocks of code have a *scope,* meaning an area of the program that's visible only by those blocks. Blocks not only have visibility of the enclosing scope, but this itself also provides visibility of the outer scopes and, by transitivity, to the outside world. Any mutation of the outside world caused by a function or method (such as mutating the enclosing scope, like the class in which the method is defined) is, therefore, an effect.

Some methods (functions) return a value. Some mutate the outer world, and some do both. When a method or function returns a value and has an effect, this is called a *side effect.* Programming with side effects is wrong in all cases. In medicine, the term "side effects" is primarily used to describe unwanted, adverse secondary outcomes. In programming, a side effect is something that's observable outside of the program and comes *in addition to* the result returned by the program.

If the program doesn't return a result, you can't call its observable effect a side effect; it's the primary effect. It can still have side (secondary) effects, although this is also generally considered bad practice, following what's called the "single responsibility" principle.

Safe programs are built by composing functions that take an argument and return a value, and that's it. We don't care about what's happening *inside* the functions because, in theory, nothing ever happens there. Some languages only offer such effect-free functions: programs written in these languages don't have any observable effects beside returning a value. But this value can, in fact, be a new program that you can run to evaluate the effect. Such a technique can be used in any language, but it's often considered inefficient (which is arguable). A safe alternative is to clearly separate effects evaluation from the rest of the program and even, as much as possible, to abstract effect evaluation. You'll learn many techniques allowing this in chapters 7, 11, and 12.

1.1.2 Making programs safer with referential transparency

Having no side effects (not mutating anything in the external world) isn't enough to make a program safe and deterministic. Programs also mustn't be affected by the external world—the output of a program should depend only on its argument. This means that programs shouldn't read data from the console, a file, a remote URL, a database, or even from the system.

Code that neither mutates nor depends on the external world is said to be *referentially transparent*. Referentially transparent code has several interesting attributes:

- *It's self-contained.* You can use it in any context; all you have to do is to provide a valid argument.
- *It's deterministic.* It always returns the same value for the same argument so you won't be surprised. It might, however, return a wrong result, but at least for the same argument, the result never changes.
- *It will never throw any kind of exception.* It might throw errors, such as out-of-memory errors (OOMEs) or stack-overflow errors (SOEs), but these errors mean that the code has a bug. This isn't a situation either you, as a programmer, or the users of your API are supposed to handle (besides crashing the application, which often won't happen automatically, and eventually fixing the bug).
- *It doesn't create conditions causing other code to unexpectedly fail.* It won't mutate arguments or some other external data, for example, causing the caller to find itself with stale data or concurrent access exceptions.
- *It doesn't depend on any external device to work.* It won't hang because some external device (whether database, filesystem, or network) is unavailable, too slow, or broken.

Figure 1.3 illustrates the difference between a referentially transparent program and one that's not referentially transparent.

1.2 The benefits of safe programming

From what I've described, you can likely guess the many benefits you can expect by using referential transparency:

- *Your programs will be easier to reason about because they'll be deterministic.* A specific input will always give the same output. In many cases, you might be able to prove a program correct rather than to extensively test it and still remain uncertain about whether it'll break under unexpected conditions.

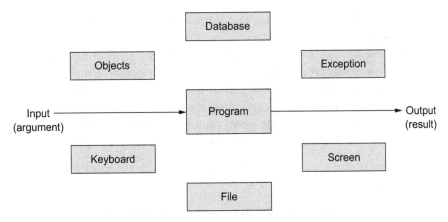

A referentially transparent program doesn't interfere with the outside world apart from taking an argument as input and outputting a result. Its result only depends on its argument.

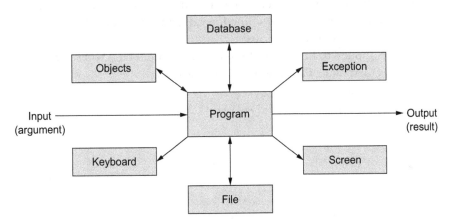

A program that isn't referentially transparent may read data from or write it to elements in the outside world, log to file, mutate external objects, read from keyboard, print to screen, and so on. Its result is unpredictable.

Figure 1.3   Comparing a program that's referentially transparent to one that's not

- *Your programs will be easier to test.* Because there are no side effects, you won't need mocks, which are generally required when testing to isolate program components from the outside.
- *Your programs will be more modular.* That's because they'll be built from functions that only have input and output; there are no side effects to handle, no exceptions to catch, no context mutation to deal with, no shared mutable state, and no concurrent modifications.
- *Composition and recombination of programs is much easier.* To write a program, you start by writing the various base functions you'll need and then combine these functions into higher-level ones, repeating the process until you have a single function corresponding to the program you want to build. And, because all these functions

are referentially transparent, they can then be reused to build other programs without any modifications.

- *Your programs will be inherently thread-safe because they avoid mutation of shared states.* This doesn't mean that all data has to be immutable, only shared data must be. But programmers applying these techniques soon realize that immutable data is always safer, even if the mutation is not visible externally. One reason is that data that's not shared at one point can become shared accidentally after refactoring. Always using immutable data ensures that this kind of problem never happens.

In the rest of this chapter, I'll present some examples of using referential transparency to write safer programs.

1.2.1 *Using the substitution model to reason about programs*

The main benefit from using functions that return a value without any other observable effect is that they're equivalent to their return value. Such a function doesn't do anything. It has a value, which is dependent only on its arguments. As a consequence, it's always possible to replace a function call or any referentially transparent expression with its value, as figure 1.4 shows.

When applied to functions, the substitution model lets you replace any function call with its return value. Consider the following code:

```
fun main(args: Array<String>) {
    val x = add(mult(2, 3), mult(4, 5))
    println(x)
}
fun add(a: Int, b: Int): Int {
    log(String.format("Returning ${a + b} as the result of $a + $b"))
    return a + b
}
fun mult(a: Int, b: Int) = a * b
fun log(m: String) {
    println(m)
}
```

Replacing mult(2, 3) and mult(4, 5) with their respective return values doesn't change the signification of the program. This is shown here:

```
val x = add(6, 20)
```

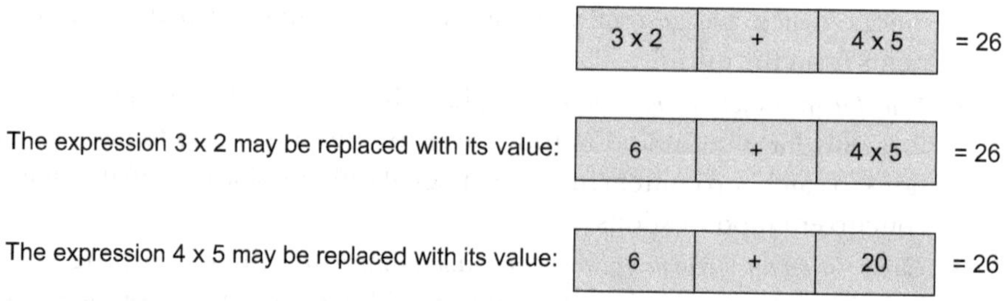

| 3 x 2 | + | 4 x 5 | = 26 |

The expression 3 x 2 may be replaced with its value:

| 6 | + | 4 x 5 | = 26 |

The expression 4 x 5 may be replaced with its value:

| 6 | + | 20 | = 26 |

Figure 1.4   Replacing referentially transparent expressions with their values doesn't change the overall meaning.

In contrast, replacing the call to the add function with its return value changes the signification of the program, because the call to log will no longer be made, so no logging takes place. This may or may not be important; in any case, it changes the outcome of the program.

1.2.2 Applying safe principles to a simple example

To convert an unsafe program into a safer one, let's consider a simple example representing the purchase of a donut with a credit card.

Listing 1.1   A Kotlin program with side effects

```
fun buyDonut(creditCard: CreditCard): Donut {
    val donut = Donut()
    creditCard.charge(donut.price)        ◀──── Charges the credit card as a side effect
    return donut    ◀──────
}                                        Returns the donut
```

In this code, charging the credit card is a side effect. Charging a credit card probably consists of calling the bank, verifying that the credit card is valid and authorized, and registering the transaction. The function returns the donut.

The problem with this kind of code is that it's difficult to test. Running the program for testing would involve contacting the bank and registering the transaction using some sort of mock account. Or you'd need to create a mock credit card to register the effect of calling the charge function and to verify the state of the mock after the test.

If you want to be able to test your program without contacting the bank or using a mock, you should remove the side effect. But because you still want to charge the credit card, the only solution is to add a representation of this operation to the return value. Your buyDonut function will have to return both the donut and this representation of the payment. To represent the payment, you can use a Payment class, as shown in the following listing.

Listing 1.2   The Payment class

```
class Payment(val creditCard: CreditCard, val amount: Int)
```

This class contains the necessary data to represent the payment, which consists of a credit card and the amount to charge. Because the buyDonut function must return both a Donut and a Payment, you could create a specific class for this, such as Purchase.

```
class Purchase(val donut: Donut, val payment: Payment)
```

You'll often need such a class to hold two (or more) values of different types because, to make programs safer, you have to replace side effects with returning a representation of these effects.

Rather than creating a specific Purchase class, you can use a generic one, Pair. This class is parameterized by the two types it contains (in this case, Donut and Payment). Kotlin provides this class, as well as Triple, which allows the representation of three values. Such a class would be useful in a language like Java because defining the Purchase class would imply writing a constructor, getters, and probably `equals` and `hashcode` methods, as well as `toString`. That's much less useful in Kotlin because the same result can be obtained with a single line of code:

```
data class Purchase(val donut: Donut, val payment: Payment)
```

The `Purchase` class already doesn't need an explicit constructor and getters. By adding the `data` keyword in front of the class definition, Kotlin additionally provides implementations of `equals`, `hashCode`, `toString`, and `copy`. But you must accept the default implementations. Two instances of a data class will be equal if all properties are equal. If this isn't what you need, you can override any of these functions with your own implementations.

```
fun buyDonut(creditCard: CreditCard): Purchase {
    val donut = Donut()
    val payment = Payment(creditCard, Donut.price)
    return Purchase(donut, payment)
}
```

You're no longer concerned at this stage with how the credit card will be charged. This adds some freedom to the way you build your application. You could process the payment immediately, or you could store it for later processing. You can even combine stored payments for the same card and process them in a single operation. This would save you some money by minimizing the bank fees for the credit card service.

The `combine` function in listing 1.3 is used to combine payments. If the credit cards don't match, an exception is thrown. This doesn't contradict what I said about safe programs not throwing exceptions. Here, trying to combine two payments with two different credit cards is considered a bug, so it should crash the application. (This isn't realistic. You'll have to wait until chapter 7 to learn how to deal with such situations without throwing exceptions.)

Listing 1.3 Composing multiple payments into a single one

```
package com.fpinkotlin.introduction.listing03
class Payment(val creditCard: CreditCard, val amount: Int) {
    fun combine(payment: Payment): Payment =
        if (creditCard == payment.creditCard)
            Payment(creditCard, amount + payment.amount)
        else
            throw IllegalStateException("Cards don't match.")
}
```

In this scenario, the `combine` function wouldn't be efficient when buying several donuts at once. For this you could replace the `buyDonut` function with `buyDonuts(n: Int, creditCard: CreditCard)` as shown in the following listing, but you need to define a new `Purchase` class. Alternatively, if you had chosen to use a `Pair<Donut, Payment>`, you'd have to replace it with `Pair<List<Donut>, Payment>`.

Listing 1.4 Buying multiple donuts at once

```
package com.fpinkotlin.introduction.listing05
data class Purchase(val donuts: List<Donut>, val payment: Payment)
fun buyDonuts(quantity: Int = 1, creditCard: CreditCard): Purchase =
        Purchase(List(quantity) {
            Donut()
        }, Payment(creditCard, Donut.price * quantity))
```

Here `List(quantity) { Donut() }` creates a list of quantity elements successively applying the function `{ Donut() }` to values 0 to quantity - 1. The `{ Donut() }` function is equivalent to

```
{ index -> Donut{} }
```

or

```
{ _ -> Donut{} }
```

When there's a single parameter, you can omit the `parameter ->` part and use the parameter as `it`. Because it's not used, the code is reduced to `{ Donut() }`. If this isn't clear, don't worry: I'll cover this more in the next chapter

Also note that the `quantity` parameter receives a default value of 1. This lets you call the buyDonuts function with the following syntax without specifying the quantity:

```
buyDonuts(creditCard = cc)
```

In Java, you'd have to overload the method with a second implementation, such as

```
public static Purchase buyDonuts(CreditCard creditCard) {
    return buyDonuts(1, creditCard);
}
public static Purchase buyDonuts(int quantity,
                                 CreditCard creditCard) {
    return new Purchase(Collections.nCopies(quantity, new Donut()),
                        new Payment(creditCard, Donut.price * quantity));
}
```

Now you can test your program without using a mock. For example, here's a test for the method buyDonuts:

```
import org.junit.Assert.assertEquals
import org.junit.Test
class DonutShopKtTest {
    @Test
    fun testBuyDonuts() {
        val creditCard = CreditCard()
        val purchase = buyDonuts(5, creditCard)
        assertEquals(Donut.price * 5, purchase.payment.amount)
        assertEquals(creditCard, purchase.payment.creditCard)
    }
}
```

Another benefit of having refactored your code is that your program is more easily composable. If the same person makes several purchases with your initial program, you'd have to contact the bank (and pay the corresponding fee) each time the person bought something. With the new version, however, you can choose to charge the card immediately for each purchase or to group all payments made with the same card and charge it only once for the total. To group payments, you'll need to use additional functions from the Kotlin `List` class:

- `groupBy(f: (A) -> B): Map<B, List<A>>`—Takes as its parameter a function from A to B and returns a map of keys and value pairs, with keys being of type B and values of type `List<A>`. You'll use it to group payments by credit cards.
- `values: List<A>`—An instance function of `Map` that returns a list of all the values in the map.
- `map(f: (A) -> B): List<B>`—An instance function of `List` that takes a function from A to B and applies it to all elements of a list of A, returning a list of B.
- `reduce(f: (A, A) -> A): A`—A function of `List` that uses an operation (represented by a function `f: (A, A) -> A`) to reduce the list to a single value. The operation could be, for example, addition. In such a case, it would mean a function such as `f(a, b) = a + b`.

Using these functions, you can now create a new function that groups payments by credit card, as shown in the next listing.

Listing 1.5 Grouping payments by credit card

Changes List<Payment> into a Map<CreditCard, List<Payment>>, where each list contains all payments for a particular credit card

```
package com.fpinkotlin.introduction.listing05;
class Payment(val creditCard: CreditCard, val amount: Int) {
    fun combine(payment: Payment): Payment =
        if (creditCard == payment.creditCard)
            Payment(creditCard, amount + payment.amount)
        else
            throw IllegalStateException("Cards don't match.")
    companion object {
        fun groupByCard(payments: List<Payment>): List<Payment> =
            payments.groupBy { it.creditCard }
                .values
                .map { it.reduce(Payment::combine) }
    }
}
```

Changes the Map<CreditCard, List<Payment>> into a List<List<Payment>>

Reduces each List<Payment> into a single Payment, leading to the overall result of a List<Payment>

Note the use of a function reference in the last line of the `groupByCard` function. Function references are similar to method references in Java. If this example isn't clear, well, that's what this book is for! When you reach the end, you'll be an expert in composing such code.

1.2.3 *Pushing abstraction to the limit*

As you've seen, you can write safer programs that are easier to test by composing *pure functions*, which mean functions without side effects. You can declare these functions using the fun keyword or as value functions, such as the arguments of methods groupBy, map, or reduce in the previous listing. *Value functions* are functions represented in such a way that, unlike fun functions, they can be manipulated by the program. In most cases, you can use these as arguments to other functions or as values returned by other functions. You'll learn how this is done in the following chapters.

But the most important concept here is *abstraction*. Look at the reduce function. It takes as its argument an operation, and uses that operation to reduce a list to a single value. Here the operation has two operands of the same type. Except for this, it could be any operation.

Consider a list of integers. You could write a sum function to compute the sum of the elements. Then you could write a product function to compute the product of the elements or a min or a max function to compute the minimum or the maximum of the list. Alternatively, you could also use the reduce function for all these computations. This is abstraction. You abstract the part that's common to all operations in the reduce function, and you pass the variable part (the operation) as an argument.

You could go further. The reduce function is a particular case of a more general function that might produce a result of a different type than the elements of the list. For example, it could be applied to a list of characters to produce a String. You'd need to start from a given value (probably an empty string). In chapters 3 and 5, you'll learn how to use this function, called fold.

The reduce function won't work on an empty list. Think of a list of integers—if you want to compute the sum, you need to have an element to start with. If the list is empty, what should you return? You know that the result should be 0, but this only works for a sum. It won't work for a product.

Also consider the groupByCard function. It looks like a business function that can only be used to group payments by credit cards. But it's not! You could use this function to group the elements of any list by any of their properties. This function then should be abstracted and put inside the List class in such a way that it could be reused easily. (It's defined in the Kotlin List class.)

Pushing abstraction to the limits allows making programs safer because the abstracted part will only be written once. As a consequence, once it's fully tested, there'll be no risk of producing new bugs by reimplementing it.

In the rest of this book, you'll learn how to abstract many things so you'll only have to define them once. You will, for example, learn how to abstract loops so you won't ever need to write loops again. And you'll learn how to abstract parallelization in a way that'll let you switch from serial to parallel processing by selecting a function in the List class.

Summary

- You can make programs safer by clearly separating functions, which return values, from effects, which interact with the outside world.
- Functions are easier to reason about and to test because their outcome is deterministic and doesn't depend on an external state.
- Pushing abstraction to a higher level improves safety, maintainability, testability, and reusability.
- Applying safe principles like immutability and referential transparency protects programs against accidental sharing of a mutable state, which is a huge source of bugs in multithreaded environments.

Functional programming in Kotlin: An overview

In this chapter, I provide a quick overview of the Kotlin language. I assume that you know a bit (at least) of Java, so I stress the differences between the two languages. The intent is not to teach you Kotlin. You'll find other books for this. If you need an in-depth coverage of Kotlin, I recommend you read Dmitry Jemerov and Svetlana Isakova's *Kotlin in Action* (Manning, 2017).

This chapter gives you a first glimpse of what to expect from Kotlin. Don't try to remember everything. Look at some of the astounding features of the Kotlin language and see how it differs from Java. In the following chapters, I come back to each feature, used in a safe programming context. In the rest of this chapter, I give you an overview of the most important benefits of using Kotlin. This presentation is certainly not exhaustive, and you'll discover additional benefits in the rest of the book.

2.1 Fields and variables in Kotlin

In Kotlin, fields are declared and initialized using the following syntax:

```
val name: String = "Mickey"
```

Note the differences with Java:

- The val keyword comes first and means that the name reference is immutable (corresponding to final in Java).
- The type (String) comes after the name, separated by a colon (:).
- There's no semicolon (;) at the end of the line. You can use semicolons, but they're not mandatory because the end of the line has the same meaning. You would use semicolons only when you want to put several instructions on the same line, which isn't a recommended practice.

2.1.1 Omitting the type to simplify

The previous example can be simplified as:

```
val name = "Mickey"
```

Here, Kotlin guesses the type by looking forward to the value used to initialize the field. This is called *type inference,* and it lets you omit the type in numerous cases. But there are places where type inference won't work, such as when the type is ambiguous or the field isn't initialized. In these cases, you must specify the type.

It's generally wise, however, to specify the type. By doing so, you can check that the type inferred by Kotlin is the type you expect. Believe me, that won't always be the case!

2.1.2 Using mutable fields

I said at the start of section 2.1 that val means that the reference is immutable. Does this mean that all references are always immutable? No, but you should use val as much as possible. The reason is that if a reference can't change, there's no way to mess with it once it's been initialized. For the same reason, you should initialize references as soon as possible. (Although, as you'll see, Kotlin generally prevents using uninitialized references. This differs from Java, which automatically sets uninitialized references to null and lets you use them.)

To use a mutable reference, you need to replace val with var, as in this example. This allows changing the value later:

```
var name = "Mickey"

...
name = "Donald"
```

Remember, though, you should avoid using var as much as possible because it's easier to reason about a program when you know that references can't change.

2.1.3 Understanding lazy initialization

Sometimes, you'll want to use a var to delay initialization of a reference that doesn't change once initialized. The reasons for delaying initialization varies. One common use case is that initialization is costly, so you don't want it to happen if the value is never used.

The solution is generally to use a var reference and set it to `null` until it's initialized to a meaningful value, which almost always never changes. This is annoying because Kotlin allows you to differentiate between nullable and non-nullable types. Non-nullable types are much safer because there's no risk of a `NullPointerException`. When the value isn't known at declaration time, and will never change after initialization, it would be sad to be forced to use var for such a use case. That would force you to use a nullable type instead of a non-nullable one, for example:

```
var name: String? = null
```

. . .

```
name = getName()
```

Here the reference is of type `String?`, which is nullable, although it could be of type `String`, which isn't. You could use a specific value to represent the uninitialized reference, such as

```
var name: String = "NOT_INITIALIZED_YET"
```

. . .

```
name = getValue()
```

Or, if the name should never be empty, you could use an empty string to denote a non-initialized reference. In any case, you're forced to use a var even if the value never changes after initialization. But Kotlin offers a better solution:

```
val name: String by lazy { getName() }
```

This way, the `getName()` function will be called only once when the name reference is used for the first time. You can also use a function reference instead of a lambda:

```
val name: String by lazy(::getName)
```

Saying when the name reference will be used for the first time means when it'll be de-referenced so that the value it points to can be used. Look at the following example:

```
fun main(args: Array<String>) {

    val name: String by lazy { getName() }
    println("hey1")
    val name2: String by lazy { name }
    println("hey2")

    println(name)
    println(name2)
    println(name)
    println(name2)
}

fun getName(): String {
    println("computing name...")
    return "Mickey"
}
```

Running this program will print

```
hey1
hey2
computing name...
Mickey
Mickey
Mickey
Mickey
```

Lazy initialization can't be used for mutable references. In case you absolutely need a lazy mutable reference, you can use the `lateinit` keyword, which has somewhat the same effect, although without the automatic on-demand initialization:

```
lateinit var name: String
```

```
...
```

```
name = getName()
```

This construction avoids using a nullable type. But it offers absolutely no benefit compared to by `lazy` except when initialization should be done externally, such as when using a dependency injection framework while working with properties. Note that constructor-based dependency injection should always be preferred because it allows using immutable properties. As you'll see in chapter 9, there's much more to learn about laziness.

2.2 *Classes and interfaces in Kotlin*

Classes in Kotlin are created with a somewhat different syntax than those in Java. A class `Person` with a property name of type `String` can be declared in Kotlin as

```
class Person constructor(name: String) {

    val name: String

    init {
        this.name = name
    }
}
```

This is equivalent to the following Java code:

```
public final class Person {

    private final String name;

    public Person(String name) {
        this.name = name;
    }

    public String getName() {
        return name;
    }
}
```

As you can see, the Kotlin version is more compact. Note some particularities:

- A Kotlin class is public by default, so there's no need for the word *public*. To make a class non-public, you can use the private, protected, or internal modifiers. The internal modifier means that the class is accessible only from inside the module where it's defined. There's no Kotlin equivalent for "package private" (corresponding to the absence of a modifier) in Java. Unlike Java, protected is restricted to extending classes and doesn't include classes in the same package.

- A Kotlin class is final by default, so the equivalent Java class would be declared with the final modifier. In Java, most classes should be declared final but programmers often forget to do that. Kotlin solves this problem by making classes final by default. To make a Kotlin class non-final, use the open modifier. This is much safer because classes opened for extension should be specifically designed for this.

- The constructor is declared after the class name, and its implementation is in an init block. This block has access to the constructor parameters.

- Accessors aren't needed. They're generated when you compile the code.

- Unlike Java, public classes need not be defined in a file with the name of the class. You can name the file as you like. Furthermore, you can define several public classes in the same file. But this doesn't mean you should do so. Having each public class in a separate file with the name of the class makes finding things easier.

2.2.1 *Making the code even more concise*

Kotlin code can be further simplified. First, because the init block is a one-liner, it can be combined with the name property declaration like this:

```
class Person constructor(name: String) {

    val name: String = name
}
```

Then you can combine the constructor declaration, the property declaration, and the property initialization like this:

```
class Person constructor(val name: String) {

}
```

Now, because the block is empty, it can be removed. And you can also remove the word *constructor* (whether the block is empty or not):

```
class Person (val name: String)
```

Additionally, you can create several properties for the same class:

```
class Person(val name: String, val registered: Instant)
```

As you can see, Kotlin removes most of the boilerplate code, resulting in concise code that's easier to read. Keep in mind that code is written once but read many times. When code is more readable, it's also easier to maintain.

2.2.2 Implementing an interface or extending a class

If you want your class to implement one or several interfaces, or to extend another class, you'll list those after the class declaration:

```
class Person(val name: String,
             val registered: Instant) : Serializable, Comparable<Person> {
    override fun compareTo(other: Person): Int {
        ...
    }
}
```

Extending a class uses the same syntax. The difference is that the extended class name is followed by the parameter names enclosed in parentheses:

```
class Member(name: String, registered: Instant) : Person(name, registered)
```

Remember, however, that classes are final by default. For this example to compile, the extended class must be declared open, which means *open for extension*:

```
open class Person(val name: String, val registered: Instant)
```

A good programming practice is to allow extension only for classes that have been specifically designed for it. As you can see, Kotlin, unlike Java, tries to enforce this principle by not letting you extend a class if it hasn't been designed for extension.

2.2.3 Instantiating a class

When creating an instance of a class, Kotlin spares you from repetitious typing, although to a lesser extent. For example, instead of writing

```
final Person person = new Person("Bob", Instant.now());
```

you can use the constructor as a function (which it is, indeed):

```
val person = Person("Bob", Instant.now())
```

This makes sense because the Person constructor is a function from the set of all possible pairs of strings and instants to the set of all possible persons. Now let's look at how Kotlin handles overloading those constructors.

2.2.4 Overloading property constructors

Sometimes, a property is optional and has a default value. In the previous example, you could decide that the date of registration defaults to the date of creation of the instance. In Java, you'd have to write two constructors as indicated in the following listing.

> Listing 2.1 A typical Java object with an optional property

```
public final class Person {

    private final String name;

    private final Instant registered;

    public Person(String name, Instant registered) {
```

```
        this.name = name;
        this.registered = registered;
    }

    public Person(String name) {
        this(name, Instant.now());
    }

    public String getName() {
        return name;
    }

    public Instant getRegistered() {
        return registered;
    }
}
```

In Kotlin, you can obtain the same result by indicating the default value after the property name:

```
class Person(val name: String, val registered: Instant = Instant.now())
```

You can also override constructors in a more traditional way:

```
class Person(val name: String, val registered: Instant = Instant.now()) {
    constructor(name: Name) : this(name.toString()) {
        // optional constructor implementation may be added
    }
}
```

As in Java, if you don't declare a constructor, a constructor without arguments is automatically generated.

PRIVATE CONSTRUCTORS AND PROPERTIES

As in Java, you can make constructors private to prevent instantiation by external code:

```
class Person private constructor(val name: String)
```

But, unlike Java, private constructors aren't needed to prevent instantiation of utility classes containing only static members. Kotlin puts static members at the package level, outside of any class.

ACCESSORS AND PROPERTIES

In Java, it's considered bad practice to expose object properties directly. Instead, you make those visible through methods that get and set property values. These methods are conveniently called *getters* and *setters* and referred to as *accessors*. The following example calls a getter for the name of a person:

```
val person = Person("Bob")
...
println(person.name) // Calling the getter
```

Although it looks like you're accessing the name field directly, you're using a generated getter. This has the same name as the field and doesn't need to be followed by parentheses.

You might remark that you can call the `println` method of `System.out` much more easily than in Java. Not that it matters much, because your programs will probably never print to the console, but it's worth noting.

2.2.5 Creating equals and hashCode methods

If the `Person` class represents data, it's likely that you'll need the `hashCode` and `equals` methods. Writing these methods in Java is tedious and error-prone. Fortunately, a good Java IDE (like IntelliJ) generates them for you. The next listing shows what IntelliJ generates if you use this functionality.

Listing 2.2   A Java data object generated by IntelliJ

```java
public final class Person {

    private final String name;

    private final Instant registered;

    public Person(String name, Instant registered) {
        this.name = name;
        this.registered = registered;
    }

    public Person(String name) {
        this(name, Instant.now());
    }

    public String getName() {
        return name;
    }

    public Instant getRegistered() {
        return registered;
    }

    @Override
    public boolean equals(Object o) {
        if (this == o) return true;
        if (o == null || getClass() != o.getClass()) return false;
        Person person = (Person) o;
        return Objects.equals(name, person.name) &&
                Objects.equals(registered, person.registered);
    }

    @Override
    public int hashCode() {
        return Objects.hash(name, registered);
    }
}
```

Having the IDE statically generate this code saves you some tedious typing, but you still have to live with this awful piece of code, which doesn't improve readability. Even worse, you have to maintain it! If you later add a new property that should be part of the hashCode and equals methods, you'll need to remove the two methods and regenerate them. Kotlin makes this much simpler:

```
data class Person(val name: String, val registered: Instant = Instant.now())
```

Yes, it's as simple as adding the word *data* in front of the class definition. The hashCode and equals functions are generated when you compile your code. You'll never see them, although you can use them as regular functions. Furthermore, Kotlin also generates a toString function, displaying a useful (human-readable) result, and a copy function, allowing you to copy an object while duplicating all its properties. Kotlin also generates additional componentN functions, letting you access each property of the class, as you'll see in the following section.

2.2.6 Destructuring data objects

In each data class with n properties, the functions component1 to componentN are automatically defined. This lets you access properties in the order they're defined in the class. The main use of this feature is to *destructure* objects, which provides much simpler access to their properties:

```
data class Person(val name: String, val registered: Instant = Instant.now())

fun show(persons: List<Person>) {
    for ((name, date) in persons)
        println(name + "'s registration date: " + date)
}

fun main(args: Array<String>) {
    val persons = listOf(Person("Mike"), Person("Paul"))
    show(persons)
}
```

The show function is equivalent to

```
fun show(persons: List<Person>) {
    for (person in persons)
        println(person.component1()
            + "'s registration date: " + person.component2())
}
```

As you can see, destructuring makes the code clearer and less verbose by avoiding de-referencing object properties each time those properties are used.

2.2.7 Implementing static members in Kotlin

In Kotlin, classes have no static members. To get the same effect, you'll have to use a special construct called a *companion object*:

```
data class Person(val name: String,
                  val registered: Instant = Instant.now()) {

    companion object {
        fun create(xml: String): Person {
```

```
        TODO("Write an implementation creating " +
            "a Person from an xml string")
    }
  }
}
```

The create function can be called on the enclosing class as you'd do with static methods in Java:

```
Person.create(someXmlString)
```

You can also call it explicitly on the companion object, but this is redundant:

```
Person.Companion.create(someXmlString)
```

On the other hand, if you use this function from Java code, you need to call it on the companion object. To be able to call it on the class, you must annotate the Kotlin function with the @JvmStatic annotation. For more information about calling Kotlin functions from Java code (and the other way round), see appendix A.

Incidentally, you can see that Kotlin offers a TODO function, which makes your code much more consistent. This method throws an exception at runtime, reminding you about the work that should have been done!

2.2.8 Using singletons

It's often necessary to create a single instance of a given class. Such an instance is called a *singleton*. The singleton pattern is a technique used to guarantee that there's possibly only one instance of a class. In Java, it's a controversial pattern because it's difficult to guarantee that only one instance can be created. In Kotlin, a singleton can be easily created by replacing the word *class* with the word *object*:

```
object MyWindowAdapter: WindowAdapter() {
    override fun windowClosed(e: WindowEvent?) {
        TODO("not implemented")
    }
}
```

An object can't have constructors. If it has properties, those must either be initialized or abstract.

2.2.9 Preventing utility class instantiation

In Java, it's common usage to create utility classes that contain only static methods. In such cases, you usually want to forbid class instantiation. The Java solution is to create a private constructor. In Kotlin, this is possible, but useless. That's because, with Kotlin, you can create functions outside of classes at the package level. To do that, create a file with any name and start with a package declaration. You can then define functions without putting them into classes:

```
package com.acme.util

fun create(xml: String): Person {
  ...
}
```

You can call such a function with its full name:

```
val person = com.acme.util.create(someXmlString)
```

Alternatively, you can import the package and use only the function's short name:

```
import com.acme.util.*

val person = create(someXmlString)
```

Because Kotlin runs on the JVM, there must be a way to call package-level functions from Java code. This is described in appendix A.

2.3 Kotlin doesn't have primitives

Kotlin has no primitives, at least not at the programmer level. Instead, it uses Java primitives under the hood to make computation faster. But you, as the programmer, will only be manipulating objects. The object class for integers is different than the object representation of integers in Java. Instead of `Integer`, you'll use the `Int` class. The other numerical and Boolean types have the same names as in Java. Also, as in Java, you can use underscores in numbers:

- Longs have a trailing *L*, and floats a trailing *F*.
- Doubles are distinguished by the use of a decimal dot such as `2.0`, or `.9`.
- Hexadecimal values must be prefixed with *0x*, such as

    ```
    0xBE_24_1C_D3
    ```

- Binary literals are prefixed with *0b*:

    ```
    0b01101101_11001010_10010011_11110100
    ```

The absence of primitives makes programming much simpler, avoiding the need for specific function classes like in Java, and allowing collections of numerical and boolean values without resorting to boxing/unboxing.

2.4 Kotlin's two types of collections

Kotlin collections are backed by Java collections, although Kotlin adds more to them. The most important aspect is that Kotlin has two types of collections: mutable and immutable. Usually, the first practical change you'll experiment with is creating collections using specific functions. This snippet creates an immutable list containing the integers 1, 2, and 3:

```
val list = listOf(1, 2, 3)
```

By default, Kotlin collections are immutable.

> **NOTE** In fact, Kotlin immutable collections aren't really immutable. They're only collections that you can't mutate. As a consequence, some prefer to call them *read-only collections*, which isn't much better because they aren't read-only either. Let's not worry about this. In chapter 5, you'll learn to create *true* immutable collections.

The listOf function is a package-level function, which means that it's not part of a class or an interface. It's defined in the kotlin.collections package so you can import it using the following syntax:

```
import kotlin.collections.listOf
```

You don't have to import it explicitly. All functions from this package are, in fact, implicitly imported as if you were using the following import:

```
import kotlin.collections.*
```

Many other packages are also automatically imported. This mechanism is similar to the automatic import of the java.lang package in Java.

Note that immutable doesn't mean that you can't do any operations with these lists, for example:

```
val list1 = listOf(1, 2, 3)
val list2 = list1 + 4
val list3 = list1 + list2
println(list1)
println(list2)
println(list3)
```

This code creates a list containing integers 1, 2, and 3. Then it creates a new list by adding an element to the first one. Finally, it creates another new list again, concatenating the two existing lists. As the result shows, no one list has been modified:

```
[1, 2, 3] [1, 2, 3, 4] [1, 2, 3, 1, 2, 3, 4]
```

If you need mutable collections, you have to specify them:

```
val list1 = mutableListOf(1, 2, 3)
val list2 = list1.add(4)
val list3 = list1.addAll(list1)
println(list1)
println(list2)
println(list3)
```

The result is totally different:

```
[1, 2, 3, 4, 1, 2, 3, 4]
true
true
```

Here, all operations were made on the first list and are then cumulative. Due to type inference, no error occurred when assigning the result of the operation (which is of type Boolean) to the references. These references were automatically made Boolean by Kotlin. This is a good reason to explicitly write the expected type. It would prevent the following code from compiling:

```
val list1: List<Int> = mutableListOf(1, 2, 3)
val list2: List<Int> = list1.add(1) // <--
Compile error
val list3: List<Int> = list1.addAll(list2) //
<-- Compile error
println(list1)
println(list2)
println(list3)
```

The + operator is an *infix* extension function called `plus`, which Kotlin declares in the `Collection` interface that `List` extends. It's translated into a static function creating a new list from its arguments. You can use the + operator with mutable lists, and you'll get the same result as if the lists where immutable, leaving the lists unchanged.

If you're aware of how immutable persistent data structures are usually implemented with data sharing, you may be disappointed to learn that Kotlin's immutable lists don't share data. (They share elements, but *not* the list data.) Adding an element to a list implies constructing a whole new list. In chapter 5, you'll learn how to create your own immutable list that implements data sharing, which lets you save memory space and obtain better performance on some operations.

2.5   *Kotlin's packages*

You already saw that functions can be declared at the package level, which is an important difference from the way Java uses packages. Another particularity of Kotlin packages is that they don't have to correspond to the directory structure where they're stored.

In the same way, classes don't need to be defined in files by the same names; package organization in the containing directory structure isn't mandatory. Packages are only identifiers. There's no notion of a *subpackage* (packages containing packages). Filenames are irrelevant (as long as they have a `.kt` extension). This said, it's a good idea to adopt the Java convention based on the package/directory correspondence for two reasons:

1   If you need to mix Java and Kotlin files, you'll have to put the Java files into directories matching the package names. You should do the same with Kotlin files.

2   Even if you create only Kotlin source files, finding a source file will be much easier. You only need to look at the package (generally indicated by an import) and convert it to a file path.

2.6   *Visibility in Kotlin*

Visibility is somewhat different from what it is in Java. Functions and properties can be defined at the package level, not only in classes. All elements defined at the package level are public by default. If an element is declared private, it's only visible from inside the same file.

An element can also be declared *internal*, meaning it's only visible from inside the same module. A *module* is a set of files compiled together, such as

- A Maven project
- A Gradle source set
- An IntelliJ module
- An Eclipse project
- A group of files compiled with a single Ant task

A module is intended to be packed into a single jar file. A module can include several packages, and a single package can spread over several modules.

Classes and interfaces have a public visibility by default. They can also be affected by one of the following visibility modifiers:

- `private`
- `protected`
- `internal`
- `public`

A `private` element is only visible from inside the class where it's defined. In Java, the private members of an *inner class* (a class defined inside another class) aren't visible from the outer class. With Kotlin, it's quite the opposite: private members of the outer class are visible from the inner class.

Class constructors are public by default. You can specify the visibility level for these constructors as shown here:

```
class Person private constructor (val name: String,
                                  val registered: Instant)
```

Unlike Java, Kotlin has no *package private* visibility (the default visibility in Java). On the other hand, the `internal` visibility is specific to Kotlin. An `internal` element can be accessed from any code in the same module. (Note that code in a Gradle test source set can access internal elements of the corresponding main source set.)

2.7   Functions in Kotlin

A function in Kotlin is equivalent to a method in Java. This isn't the same meaning as a function in math or in functional programming.

> **NOTE** In Kotlin the word *function* is used even for things that aren't true functions, or that aren't functions at all. In the next chapter, you'll learn what a true function is. For the rest of this chapter, I'll use function in the Kotlin sense (meaning as equivalent to a Java method).

2.7.1   Declaring functions

Like Kotlin properties, you can declare Kotlin functions at the package level or in classes or objects. Functions are introduced by the keyword `fun` as in the following example:

```
fun add(a: Int, b: Int): Int {
  return a + b
}
```

When the body can be expressed as a single line, the block delimited with curly braces can be replaced with the following syntax:

```
fun add(a: Int, b: Int): Int = a + b
```

This is called the *expression syntax*. When using this syntax, you can omit the return type if it can be inferred from the body:

```
fun add(a: Int, b: Int) = a + b
```

Be aware that mixing the two syntaxes may have unexpected results. The following example is perfectly valid

```
fun add(a: Int, b: Int) = {
    a + b
}
```

but the return type is probably not what you'd expect. I'll explain this in the next chapter. In such an example, using an explicit return type allows the compiler to warn you about the error (although you can't use `return` in this example).

2.7.2 Using local functions

Functions can be defined inside classes and objects. Furthermore, they can also be declared inside other functions. The following code is an example of a somewhat complex function returning the number of divisors of an integer. For now, you don't have to understand how this function works. We'll get to that in the next chapters. But the important fact to note is that the `sumOfPrimes` function definition contains the definition of the `isPrime` function:

```
fun sumOfPrimes(limit: Int): Long {

    val seq: Sequence<Long> = sequenceOf(2L) +
            generateSequence(3L, {
                it + 2
            }).takeWhile{
                it < limit
            }

    fun isPrime(n: Long): Boolean =
            seq.takeWhile {
                it * it <= n
            }.all {
                n % it != 0L
            }

    return seq.filter(::isPrime).sum()
}
```

The `isPrime` function can't be defined outside the `sumOfPrimes` function because it *closes over* the seq variable. Such a construct is called a *closure*. As you'll learn in the next chapter, closures cause the closed-over variable(s) to be part of the function argument. This code is equivalent to the following:

```
fun sumOfPrimes(limit: Int): Long {
    val seq: Sequence<Long> = sequenceOf(2L) +
            generateSequence(3L, {
                it + 2
            }).takeWhile{
                it < limit
            }

    return seq.filter {
        x -> isPrime(x, seq)
    }.sum()
}
```

```
fun isPrime(n: Long, seq: Sequence<Long>): Boolean =
    seq.takeWhile {
        it * it <= n
    }.all {
        n % it != 0L
    }
```

Using a closure lets you use a function reference (equivalent to a Java method reference) instead of a lambda to call the isPrime function. On the other hand, it makes the isPrime function unusable outside of the sumOfPrimes function. This may or may not be what you want.

Here, the isPrime function, which takes (n: Long, seq: Sequence<Long>) as its parameter, would probably be useless outside of sumOfPrimes. In this case, it's better to declare isPrime as a local function, allowing for its use of a closure and a function reference.

2.7.3   *Overriding functions*

When extending a class or implementing an interface, you'll often override functions. Unlike Java, overriding must be explicitly specified using the override keyword:

```
override fun toString() = ...
```

This is one of the rare cases where Kotlin is more verbose than Java. But this makes your programs much safer by preventing your code from inadvertently overriding functions. (In Java, the same effect can be obtained with the @Override annotation.)

2.7.4   *Using extension functions*

Extension functions are functions that can be called on objects as if they were instance functions of the corresponding class. Kotlin uses this mechanism frequently. Let's say you want to define a length function that gives the length of a list like this:

```
fun <T> length(list: List<T>) = list.size
```

This is, of course, totally useless, but it's just an example. Kotlin lets you define this function as

```
fun <T> List<T>.length() = this.size
```

In this example, length is an extension function because it extends the List interface by adding a function that can be used as if it were an instance function:

```
fun <T> List<T>.length() = this.size

val ints = listOf(1, 2, 3, 4, 5, 6, 7)

val listLength = ints.length()
```

Unlike the size function, which can be called with the property syntax, parentheses are mandatory when calling length(). Additionally, such extension functions can't be called as instance methods from Java code; it must be called as a static method. With Kotlin, it's even possible to add functions to parameterized classes such as

```
fun List<Int>.product(): Int = this.fold(1) { a, b -> a * b }
```

```
val ints = listOf(1, 2, 3, 4, 5, 6, 7)

val product = ints.product()
```

As you can see, extension functions are just like static functions in Java. But instead of being called on a class, they can be called on an instance, letting you chain function calls instead of embedding one in another.

2.7.5 *Using lambdas*

Like in Java, *lambdas* are anonymous functions, meaning function implementations that aren't referenced by a name. The syntax of Kotlin lambdas is slightly different than Java syntax, though. Lambdas are included between curly braces, as you can see in the following example:

```
fun triple(list: List<Int>): List<Int> = list.map({ a -> a * 3 })
```

When the lambda is the last argument of a function, it can be put outside of the parentheses:

```
fun triple(list: List<Int>): List<Int> = list.map { a -> a * 3 }

fun product(list: List<Int>): Int = list.fold(1) { a, b -> a * b }
```

In the map example, the lambda is not only the last argument, but the only one, so the parentheses can be removed. As you may have noticed in the second example, the arguments of the lambda don't need to be put between parentheses. In fact, you can't put parentheses around them because it would change the meaning. This would not compile:

```
fun List<Int>.product(): Int = this.fold(1) { (a, b) -> a * b }
```

LAMBDA PARAMETER TYPES

Kotlin infers the lambda parameter types, but it often doesn't make the best effort in this domain. This is done on purpose to speed up compilation. When inferring the correct types could potentially take too much time, Kotlin gives up, and it's up to you to specify the parameter types. Here's how to do this:

```
fun List<Int>.product(): Int = this.fold(1) { a: Int, b: Int -> a * b }
```

Although you might often avoid specifying the types and rely upon type inference, you'll soon realize that there's another way to benefit. By specifying the types, if your code doesn't compile, the compiler (or the IDE) will tell you how the inferred types differ from the types you've specified.

MULTI-LINE LAMBDAS

A lambda implementation can spread over multiple lines as in the following example:

```
fun List<Int>.product(): Int = this.fold(1) { a, b ->
        val result = a * b
        result
}
```

The value returned by the lambda is the value of the expression on the last line. You can use the return keyword, but it can be safely omitted.

SIMPLIFIED SYNTAX FOR LAMBDAS

Kotlin offers a simplified syntax for lambdas with a single parameter. This parameter is implicitly named `it`. The previous `map` example can be written:

```
fun triple(list: List<Int>): List<Int> = list.map { it * 3 }
```

But it might not always be wise to use this syntax. It's often a good simplification to use when lambdas aren't nested; otherwise, it might become difficult to guess what `it` is! In any case, a good practice is to write lambdas on several lines:

```
fun triple(list: List<Int>): List<Int> = list.map {
    it * 3
}

fun triple(list: List<Int>): List<Int> = list.map { a ->
    a * 3
}
```

Splitting the line after the arrow (`->`) makes it clear which syntax you're using.

LAMBDAS IN CLOSURES

Like Java, Kotlin allows for lambdas to close over variables in the enclosing scope:

```
val multiplier = 3

fun multiplyAll(list: List<Int>): List<Int> = list.map { it * multiplier }
```

Be aware that closures should generally be replaced with function arguments, which makes your code safer. Take this example, for instance:

```
fun multiplyAll(list: List<Int>, multiplier:
int): List<Int> = list.map { it * multiplier }
        list.map { it * multiplier }
```

You should use a closure only when it closes over a narrow scope (for example, in functions defined inside other functions). In such cases, it might be safe to close over the arguments or the temporary result of the enclosing function. Unlike Java, Kotlin allows closing over mutable variables. But if you want to write safer programs, avoid using mutable references in any case.

2.8   *Nulls in Kotlin*

Kotlin handles null references in a specific way. As you'll see in chapter 6, null references are one of the most frequent sources of bugs in computer programs. Kotlin attempts to solve the problem by forcing you to handle null references.

Kotlin makes a distinction between nullable and non-nullable types. Take the example of integers. To represent integers in the range [–2,147,483,648 to 2,147,483,647], Kotlin uses the type `Int`. A reference of this type can have any value in this range, but nothing else. In particular, it can't have the value `null` because `null` is not a value in this range. On the other hand, Kotlin also has the type `Int?` that can take any value in this range, plus `null`.

`Int` is said to be a non-nullable type, whereas `Int?` is a nullable type. Kotlin uses this mechanism for all types, which exist in two versions: nullable (postfixed with a `?`) and non-nullable. The most interesting part of the story is that any non-nullable type is a child type of the corresponding nullable type, so the following is correct:

```
val x: Int = 3
val y: Int? = x
```

But this is not:

```
val x: Int? = 3
val y: Int = x
```

2.8.1 Dealing with nullable types

When using non-nullable types, you can't throw a NullPointerException. On the other hand, if you use nullable types, you can get a NullPointException. Kotlin forces you to handle the exception or to take full responsibility. The following code won't compile:

```
val s: String? = someFunctionReturningAStringThatCanBeNull()
val l = s.length
```

The dot . operator, also called the *dereferencing* operator, can't be used here because it could cause an NPE (NullPointerException). What you might want to do instead is this:

```
val s: String? = someFunctionReturningAStringThatCanBeNull()
val l = if (s != null) s.length else null
```

Kotlin simplifies this use case thanks to the *safe call* operator, ?.:

```
val s: String? = someFunctionReturningAStringThatCanBeNull()
val l = s?.length
```

Note that Kotlin infers the type of l to be Int?. This syntax, however, is more practical when chaining calls:

```
val city: City? = map[companyName]?.manager?.address?.city
```

In such cases, the companyName could be absent from the map, or it could have no manager, or the manager could have no address, or the city could be missing. Null safety could be obtained by nesting if...else constructs, but the Kotlin syntax is much more convenient. It's also more compact than the equivalent Java solution:

```
City city = Optional.ofNullable(map.get(companyName))
                .flatMap(Company::getManager)
                .flatMap(Employee::getAddress)
                .flatMap(Address::getCity)
                .getOrElse(null);
```

As I mentioned, Kotlin also offers you the opportunity to take full responsibility for throwing NPEs:

```
val city: City? = map[companyName]!!.manager!!.address!!.city
```

With this syntax, if anything is null (except for the city), an NPE will be thrown.

2.8.2   *Elvis and the default value*

Sometimes, you'll want to use a specific default value instead of `null`, which is what the Java `Optional.getOrElse()` method allows. But Elvis can do this for you:

```
val city: City = map[company]?.manager?.address?.city ?: City.UNKOWN
```

Here, if anything is `null`, a special default value is used. This default value is provided by `?:`, called the *Elvis operator.* If you're wondering why it's called Elvis, rotate your screen 90 degrees to the right. (Alternatively, if you're young enough, you can rotate your head 90 degrees to the left.)

2.9   *Program flow and control structures*

Control structures are elements controlling the program flow. These are the basis of imperative programming: where a program expresses how a computation is to be done. As you'll see in the next chapters, control structures are a major source of bugs in computer programs, so you should avoid them as much as possible. You'll see that it's possible to write much safer programs by totally avoiding the use of control structures.

Primarily, you can ignore the notion of control flow. You replace control structures with expressions and functions. Unlike some languages specifically designed to promote safe programming, Kotlin has both control structures (like Java) and functions that can be used to replace those structures. But some of these control structures are, in fact, different from their Java versions.

2.9.1   *Using conditional selectors*

In Java, the `if...else` construct is a control structure. It tests a condition and directs the program flow to execute one of two blocks of instructions, depending on whether the condition holds. Here's a simple Java example:

```
int a = ...
int b = ...

if (a < b) {
  System.out.println("a is smaller than b");
} else {
  System.out.println("a is not smaller than b");
}
```

In Kotlin, the `if...else` construct is an expression that can be evaluated to a value. It has the same form as in Java, although it returns the value in the first block if the condition holds. If not, it returns the value in the second block:

```
val a: Int = ...
val b: Int = ...

val s = if (a < b) {
  "a is smaller than b"
} else {
  "a is not smaller than b"
}

println(s)
```

Like Java, you can omit the curly braces if the blocks have only one line:

```
val a: Int = ...
val b: Int = ...

val s = if (a < b)
            "a is smaller than b"
        else
            "a is not smaller than b"

println(s)
```

Although this is often considered bad practice in Java, it's not in Kotlin. If the braces are omitted, there can't be an `if` without a corresponding `else` clause. Mistakenly adding a line to a branch without adding the curly braces would not compile. When the branches of the `if...else` expression comprise several lines, however, they must be enclosed in blocks (like in Java). In this case, the `return` keyword shouldn't be used:

```
val a: Int = 6
val b: Int = 5

val percent = if (b != 0) {
                  val temp = a / b
                  temp * 100
              } else {
                  0
              }
```

Here, the first branch has two lines, so it's enclosed in a block. The value of the block is the value of the expression on the last line of the block. Braces delimiting the second block aren't mandatory because it has only one line. For consistency and readability, programmers generally use braces for the two branches even if only one of them needs the braces.

It's possible to add effects in the `if` block, making this function much more like the Java control structure. But avoid this practice as much as possible. In the previous chapter, I said that effects should be used only in delimited, "non-safe" parts of the program. Outside of these parts, you should only use the `if...else` function as an expression, with no side effects.

2.9.2 Using multi-conditional selectors

When there are more than two conditional branches, Java uses the `switch...case` structure. This lets you test for integer values, enums, or strings:

```
// Java code
String country = ...
String capital;

switch(country) {
  case "Australia":
    capital = "Canberra";
    break;
  case "Bolivia":
    capital = "Sucre";
    break;
```

```
    case "Brazil":
      capital = "Brasilia";
      break;
    default:
      capital = "Unknown";
  }
```

Kotlin uses the when construct, which is not a control structure, but an expression:

```
val country = ...

val capital = when (country) {
    "Australia" -> "Canberra"
    "Bolivia"   -> "Sucre"
    "Brazil"    -> "Brasilia"
    else        -> "Unknown"
}
```

Instead of a value to the right of each arrow, you can use a multi-line block; in which case, the value returned will be the last line of the block. You don't have to use a break at the end of each case. As with the if...then expression, you shouldn't use effects in these blocks.

One important thing to note is that Kotlin won't let you use a non-exhaustive when. All possible cases must be handled. If using an enum, you can create one case for each possible value of the enum. If you add a new value later to the enum, and the when code isn't updated to handle that value, the code will no longer compile. (The else case is the simplest way to handle all cases.) You can also use the when construct with a different syntax:

```
val country = ...

val capital = when {
    tired                     -> "Check for yourself"
    country == "Australia" -> "Canberra"
    country == "Bolivia"   -> "Sucre"
    country == "Brazil"    -> "Brasília"
    else                      -> "Unknown"
}
```

Using the when construct this way can be useful if not all of the conditions depend on the same argument. In the previous example, tired is a Boolean value that was initialized somewhere else. If it's true, the value to the right of the corresponding arrow is returned. Conditions are tested in the order they're listed. The first condition that holds determines the value of the expression.

2.9.3 *Using loops*

Java uses several kinds of loops:

- Indexed loops, iterating over a range of numerical values
- Loops iterating over a collection of values
- Loops iterating as long as a condition holds

Kotlin also has similar control structures. The `while` loop in Kotlin is like its Java counterpart. It's a control structure and is used if you want your program to describe *how* things should be done. This comes with a responsibility. If your description of how things should be done is inaccurate, your program will be wrong or buggy, even if your intention was correct. That's why it's safer to replace control structures with functions saying *what* should be done (not how it should be done).

Indexed loops also exist in Kotlin, although an indexed loop is, in fact, an iteration over a collection of indexes:

```
for(i in 0 until 10 step 2) {
    println(i)
}
```

This is equivalent to

```
val range = 0 until 10 step 2
for (i in range) println(i)
```

This control structure iterates over a range of indexes. Kotlin offers three main functions for creating ranges. `until` builds an ascending range, using a default step 1 or an explicit step. The starting value is included, whereas the ending value is excluded. `until` and `step` are functions of `Int` and can be used as shown here:

```
for (i in 0.until(10).step(2)) println(i)
```

Like many other functions, they can also be used with infix notation:

```
for (i in 0 until 10 step 2) println(i)
```

Two other useful functions for creating ranges are the `..` operator (two consecutive dots), which is like `until` but includes the upper bounds, and `downTo`, for descending ranges. For safer programming, you shouldn't use ranges with `for` loops but with special functions that abstract iterations, such as `fold`. You'll learn more about this in chapter 4.

2.10 *Kotlin's unchecked exceptions*

Unlike Java, Kotlin has no checked exceptions. All exceptions are unchecked. This is in line with what most Java programmers do nowadays: wrapping checked exceptions into unchecked ones. Beside this, the main difference between Kotlin and Java is that the `try..catch..finally` construct is an expression returning a value. You can use it like this:

```
val num: Int = try {
    args[0].toInt()
} catch (e: Exception) {
    0
} finally {
    // Code in this block is always executed
}
```

As you already saw with `if...else`, the value returned by each block is the result of evaluating the last line of the block. The difference is that for the `try...catch...finally`, braces are *mandatory*. The value returned is either the result of the evaluation of the last line of the try block, if there's no exception, or the evaluation of the last line of the catch block otherwise.

2.11 Automatic resource closure

Kotlin is able to automatically close resources in the same way as Java does with the *try with resource* construct, provided these resources implement either Closable or Auto-Closable. The main difference is that to achieve this, Kotlin offers the use function:

```
File("myFile.txt").inputStream()
                .use {
                     it.bufferedReader()
                        .lineSequence()
                        .forEach (::println)
              }
```

This specific code is only an example of automatically handling closable resources. It's not of great interest beside this because the lineSequence function returns a Sequence, which is a lazy construct. *Lazy* means that evaluation (reading the file lines) occurs only later, when the lines are used.

Outside of the use function block, the input stream must automatically close or the sequence would be useless. This forces you to apply the effect (println\) immediately, contradicting safe programming principles. The following code will compile, but it throws an IOException: Stream Closed at runtime:

```
val lines: Sequence<String> = File("myFile.txt")
        .inputStream()
        .use {
            it.bufferedReader()
               .lineSequence()
        }

lines.forEach(::println)
```

The solution is to force stream evaluation before exiting the block:

```
val lines: List<String> = File("myFile.txt")
        .inputStream()
        .use {
            it.bufferedReader()
               .lineSequence()
               .toList()
        }

lines.forEach(::println)
```

The main problem is that the whole file must be held in memory. By the way, if you want to process the file as a sequence of lines, Kotlin offers a much simpler way to do this, using the forEachLine function:

```
File("myFile.txt").forEachLine { println(it) }
```

You can also use `useLines`, which returns a `Sequence`. The equivalent of the previous example would be

```
File("myFile.txt").useLines{ it.forEach(::println) }
```

2.12 *Kotlin's smart casts*

In Java, it's sometimes necessary to cast a reference to some given type. As this might produce a `ClassCastException` if the referenced object is not of the right type, you must first check the type using the `instanceof` operator:

```
Object payload = message.getPayload();
int length = -1;
if (payload intanceof String) {
    String stringPayload = (String) payload;
    length = stringPayload.length();
}
```

This type of code is clumsy. In true object-oriented programming, checking the type and casting is often considered bad practice. This might be the reason why not much effort has been made to make casting easier to use. But Kotlin has a special technique called smart casts. Here's how you'd use a smart cast for the same example:

```
val payload: Any = message.payload

val length: Int = if (payload is String)
    payload.length
else
    -1
```

This is called a *smart cast* because in the first branch of the `if` function, Kotlin knows that `payload` is of type `String`, so it performs the cast automatically. You can also use smart casts with the `when` function:

```
val result: Int = when (payload) {
        is String -> payload.length
        is Int    -> payload
        else      -> -1
    }
```

Casting can also be done in a normal, *unsafe* way, using the as operator:

```
val result: String = payload as String
```

If the object isn't of the right type, a `ClassCastException` is thrown. Kotlin offers another safe syntax for these kinds of casts:

```
val result: String? = payload as? String
```

If the cast doesn't succeed, the result will be `null` instead of an exception. If you want to write safer programs in Kotlin, you should avoid using the `as?` operator in the same way you should avoid nullable types.

2.13 *Equality versus identity*

One of the classical pitfalls in Java is the possible confusion between equality and identity. This problem is made even trickier due to the presence of primitives, the fact that strings are interned, and the way in which Integers are handled:

```
// Java code
int a = 2;
System.out.println(a == 2); // true
Integer b = Integer.valueOf(1);
System.out.println(b == Integer.valueOf(1)); // true
System.out.println(b == new Integer(1)); // false
System.out.println(b.equals(new Integer(1))); // true
Integer c = Integer.valueOf(512);
System.out.println(c == Integer.valueOf(512)); // false
System.out.println(c.equals(Integer.valueOf(512))); // true
String s = "Hello";
System.out.println(s == "Hello"); // true
String s2 = "Hello, World!".substring(0, 5);
System.out.println(s2 == "Hello"); // false
System.out.println(s2.equals("Hello")); // true
```

What a mess! (In case you wonder why the integers b and c behave differently, it's because Java returns a memoized shared version of integers for low values, so Integer.valueOf(1) always returns the same object, whereas Integer.valueOf(512) returns a new distinct object on each call.) To be safe in Java, always test equality with equals for objects and with == for primitives. The == symbol tests equality for primitives and identity for objects.

Kotlin is simpler. Identity (also called *referential equality*) is tested with ===. Equality (sometimes called *structural equality*) is tested with ==, which is a shorthand for equals. The simple fact that testing for equality (==) is simpler than testing for identity (===) will prevent many mistakes. You can negate both == and === by replacing the first = with a !.

2.14 *String interpolation*

Kotlin offers a much simpler syntax than Java for mixing values with strings. In a previous example, I used the + operator to construct a parameterized string, which is somewhat impractical. A better form in Java would be to use the String.format() method, such as

```
// Java code
System.out.println(String.format("%s's registration date: %s",
                                            name, date));
```

Kotlin makes this much simpler:

```
println("$name's registration date: $date")
```

Or you can also use expressions, provided they're enclosed in curly braces:

```
println("$name's registration date: ${date.atZone(
                        ZoneId.of("America/Los_Angeles"))}")
```

This technique, called *string interpolation*, makes handling of strings much easier and more readable.

2.15 *Multi-line strings*

Kotlin makes it easy to format multi-line strings by using the triple-quoted string (""") with the `trimMargin` function:

```
println("""This is the first line
         |and this is the second one.""".trimMargin())
```

This code will print

```
This is the first line
and this is the second one.
```

The `trimMargin` function takes as an optional parameter, a string, to use as the margin limit. As you can see in this example, the default value is "|".

2.16 *Variance: parameterized types and subtyping*

Variance describes how parameterized types behave in relation to subtyping. *Covariance* means that a `Matcher<Red>` is considered a subtype of `Matcher<Color>` if Red is a subtype of Color. In such cases, `Matcher<T>` is said to be a covariant on T. If, on the contrary, `Matcher<Color>` is considered a subtype of `Matcher<Red>`, then `Matcher<T>` is said to be a *contravariant* on T.

In Kotlin, you can indicate variance using the keywords in and out, which are shorter and hopefully simpler to understand than covariant and contravariant. (The absence of a keyword means *invariant*.)

Think about a `List<String>`. As String is a subtype of Any, it's clear that a `List<String>` could also be considered a `List<Any>`. In Java, which doesn't handle variance, one has to use wildcards for this.

2.16.1 *Why is variance a potential problem?*

An instance of String is an instance of Any, so you can write

```
val s = "A String"
val a: Any = s
```

This is because Any is a parent of String. If `MutableList<Any>` was a parent of `MutableList<String>`, you could write

```
val ls = mutableListOf("A String")
val la: MutableList<Any> = ls  // <- compile error
la.add(42)
```

If this code compiled, you could insert an Int into a list of strings. This isn't a problem when using immutable lists. Adding an Int element to an immutable list of strings produces a new list of type List<Any>, without changing the type of the original list:

```
val ls = listOf("A String")
val la = ls + 42 // <- Kotlin infers the type `List<Any>` for `la`
```

In Java, types are *invariant*, which means that if A is a parent type of B, List<A> is neither a parent type nor a child type of List<B>. List<A> and List<B> are two different types at compile time (and the same type at runtime). The problem with invariant types is that you can't write the following:

```
fun <T> addAll(list1: MutableList<T>,
               list2: MutableList<T>) {
  for (elem in list2) list1.add(elem)
}


val ls = mutableListOf("A String")
val la: MutableList<Any> = mutableListOf()
addAll(la, ls)  // <-- won't compile !
```

Although each elem of type String would be added to a List<Any>, which is perfectly valid, Kotlin can't make MutableList<Any> and MutableList<String> both fit for MutableList<T>. To make this work, you need to specifically tell the compiler that MutableList<Any> can be used as if it were a supertype of MutableList<String> because it'll only be read from (out) and never written to (in). You can do this with the qualifier out as in the following code:

```
fun <T> addAll(list1: MutableList<T>,
               list2: MutableList<out T>) { // <-- Make T covariant
  for (elem in list2) list1.add(elem)
}


val ls = mutableListOf("A String")
val la: MutableList<Any> = mutableListOf()
addAll(la, ls)  // <-- No more error
```

Here, the out keyword is used to indicate that list2 is a covariant on T. As you may guess, contravariance is indicated with the keyword in. So another solution to the problem would be to make list1 an in type (consumed but never produced).

2.16.2 *When to use covariance and when to use contravariance*

The Kotlin words for covariant and contravariant are out and in, respectively. Suppose you have the following interface:

```
interface Bag<T> {
  fun get(): T
}
```

As this interface has only a function returning T (and no function taking T as its argument), you could securely assign a Bag<T> to any Bag<V> reference, where V is a supertype of T. But you must specify your intention of making the type parameter covariant by using the out keyword:

```
open class MyClassParent

class MyClass: MyClassParent()

interface Bag<out T> {
  fun get(): T
}
```

```
class BagImpl : Bag<MyClass> {
  override fun get(): MyClass = MyClass()
}

val bag: Bag<MyClassParent>  = BagImpl()
```

NOTE If the type parameter can have an out variance and you don't specify it, a good IDE (such as IntelliJ) will warn you that you can make it covariant.

Conversely, if the interface only has functions taking arguments of type T and never returning T, you can make the type parameter contravariant by using the keyword in:

```
open class MyClassParent

class MyClass: MyClassParent()

interface Bag<in T> {
  fun use(t: T): Boolean
}

class BagImpl : Bag<MyClassParent> {
  override fun use(t: MyClassParent): Boolean = true
}

val bag: Bag<MyClass> = BagImpl()
```

If neither in nor out is specified, the type is invariant. The choice of out and in is simple if memorizing that covariance is used when the type is only output (return values), and contravariance is used when the type is only input (arguments).

2.16.3 *Declaration-site variance versus use-site variance*

As useful as a declaration-site variance can be, you'll find many times when it can't be used. If the Bag interface both consumes and produces a type T, it can't be variant:

```
interface Bag<T> {

  fun get(): T
  fun use(t: T): Boolean
}
```

Parameter T can't be made variant because it should be covariant for the method get and contravariant for the method use. In this case, declaration-site variance can't be used. But it's still possible to declare use-site variance. Consider the following useBag function:

```
open class MyClassParent

class MyClass: MyClassParent()

interface Bag<T> {
  fun get(): T
  fun use(t: T): Boolean
}
```

```
class BagImpl : Bag<MyClassParent> {
  override fun get(): MyClassParent =  MyClassParent()

  override fun use(t: MyClassParent): Boolean = true
}

fun useBag(bag: Bag<MyClass>): Boolean {
  // do something with bag
  return true
}

val bag3 = useBag(BagImpl()) // <-- Compile error !
```

Here, you'll get a compiler error because `useBag` wants an argument of type `Bag<MyClass>` and all you have is a `Bag<MyClassParent>`. To make it work, you need to specify contravariance for `T`. But this can't be done in the `Bag<T>` interface declaration because it would clash with the `get(t: T)` function, where `T` is in the `out` position. The solution is to restrict the type on the use site:

```
fun useBag(bag: Bag<in MyClass>): Boolean {
  // do something with bag
  return true
}
```

The opposite is also possible:

```
fun createBag(): Bag<out MyClassParent> = BagImpl2()

class BagImpl2 : Bag<MyClass> {
  override fun use(t: MyClass): Boolean = true
  override fun get(): MyClass = MyClass()
}
```

You can see `in MyClass` and `out MyClassParent` as restricted types: `in MyClass` is a subtype of `MyClass` that can only be used in the `in` position, whereas `out MyClassParent` is a subtype of `MyClassParent` that can only be used in the `out` position. These restrictions are checked by the compiler. You can say that `in MyClass` and `out MyClassParent` are type projections of `MyClass` and `MyClassParent`.

As I said, this chapter is only an overview of Kotlin. In the following chapters, I talk about Kotlin's other specifics from the perspective of safe programs. On the other hand, if you'd like an in-depth study of the Kotlin language, I'd suggest reading Dmitry Jemerov and Svetlana Isakova's *Kotlin in Action* (Manning, 2017), which was written by members of the Kotlin development team.

Summary

- Fields and variables have different syntax and different visibility.
- Classes and interfaces save you most boilerplate code, especially for data classes. This lets you create the equivalent of a Java object with properties, getters and setters, constructors, `equals`, `hashCode`, `toString`, and `copy` functions (and more), all in a single line.

- You can define functions at the package level (replacing Java static methods) in classes, objects, or even locally in other functions.
- Using extension functions, you can add functions to existing classes, and you can call them as if they were instance functions.
- In Kotlin, conditional control structures are replaced with expressions that can be evaluated.
- Kotlin has looping control structures, but you can nearly always replace them with functions.
- Kotlin distinguishes between nullable and non-nullable types and provides operators to safely compose null values.

Programming with functions

In chapter 1, you learned that one of the most important techniques for safer programming is to clearly separate the parts of the programs that don't depend on anything other than the input data from the part which depends on the state of the outside world. With programs composed of *subprograms* (called procedures, methods, or functions), this separation transitively applies to these subprograms as well. In Java these are called methods, but in Kotlin they're called functions, which is probably more appropriate because function is a mathematical term with a precise definition (as is usual with mathematics). Kotlin functions can be compared to mathematical functions when they've no effect beside returning a value that's only dependent on their argument. Such functions are often called *pure functions* by programmers. To write safer programs, therefore, one must

- Use pure functions for computations
- Use pure effects for making the result of computations available to the outside world

46

Pure functions are necessary in order to ensure that they always return the same result given the same argument. Otherwise, your program would be *nondeterministic*, which means you can never check whether the program is correct. Pure effects might seem less important, but if you think about it, *impure effects* are effects that include computations, and these computational parts aren't easily testable, so they should be put in separate (pure) functions.

For some programmers seeking ways to write safer programs, clearly differentiating pure functions from pure effects and never mixing them isn't the ultimate goal. Pure functions are easy to test, but pure effects aren't. Is it possible to change this? Yes, it is, by treating effects in a different way. That's what pure functional programming does. In this paradigm, everything is a function. Values are functions, functions are functions, and effects are functions. Instead of applying effects, functional programmers use functions returning data representing the intended effect in a non-evaluated form. In such a programming paradigm, everything is a function and everything is data because there's no difference between data and functions.

Why not simply use pure functional programming? Although it's possible, it's sometimes difficult if you're not using a language that was specifically designed for this. Languages like Java and Kotlin offer many tools for adopting some functional programming techniques, but the support of functional effects is limited. In chapter 12, I'll show you how to process effects functionally because this technique is used in all types of programming (often without the programmer realizing it). Although this is something you can do, and something you should sometimes do, you probably shouldn't always treat effects that way.

In this chapter, you'll learn how to use pure functions for computations and how to use curried versions of functions. You might have trouble understanding some parts of the code presented in this chapter. That's to be expected because it's difficult to introduce functions without using other functional constructs like List, Option, and others. Be patient. All the unexplained components will be discussed in the following chapters.

3.1 What's a function?

In this section, we'll take a deeper look at functions. A *function* is primarily a mathematical concept. It represents a relationship between a source set (called the function *domain*) and a target set (called the function *codomain*). The domain and the codomain need not be distinct. A function, for example, can have the same set of integer numbers for its domain and its codomain.

3.1.1 Understanding the relationship between two function sets

To be a function, a relationship must fulfill one condition: all elements of the domain must have one and only one corresponding element in the codomain, as shown in figure 3.1. This has some interesting implications:

- There can't be elements in the domain with no corresponding value in the codomain.

- There can't be two elements in the codomain corresponding to the same element of the domain.
- There can be elements in the codomain with no corresponding element in the source set.
- There can be elements in the codomain with more than one corresponding element in the source set.

NOTE   The set of elements of the codomain that have a corresponding element in the domain is called the *image* of the function.

Figure 3.1 illustrates a function. You can, for example, define the function

```
f(x) = x + 1
```

where x is a positive integer. This function represents the relationship between each positive integer and its successor. You can give any name to this function. In particular, you can give it a name that'll help you to remember what it is, such as:

```
successor(x) = x + 1
```

This may seem like a good idea, but you shouldn't blindly trust a function name. You could alternatively have defined the function as follows:

```
predecessor(x) = x + 1
```

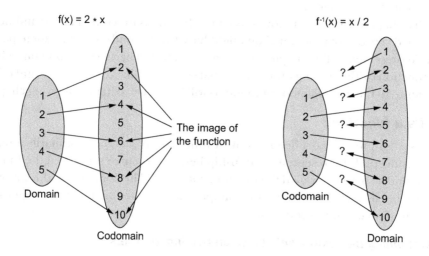

f(x) is a function from N to N.

f⁻¹(x) isn't a function considering N as the domain. It is, however, a function considering the set of even numbers (the image of f) as the domain.

Figure 3.1   All elements of a function's domain must have one and only one corresponding element in the codomain.

No error occurs here because no mandatory relationship exists between a function name and the definition of the function. But it would be a bad idea to use such a name. In fact, the name you give to a function isn't part of the function. It's a convenient way to refer to it.

Note that I'm talking about what a function *is* (its definition) and not what it *does*. A function does nothing. The successor function doesn't add 1 to its argument x. You can add 1 to an integer to calculate its successor, but the successor function doesn't do this. The successor function is merely the relationship between an integer and the next one in ascending order:

```
successor(x)
```

The expression successor(x) is only equivalent to x + 1, which means that each time you encounter successor(x), you can replace it with (x + 1). Note the parentheses that are used to isolate the expression. They aren't needed when the expression is used alone, but they might be necessary on some occasions.

3.1.2 An overview of inverse functions in Kotlin

A function may or may not have an inverse function. If f(x) is a function from A to B (A being the domain and B the codomain), the inverse function is noted as $f^{-1}(x)$ and has B as its domain and A as its codomain. If you represent the type of the function as A -> B, the inverse function (if it exists) has the type B -> A.

> **NOTE** Kotlin uses a slightly different syntax to represent function types, with the origin type in parentheses: (A) -> B and (B) -> A. From now on, I'll use the Kotlin syntax.

The inverse of a function is a function if it fulfills the same requirements as any function: having one and only one target value for each source value. As a result, the inverse of successor(x), a relationship that you'll call predecessor(x) (although you could just as well call it xyz), isn't a function in N (the set of positive integers including 0) because 0 has no predecessor in N. Conversely, if successor(x) is considered with the set of signed integers (positive and negative, noted as Z), the inverse of successor is a function.

Some other simple functions have no inverse. For example, the function

```
f(x) = (2 * x)
```

has no inverse if defined from N to N because the inverse of f would be f'(x) = x / 2, which doesn't belong to N when x is odd. It has an inverse if you define it as a function from N to the set of even integers.

3.1.3 Working with partial functions

To be a function, a relationship has two requirements:

1 It must be defined for all elements of the domain.
2 No element of the domain can have a relationship with more than one element of the codomain.

A relationship that isn't defined for all elements of the domain but that fulfills the rest of the requirement is often called a *partial function*. And, by analogy, a nonpartial function is sometimes called a *total function*, which is redundant. Strictly speaking, a true function is always total, and a partial function is not a function. But it's useful to know the vocabulary used by many programmers.

The relation `predecessor(x)` is a partial function on N (the set of positive integers plus 0), but it's a total function on N*, which is the set of positive integers without 0, and its codomain is N. Partial functions are important in programming because many bugs are the result of using a partial function as if it were a total function. For example, the relation `f(x) = 1/x` is a partial function from N to Q (the rational numbers) because it isn't defined for 0. It's a total function from N* to Q, but it's also a total function from N to (Q plus error). By adding an element to the codomain (the error condition), you can transform the partial function into a total one. But to do this, the function needs a way to return an error. Can you see an analogy with computer programs? Later in this book, you'll see that turning partial functions into total ones is an important part of safe programming.

3.1.4   *Understanding function composition*

Functions are building blocks that can be composed to build other functions. The composition of functions f and g is noted as f ∘ g, which reads as f *round* g. If f (x) = x * 2 and g(x) = x + 1, then

```
f ° g (x) = f(g(x)) = f(x + 1) = (x + 1) * 2
```

The two notations f ∘ g (x) and f(g(x)) are equivalent. But writing a composition as f(g(x)) implies using x as a placeholder for the argument. Using the f ∘ g notation, you can express a function composition without using this placeholder. If you apply this function to 5, you'll get the following:

```
f ° g (5) = f(g(5)) = f(5 + 1) = 6 * 2 = 12
```

It's interesting to note that f ∘ g is generally different from g ∘ f, although they can sometimes be equivalent. For example:

```
g ° f (5) = g(f(5)) = g(5 * 2) = 10 + 1 = 11
```

Functions are applied in the inverse of the writing order. If you write f ∘ g, you first apply g and then f.

3.1.5   *Using functions of several arguments*

Thus far I've spoken only about functions of one argument. What about functions of several arguments? Simply put, there's no such thing as a function of several arguments. Remember the definition of a function? A function is a relationship between a source set and a target set. It isn't a relationship between two or more source sets and a target set. A function can't have several arguments. But the product of two sets is itself a set. A function from such a product of sets into a set may seem like a function of several arguments. Let's consider the following function:

```
f(x, y) = x + y
```

There can be a relationship between N x N and N; in which case, it's a function. But it has only one argument that's an element of N x N. N x N is the set of all possible pairs of integers. An element of this set is a pair of integers, and a pair is a special case of the more general *tuple* concept that's used to represent combinations of several elements. A *pair* is a tuple of two elements.

Tuples are usually noted between parentheses, so (3, 5) is a tuple and an element of N x N. The function f can be applied to this tuple:

```
f((3, 5)) = 3 + 5 = 8
```

In such a case, you can by convention simplify writing by removing one set of the parentheses:

```
f(3, 5) = 3 + 5 = 8
```

Nevertheless, it's still a function of one tuple and not a function of two arguments.

3.1.6 *Currying functions*

Functions of tuples can be thought of differently. The function f(3, 5) might be considered as a function from N to a set of functions of N. The previous example, therefore, could be rewritten as

```
f(x)(y) = x + y
```

In such a case, you can write

```
f(x) = g
```

which means that the result of applying the function f to the argument x is a new function g. Applying this g function to y gives the following:

```
g(y) = x + y
```

When applying g, x is no longer a variable but a *constant*. It doesn't depend on the argument or on anything else. If you apply this to (3, 5), you get the following:

```
f(3)(5) = g(5) = 3 + 5 = 8
```

The only new thing here is that the codomain of f is a set of functions instead of a set of numbers. The result of applying f to an integer is a function. The result of applying this resulting function to an integer is an integer.

f(x)(y) is the curried form of the function f(x, y). Applying this transformation to a function of a tuple (which you can call a function of several arguments if you prefer) is called *currying*, after the mathematician Haskell Curry, although he wasn't the inventor of this transformation.

3.1.7 *Using partially-applied functions*

The curried form of the addition function may not seem natural, and you might wonder if it corresponds to something in the real world. With the curried version, you're considering both arguments separately. One of the arguments is considered first and applying the function to it gives you a new function. Is this new function useful by itself or is it simply a step in the global calculation?

In the case of an addition, currying doesn't seem that useful. And, by the way, you could start with either of the two arguments and it'd make no difference. The intermediate function would be different, but not the end result.

To help you understand the usefulness of currying, imagine you're traveling in a foreign country, using a handheld calculator (or your smartphone) to convert from one currency to another. Would you prefer having to type the conversion rate each time you want to compute a price or would you rather put the conversion rate into memory? Which solution would be less error-prone? Consider a new function of a pair of values:

```
f(rate, price) = price / 100 * (100 + rate)
```

That function seems to be equivalent to this:

```
g(price, rate) = price / 100 * (100 + rate)
```

Let's now consider the curried versions of these two functions:

```
f(rate)(price) g(price)(rate)
```

You know that f and g are functions. But what are `f(rate)` and `g(price)`? Yes, for sure, those are the results of applying `f` to `rate` and `g` to `price`. But what are the types of these results?

`f(rate)` is a function of a rate to a price. If `rate = 9`, this function applies a tax of 9% to a price, returning a new price. You could call the resulting function `apply9percentTax(price)`, and it'd probably be a useful tool because the tax rate doesn't change often.

On the other hand, `g(price)` is a function of a rate to a price. If the price is $100, it gives a new function applying a price of $100 to a variable tax. It might not seem as useful, although this depends on the problem you need to solve. If the problem is to compute how much a fixed amount will grow given a variable interest rate, this version would be the more useful.

Functions like `f(rate)` and `g(price)` are sometimes called partially-applied functions, in reference to the forms `f(rate, price)` and `g(price, rate)`. Partially-applied functions can have huge consequences regarding argument evaluation. I'll come back to this subject in section 3.2.4.

3.1.8   *Functions have no effects*

Remember that pure functions only return a value and do nothing else. They don't mutate any element of the outside world (with *outside* being relative to the function itself), they don't mutate their arguments, and they don't explode (or throw an exception or anything else) if an error occurs. They can, however, return an exception or anything else, such as an error message. But they must return it, not throw it, nor log it, nor print it. I go into more detail on pure functions in section 3.2.4.

3.2   *Functions in Kotlin*

In chapter 1, you used what Kotlin calls functions but which are, in fact, methods. In many languages, methods are a way to represent (to a certain extent) functions. As discussed in chapter 2, Kotlin calls methods functions and uses the keyword `fun` to introduce functions. But there are two problems with these *functions*. Data and functions are fundamentally the same thing. Any piece of data is, in fact, a function, and any function is a piece of data.

3.2.1   Understanding functions as data

Functions have types, like any other data such as String or Int, and these can be assigned to a reference. Data types also can be passed as arguments to other functions, and they can be returned by functions, as you'll soon see. Functions can also be stored in data structures like lists or maps, or even in a database. But functions declared with fun (like Java methods) can't be manipulated in such ways. Kotlin has all the necessary mechanisms to transform any such method into a true function.

3.2.2   Understanding data as functions

Remember the definition of a function? A *function* is a relationship between a source set and a target set that must fulfill some specific requirement. Now imagine a function having the set of all possible elements as its source set and the integer 5 as its target set. Believe it or not, this is a function that fulfills all the requirements of the definition of a function. It's a specific type of function whose result doesn't depend on its argument. This is called a *constant function.* You don't need to specify any argument to call it and there's no need to give it a special name. Let's call it 5. This is pure theory, but it's worth remembering. It will be useful later.

3.2.3   Using object constructors as functions

Objects constructors are, in fact, functions. Unlike Java, which uses a special syntax for creating objects, Kotlin uses the function syntax for this. (But it's not the syntax that makes objects functions; Java objects are functions, too.) In Kotlin, you can obtain an instance of object by using the name of the class followed by the constructor argument list enclosed in parentheses, like so:

```
val person = Person("Elvis")
```

This raises an important question. I said that a pure function should always return the same value for the same argument. You may wonder if constructors are pure functions. Consider the following example:

```
val elvis = Person("Elvis")
val theKing = Person("Elvis")
```

Two objects are created with the same argument, so it should return the same value.

```
val elvis = Person("Elvis")
val theKing = Person("Elvis")

println(elvis == theKing) // should return "true"
```

The test for equality returns true only if an equals function has been defined accordingly. This will be the case if Person is a data class (as seen in chapter 2):

```
data class Person(val name: String)
```

Otherwise, it's up to you to define equality.

3.2.4   *Using Kotlin's fun functions*

You may recall that I've mentioned pure functions before. Whichever way you declare those, Kotlin functions declared with the `fun` keyword aren't guaranteed to be real functions. What programmers call functions are so rarely real functions that programmers have coined an expression to mean real functions. They call them *pure functions*. (By analogy, the other functions are called *impure functions*.) In this section, I'll explain what makes a function pure and give you some examples of pure functions.

Here's what's needed for a function/method to be a pure function:

- It mustn't mutate anything outside the function. No internal mutation can be visible from the outside.
- It mustn't mutate its argument.
- It mustn't throw errors or exceptions.
- It must always return a value.
- When called with the same argument, it must always return the same result.

Let's look at an example of pure and impure functions as shown in the next listing.

Listing 3.1   Pure and impure functions

```
class FunFunctions {

    var percent1 = 5
    private var percent2 = 9
    val percent3 = 13

    fun add(a: Int, b: Int): Int = a + b

    fun mult(a: Int, b: Int?): Int = 5

    fun div(a: Int, b: Int): Int = a / b

    fun div(a: Double, b: Double): Double = a / b

    fun applyTax1(a: Int): Int = a / 100 * (100 + percent1)

    fun applyTax2(a: Int): Int = a / 100 * (100 + percent2)

    fun applyTax3(a: Int): Int = a / 100 * (100 + percent3)

    fun append(i: Int, list: MutableList<Int>): List<Int> {
        list.add(i)
        return list
    }

    fun append2(i: Int, list: List<Int>) = list + i
}
```

Can you say which of these functions/methods represent pure functions? Think for a few minutes before reading the answer that follows. Think about all the conditions and all the processing done inside the functions. Remember that what counts is what's visible from the outside. Don't forget to consider exceptional conditions:

```
fun add(a: Int, b: Int): Int = a + b
```

The first function, add, is a pure function because it always returns a value that depends only on its arguments. It doesn't mutate its arguments and doesn't interact in any way with the outside world. This function can cause an error if the sum a + b overflows the maximum Int value. But it won't throw an exception. The result will be erroneous (a negative value); this is another problem. The result must be the same each time the function is called with the same arguments. This doesn't mean that the result must be exact!

Exactness

The term *exact* doesn't mean anything by itself. It generally means that it fits what's expected. To say whether the result of a function implementation is exact, you must know the intention of the implementer. Usually you'll have nothing but the function name to determine the intention, which can be a source of misunderstanding.

The second function

```
fun mult(a: Int, b: Int?): Int = 5
```

is a pure function. The fact that it always returns the same value whatever the arguments are is irrelevant, as is the fact that the function name has nothing to do with what the function returns. This function is a constant.

The div function working on Int isn't a pure function because it'll throw an exception if the divisor is 0:

```
fun div(a: Int, b: Int): Int = a / b
```

To make div a pure function, you could test the second parameter and return a value if it's null. It would have to be an Int, so it would be difficult to find a meaningful value, but that's another problem. The div function working on doubles is a pure function because dividing by 0.0 won't throw an exception, but will return Infinity, which is an instance of Double:

```
fun div(a: Double, b: Double): Double = a / b
```

Infinity is absorbing for addition, meaning that adding Infinity to anything returns Infinity. It's not fully absorbing for multiplication because multiplying Infinity by 0.0 results in NaN (Not a Number). Despite its name, NaN is an instance of Double. Let's consider the next code snippet:

```
var percent1 = 5
fun applyTax1(a: Int): Int = a / 100 * (100 + percent1)
```

The applyTax1 method doesn't seem to be a pure function because its result depends on the value of percent1, which is public, and can be modified between two function calls. As a consequence, two function calls with the same argument could return different values: percent1 can be considered an implicit parameter, but this parameter isn't evaluated at the same time as the explicit argument. This isn't a problem if you use the percent1 value only once inside the function, but if you read it twice, it could change between the two read operations. If you need to use the value twice, you must read it once and keep it in a local variable. This means the method applyTax1 is a pure function of the pair (a, percent1), but it's not a pure function of a.

In this example, the class itself can be considered a supplemental implicit argument because all its properties are accessible from inside the function. This is an important notion. All instance methods/functions can be replaced with non-instance methods/functions by adding an argument of the type of the enclosing class. The applyTax1 function can be rewritten outside the FunFunctions (or even inside) as

```
fun applyTax1(ff: FunFunctions, a: Int): Int = a / 100 * (100 + ff.percent1)
```

This function can be called from inside the class, passing a reference to this for the arguments, such as applyTax1(this, a). It can also be called from the outside because it's public, provided a reference to a FunFunctions instance is available. Here, applyTax1 is a pure function of the pair (this, a):

```
private var percent2 = 9

fun applyTax2(a: Int): Int = a / 100 * (100 + percent2)
```

The result of the applyTax2 function depends on the value of percent2, which is mutable (declared with var). The result of applyTax2 varies if percent2 is modified. No code actually mutates this variable, however, so applyTax2 is a pure function. It's unsafe, however, because it could become impure without any modification of the function itself by adding another function mutating percent2. This is a good reason for always making everything immutable unless you really need mutations. By default, always use the val keyword:

```
val percent3 = 13
fun applyTax3(a: Int): Int = a / 100 * (100 + percent3)
```

The applyTax3 function is a pure function of a because unlike applyTax1, it uses percent3, which is immutable:

```
fun append1(i: Int, list: MutableList<Int>): List<Int> {
    list.add(i)
    return list
}
```

The append1 function mutates its argument before returning it, and this mutation is visible from outside the function, so it isn't a pure function:

```
fun append2(i: Int, list: List<Int>) = list + i
```

The append2 function seems to add an element to its argument. But this is not the case. The expression list + i is evaluated to a new (immutable) list containing the same elements as the original list plus the added element. Nothing is mutated. append2 is a pure function.

3.2.5 *Using object notation versus functional notation*

You've seen that instance functions accessing class properties can be considered as having the enclosing class instance as an implicit parameter. Functions that don't access the enclosing class instance can be safely moved out of the class. You can put such functions in the companion object (making them roughly equivalent to Java static methods) or at the package level, outside of any class. You can also put functions accessing the enclosing instance in the companion object or at package level if their implicit parameter (the enclosing instance) is made explicit. Consider the `Payment` class from chapter 1:

```kotlin
class Payment(val creditCard: CreditCard, val amount: Int) {
    fun combine(payment: Payment): Payment =
            if (creditCard == payment.creditCard)
                Payment(creditCard, amount + payment.amount)
            else
                throw IllegalStateException("Cards don't match.")

    companion object {
        fun groupByCard(payments: List<Payment>): List<Payment> =
                payments.groupBy { it.creditCard }
                    .values
                    .map { it.reduce(Payment::combine) }
    }
}
```

The `combine` function accesses the enclosing class's `creditCard` and `amount` fields. As a result, it can't be put outside of the class or in the companion object. This function has the enclosing class as an implicit parameter. You could make this parameter explicit, which would allow you to define the function at the package level or in the companion object:

```kotlin
fun combine(payment1: Payment, payment2: Payment): Payment =
        if (payment1.creditCard == payment2.creditCard)
            Payment(payment1.creditCard, payment1.amount + payment2.amount)
        else
            throw IllegalStateException("Cards don't match.")
```

A function declared in the companion object or at package level lets you make sure no unwanted access exists to the enclosing scope. But it changes the way the function can be used. If used from inside the class, the function can be called passing it the `this` reference:

```kotlin
val newPayment = combine(this, otherPayment)
```

This makes little difference, but it all changes when you need to compose function calls. If you need to combine several payments, an instance function written as

```kotlin
fun combine(payment: Payment): Payment =
        if (creditCard == payment.creditCard)
            Payment(creditCard, amount + payment.amount)
        else
            throw IllegalStateException("Cards don't match.")
```

can be used with object notation like this:

```kotlin
val newPayment = payment1.combine(payment2).combine(payment2)
```

That's much easier to read than this:

```
import ...Payment.Companion.combine
```

```
val newPayment = combine(combine(payment1, payment2), payment3)
```

This example throws an exception if the credit cards don't match, but this is only because you've not yet learned how to handle errors functionally. This will be the subject of chapter 7.

3.2.6   *Using value functions*

I said previously that functions can be used as data, but this isn't the case for functions declared with the `fun` keyword. Kotlin allows treating functions as data. Kotlin has function types, and functions can be assigned to references of the corresponding types in the same way other types of data are treated. Consider the following function:

```
fun double(x: Int): Int = x * 2
```

The same function might be declared as

```
val double: (Int) -> Int = { x -> x * 2 }
```

The type of the `double` function is `(Int) -> Int`. At the left of the arrow is the parameter type, enclosed in parentheses. The return type is indicated on the right side of the arrow. The definition of the function comes after the equals sign. It's enclosed between braces and takes the form of a lambda expression.

In the previous example, the lambda consists of a name given to the parameter, an arrow, and an expression that when evaluated will be the result returned by the function. Here, this expression is simple, so it can be written on a single line. If the expression were more complex, it could be written on several lines. In such a case, the result would be the evaluation of the last line as in the following example:

```
val doubleThenIncrement: (Int) -> Int = { x ->
    val double = x * 2
    double + 1
}
```

The last line shouldn't have a `return`.

Functions of tuples are no different. Here's a function representing addition of integers:

```
val add: (Int, Int) -> Int = { x, y -> x + y }
```

As you can see, in the function type, the (single) argument is included between parentheses. By contrast, no parentheses can be used to enclose the parameter in the lambda expression.

When the parameter is not a tuple (or, more precisely, when it's a tuple of one single element), you can use the special name `it`:

```
val double: (Int) -> Int = { it * 2 }
```

This simplifies the syntax, although it sometimes makes the code less readable, particularly when several function implementations are nested.

> **NOTE** In this example, double isn't the name of the function. A function has no name. Here, it's assigned to a reference of the corresponding type, so that you can then manipulate it in the same way you'd do for any other piece of data. When you write
>
> ```
> val number: Int = 5
> ```
>
> you wouldn't say that number is the name of 5. It's the same for functions.

You might wonder why Kotlin has two kinds of functions. Because functions are values, why should you use the fun keyword to define functions?

As I said at the start of section 3.2.4, functions defined with fun aren't really functions. You can call them methods, subprograms, procedures, or whatever. They can represent pure functions (always returning the same value for a given argument without any other effect visible from outside), but you can't treat them as data.

Why should you use them? Because fun functions are much more efficient. They are an optimization. Each time you use a function only to pass it an argument and get the corresponding return value, you'll be using the version defined with fun. This is absolutely not mandatory, but it's wise.

On the other hand, each time you want to use a function as data (for example, to pass it to another function—an argument you'll see soon), or to get it as the return value of another function, or to store it in a variable, a map, or any other data structure, you'll be using an expression of the function type.

You may wonder how you can convert from one form to the other. It's quite simple. You'll only need to convert from fun to the expression type because you can't create fun at runtime.

3.2.7   *Using function references*

Kotlin offers the same functionality as Java does under the name of method references. But, as you may recall, in Kotlin methods are called functions, so method references are called function references in Kotlin. Here's an example of using a fun function in a lambda:

```
fun double(n: Int): Int = n * 2

val mutliplyBy2: (Int) -> Int = { n -> double(n) }
```

You could have also written

```
val mutliplyBy2: (Int) -> Int = { double(it) }
```

Using a function reference simplifies the syntax:

```
val mutliplyBy2: (Int) -> Int = ::double
```

Here, the `double` function is called on the same object, class, or package as the `mutliplyBy2` function. If it were an instance function of another class, you could use the following syntax, provided you have a reference to an instance of this class available:

```
class MyClass {
    fun double(n: Int): Int = n * 2
}

val foo = MyClass()
val mutliplyBy2: (Int) -> Int = foo::double
```

Alternatively, if `double` is defined in another package, you have to import it:

```
import other.package.double

val mutliplyBy2: (Int) -> Int = ::double
```

In the case of a function defined in the companion object of a class (somewhat equivalent to a Java static method), you can either import it or you can use the following syntax:

```
val mutliplyBy2: (Int) -> Int = (MyClass)::double
```

This is a shorthand for

```
val mutliplyBy2: (Int) -> Int = MyClass.Companion::double
```

Don't forget `.Companion` or the parentheses. Otherwise, you'll get a completely different result:

```
class MyClass {
    companion object {
        fun double(n: Int): Int = n * 2
    }
}

val mutliplyBy2: (MyClass, Int) -> Int = MyClass::double
```

In such a case, the `multiplyBy2` function type is not `(Int) -> Int`, but `(MyClass, Int) -> Int`.

3.2.8   *Composing functions*

If you use `fun` functions, composing them seems simple:

```
fun square(n: Int) = n * n

fun triple(n: Int) = n * 3

println(square(triple(2)))
```

36

But this isn't function composition. In this example, you're composing function applications. Function composition is a binary operation on functions, just as addition is a binary operation on numbers, so you can compose functions programmatically, using another function.

EXERCISE 3.1

Write the compose function (declared with 'fun'), allowing to compose functions from Int to Int.

> **NOTE** Solutions follow each exercise, but you should first try to solve the exercise without looking at the answer. The solution code also appears on the book's website. This exercise is simple, but some exercises will be quite hard, so it might be difficult to refrain from cheating. Remember that the harder you search, the more you learn.

HINT

The compose function will take as its parameters two functions of type (Int) -> Int and will return a function of the same type. The compose function can be declared with fun, but the parameters need to be values. You can transform a function myFunc declared with fun into a value (val) function, prefixing its name with ::.

SOLUTION

Here's the solution using a lambda:

```
fun compose(f: (Int) -> Int, g: (Int) -> Int): (Int) -> Int = { x -> f(g(x)) }
```

Alternatively, it can be simplified as

```
fun compose(f: (Int) -> Int, g: (Int) -> Int): (Int) -> Int = { f(g(it)) }
```

You can use this function to compose square and triple:

```
val squareOfTriple = compose(::square, ::triple)
println(squareOfTriple(2))
36
```

Now you can start to see how powerful this concept is! But two big problems remain. The first is that your functions can only take integer (Int) arguments and return integers. Let's deal with this first.

3.2.9 Reusing functions

To make your function more reusable, you can change it into a polymorphic function by using type parameters.

EXERCISE 3.2

Make the compose function polymorphic by using type parameters.

HINT

Declare the type parameters between the fun keyword and the name of the function. Then replace the Int types with the right parameters, taking care of the order of execution. Remember you're defining f ° g, meaning that you must first apply g, and then apply f to the result. Specify the return type. If the types don't match, it won't compile.

SOLUTION

The exercise doesn't consist in writing the implementation of the function. It's the same implementation as the nonpolymorphic one. It's about finding the right signature:

```
fun <T, U, V> compose(f: (U) -> V, g: (T) -> U): (T) -> V = { f(g(it)) }
```

Here, you're seeing the benefit of a strong type system with parameterized types. With type parameters, you can not only define a compose function that works for any types (provided the types match), but, unlike the Int version, you can't get it wrong. If you switch f and g, it'll no longer compile.

3.3   *Advanced function features*

Thus far, you've seen how to create, apply, and compose functions. But you haven't answered a fundamental question: Why do you need functions represented as data? Couldn't you simply use the fun version? Before answering this question, you need to consider the problem of *multi-argument* functions.

3.3.1   *What about functions of several arguments?*

In section 3.1.5, I said that there are no functions of several arguments, but only functions of one tuple of elements. The cardinality of a tuple can be whatever you need, and there are specific names for tuples with a few elements: pair, triplet, quartet, and so on. Other possible names exist, and some prefer to call them tuple2, tuple3, tuple4, and so forth. Kotlin has predefined Pair and Triple. But I also said that elements of the argument can be applied one by one, with each application of one element returning a new function, except for the last one.

Let's try to define a function for adding two integers. You'll apply a function to the first integer, and this will return a function. The type is as follows:

```
(Int) -> (Int) -> Int
```

In this syntax, (Int) is the type of the argument, and (Int) -> Int is the type of the return value. To remember how the -> symbol associates, you can think of this as if there were parentheses around the return value so it's equivalent to

```
(Int) -> ((Int) -> Int)
```

The argument type is Int and the return type is a function taking an argument of type Int, and returning an Int.

EXERCISE 3.3

Write a function to add two Int values.

SOLUTION

This function will take an Int as its argument and return a function from Int to Int, so the type will be (Int) -> (Int) -> Int. Let's give it the name add. It'll be implemented using lambdas. The end result is shown here:

```
val add: (Int) -> (Int) -> Int = { a -> { b -> a + b} }
```

If you prefer a shorter type name, you can create an alias:

```
typealias IntBinOp = (Int) -> (Int) -> Int

val add: IntBinOp = { a -> { b -> a + b} }
val mult: IntBinOp = { a -> { b -> a * b} }
```

Here `IntBinOp`, the type alias, stands for *Integer Binary Operator*. The number of arguments isn't limited. You can define functions with as many arguments as you need. As I said in the first part of this chapter, functions such as the `add` function or the `mult` function are said to be the curried form of the equivalent functions of tuples.

3.3.2 Applying curried functions

You've seen how to write curried function types and how to implement them. But how do you apply them? Well, you apply them like any function. You apply the function to the first argument, then apply the result to the next argument, and so on until the last one. For example, you can apply the `add` function to 3 and 5:

```
println(add(3)(5))
```

8

3.3.3 Implementing higher-order functions

In section 3.2.8, you wrote a `fun` function to compose functions. This function took as its argument a tuple of two functions and returned a function. But instead of using a `fun` function (actually a method), you could use a value function. This special kind of function, taking functions as its arguments and returning functions, is called a *higher-order function* (HOF).

EXERCISE 3.4

Write a value function to compose two functions; for example, the `square` and `triple` functions used previously.

SOLUTION

This exercise is easy if you follow the right procedure. The first thing to do is to write the type. This function will work on two arguments, so it'll be a curried function. The two arguments and the return type will be functions from `Int` to `Int`:

```
(Int) -> Int
```

You can call this `T`. You want to create a function taking an argument of type `T` (the first argument) and returning a function from `T` (the second argument) to `T` (the return value). The type of the function is then as follows:

```
(T) -> (T) -> T
```

If you replace `T` with its value, you obtain the real type:

```
((Int) -> Int) -> ((Int) -> Int) -> (Int) -> Int
```

The main problem here is the line length! Let's now add the implementation, which is much easier than the type:

```
x -> { y -> { z -> x(y(z)) } } }
```

The complete code is shown here:

```
val compose: ((Int) -> Int) -> ((Int) -> Int) -> (Int) -> Int =
                              { x -> { y -> { z -> x(y(z)) } } }
```

If you prefer, you can take advantage of type inference and omit specifying the return type. But you'll then have to specify the type of each argument:

```
val compose = { x: (Int) -> Int -> { y: (Int) -> Int ->
                              { z: Int -> x(y(z)) } } }
```

Or you can use an alias:

```
typealias IntUnaryOp = (Int) -> Int

val compose: (IntUnaryOp) -> (IntUnaryOp) -> IntUnaryOp =
                              { x -> { y -> { z -> x(y(z)) } } }
```

You can test this code with the square and triple functions:

```
typealias IntUnaryOp = (Int) -> Int

val compose: (IntUnaryOp) -> (IntUnaryOp) -> IntUnaryOp =
                              { x -> { y -> { z -> x(y(z)) } } }

val square: IntUnaryOp = { it * it }

val triple: IntUnaryOp = { it * 3 }

val squareOfTriple = compose(square)(triple)
```

In this code, you start by applying the first argument, which gives you a new function to apply to the second argument. The result is a function, which is the composition of the two function arguments. Applying this new function to (for example) 2 gives you the result of first applying triple to 2 and then applying square to the result (which corresponds to the definition of function composition):

```
println(squareOfTriple(2))
```

36

Pay attention to the order of the parameters: triple is applied first and then square is applied to the result returned by triple.

3.3.4 *Creating polymorphic HOFs*

Your compose function is fine, but it can compose only functions from Int to Int. A polymorphic compose function would also allow you to compose functions of different types, provided that the return type of one is the same as the argument type of the other.

EXERCISE 3.5 (HARD)

Write a polymorphic version of the compose function.

HINT

You'll face a problem with this exercise due to the lack of polymorphic properties in Kotlin. In Kotlin, you can create polymorphic classes, interfaces, and functions, but you can't define polymorphic properties. The solution is to store the function in a function, class, or interface, instead of in a property.

SOLUTION

The first step seems to be to "type parameterize" the example of Exercise 3.3:

```
val <T, U, V> higherCompose: ((U) -> V) -> ((T) -> U) -> (T) -> V =
    { f ->
        { g ->
            { x -> f(g(x)) }
        }
    }
```

But this isn't possible because Kotlin doesn't allow standalone parameterized properties. To be parameterized, a property must be created in a scope defining the type parameters. Only classes, interfaces, and functions declared with fun can define type parameters, so you need to define your property inside one of those elements. The most practical is a fun function:

```
fun <T, U, V> higherCompose(): ((U) -> V) -> ((T) -> U) -> (T) -> V =
    { f ->
        { g ->
            { x -> f(g(x)) }
        }
    }
```

The fun function called higherCompose() takes no parameter and always returns the same value. It's a constant. The fact that it's defined as a fun function is irrelevant from this point of view. It isn't a function for composing functions. It's only a fun function returning a value function that composes value functions. You may prefer to avoid indicating the return type. In such a case, you must indicate parameter types:

```
fun <T, U, V> higherCompose() =
    { f: (U) -> V ->
        { g: (T) -> U ->
            { x: T -> f(g(x)) }
        }
    }
```

Now you could use this function to compose triple and square:

```
val squareOfTriple = higherCompose()(square)(triple)
```

But this doesn't compile, producing the following error:

```
Error:(79, 24) Kotlin: Type inference failed:
    Not enough information to infer parameter T in fun <T, U, V>
    higherCompose(): ((U) -> V) -> ((T) -> U) -> (T) -> V
Please specify it explicitly.
```

The compiler is saying that it couldn't infer the real types for the T, U, and V type parameters. If you think that the type of the parameters ((Int) -> Int) should be enough information to infer the T, U, and V types, then you're smarter than Kotlin!

The solution is to help the compiler by telling it what real types T, U, and V are. Inserting the type information after the function name can do this:

```
val squareOfTriple = higherCompose<Int, Int, Int>()(square)(triple)
```

EXERCISE 3.6 (EASY NOW!)

Write the higherAndThen function that composes the functions the other way around, which means that higherCompose(f, g) is equivalent to higherAndThen(g, f).

SOLUTION

```
fun <T, U, V> higherAndThen(): ((T) -> U) -> ((U) -> V) -> (T) -> V =
    { f: (T) -> U ->
        { g: (U) -> V ->
            { x: T -> g(f(x)) }
        }
    }
```

Testing function parameters

If you have any doubt concerning the order of the parameters, you should test these HOFs with functions of different types. Testing with functions from Int to Int will be ambiguous because you'll be able to compose the functions in both orders, so an error will be difficult to detect. Here's a test using functions of different types:

```
fun testHigherCompose() {

    val f: (Double) -> Int = { a -> (a * 3).toInt() }
    val g: (Long) -> Double = { a -> a + 2.0 }

    assertEquals(Integer.valueOf(9), f(g(1L)))
    assertEquals(Integer.valueOf(9),
        higherCompose<Long, Double, Int>()(f)(g)(1L))
}
```

3.3.5 *Using anonymous functions*

Up to now, you've been using named functions. Often, you won't define names for functions; you'll use them as anonymous functions. Let's look at an example. Instead of writing

```
val f: (Double) -> Double = { Math.PI / 2 - it }
val sin: (Double) -> Double = Math::sin
val cos: Double = compose(f, sin)(2.0)
```

you can use anonymous functions as shown here:

```
val cosValue: Double =
        compose({ x: Double -> Math.PI / 2 - x }, Math::sin)(2.0)
```

Here, you're using the `compose` function defined with `fun` at the package level. But this also applies to HOFs:

```
val cos = higherCompose<Double, Double, Double>()
                ({ x: Double -> Math.PI / 2 - x })( Math::sin)

val cosValue = cos(2.0)
```

The two parameters in the `cos` function definition are enclosed in separate sets of parentheses. Unlike the `compose` function, `higherCompose` is defined in curried form, applying one parameter at a time. Also note that the lambda can be put outside of the parentheses:

```
val cos = higherCompose<Double, Double, Double>()()
                { x: Double -> Math.PI / 2 - x }( Math::sin)
```

Beside the fact that lines are broken due to limited line length in this book, the last form might seem a bit awkward, but it's the recommended formatting in Kotlin.

WHEN TO USE ANONYMOUS FUNCTIONS AND WHEN TO USE NAMED FUNCTIONS

Apart from special cases when anonymous functions can't be used, it's up to you to choose between anonymous and named value functions. (Functions declared with `fun` always have a name.) As a general rule, functions that are used only once are defined as anonymous instances. But *used once* means that you write the function once. It doesn't mean that it's instantiated only once.

In the following example, you define a `fun` function to compute the cosine of a `Double` value. The function implementation uses two anonymous functions because you're using a lambda expression and a function reference:

```
fun cos(arg: Double) = compose({ x -> Math.PI / 2 - x }, Math::sin)(arg)
```

Don't worry about the creation of anonymous functions. Kotlin won't always create new objects each time the function is called. Instantiating such objects is cheap. Instead, you should decide whether to use anonymous or named functions by considering only the clarity and maintainability of your code. If you're concerned with performance and reusability, you should use function references as often as possible.

IMPLEMENTING TYPE INFERENCE

Type inference can also be an issue with anonymous functions. In the previous example, the types of the two anonymous functions can be inferred by the compiler because it knows that the compose function takes two functions as arguments:

```
fun <T, U, V> compose(f: (U) -> V, g: (T) -> U): (T) -> V = { f(g(it)) }
```

But this won't always work. If you replace the second argument with a lambda instead of a function reference

```
fun cos(arg: Double) =
    compose({ x -> Math.PI / 2 - x }, { y -> Math.sin(y)})(arg)}
```

the compiler is lost and displays the following error message:

```
Error:(48, 28) Kotlin: Type inference failed: Not enough information to infer
    parameter T in fun <T, U, V> compose(f: (U) -> V, g: (T) -> U): (T) -> V
```

```
Please specify it explicitly.
Error:(48, 38) Kotlin: Cannot infer a type for this parameter.
                      Please specify it explicitly.
Error:(48, 64) Kotlin: Cannot infer a type for this parameter.
                      Please specify it explicitly.
```

Kotlin is now unable to infer the types of both arguments. To make this code compile, you need to add type annotations:

```
fun cos(arg: Double) =
    compose({ x: Double -> Math.PI / 2 - x },
            { x: Double -> Math.sin(x) })(arg)
```

This is a good reason to prefer function references.

3.3.6   *Defining local functions*

You saw that you can define value functions locally in functions, but Kotlin also allows defining fun functions inside functions, as seen in the following example:

```
fun cos(arg: Double): Double {
    fun f(x: Double): Double = Math.PI / 2 - x
    fun sin(x: Double): Double = Math.sin(x)
    return compose(::f, ::sin)(arg)
}
```

3.3.7   *Implementing closures*

You've seen that pure functions mustn't depend on anything other than their arguments to evaluate their return values. Kotlin functions often access elements outside the function itself, either at the package level or as class or object properties. Functions can even access members of other classes's companion objects or other packages.

I've said that pure functions are functions that respect referential transparency, which means they have no observable effects besides returning a value. But what about functions with return values depending not only on their arguments, but also on elements belonging to the enclosing scope? You've already seen this case, and these elements of the enclosing scope could be considered implicit parameters of the functions using them.

This also applies to lambdas, and Kotlin lambdas don't have the same limitation as Java lambdas: they can access mutable variables of the enclosing scope. Let's look at an example:

```
val taxRate = 0.09
fun addTax(price: Double) = price + price * taxRate
```

In this example, the addTax function *closes* over the taxRate variable. It's important to note that addTax isn't a function of price because it won't always give the same result for the same argument. But it can be seen as a function of the tuple (price, taxRate).

Closures are compatible with pure functions if you consider them as additional implicit arguments. They can cause problems when refactoring the code, and also when functions are passed as parameters to other functions. This can result in programs that are difficult to read and maintain.

One way to make programs easier to read and maintain is to make them more modular, meaning that each part of the programs might be used as independent modules. This can be achieved by using functions of tuples of arguments:

```
val taxRate = 0.09

fun addTax(taxRate: Double, price: Double) = price + price * taxRate

println(addTax(taxRate, 12.0))
```

This applies also to value functions:

```
val taxRate = 0.09

val addTax = { taxRate: Double, price: Double -> price + price * taxRate }

println(addTax(taxRate, 12.0))
```

The `addTax` function takes a single argument, which is a pair of `Double`. Unlike Java, Kotlin allows the use of arguments of cardinality greater than 2. (In Java, you can use the `Function` interface for a single argument and the `BiFunction` interface for a pair of arguments. If you want triples or more, you have to define your own interfaces.)

But you've already seen that you could use the curried version to get the same result. A curried function takes a single argument and returns a function taking a single argument, returning… and so on until returning the final value. Here's the curried version of the `addTax` value function:

```
val taxRate = 0.09

val addTax = { taxRate: Double ->
                 { price: Double ->
                     price + price * taxRate
                 }
             }

println(addTax(taxRate)(12.0))
```

A curried version of a `fun` function makes little sense. You could use a `fun` for the first function, but you're forced to return a value function. `fun` function aren't values.

3.3.8 *Applying functions partially and automatic currying*

The closure and curried versions in the previous example give the same results and might be seen as equivalent. In fact, they're *semantically* different. As I've already said, the two parameters play totally different roles. The tax rate isn't supposed to change often, whereas the price is supposed to be different on each invocation. This appears clearly in the closure version. The function closes over a parameter that doesn't change (because it's a `val`). In the curried version, both arguments can change on each invocation, although the tax rate won't change more often than in the closure version.

It's common to need a changing tax rate, such as when you have several tax rates for different categories of products or for different shipping destinations. In traditional object programming, turning the class into a parameterized *tax computer* could accommodate this. Here's an example:

```
class TaxComputer(private val rate: Double) {

    fun compute(price: Double): Double = price * rate + price
}
```

With this class, you can create several `TaxComputer` instances for several tax rates, and these instances can be reused as often as needed:

```
val tc9 = TaxComputer(0.09)
val price = tc9.compute(12.0)
```

You can achieve the same thing with a curried function by partially applying it:

```
val tc9 = addTax(0.09)
val price = tc9(12.0)
```

Here, the `addTax` function is the one from the end of section 3.3.7. The type of `tc9` is now `(Double) -> Double`; it's a function taking a `Double` as its argument and returning a `Double` with the tax added.

You can see that currying and partial application are closely related. Currying consists in replacing a function of a tuple with a new function that you can partially apply, one argument after another. This is the main difference between a curried function and a function of a tuple. With a function of a tuple, all arguments are evaluated before the function is applied.

With the curried version, all arguments must be known before the function is totally applied, but a single argument can be evaluated and the function partially applied to it. You aren't obligated to totally curry the function. A function of three arguments can be curried into a function of a tuple that produces a function of a single argument.

Abstraction being the essence of programming, currying and partially applying functions can be abstracted in order to do this automatically. In the preceding sections, you used mostly curried functions and not functions of tuples. Using curried functions presents a great advantage: partially applying this kind of function is absolutely straightforward.

EXERCISE 3.7 (EASY)

Write a `fun` function to partially apply a curried function of two arguments to its first argument.

SOLUTION

You have nothing to do! The signature of this function is as follows:

```
fun <A, B, C> partialA(a: A, f: (A) -> (B) -> C): (B) -> C
```

You can see immediately that partially applying the first argument is as simple as applying the second argument (a function) to the first one:

```
fun <A, B, C> partialA(a: A, f: (A) -> (B) -> C): (B) -> C = f(a)
```

(If you'd like to see an example of how `partialA` can be used, look at the unit test for this exercise in the accompanying code.)

You might have noticed that the original function was of type `(A) -> (B) -> C`. What if you want to partially apply this function to the second argument?

EXERCISE 3.8

Write a `fun` function to partially apply a curried function of two arguments to its second argument.

SOLUTION

With your previous function, the answer to the problem would be a function with the following signature:

```
fun <A, B, C> partialB(b: B, f: (A) -> (B) -> C): (A) -> C
```

This exercise is slightly more difficult, but still simple if you carefully consider the types. Remember, you should always trust the types! They won't give you an immediate solution in all cases, but they'll lead you to the solution. This function has only one possible implementation, so if you find an implementation that compiles, you can be sure it's correct!

What you know is that you must return a function from A to C. You can start the implementation by writing this:

```
fun <A, B, C> partialB(b: B, f: (A) -> (B) -> C): (A) -> C =
    { a: A ->

    }
```

Here, a is a variable of type A. After the right arrow, you must write an expression that's composed of the function f and the variables a and b, and it must evaluate to a function from A to C. The function f is a function from A to `(B) -> C`, so you can start by applying it to the A you have:

```
fun <A, B, C> partialB(b: B, f: (A) -> (B) -> C): (A) -> C =
    { a: A ->
        f(a)
    }
```

This gives you a function from B to C. You need a C and you already have a B, so once again, the answer is straightforward:

```
fun <A, B, C> partialB(b: B, f: (A) -> (B) -> C): (A) -> C =
    { a: A ->
        f(a)(b)
    }
```

That's it! In fact, you had nearly nothing to do but to follow the types.

As I said, the most important thing is that you had a curried version of the function. You'll probably learn quickly how to write curried functions directly. One task that comes back frequently when trying to push abstraction to the limit in order to write more reusable programs is converting functions with tuple arguments into curried functions. As you just saw, this is extremely simple.

EXERCISE 3.9 (EASY)

Convert the following function into a curried function:

```
fun <A, B, C, D> func(a: A, b: B, c: C, d: D): String = "$a, $b, $c, $d"
```

(I agree that this function is totally useless, but it's only an exercise.)

SOLUTION

Once again, you don't have much to do besides replacing the commas with right arrows and adding parentheses. Remember, however, that you must define this function in a scope that accepts type parameters, which isn't the case for a property. You must then define it in a class, an interface, or a 'fun' function with all needed type parameters.

Here's a solution using a function. First, write the enclosing fun function declaration with the type parameters:

```
fun <A,B,C,D> curried()
```

Then, think about the signature of the resulting function. The first parameter will be an A, so you can write

```
fun <A,B,C,D> curried(): (A) ->
```

Then do the same thing with the second parameter type:

```
fun <A,B,C,D> curried(): (A) -> (B) ->
```

Then continue until no parameters are left:

```
fun <A,B,C,D> curried(): (A) -> (B) -> (C) -> (D) ->
```

Add the return type of the resulting function:

```
fun <A,B,C,D> curried(): (A) -> (B) -> (C) -> (D) -> String
```

For the implementation, list as many parameters as needed, separating them with right arrows and opening braces (starting with a brace and ending with an arrow):

```
fun <A,B,C,D> curried() =
        { a: A ->
            { b: B ->
                { c: C ->
                    { d: D ->

                    }
                }
            }
        }
```

Finally, add the implementation, which is the same as in the original function, and close all braces:

```
fun <A,B,C,D> curried() =
        { a: A ->
            { b: B ->
                { c: C ->
                    { d: D ->
                        "$a, $b, $c, $d"
                    }
```

```
            }
        }
    }
```

The same principle can be applied to curry a function of any tuple.

EXERCISE 3.10

Write a function to curry a function of a `(A, B)` to `C`.

SOLUTION

Again, you have to follow the types. You know the function will take a parameter of type `(A, B) -> C` and will return `(A) -> (B) -> C`, so the signature is as follows:

```
fun <A, B, C> curry(f: (A, B) -> C): (A) -> (B) -> C
```

Now, for the implementation, you'll have to return a curried function of two arguments, so you can start with this:

```
fun <A, B, C> curry(f: (A, B) -> C): (A) -> (B) -> C =
    { a ->
        { b ->

        }
    }
```

Eventually, you'll need to evaluate the return type. For this, you can use the function `f` and apply it to parameters a and b:

```
fun <A, B, C> curry(f: (A, B) -> C): (A) -> (B) -> C =
    { a ->
        { b ->
            f(a, b)
        }
    }
```

Once again, if it compiles, it can't be wrong. This is one of the numerous benefits of relying on a strong type system! (This isn't always true, but you'll learn in the next chapters how to make this happen more often.)

3.3.9 *Switching arguments of partially-applied functions*

If you have a function of two arguments, you might want to apply only the first argument to get a partially-applied function. Let's say you have the following function:

```
val addTax: (Double) -> (Double) -> Double =
    { x ->
        { y ->
            y + y / 100 * x
        }
    }
```

You might want to first apply the tax to get a new function of one argument that you can then apply to any price:

```
val add9percentTax: (Double) -> Double = addTax(9.0)
```

Then, when you want to add tax to a price, you can do this:

```
val priceIncludingTax = add9percentTax(price);
```

This is fine, but what if the initial function was as follows:

```
val addTax: (Double) -> (Double) -> Double =
    { x ->
        { y ->
            x + x / 100 * y
        }
    }
```

In this case, the price is the first argument. Applying the price only is probably useless, but how can you apply the tax only? (Suppose you don't have access to the implementation.)

EXERCISE 3.11

Write a 'fun' function to swap the arguments of a curried function.

SOLUTION

The following function returns a curried function with the arguments in reverse order. It could be generalized to any number of arguments and to any arrangement of them:

```
fun <T, U, V> swapArgs(f: (T) -> (U) -> V): (U) -> (T) -> (V) =
                                    { u -> { t -> f(t)(u) } }
```

Given this function, you can partially apply any of the two arguments. For example, if you have a function computing the monthly payment for a loan from an interest rate and an amount

```
val  payment = { amount -> { rate -> ... } }
```

You can easily create a function of one argument to compute the payment for a fixed amount and a varying rate, or a function computing the payment for a fixed rate and a varying amount.

3.3.10 *Declaring the identity function*

You've seen that you can treat functions as data. They can be passed as arguments to other functions, they can be returned by functions, and they can be used in operations exactly like integers or strings. In future exercises, you'll apply operations to functions, and you'll need a neutral element for these operations. A *neutral element* acts as the 0 for addition, or 1 for multiplication, or the empty string for string concatenation.

A neutral element is only neutral for a given operation. For integer addition, 1 is not neutral, and for multiplication, 0 is even less neutral. Here, I'm speaking of a neutral element for function composition. This specific function is a function returning its argument. For this reason, it's called the *identity* function. By extension, the term *identity element* is often used instead of neutral element for operations such as addition multiplication or string concatenation. The identity function in Kotlin can be expressed simply:

```
val identity = { it }
```

3.3.11 *Using the right types*

In the previous examples, you've used standard types such as `Int`, `Double`, and `String` to represent business entities such as prices and tax rates. Although this is common practice in programming, it causes problems that should be avoided. As I said, you should trust types more than names. Calling a `Double` "price" doesn't make it a price. It only shows your intention. Calling another `Double` "taxRate" shows a different intention, which no compiler can enforce.

To make programs safer, you need to use more powerful types that the compiler can check. This prevents messing with types such as adding `taxRate` to a `price`. If you inadvertently do this, the compiler will only see a `Double` being added to a `Double`, which is perfectly legit, but totally wrong.

AVOIDING PROBLEMS WITH STANDARD TYPES

Let's examine a simplified problem and see how solving it by using standard types leads to problems. Imagine you have products with a name, a price, and a weight, and you need to create invoices representing product sales. These invoices must mention the products, the quantities, the total price, and the total weight. You could represent a `Product` with the following class:

```
data class Product(val name: String, val price: Double, val weight: Double)
```

Next, you can use an `OrderLine` class to represent each line of an order:

```
data class OrderLine(val product: Product, val count: Int) {

    fun weight() = product.weight * count

    fun amount() = product.price * count
}
```

This looks like a good old object, initialized with a `Product` and an `Int`, and representing one line of an order. It also has functions for returning the total price and the total weight for the line.

Continuing with the decision to use standard types, you'll use `List<OrderLine>` to represent an order. The following listing shows how you can handle orders.

Listing 3.2 Handling orders

```
package com.fpinkotlin.functions.listing03_02

data class Product(val name: String, val price: Double, val weight: Double)

data class OrderLine(val product: Product, val count: Int) {

    fun weight() = product.weight * count

    fun amount() = product.price * count
}

object Store {          ◀───┐  Store is a singleton object.
```

```
@JvmStatic  ◄─────────────────────────────────
fun main(args: Array<String>) {
    val toothPaste = Product("Tooth paste", 1.5, 0.5)
    val toothBrush = Product("Tooth brush", 3.5, 0.3)
    val orderLines = listOf(
            OrderLine(toothPaste, 2),
            OrderLine(toothBrush, 3))
    val weight = orderLines.sumByDouble { it.amount() }
    val price = orderLines.sumByDouble { it.weight() }
    println("Total price: $price")
    println("Total weight: $weight")
  }
}
```

The @JvmStatic annotation makes the main function callable as if it were a Java static method.

Running this program displays the following result on the console:

```
Total price: 1.9
Total weight: 13.5
```

This is fine, but wrong! Although the error is obvious, the problem is that the compiler didn't tell you anything about it. (You can see the error by looking at the Store code.) But the same error could have been made when creating a Product, and the creation of a Product could have happened far away.

The only way to catch this error is to test the program, but tests can't prove a program to be correct. They can only prove that you haven't been able to prove it incorrect through writing another program (which, by the way, could be incorrect too). In case you didn't notice it (which is unlikely), the problem is in the following lines:

```
val weight = orderLines.sumByDouble { it.amount() }
val price = orderLines.sumByDouble { it.weight() }
```

You have incorrectly mixed prices and weights, which the compiler couldn't notice because those are both doubles.

NOTE If you've learned about modeling, you might recall an old rule: classes shouldn't have several properties of the same type. Instead, they should have one property with a specific cardinality. Here, this would mean that a Product should have one property of type Double with a cardinality of 2. This is clearly not the right way to solve the problem, but it's a good rule to remember. If you find yourself modeling objects with several properties of the same type, you're probably doing it wrong.

What can you do to avoid such problems? First, you have to realize that prices and weights aren't numbers; they're quantities. Quantities can be numbers, but prices are quantities of money units and weights are quantities of weight units. You should never be in the situation of adding ounces and dollars.

DEFINING VALUE TYPES

To avoid this problem, you should use value types. *Value types* are types representing values. You can define a value type to represent a price like this:

```
data class Price(val value: Double)
```

You can do the same for the weight:

```
data class Weight(val value: Double)
```

But this doesn't solve the problem because you could write this:

```
val total = price.value + weight.value
```

What you need to do is to define addition for `Price` and for `Weight`, and you can do that with a function:

```
data class Price(val value: Double) {

    operator fun plus(price: Price) = Price(this.value + price.value)
}

data class Weight(val value: Double) {

    operator fun plus(weight: Weight) = Weight(this.value + weight.value)
}
```

The `operator` keyword means that you'll be able to use the function name in an infix position. Furthermore, as the function is named `plus`, you'll be able to replace this name with the + symbol, like this:

```
val totalPrice = Price(1.0) + Price(2.0)
```

You also need multiplication, but multiplication is a bit different. Addition adds things of the same type, whereas multiplication multiplies things of one type by a number. Multiplication isn't commutative when it isn't applied only to numbers. Here's an example of multiplication for `Price`:

```
data class Price(val value: Double) {

    fun plus(price: Price) = Price(this.value + price.value)

    fun times(num: Int) = Price(this.value * num)
}
```

Now, you no longer use `sumByDouble` to compute the sum of `Price` list. You could define an equivalent function `sumByPrice`. If you're interested, you might look at the implementation of `sumByDouble` and adapt it to prices. But there's a much better way to go.

Reducing a collection to a single element is called either `fold` or `reduce`. The distinction isn't always made clear, but most often, it's understood as depending on two conditions:

- Whether you provide an element to start with (`fold`) or not (`reduce`)
- Whether the result has to be of the same type as the elements (`reduce`) or not (`fold`)

The difference is that if the collection is empty, `reduce` will have no result, whereas `fold` will result in the starting element you provide. In chapter 6, you'll learn more about how this works. For now, you need to use the `fold` function offered by Kotlin collections. This function takes two parameters: the starting value and a function allowing you to compose the current result with the current element, while iterating over each element.

A reduce function is much like a fold, although it has no starting value. It must then take the first element as the starting value, which implies that the result type is the same as the element type. If applied to an empty collection, the result is null or an error, or any other representation of the fact that there's no result.

In the following example, because you'll use fold, you'll use a zero price—Price(0.0)—and a zero weight—Weight(0.0)—for the starting values. The function used as the second parameter uses the addition you just defined. To make it a value function, you can use a lambda:

```
val zeroPrice = Price(0.0)
val zeroWeigth = Weight(0.0)
val priceAddition = { x, y -> x + y }
```

The Product class needs to be modified as follows:

```
data class Product(val name: String, val price: Price, val weight: Weight)
```

OrderLine doesn't need any modifications:

```
data class OrderLine(val product: Product, val count: Int) {

    fun weight() = product.weight * count

    fun amount() = product.price * count
}
```

The * operator is now automatically replaced by a call to the times functions you've defined. You can now rewrite the Store object with these types and operations:

```
object Store {

    @JvmStatic
    fun main(args: Array<String>) {
        val toothPaste = Product("Tooth paste", Price(1.5), Weight(0.5))
        val toothBrush = Product("Tooth brush", Price(3.5), Weight(0.3))
        val orderLines = listOf(
            OrderLine(toothPaste, 2),
            OrderLine(toothBrush, 3))
        val weight: Weight =
            orderLines.fold(Weight(0.0)) { a, b -> a + b.weight() }
        val price: Price =
            orderLines.fold(Price(0.0)) { a, b -> a + b.amount() }
        println("Total price: $price")
        println("Total weight: $weight")
    }
}
```

You can't mess with types anymore without the compiler warning you. This implies that you specify the types for val weight: Weight and val price: Price. Kotlin is able to infer the types, but by specifying them, you make it possible for the compiler to tell you if the inferred types differ from what you expect.

But you can do far better than this. First, you can add validation to `Price` and `Weight`. Neither of them should be constructed with a 0 value, except from inside the class itself, for the identity element. You can use a private constructor and a factory function. Here's how it goes for `Price`:

```
data class Price private constructor (private val value: Double) {

    override fun toString() = value.toString()

    operator fun plus(price: Price) = Price(this.value + price.value)

    operator fun times(num: Int) = Price(this.value * num)

    companion object {
        val identity = Price(0.0)

        operator fun invoke(value: Double) =
            if (value > 0)
                Price(value)
            else
                throw IllegalArgumentException(
                  "Price must be positive or null")
    }
}
```

The constructor is now private, and the `invoke` function of the companion object is declared as `operator` and contains the validation code. The name `invoke` is a special name like `plus` and `times` that, when used with the `operator` keyword, makes it possible for you to override an operator.

Here, the operator that's overloaded is `()`, which corresponds to the invocation of a function. As a result, you can use the factory function exactly like the constructor, which is now private. The private constructor is used from the companion object to create the result of the function. It's also used to create the `identity` value used for folding. Here's the final code of the `Store` object:

```
object Store {

    @JvmStatic
    fun main(args: Array<String>) {
        val toothPaste = Product("Tooth paste", Price(1.5), Weight(0.5))
        val toothBrush = Product("Tooth brush", Price(3.5), Weight(0.3))
        val orderLines = listOf(
            OrderLine(toothPaste, 2),
            OrderLine(toothBrush, 3))
        val weight: Weight =
            orderLines.fold(Weight.identity) { a, b ->
                a + b.weight()
            }
        val price: Price =
            orderLines.fold(Price.identity) { a, b ->
                a + b.amount()
            }
        println("Total price: $price")
```

```
        println("Total weight: $weight")
    }
}
```

Nothing has changed for the creation of a price or a weight. The syntax to call the `invoke` function is similar to the way you previously used the constructor, which is now private. The "zero" value (called `identity`) used for the fold is read from the companion object. It couldn't be created from the `invoke` function due to the validation code throwing an exception.

> **NOTE** The private constructor of a data class isn't private because it's exposed by the generated copy function. But this isn't a problem. You can only copy an object that has already been validated.

Summary

- A function represents a relationship between a source set and a target set. It establishes a correspondence between the elements of the source set (the domain) and the elements of the target set (the codomain).
- Pure functions have no visible effects besides returning a value.
- Functions have only one argument, which can be a tuple of several elements.
- You can curry functions of tuples in order to apply them to one element of the tuple at a time.
- When a curried function is applied to only some of its arguments, it's said to be partially applied.
- In Kotlin, functions can be represented by `fun` functions, which are methods, or by value functions, which can be handled as data.
- Value functions can be implemented by using lambdas or by using references to `fun` functions.
- You can compose functions to create new functions.
- You can use lambdas and function references in places where a value function is expected.
- You can use value types to make programs safer by allowing the compiler to detect type problems.

Recursion, corecursion, and memoization

Recursive functions are a ubiquitous feature in many programming languages, although those are seldom used in Java. That's because of the poor implementation of this functionality. Fortunately, Kotlin offers a much better implementation, so that you can use recursion widely.

With recursion, many algorithms are defined recursively. Implementing these algorithms in non-recursive languages consists mainly of translating recursive algorithms into non-recursive ones. Using a language capable of handling recursion not only simplifies coding, but also allows writing programs that reflect the intention (the original algorithm). Such programs are generally much easier to read and to understand. And programming is much more about reading programs that writing them, so it's important to create programs that clearly show what's done rather than how it's done.

> **IMPORTANT** Be aware that, like loops, recursion should often be abstracted into functions, rather than used directly.

4.1 Corecursion and recursion

Corecursion is composing computation steps by using the output of one step as the input of the next one, starting with the first step. *Recursion* is the same operation but starts with the last step. Let's take as an example a list of characters that you want to join into a string representation.

4.1.1 Implementing corecursion

Let's suppose you have at your disposal an append function taking a pair of (String, Char) as its arguments and returning the argument string with the argument character appended to it:

```
fun append(s: String, c: Char): String = "$s$c"
```

You can't do anything with this function because you've no string to start with. You need an additional element: the empty string "". With these two elements, you can now construct the intended result. Figure 4.1 shows the processing of the list.

This process can be described in code as

```
fun toString(list: List<Char>, s: String): String =
        if (list.isEmpty())
            s
        else
            toString(list.subList(1, list.size), append(s, list[0]))
```

With corecursion, computation can be carried on at each step.

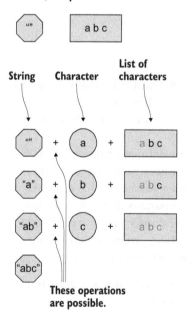

These operations are possible.

Figure 4.1   Corecursively transforming a list of characters into a string

Note that list [0] returns the first element of the list, which corresponds to a function generally known by the name head. On the other hand, list.subList(1, list.size) corresponds to a function named tail, which returns the rest of the list. You could abstract these into separate functions, but you'd have to handle the case of an empty list. Here, this won't happen because the list is filtered by the if..else expression.

A more idiomatic solution would be to use the functions drop and first:

```
fun toString(list: List<Char>, s: String): String =
        if (list.isEmpty())
            s
        else
            toString(list.drop(1), append(s, list.first()))
```

Using indexed access makes comparing corecursion and recursion easier. The only problem with this implementation is that you have to call the toString function with the empty string as an additional argument (or more precisely, as an additional part of its argument). The simple solution is to write another function for this, taking advantage of the fact that Kotlin lets you declare functions inside functions:

```
fun toString(list: List<Char>): String {
    fun toString(list: List<Char>, s: String): String =
            if (list.isEmpty())
                s
            else
                toString(list.subList(1, list.size), append(s, list[0]))
    return toString(list, "")
}
```

Here you'll have to use a block function, meaning a function with curly braces, for the enclosing toString function. You also have to indicate explicitly the return type of both functions for two reasons:

- For the enclosing function, block functions must have an explicit return type; otherwise, Unit is assumed. (Unit is the Kotlin equivalent of Java void, or more exactly Void.)
- For the enclosed function, you must indicate the type, because the function is calling itself. In such a case, Kotlin can't infer the return type.

Another solution would be to add a second parameter to the function with a default value:

```
fun toString(list: List<Char>, s: String = ""): String =
        if (list.isEmpty())
            s
        else
            toString(list.subList(1, list.size), append(s, list[0]))
```

4.1.2 *Implementing recursion*

The previous implementation was possible only because you had at your disposal the append function, which appends a character to a string, meaning adding the character to the end of the string. Now think about what you'd do if you only had access to the following function:

```kotlin
fun prepend(c: Char, s: String): String = "$c$s"
```

You could start with the end of the list. For this, you could either reverse the list before starting the computation, or you could change the implementation to return the last element of the list and the list without its last element. Here's a possible implementation:

```kotlin
fun toString(list: List<Char>): String {
    fun toString(list: List<Char>, s: String): String =
            if (list.isEmpty())
                s
            else
                toString(list.subList(0, list.size - 1),
                        prepend(list[list.size - 1], s))
    return toString(list, "")
}
```

This would, however, only work with lists offering this type of access, such as the indexed list or the doubly-linked list, also known as *deque* (pronounced *dek* and meaning *double-ended queue*). If you were working with singly-linked lists, you'd have no choice but to reverse the list, which is far from efficient.

As a worst case scenario, take infinite lists. You might think that there's nothing you can do with infinite lists, but this isn't true. With Kotlin, you can apply functions to infinite lists, which produces other infinite lists. You can compose such functions to get the intended result, and then truncate the result before it's computed.

Think of this example: if you want to compute the list of the 100 first primes (not that this would be extremely useful, but it's only an example), you'd have to iterate the list of integers (which is infinite), testing which are primes, and stopping after the 100th prime. In this example, you could certainly not start with reversing the list. The solution is to use recursion instead of corecursion as shown in figure 4.2.

As you can see in the figure, no computation can be carried on until the terminal condition (here, the last element of the list) is encountered. As a result, intermediate steps must be stored somewhere until they can be evaluated. This process might be expressed in code as

```kotlin
fun toString(list: List<Char>): String =
    if (list.isEmpty())
        ""
    else
        prepend(list[0], toString(list.subList(1, list.size)))
```

As you'll see, the main problem with this type of code is storing the intermediate steps. That's because the JVM uses very limited memory space for this.

4.1.3   *Differentiating recursive and corecursive functions*

Considering what you've learned at school, you may think that both the recursive and corecursive examples are, in fact, *recursive functions*, meaning functions calling

With recursion, computation must be delayed until the terminal condition is reached.

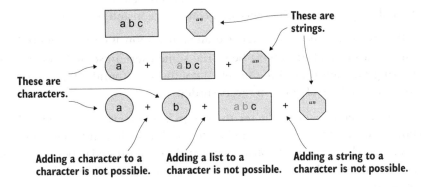

Up to this step, no operation may be computed.

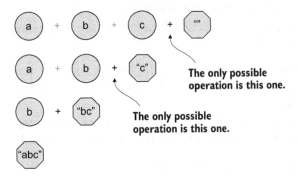

Figure 4.2 Recursively transforming a list of characters into a string

themselves. Well, if you stick by this definition of recursion, you're right. But this isn't what recursion is.

A function is recursive if it calls itself as part of a computation. Otherwise, it's not true recursion. At least, it isn't a recursive process. It might be a corecursive one. Think of a method printing "Hello, World!" on the screen and eventually calling itself recursively:

```
fun hello() {
    println("Hello, World!")
    hello()
}
```

Doesn't this look more like an infinite loop than a recursive method? Although it's implemented as a recursive method, it is in fact a corecursive one that could translate into an infinite loop! The good news is that Kotlin is able to do this translation automatically.

4.1.4   *Choosing recursion or corecursion*

The problem with recursion is that all languages impose a limit to the number of recursive steps. In theory, the main difference between recursion and corecursion is as follows:

- With corecursion, each step can be evaluated as soon as it's encountered.
- With recursion, all steps must be stored somewhere in some form. This allows delaying evaluation until the terminal condition is found. Only then can each previous step be evaluated, in reverse order.

The memory needed for storing the recursive steps is often severely limited and can easily overflow. To prevent this problem, it's best to avoid recursion and prefer corecursion.

The distinction between recursion and corecursion is illustrated in figures 4.3 and 4.4. These figures represent the computation of the sum of a list of integers. Addition is a bit special because

- It's commutative, meaning $a + b = b + a$, which isn't the case for most operations, such as adding a character to a string.
- The two parameters, as well as the result, are of the same type. Once again, this isn't generally the case.

You might think the operations on the figures could be transformed, for example, by removing parentheses. Let's say it's not possible. (This is only an example to show what's happening.)

In figure 4.3, you can see a corecursive process. Each step is evaluated as soon as it's encountered. As a result, the amount of memory needed for the whole process is

Corecursive computation of the sum of the first 10 integers

```
sum(1 to 10)
= 1 + sum(2 to 10)
= (1 + 2) + sum(3 to 10)
= 3 + sum(3 to 10)
= (3 + 3) + sum(4 to 10)
= 6 + sum(4 to 10)
= (6 + 4) + sum(5 to 10)
= 10 + sum(5 to 10)
= (10 + 5) + sum(6 to 10)
= 15 + sum(6 to 10)
= (15 + 6) + sum(7 to 10)
= 21 + sum(7 to 10)
= (21 + 7) + sum(8 to 10)
= 28 + sum(8 to 10)
= (28 + 8) + sum(9 to 10)
= 36 + sum(9 to 10)
= (36 + 9) + sum(10 to 10)
= 45 + sum(10 to 10)
= 45 + 10
= 55
```

Memory needed

Figure 4.3   A corecursive computation

constant, symbolized by the rectangle at the bottom of the figure. Figure 4.4, on the other hand, shows how a recursive process can be used to compute the same result.

No intermediate result can be evaluated until all steps are developed. As a consequence, the memory needed for the recursive computation is much higher; the intermediate steps must be stacked somewhere before being processed in reverse order.

Using more memory isn't the worst problem of recursion. What makes the problem even worse is that computer languages use the stack for storing computation steps. This is smart because computation steps must be evaluated in reverse order compared to the order in which they were stacked. Unfortunately, the stack size is limited, so if there are too many steps, the stack will overflow, crashing the computation thread.

How many computation steps can safely be pushed onto the stack is language-dependent and can be configured. In Kotlin, it's about 20,000; in Java, it's about 3,000. Configuring the stack size to a higher value might not be a good idea because the same stack size (but not the same stack area) is used by all threads. And a higher stack size is often a waste of memory, given that nonrecursive processes use little stack space.

As you see by looking at the two figures, the memory needed for the corecursive process is constant. It won't grow if the number of computation steps increases. On the other hand, the memory needed for the recursive process grows with the number of steps (and it can be much worse than a linear growth, as you'll soon see). This is why you should avoid recursive processes except when you're sure that the number of steps will remain low *in all cases*. As a consequence, you must learn to replace recursion with corecursion each time it's possible.

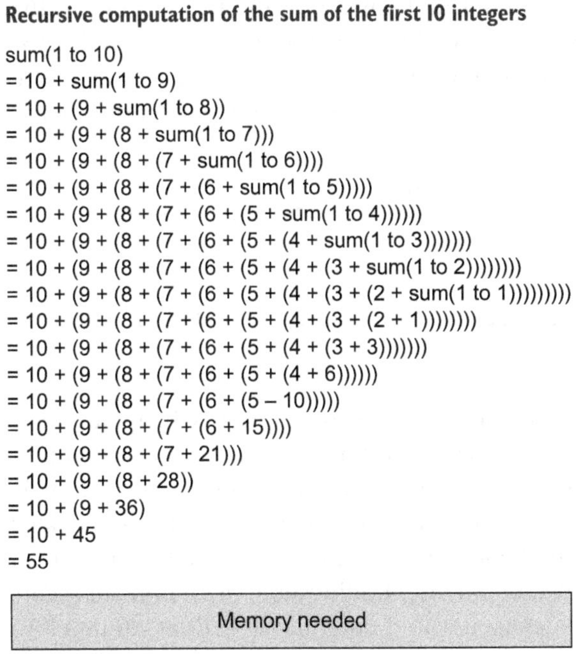

Recursive computation of the sum of the first 10 integers

```
sum(1 to 10)
= 10 + sum(1 to 9)
= 10 + (9 + sum(1 to 8))
= 10 + (9 + (8 + sum(1 to 7)))
= 10 + (9 + (8 + (7 + sum(1 to 6))))
= 10 + (9 + (8 + (7 + (6 + sum(1 to 5)))))
= 10 + (9 + (8 + (7 + (6 + (5 + sum(1 to 4))))))
= 10 + (9 + (8 + (7 + (6 + (5 + (4 + sum(1 to 3)))))))
= 10 + (9 + (8 + (7 + (6 + (5 + (4 + (3 + sum(1 to 2))))))))
= 10 + (9 + (8 + (7 + (6 + (5 + (4 + (3 + (2 + sum(1 to 1)))))))))
= 10 + (9 + (8 + (7 + (6 + (5 + (4 + (3 + (2 + 1))))))))
= 10 + (9 + (8 + (7 + (6 + (5 + (4 + (3 + 3)))))))
= 10 + (9 + (8 + (7 + (6 + (5 + (4 + 6))))))
= 10 + (9 + (8 + (7 + (6 + (5 – 10)))))
= 10 + (9 + (8 + (7 + (6 + 15))))
= 10 + (9 + (8 + (7 + 21)))
= 10 + (9 + (8 + 28))
= 10 + (9 + 36)
= 10 + 45
= 55
```

```
Memory needed
```

Figure 4.4 A recursive computation

4.2   *Tail Call Elimination*

At this point, you may have doubts. I said that corecursion uses constant stack space. But you might know that a function calling itself eventually uses stack space, even if it doesn't have much to push onto the stack. It seems that corecursion would also exhaust the stack, although more slowly. It is possible to completely eliminate the problem. The trick is to transform a corecursive function into a good old loop. This couldn't be easier—just replace the corecursive implementation

```
fun toString(list: List<Char>): String {
    fun toString(list: List<Char>, s: String): String =
        if (list.isEmpty())
            s
        else
            toString(list.subList(1, list.size), append(s, list[0]))
    return toString(list, "")
}
```

with an imperative loop and mutable references:

```
fun toStringCorec2(list: List<Char>): String {
    var s = ""
    for (c in list) s = append(s, c)
    return s
}
```

But don't worry: Kotlin can automatically translate corecursion into loops for you!

4.2.1   *Using Tail Call Elimination*

Unlike Java, Kotlin implements Tail Call Elimination (TCE). This means that when a function call to itself is the last thing the function does (meaning that the result of this call isn't used in a further computation), Kotlin eliminates this tail call. But it won't do it without you asking for it, which you can do by prefixing the function declaration with the `tailrec` keyword:

```
fun toString(list: List<Char>): String {
    tailrec fun toString(list: List<Char>, s: String): String =
        if (list.isEmpty())
            s
        else
            toString(list.subList(1, list.size), append(s, list[0]))
    return toString(list, "")
}
```

Kotlin detects that this function is tail recursive and applies TCE. Again, you must indicate that this is your intention. It may seem boring at first, and you might prefer to have Kotlin handle this silently. As you'll soon discover, thinking that a function implementation is tail recursive when it's not is a common bug. But if you indicate that your function has a tail-recursive implementation, Kotlin can check the function and let you know if you've made a mistake. Otherwise, Kotlin would use a non-tail recursive function and a `StackOverflowException` would potentially occur at runtime. And worse, this could appear only once in production because it depends on the input data.

4.2.2 *Switching from loops to corecursion*

Using corecursion instead of loops is a paradigm shift. At first, you'll think in your original paradigm and then translate it to the new one. Only later will you start thinking directly in your new paradigm. This is true of all learning, and learning to use corecursion instead of loops is no different.

In the previous sections, I presented recursion and corecursion as native concepts. At this point, a rationale for translating imperative loops into recursive functions will probably be useful. (But remember that this is only an intermediate step. You'll soon learn how to abstract recursion and corecursion in order to avoid manipulating them.)

Although you've seen that recursion is much less useful than corecursion, due to the implied memory limitations, recursion has a big advantage: it's often much simpler to write. The recursive version of the sum of integers from 1 to 10 can be written as in the following example, assuming that sum(n) means sum of integers from 1 to *n*:

```
fun sum(n: Int): Int = if (n < 1) 0 else n + sum(n - 1)
```

It couldn't be simpler. But as you've seen, the addition can't be performed until you know the result of sum(n - 1). The state of the computation at this stage has to be stored on the stack until all steps have been processed. You'll want to transform this into a corecursive implementation in order to benefit from TCE. Many programmers learning to use corecursion have problems with this transformation, although it's straightforward.

Let's take a break and look at how traditional programmers would solve the problem. Traditional programmers would draw a flowchart of the computation using state mutation and condition testing. The problem is so simple that they'd probably draw the flowchart only in their heads, but let's look at the flowchart (figure 4.5).

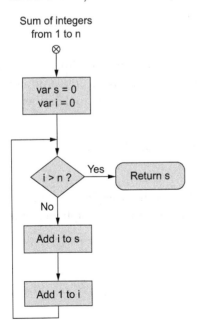

Figure 4.5   A flow chart of the imperative computation of the sum of *n* first integers

The corresponding imperative implementation is ubiquitous, using what imperative programmers call *control structures* such as `for` or `while` loops. As Kotlin has no `for` loop (at least not the traditional `for` loop that corresponds to this flowchart), I'll use a `while` loop in this code:

```kotlin
fun sum(n: Int): Int {
    var sum = 0
    var idx = 0
    while(idx <= n) {
        sum += idx
        idx += 1
    }
    return sum
}
```

Not a big deal, but this code contains many places where it could go wrong, especially since I had to translate the flowchart into a `while` loop implementation. It's easy to mess with the conditions. Should it be `<=` or `<`? Should i be incremented before or after s? Obviously, this style of programming is for smart programmers who don't make these kinds of mistakes. But for the rest of us, who'd need to write many tests to check for potential errors, is it possible to write a corecursive implementation doing the same thing? Sure.

What you can do is replace the variables with parameters added to the function. Instead of a function `sum(n)`, you must write a helper function: `sum(n, sum, idx)`:

```kotlin
fun sum(n: Int, sum: Int, idx: Int): Int = ...
```

Then your main function `sum(n: Int)` will call the helper function with the starting values:

```kotlin
fun sum(n: Int, sum: Int, idx: Int): Int =
        if (idx < 1)  sum else sum(n, sum + idx, idx - 1)

fun sum(n: Int) = sum(n, 0, n)
```

But, in fact, n will never change. You can benefit from Kotlin local functions to remove one parameter, making the helper function local to the main function and closing over the main function parameter. This is a lot easier to do than to describe:

```kotlin
fun sum(n: Int): Int {
    fun sum(sum: Int, idx: Int): Int =
            if (idx < 1)  sum else -sum(sum + idx, idx - 1)
    return sum(0, n)
}
```

As I said earlier, you now need a block function with an explicit `return` at the end of the block and an explicit return type. Then, you need to implement the helper function.

Think about the looping version. On each iteration of the loop, you get modified versions of the variables: s + i and i + 1. All you have to do is make the helper function call itself with these modified parameters:

```
fun sum(n: Int): Int {
    fun sum(s: Int, i: Int): Int = sum(s + i, i + 1)
    return sum(0, 0)
}
```

This won't work because it never terminates. What you're missing is the terminal condition testing:

```
fun sum(n: Int): Int {
    fun sum(s: Int, i: Int): Int = if (i > n) s else sum(s + i, i + 1)
    return sum(0, 0)
}
```

All that's left to do is to tell Kotlin that you want TCE to be applied to the helper function. You do this by adding the `tailrec` keyword:

```
fun sum(n: Int): Int {
    tailrec fun sum(s: Int, i: Int): Int =
        if (i > n) s else sum(s + i, i + 1)
    return sum(0, 0)
}
```

In case TCE can't be applied, Kotlin displays a warning:

```
Warning:(16, 5) Kotlin: A function is marked as tail-recursive
                    but no tail calls are found
```

This won't stop your program from compiling, but it'll produce code that might overflow the stack! You should watch such warnings closely.

EXERCISE 4.1

Implement a corecursive add function working with positive integers. The implementation of the add function shouldn't use the plus (+) or minus (-) operators, but only two functions:

```
fun inc(n: Int) = n + 1
fun dec(n: Int) = n - 1
```

Here's the function signature:

```
fun add(a: Int, b: Int): Int
```

HINT

You should be able to directly write the corecursive implementation. If not, write an implementation using a loop and translate it as you've done for the sum function.

SOLUTION

To add two numbers, *x* and *y*, you can do the following:

- If $y = 0$, return *x*.
- Otherwise, add 1 to *x*, subtract 1 from *y*, and start again.

This can be written using a loop as follows:

```
fun add(a: Int, b: Int): Int {
  var x = a
  var y = b
  while(y != 0) {
    x = inc(x)
    y = dec(y)
  }
  return x
}
```

Here the condition has been changed to better fit a `while` loop. It would be possible to use the original condition but with an ugly result:

```
fun add(a: Int, b: Int): Int {
  var x = a
  var y = b
  while(true) {
    if (y == 0) return x
    x = inc(x)
    y = dec(y)
  }
}
```

Also note that unlike Java, Kotlin doesn't allow using the parameters x and y directly because parameters can only be `val` references. You'll have to make copies. Then all you have to do is to replace the variables with parameters in a call to the add function:

```
tailrec fun add(x: Int, y: Int): Int = if (y == 0) x else add(inc(x), dec(y))
```

In this exercise, you don't need to mutate anything. Instead of storing the current values in mutable `var` references, you need to recursively call the function with the new values as parameters. Now you can call your function with any argument value without causing a `StackOverflowException`. As you'll see soon, writing safer programs often involves a lot of effort to change a (non-tail) recursive function implementation into a tail recursive one. And sometimes, it won't be possible!

4.2.3   *Using recursive value functions*

As you've just seen, defining a recursive function is simple. Sometimes the simplest implementation is tail recursive, as you saw in the previous example. But this wasn't a real example. No one would ever create that sort of function to perform an addition. Let's try with a more useful example. The function `factorial(int n)` can be defined as returning 1 if its argument is 0, and n * `factorial(n - 1)` otherwise:

```
fun factorial(n: Int): Int = if (n == 0) 1 else n * factorial(n - 1)
```

This function, obviously, isn't tail recursive, so be aware that it'll overflow the stack if n is higher that a few thousand. And don't use this kind of code in production unless you know for sure that the number of recursion steps will stay low.

Writing recursive fun functions is easy. What about recursive value functions?

EXERCISE 4.2 (HARD)

Write a recursive factorial value function. Remember that a value function is a function declared with the val keyword:

```
val factorial: (Int) -> Int =
```

As this is an exercise, using a function reference would be considered cheating!

HINT

You may want to refer to chapter 2, sections "Lazy initialization" and "Delayed initialization," to solve this exercise.

SOLUTION

As the function must call itself, it should already be defined when this call happens, which implies that it should be defined before you try to define it! Put aside this chicken-and-egg problem for the moment. Converting a single argument fun function into a value function is straightforward. It uses a lambda with the same implementation as the fun function:

```
val factorial: (Int) -> Int =
    { n -> if (n <= 1) n else n * factorial(n - 1) }
```

> **NOTE** You need to indicate explicitly either the type of the function or the type of the lambda argument.

Now for the tricky part. This code won't compile because the compiler will complain about the variable factorial not being initialized yet. What does this mean? When the compiler reads this code, it's in the process of defining the factorial function. During this process, it encounters a call to the factorial function, which isn't yet defined. This is the same problem as

```
val x: Int = x + 1
```

You can solve this problem by first declaring the variable and then changing its value, which can be done in an initializer such as the following:

```
lateinit var x: Int
init {
  x = x + 1;
}
```

This works because members are defined before initializers are executed. The lateinit keyword declares that the variable will be initialized later. If you call it before it's initialized, you'll get an exception. But this function allows using a non-nullable type. Without lateinit, you'd be forced to use a nullable type, or to initialize the reference to a dummy value. This trick is totally useless in the previous case, but you can use it to define the factorial function:

```
object Factorial {
    lateinit var factorial: (Int) -> Int
    init {
        factorial = { n -> if (n <= 1) n else n * factorial(n - 1) }
    }
}
```

Another more elegant solution is to use lazy initialization:

```
object Factorial {
    val factorial: (Int)-> Int by lazy { { n: Int ->
        if (n <= 1) n else n * factorial(n - 1)
    } }
}
```

The double braces are mandatory! Lazy initialization is achieved with the following:

```
object Factorial {
    val factorial: (Int)-> Int by lazy { ... }
}
```

The ... must now be replaced by the lambda, which is nearly the same as in the previous example, including the braces:

```
{ n: Int -> if (n <= 1) n else n * factorial(n - 1) }
```

The only difference is that Kotlin is now unable to infer the type of n, so you must write it explicitly. The only problem with this trick is that the field can't be declared as a val, which is annoying because immutability is one of the fundamental techniques for safe programming. With a var, nothing guarantees that the value of the factorial variable won't change later. A solution is to make the var private and then copy its value to a val:

```
object Factorial {
    private lateinit var fact: (Int) -> Int
    init {
        fact = { n -> if (n <= 1) n else n * fact(n - 1) }
    }
    val factorial = fact
}
```

This way, you can be sure that nothing can change the value of factorial once it's initialized. But remember, a recursive value function, although it can be tail recursive, can't be optimized through TCE, so it might overflow the stack. If you need a tail-recursive value function, use a function reference.

Also note that this function will not work in any case for values over 16 because it'll cause an arithmetic overflow, producing a negative result. Worst, above 33, it'll produce a 0 result because multiplying –2,147,483,648 (the result of calling the function with parameter 33) by 34 results in 0. This causes all subsequent results to be 0. (This happens because Kotlin Int values are 32-bit numbers.)

4.3   *Recursive functions and lists*

Recursion and tail recursion are often used to process lists. Such processes generally involve splitting a list in two parts: the first element, called the *head*, and the rest of the list, called the *tail.* You already saw an example of this when defining a function converting a list of characters into a string. Consider the following function, which computes the sum of the elements of a list of integers:

```
fun sum(list: List<Int>): Int =
        if (list.isEmpty()) 0 else list[0] + sum(list.drop(1))
```

If the list is empty, the function returns 0. Otherwise, it returns the value of the first element (the head of the list) plus the result of applying the sum function to the rest of the list (the tail of the list). It might be clearer if you define helper functions to return the head and the tail of a list. You don't have to restrict these functions to lists of integers because they can be made to work on any lists:

```
fun <T> head(list: List<T>): T =
        if (list.isEmpty())
            throw IllegalArgumentException("head called on empty list")
        else
            list[0]

fun <T> tail(list: List<T>): List<T> =
        if (list.isEmpty())
            throw IllegalArgumentException("tail called on empty list")
        else
            list.drop(1)

fun sum(list: List<Int>): Int =
        if (list.isEmpty())
            0
        else
            head(list) + sum(tail(list))
```

Or, even better, you can create the head and tail function as extension functions of the List class:

```
fun <T> List<T>.head(): T =
        if (this.isEmpty())
            throw IllegalArgumentException("head called on empty list")
        else
            this[0]

fun <T> List<T>.tail(): List<T> =
        if (this.isEmpty())
            throw IllegalArgumentException("tail called on empty list")
        else
            this.drop(1)

fun sum(list: List<Int>): Int =
        if (list.isEmpty())
            0
        else
            list.head() + sum(list.tail())
```

In this example, the recursive call to the sum function isn't the last thing the function does. The four last things the function does are as follows:

- Calls the head function
- Calls the tail function
- Calls the sum function with the result of tail as its argument
- Adds the result of head and the result of sum

This function isn't tail recursive, so you can't use the `tailrec` keyword, and you won't be able to use this function with lists of more than a few thousand elements. But you can rewrite this function in order to put the call to sum in the tail position:

```
fun sum(list: List<Int>): Int {
    tailrec fun sumTail(list: List<Int>, acc: Int): Int =
            if (list.isEmpty())
                acc
            else
                sumTail(list.tail(), acc + list.head())
    return sumTail(list, 0)
}
```

Here, the `sumTail` helper function is tail recursive and can be optimized through TCE. As this helper function will never be used elsewhere, the best place to put it is inside the sum function.

You could define the helper function alongside the main function. But you'd have to make the helper function `private` or `internal` and the main function public. In such a case, the call to the helper function by the main function would be a closure. The primary reasons for preferring a locally-defined helper function over a private helper function is to avoid name clashes and to be able to close over some parameters of the enclosing function.

In languages that allow locally-defined functions, a current practice is to call all helper functions with a single name, such as go or process. This can't always be done with nonlocal functions; the names could clash if the argument types were identical. In the previous example, the helper function for sum was called `sumTail`.

Another current practice is to call the helper function with the same name as the main function with an appended underscore, such as sum_. It's also possible to give the helper function the same name as the main function because the functions will have a different signature. Whatever system you choose, it's useful to be consistent. In the rest of this book, I'll use the underscore to denote tail-recursive helper functions.

4.3.1   *Using doubly recursive functions*

No book talking about recursive functions can avoid the Fibonacci series example. Although it's totally useless to most of us, it's ubiquitous because it's one of the simplest examples of a *doubly recursive function*, meaning a function which calls itself twice on each step. Let's start with the requirements in case you've never met this function.

The Fibonacci series is a suite of numbers in which each number is the sum of the two previous ones. This is a recursive definition. You need a terminal condition, so the full requirements are as follows:

- $f(0) = 1$
- $f(1) = 1$
- $f(n) = f(n-1) + f(n-2)$

This is the original Fibonacci series, in which the first two numbers are equal to 1. Each number is supposed to be a function of its position in the series. Most programmers generally prefer to start at 0 rather than 1. You'll often find definitions where $f(0) = 0$, which is not part of the original Fibonacci series. Anyway, this doesn't change the problem.

Why is this function so interesting? Instead of answering this question right now, let's try a naive implementation:

```kotlin
fun fibonacci(number: Int): Int =
        if (number == 0 || number == 1)
            1
        else
            fibonacci(number - 1) + fibonacci(number - 2)
```

Now you'll write a simple program to test this function:

```kotlin
fun main(args: Array<String>) {
    (0 until 10).forEach { print("${fibonacci(it)} ") }
}
```

If you run this test program, you'll get the first ten Fibonacci numbers:

```
1 1 2 3 5 8 13 21 34 55
```

Based on what you know about recursion in Kotlin, you may think that this function will succeed in calculating f(n) for n, up to a few thousands before overflowing the stack. Well, let's check it. Replace 10 with 1000 and see what happens. Launch the program and take a coffee break. When you return, you'll realize that the program is still running. It'll have reached somewhere around 1,836,311,903, which is only the 47th step (your mileage may vary—you may even get a negative number!), but it'll never finish. No stack overflow, no exception—just hanging in the wild. What's happening?

The problem is that each call to the function creates two recursive calls. To calculate f(n), you need $2n$ recursive calls. Let's say your function needs 10 nanoseconds to execute. (Just guessing, but you'll soon see that it doesn't change anything.) Calculating f(5000) will take $2^{5000} \times 10$ nanoseconds. Do you have any idea how long that is? The program will never terminate because it would need longer than the expected duration of the solar system (if not the universe).

To make a usable Fibonacci function, you have to change it so it uses a single tail recursive call. There's also another problem: the results are so big that you'll soon get an arithmetic overflow, first resulting in negative numbers, and then soon into 0.

EXERCISE 4.3

Create a tail-recursive version of the Fibonacci function.

HINT

If you think about a loop-based implementation, as when you created the sum function, you know that you should use two variables for keeping track of the two previous values. These variables would then translate into parameters for a helper function. These parameters will be of type BigInteger in order to allow computing big values.

SOLUTION

Let's first write the signature of the helper function. It'll take two `BigInteger` instances as parameters, and one for the original argument, and it'll return a `BigInteger`:

```
tailrec fun fib(val1: BigInteger, val2: BigInteger, x: BigInteger): BigInteger
```

You must deal with the terminal conditions. If the argument is 0, you return 1:

```
tailrec
fun fib(val1: BigInteger, val2: BigInteger, x: BigInteger): BigInteger =
    when {
        (x == BigInteger.ZERO) -> BigInteger.ONE
        ...
    }
}
```

If the argument is 1, you return the sum of the two parameters `val1` and `val2`:

```
tailrec
fun fib(val1: BigInteger, val2: BigInteger, x: BigInteger): BigInteger =
    when {
        (x == BigInteger.ZERO) -> BigInteger.ONE
        (x == BigInteger.ONE) -> val1 + val2
        ...
    }
}
```

Eventually, you have to deal with recursion. To do that, you must do the following:

- Take `val2` and make it `val1`.
- Create a new `val2` by adding the two previous values.
- Subtract 1 from the argument.
- Recursively call the function with the three computed values as its arguments.

Here is the transcription in code:

```
tailrec
fun fib(val1: BigInteger, val2: BigInteger, x: BigInteger): BigInteger =
    when {
        (x == BigInteger.ZERO) -> BigInteger.ONE
        (x == BigInteger.ONE) -> val1 + val2
        else -> fib(val2, val1 + val2, x - BigInteger.ONE)
    }
```

The two parameters `val1` and `val2` accumulate the results `fib(n - 1)` and `fib(n - 2)`. For this reason, those are often called acc (for *accumulator*). Here you can rename them `acc1` and `acc2`. The last thing to do is to create the main function that calls this helper function with the initial parameters, and put the helper function inside the body of the main function:

```
fun fib(x: Int): BigInteger {
    tailrec
    fun fib(val1: BigInteger, val2: BigInteger, x: BigInteger): BigInteger =
        when {
            (x == BigInteger.ZERO) -> BigInteger.ONE
            (x == BigInteger.ONE) -> val1 + val2
            else -> fib(val2, val1 + val2, x - BigInteger.ONE)
        }
    return fib(BigInteger.ZERO, BigInteger.ONE, BigInteger.valueOf(x.toLong()))
}
```

This is only one possible implementation. You can organize parameters, initial values, and conditions in a slightly different manner, as long as it works. Now you can call `fib(10_000)` and it'll give you the result in a couple of nanoseconds. Well, it'll take a few dozen milliseconds but only because printing to the console is a slow operation. I'll come back to this shortly. In any case, the result is impressive, whether it's the result of the computation (2,090 digits) or the increase in speed due to the transformation of a dual recursive call into a single corecursive one.

4.3.2 *Abstracting recursion on lists*

One main use of recursion consists of combining the first element (the head) of a list with the result of applying the same process to the rest of the list (the tail). You've already seen an example of this when you computed the sum of a list of integers, which you defined as

```
fun sum(list: List<Int>): Int =
        if (list.isEmpty())
            0
        else
            list.head() + sum(list.tail())
```

The same principle could be applied to any operation on any types and not only to the addition of integers. You already saw an example consisting in processing a list of characters in order to build a string out of them. You could use the same technique to copy a list of any type into a delimited string:

```
fun <T> makeString(list: List<T>, delim: String): String =
    when {
        list.isEmpty() -> ""
        list.tail().isEmpty() ->
            "${list.head()}${makeString(list.tail(), delim)}"
        else -> "${list.head()}$delim${makeString(list.tail(), delim)}"
    }
```

EXERCISE 4.4

Write a tail-recursive version of the `makeString` function. (Try not to look at the tail-recursive version of `sum`.)

SOLUTION

You need to apply the same technique that you used for the previous example: create a helper function with an additional parameter accumulating the result. If you put this helper function inside the main function, you can make it close over the `delim` parameter because it doesn't change on each recursive step:

```
fun <T> makeString(list: List<T>, delim: String): String {
    tailrec fun makeString_(list: List<T>, acc: String): String = when {
        list.isEmpty() -> acc
        acc.isEmpty() -> makeString_(list.tail(), "${list.head()}")
        else -> makeString_(list.tail(), "$acc$delim${list.head()}")
    }
    return makeString_(list, "")
}
```

Okay, it was simple, but repeating this for every recursive function would be tedious. Can you abstract this? You can. The first thing to do is to step back and have a look at the whole figure. What do you have?

- A function working on a list of elements of a given type, returning a single value of another type. These types could be abstracted into type parameters T and U.
- An operation between an element of type T and an element of type U, producing a result of type U. Note that such an operation is a function from a pair (U, T) to a U.

This seems to be different from what you had in the sum example, but it is indeed the same, although T and U were the same type (Int). For the string example, T was Char and U was String. For the makeString function, T was already generic and U was String.

EXERCISE 4.5

Create a generic version of your tail-recursive function that can be used for sum, string, and makeString. Call this function foldLeft, then write sum, string, and makeString in terms of this new function.

HINT

You'll have to introduce the starting value of type U (for the accumulator) and the function from (U, T) to U as additional parameters.

SOLUTION

Here is the foldLeft function implementation and the three modified functions to use the foldLeft abstraction:

```
fun <T, U> foldLeft(list: List<T>, z: U, f: (U, T) -> U): U {
    tailrec fun foldLeft(list: List<T>, acc: U): U =
            if (list.isEmpty())
                acc
            else
                foldLeft(list.tail(), f(acc, list.head()))
    return foldLeft(list, z)
}

fun sum(list: List<Int>) = foldLeft(list, 0, Int::plus)

fun string(list: List<Char>) = foldLeft(list, "", String::plus)

fun <T> makeString(list: List<T>, delim: String) =
    foldLeft(list, "") { s, t -> if (s.isEmpty()) "$t" else "$s$delim$t" }
```

The function you created here is one of the most important when programming without loops. This function lets you abstract corecursion in a stack-safe way, so that you'll seldom have to think about making functions tail recursive. But sometimes you'll need to make things in the opposite way, using recursion instead of corecursion.

Suppose you've a list of chars [a, b, c] and you want to build the string "abc" using only the head and tail and prepend functions you've developed in the previous section. You can't access list elements by their index. But you could write the following recursive implementation:

```
fun string(list: List<Char>): String =
    if (list.isEmpty())
        ""
    else
        prepend(list.head(), string(list.tail()))
```

You can abstract several things in this code in the same way you abstracted the fold-Left function. You could abstract the Char type to type T so that the function would work with lists of any type. You could abstract the String return type to U so that you can build a result of any type. And you'd have to abstract the prepend function into a generic (T, U) -> U function. You should also replace the initial value "" with the identity value of type U corresponding to this function.

EXERCISE 4.6

Write this abstracted function and call it foldRight. Then write the string function in terms of foldRight.

SOLUTION

Write the signature of the function, taking as additional parameters the identity and the function to use for folding:

```
fun <T, U> foldRight(list: List<T>, identity: U, f: (T, U) -> U): U =
```

If the list is empty, return the identity value:

```
fun <T, U> foldRight(list: List<T>, identity: U, f: (T, U) -> U): U =
    if (list.isEmpty())
        identity
```

If the list isn't empty, use the same code as in the string function, replacing prepend with the parameter function:

```
fun <T, U> foldRight(list: List<T>, identity: U, f: (T, U) -> U): U =
    if (list.isEmpty())
        identity
    else
        f(list.head(), foldRight(list.tail(), identity, f))
```

That's it! Now you can define string in terms of foldRight by calling it with the values you replaced with the generic types:

```
fun string(list: List<Char>): String =
    foldRight(list, "", { c, s -> prepend(c, s) })
```

It's more idiomatic in Kotlin to write the last argument outside of the parenthesis when this argument is a function. In such a case, no comma is used before the function:

```
fun string(list: List<Char>): String =
    foldRight(list, "") { c, s -> prepend(c, s) }
```

> **NOTE** The foldRight function is recursive; it isn't tail recursive, so it can't be optimized using TCE. You can't create a real tail-recursive version of foldRight. The only possibility is to define a function returning the same result as foldRight, but using a left fold, for example, after reversing the list.

When using Kotlin's `List` class, you don't need to create `foldRight` and `foldLeft` because Kotlin already defines these functions (although `foldLeft` is simply called `fold`).

4.3.3   *Reversing a list*

Reversing a list is sometimes useful, although this operation is generally not optimal in terms of performance. Finding other solutions that don't require reversing a list is preferable, but not always possible. One such solution is to use a different data structure that allows access from both ends.

Defining a `reverse` function with a loop-based implementation is easy: iterate backward over the list. You must be careful, though, not to mess with the indexes:

```
fun <T> reverse(list: List<T>): List<T> {
    val result: MutableList<T> = mutableListOf()
    (list.size downTo 1).forEach {
        result.add(list[it - 1])
    }
    return result
}
```

But this isn't the way it's supposed to be done in Kotlin. Kotlin already has a `reversed` function on lists.

EXERCISE 4.7

Define a `reverse` function using a fold.

HINT

Remember that `foldRight` might overflow the stack when used with long lists, so you should prefer `foldLeft` as often as possible. You should also create the `prepend` function working on the list and adding an element in front of the list. Don't worry about performance. This is a problem you'll address in chapter 5. Make your function work with immutable lists using the + operator.

SOLUTION

The `prepend` function is easy to define, although there's a little trick. The + operator in Kotlin allows concatenating lists or adding an element at the end of a list, but not adding an element to the head of the list. One solution to this problem is to first make a single item list of the element to prepend:

```
fun <T> prepend(list: List<T>, elem: T): List<T> = listOf(elem) + list
```

Then, all you need to do to reverse a list is to fold it to the left using this function:

```
fun <T> reverse(list: List<T>): List<T> =
        foldLeft(list, listOf(), ::prepend)
```

This works, but it's kind of cheating. Could you define the `reverse` function without creating this single item list?

EXERCISE 4.8

Define the `reverse` function using only the append version of + without resorting to concatenation.

HINT

What you need for this exercise is to define the prepend function while not using concatenation. Try to start with a function copying a list through a left fold.

SOLUTION

Copying a list through a left fold is easy:

```
fun <T> copy(list: List<T>): List<T> =
        foldLeft(list, listOf()) { lst, elem -> lst + elem }
```

The prepend function that adds an element in front of a list can be implemented by left folding the list, using an accumulator containing the element to add instead of the empty list:

```
fun <T> prepend(list: List<T>, elem: T): List<T> =
        foldLeft(list, listOf(elem)) { lst, elm -> lst + elm }
```

Now you can use the same reverse implementation with this new prepend function:

```
fun <T> reverse(list: List<T>): List<T> =
        foldLeft(list, listOf(), ::prepend)
```

Don't use these implementations of reverse and prepend in production code. Both imply traversing the whole list several times, so these are slow. If you're working with Kotlin lists, use the standard reversed function on List. In chapter 5, you'll learn how to create functional immutable lists that perform well on all occasions.

4.3.4 *Building corecursive lists*

One thing programmers do again and again is build corecursive lists, and most of these are lists of integers. Consider the following example in Java:

```
for (int i = 0; i < limit; i++) {
  // some processing...
}
```

This code is a composition of two abstractions: a corecursive list and some processing. The corecursive list is a list of integers from 0 (included) to `limit` (excluded). As I've said, one way to make programs safer is, among other things, pushing abstraction to the limit so that you can reuse a maximum of code. Let's abstract the construction of this corecursive list.

Corecursive lists are easy to construct. You start from the first element (int i = 0) and apply the chosen function (i -> i++).

You could have constructed the list first and then mapped it to a function corresponding to some processing..., or to a composition of functions, or to an effect. Let's do this with a concrete limit. Consider this Java example:

```
for (int i = 0; i < 5; i++) {
  System.out.println(i);
}
```

This is nearly equivalent to the following Kotlin code:

```
listOf(0, 1, 2, 3, 4).forEach(::println)
```

Both the list and the effect have been abstracted. But you can push abstraction even further.

EXERCISE 4.9

Write a loop-based implementation of a function that produces a list using a starting value, a limit, and the function x -> x + 1. You'll call this function range, and it'll have the following signature:

```
fun range(start: Int, end: Int): List<Int>
```

SOLUTION

You can use a while loop to implement the range function:

```
fun range(start: Int, end: Int): List<Int> {
    val result: MutableList<Int> = mutableListOf()
    var index = start
    while (index < end) {
        result.add(index)
        index++
    }
    return result
}
```

EXERCISE 4.10

Write a generic version of a range-like function that works for any type and any condition. As the notion of range works only for numbers, let's call this function unfold and give it the following signature:

```
fun <T> unfold(seed: T, f: (T) -> T, p: (T) -> Boolean): List<T>
```

SOLUTION

Starting from the range function implementation, all you have to do is to replace the specific parts with generic ones:

```
fun <T> unfold(seed: T, f: (T) -> T, p: (T) -> Boolean): List<T> {
    val result: MutableList<T> = mutableListOf()
    var elem = seed
    while (p(elem)) {
        result.add(elem)
        elem = f(elem)
    }
    return result
}
```

EXERCISE 4.11

Implement the range function in terms of unfold.

SOLUTION

There's nothing difficult here. You need to provide

- The seed, which is the start parameter of range
- The function f, which is { x -> x + 1 } or the equivalent { it + 1 }
- The predicate p, which resolves to { x -> x < end } or the equivalent { it < end }:

```
fun range(start: Int, end: Int): List<Int> =
            unfold(start, { it + 1 }, { it < end })
```

Corecursion and recursion have a dual relationship. One is the counterpart of the other, so it's always possible to change a recursive process into a corecursive one, and vice versa. For now, let's do the inverse process.

EXERCISE 4.12

Write a recursive version of range based on the functions you've defined in previous sections.

HINT

The only function you need is prepend, although you can choose other implementations using different functions.

SOLUTION

Defining a recursive implementation is extremely simple. You prepend the start parameter to the same function, using the same end parameter and replacing the start parameter with the result of applying the f function to it. It's much easier to do than to explain in words:

```
fun range(start: Int, end: Int): List<Int> =
    if (end <= start)
        listOf()
    else
        prepend(range(start + 1, end), start)
```

EXERCISE 4.13

Write a recursive version of unfold.

HINT

Again, start from the range function recursive implementation and try to generify it.

SOLUTION

The solution is simple:

```
fun <T> unfold(seed: T, f: (T) -> T, p: (T) -> Boolean): List<T> =
        if (p(seed))
            prepend(unfold(f(seed), f, p), seed)
        else
            listOf()
```

You can now redefine range in term of this function. Be aware, however, that the recursive unfold function will blow the stack after a few thousand recursive steps.

EXERCISE 4.14

Can you make a tail recursive version of this function? Try to answer this question in theory before doing the exercise.

HINT

Think about this: Is unfold a recursive function or a corecursive one?

SOLUTION

The unfold function is in fact corecursive, like the foldLeft function you developed earlier. You might guess that you can make a tail-recursive version using a helper function taking an accumulator as an additional parameter:

```
fun <T> unfold(seed: T, f: (T) -> T, p: (T) -> Boolean): List<T> {
    tailrec fun unfold_(acc: List<T>,
                        seed: T,
                        f: (T) -> T, p: (T) -> Boolean): List<T> =
            if (p(seed))
                unfold_(acc + seed, f(seed), f, p)
            else
                acc
    return unfold_(listOf(), seed, f, p)
}
```

The use of a local function allows simplifying this code by removing the constant parameters from the helper function (f and p) and making this function close over the enclosing function parameters:

```
fun <T> unfold(seed: T, f: (T) -> T, p: (T) -> Boolean): List<T> {
    tailrec fun unfold_(acc: List<T>, seed: T): List<T> =
            if (p(seed))
                unfold_(acc + seed, f(seed))
            else
                acc
    return unfold_(listOf(), seed)
}
```

4.3.5   *The danger of strictness*

None of these versions (recursive and corecursive) are equivalent to the for loop. This is because even with strict languages like Java and Kotlin (they're strict regarding method or function arguments), the for loop, like most control structures, is lazy. This means that in the for loop you used as an example, the order of evaluation will be index, computation, index, computation ..., although using the range function will first compute the complete list of indexes before mapping the function.

This problem arises because you shouldn't be using lists for this. Lists are strict data structures. But you have to start somewhere. In chapter 9, you'll learn how to use lazy collections that will solve this problem.

4.4 Memoization

In section 4.3.1, you implemented a function to display a series of Fibonacci numbers. One problem with this implementation of the Fibonacci series is that if you want to print the string representing the series up to f(n), you'll have to compute f(1), f(2), until f(n). But to compute f(n), you have to recursively compute the function for all preceding values. Eventually, to create the series up to n, you'll have computed f(1) n times, f(2) $n-1$ times, and so on. The total number of computations will then be the sum of the integers 1 to n.

In this section, you'll learn how memoization can help. *Memoization* is the technique of keeping the result of a computation in memory so it can be returned immediately if you have to redo the same computation in the future. Can you do better? One possibility would be to implement a special function called scan. You'll do this in chapter 8. For now, we'll look at another solution. Could you possibly keep the computed values in memory so you don't have to compute them again if they're needed several times?

4.4.1 Using memoization in loop-based programming

In loop-based programming, you wouldn't have this problem. The obvious way to proceed would be as follows:

```kotlin
fun main(args: Array<String>) {
    println(fibo(10))
}

fun fibo(limit: Int): String =
    when {
        limit < 1 -> throw IllegalArgumentException()
        limit == 1 -> "1"
        else -> {
            var fibo1 = BigInteger.ONE
            var fibo2 = BigInteger.ONE
            var fibonacci: BigInteger
            val builder = StringBuilder("1, 1")
            for (i in 2 until limit) {
                fibonacci = fibo1.add(fibo2)
                builder.append(", ").append(fibonacci)
                fibo1 = fibo2
                fibo2 = fibonacci
            }
            builder.toString()
        }
    }
```

Accumulates the present result into the accumulator (the StringBuffer)

Stores f(n − 1) for the next pass

Stores f(n) for the next pass

Although this program concentrates most of the problems that functional programming is supposed to avoid or solve, it works, and it's much more efficient than the functional version. The reason is memoization.

As I said, memoization is the technique of keeping the result of a computation in memory so it can be returned immediately if you have to redo the same computation in the future. Applied to functions, memoization makes the functions memorize the results of previous calls, so they can return the results much faster if they're called again with the same arguments.

This might seem incompatible with the principles I exposed previously because a memoized function maintains a mutable state, which is a side effect. But it isn't incompatible because the result of the function is the same when it's called with the same argument. (You could argue that it's even more the same because it isn't computed again!) The side effect of storing the results must not be visible from outside the function. In traditional programming, because maintaining state is the universal way of computing results, memoization isn't even noticed.

4.4.2   *Using memoization in recursive functions*

Recursive functions often use memoization implicitly. In the example of the recursive Fibonacci function, you wanted to return the series, so you calculated each number in the series, leading to unnecessary recalculations. A simple solution is to rewrite the function in order to directly return the string representing the series.

EXERCISE 4.15

Write a tail-recursive function taking an integer n as its argument and returning a string representing the values of the Fibonacci numbers from 0 to n, separated by a comma and a space.

HINT

One solution is to use an instance of StringBuilder as the accumulator. StringBuilder is a mutable structure, but this mutation won't be visible from the outside. Another solution is to return a list of numbers and then transform it into a String. This solution is easier because you can abstract the problem of the separators by first returning a list and then writing a function to turn the list into a comma-separated string.

SOLUTION

The following listing shows the solution using List as the accumulator.

Listing 4.1   **Recursive Fibonacci with implicit memoization**

Calls the fibo helper function to get the list of Fibonacci numbers

The first + sign on this line is the list concatenation operator; others represent BigIntegers addition.

```
fun fibo(number: Int): String {
    tailrec fun fibo(acc: List<BigInteger>,
                     acc1: BigInteger,
                     acc2: BigInteger, x: BigInteger): List<BigInteger> =
        when (x) {
            BigInteger.ZERO -> acc
            BigInteger.ONE -> acc + (acc1 + acc2)
            else -> fibo(acc + (acc1 + acc2), acc2, acc1 + acc2,
                    x - BigInteger.ONE)
        }
    val list = fibo(listOf(),
```

```
                        BigInteger.ONE, BigInteger.ZERO, BigInteger.
        valueOf(number.toLong())))
        return makeString(list, ", ")
}

fun <T> makeString(list: List<T>, separator: String): String =
    when {
        list.isEmpty() -> ""
        list.tail().isEmpty() -> list.head().toString()
        else -> list.head().toString() +
                    foldLeft(list.tail(), "") { x, y -> x + separator + y }
    }
```

The + sign must be at the end of this line and not at the beginning of the next line; otherwise the code won't compile.

Formats the list into a comma-separated string through a call to makeString. This is only for an exercise. You could have used the standard Kotlin list.joinToString (", ") function instead.

4.4.3 *Using implicit memoization*

This example demonstrates the use of implicit memoization. Don't conclude that this is the best way to solve the problem. Many problems are much easier to solve when twisted—looked at from another perspective. Let's twist this one.

Instead of a suite of numbers, you could see the Fibonacci series as a suite of pairs (tuples of two elements). Instead of trying to generate this

```
1, 1, 2, 3, 5, 8, 13, 21, ...
```

you could try to produce this:

```
(1, 1), (1, 2), (2, 3), (3, 5), (5, 8), (8, 13), (13, 21), ...
```

In this series, each tuple can be constructed from the previous one. The second element of tuple n becomes the first element of tuple $n + 1$. The second element of tuple $n + 1$ is equal to the sum of the two elements of tuple n. In Kotlin, you can write a function for this:

```
val f = { x: Pair<BigInteger, BigInteger> ->
            Pair(x.second, x.first + x.second) }
        }
```

Or using a destructuring declaration, it'd look like this:

```
val f = { (a, b): Pair<BigInteger, BigInteger> -> Pair(b, a + b)}
```

To replace the recursive function with a corecursive one, you'll need two additional functions: map and iterate.

EXERCISE 4.16

Define the iterate function that works like unfold, except instead of calling itself recursively until a condition is met, it calls itself a given number of times.

HINT

Start with a copy of the unfold function and change the last parameter and the condition.

SOLUTION

Instead of a predicate, the function takes an integer as its third argument:

```
fun <T> iterate(seed: T, f: (T) -> T, n: Int): List<T> {
```

The function uses a tail-recursive helper function that's identical to the one used by unfold except for the condition:

```
fun <T> iterate(seed: T, f: (T) -> T, n: Int): List<T> {
    tailrec fun iterate_(acc: List<T>, seed: T): List<T> =
            if (acc.size < n)
                iterate_(acc + seed, f(seed))
            else
                acc
    return iterate_(listOf(), seed)
}
```

EXERCISE 4.17

Define a map function that applies a function (T) -> U to each element of a List<T>, producing a List<U>.

HINT

You can define a tail-recursive function or you can define your function in terms of foldLeft or foldRight. A good idea would be to start from the copy function you created when defining reverse.

SOLUTION

An explicitly recursive solution could be

```
fun <T, U> map(list: List<T>, f: (T) -> U): List<U> {
    tailrec fun map_(acc: List<U>, list: List<T>): List<U> =
            if (list.isEmpty())
                acc
            else
                map_(acc + f(list.head()), list.tail())
    return map_(listOf(), list)
}
```

It's simpler and safer to reuse foldLeft because it abstracts recursion. Recall the copy function:

```
fun <T> copy(list: List<T>): List<T> =
        foldLeft(list, listOf()) { lst, elem -> lst + elem}
```

All you have to do is to apply the function argument to each element during the copy:

```
fun <T, U> map(list: List<T>, f: (T) -> U): List<U> =
        foldLeft(list, listOf()) { acc, elem -> acc + f(elem) }
```

EXERCISE 4.18

Define a corecursive version of the Fibonacci function producing a string representing the first n Fibonacci numbers.

SOLUTION

You need to iterate using a pair of the two first numbers and a function computing the next pair from the previous one. This will give you a list of pairs. You can then map this list with a function returning the first element of each pair and convert the resulting list into a string:

```
fun fiboCorecursive(number: Int): String {
    val seed = Pair(BigInteger.ZERO, BigInteger.ONE)
    val f = { x: Pair<BigInteger, BigInteger> -> Pair(x.second, x.first +
    x.second) }
    val listOfPairs = iterate(seed, f, number + 1)
    val list = map(listOfPairs) { p -> p.first }
    return makeString(list, ", ")
}
```

4.4.4 Using automatic memoization

Memoization isn't only used for recursive functions. It can be used to speed up any function. Think about how you perform multiplication. If you need to multiply 234 by 686, you'll probably need a pen and some paper, or a calculator. But if you're asked to multiply 9 by 7, you can answer immediately, without doing any computation. This is because you're using a memoized multiplication.

A memoized function works the same way, although it needs to make the computation once to retain the result. Imagine you've a function double that multiplies its argument by 2:

```
fun double(x: Int) = x * 2
```

You could memoize this function by storing the result into a map. Here's how it could be done using traditional programming techniques involving testing conditions and controlling program flow:

```
val cache = mutableMapOf<Int, Int>()          ◄——— Uses a mutable map to store the results

fun double(x: Int) =                           ◄——— Looks in the map to see if the result has
    if (cache.containsKey(x)) {                        already been computed
        cache[x]                               ◄——— If found, returns the result
    } else {
        val result = x * 2                     ◄——— If not found, computes the result
        cache.put(x, result)                   ◄——— Puts the result in the map
        result                                 ◄——— Returns the result
    }
```

It happens that in this particular case, testing and control flow have already been abstracted into the computeIfAbsent function:

```
val cache: MutableMap<Int, Int> = mutableMapOf()

fun double(x: Int) = cache.computeIfAbsent(x) { it * 2 }
```

Or you might prefer a value function such as

```
val double: (Int) -> Int = { cache.computeIfAbsent(it) { it * 2 } }
```

But two problems arise:

- You have to repeat this modification for all functions you want to memoize.
- The map you use is exposed to the outside.

The second problem is easy to address. You can put the function in a separate object, including the map, with private access. Here's an example in the case of a fun function:

```
object Doubler {

    private val cache: MutableMap<Int, Int> = mutableMapOf()

    fun double(x: Int) = cache.computeIfAbsent(x) { it * 2 }
}
```

You can then use this object each time you want to compute a value:

```
val y = Doubler.double(x);
```

With this solution, the map is no longer accessible from the outside. You've now addressed the second problem. What can you do to address the first one?

Let's start with the requirements. What you need is a way to do the following:

```
val f: (Int) -> Int = { it * 2 }
val g: (Int) -> Int = Memoizer.memoize(f)
```

Then you can use the memoized function as a drop-in replacement for the original one. All values returned by function g are calculated through the original function f the first time and returned from the cache for all subsequent accesses. By contrast, if you create a third function

```
val f: (Int) -> Int = { it * 2 }
val g: (Int) -> Int = Memoizer.memoize(f)
val h: (Int) -> Int = Memoizer.memoize(f)
```

the values cached by g won't be returned by h; g and h will use separate caches (unless you memoize the memoize function!).

The following listing shows the implementation of the Memoizer class, which is quite simple.

Listing 4.2   The Memoizer class

```
class Memoizer<T, U> private constructor() {

    private val cache = ConcurrentHashMap<T, U>()

    private fun doMemoize(function: (T) -> U): (T) -> U =
        { input ->
            cache.computeIfAbsent(input) {      ◄─── Handles the computation, calling the
                function(it)                         original function if necessary
            }
        }

    companion object {
```

```
fun <T, U> memoize(function: (T) -> U): (T) -> U =
    Memoizer<T, U>().doMemoize(function)
}
}
```

Returns a memoized version of its function argument

The following listing shows how this class can be used. The program simulates a long computation to show the result of memoizing the function.

Listing 4.3 Demonstrating the memoizer

```
fun longComputation(number: Int): Int {
    Thread.sleep(1000)
    return number
}
```

The function to memoize

Simulates a long computation

```
fun main(args: Array<String>) {
    val startTime1 = System.currentTimeMillis()
    val result1 = longComputation(43)
    val time1 = System.currentTimeMillis() - startTime1
    val memoizedLongComputation =
        Memoizer.memoize(::longComputation)
    val startTime2 = System.currentTimeMillis()
    val result2 = memoizedLongComputation(43)
    val time2 = System.currentTimeMillis() - startTime2
    val startTime3 = System.currentTimeMillis()
    val result3 = memoizedLongComputation(43)
    val time3 = System.currentTimeMillis() - startTime3
    println("Call to nonmemoized function: result = " +
            "$result1, time = $time1")
    println("First call to memoized function: result = " +
            "$result2, time = $time2")
    println("Second call to nonmemoized function: result = " +
            "$result3, time = $time3")
}
```

The memoized function

Running this program produces the following result:

```
Call to non memoized function: result = 43, time = 1000
First call memoized function: result = 43, time = 1001
Second call to nonmemoized function: result = 43, time = 0
```

You can now make memoized functions out of ordinary ones by calling a single function on `Memoizer`, but to use this technique in production, you'd have to handle potential memory problems. This code is acceptable if the number of possible inputs is low, so you can keep all results in memory without causing memory overflow. Otherwise, you can use soft references or weak references to store memoized values.

4.4.5   *Implementing memoization of multi-argument functions*

As I said before, there's no such thing in this world as a function with several arguments. Functions represent relationships between one set (the source set) and another set (the target set). They can't have several arguments. Functions that appear to have several arguments are either

- Functions of tuples
- Functions returning functions returning functions ... returning a result

In either case, you're concerned only with functions of one argument, so you can easily use your `Memoizer` object.

Using functions of tuples may seem the simplest choice. You could use the `Pair` or `Triple` classes offered by Kotlin, or you could define your own if you need to group more than three elements. The second option is much easier, but you need to use the curried version of the functions as you did in the section, "Currying functions" (chapter 3).

Memoizing curried functions is easy, although you can't use the same simple form as previously. You have to memoize each function:

```
val mhc = Memoizer.memoize { x: Int ->
              Memoizer.memoize { y: Int ->
                  x + y
              }
          }
```

You can use the same technique to memoize a function of three arguments:

```
val f3 = { x: Int -> { y: Int -> { z: Int -> x + y - z } } }

val f3m = Memoizer.memoize { x: Int ->
              Memoizer.memoize { y: Int ->
                  Memoizer.memoize { z: Int -> x + y - z }
              }
          }
```

The following listing shows an example of testing the memoized function with three arguments.

> **Listing 4.4   Testing a memoized function with three arguments**

```
val f3m = Memoizer.memoize { x: Int ->
    Memoizer.memoize { y: Int ->
        Memoizer.memoize { z: Int ->
            longComputation(z) - (longComputation(y) + longComputation(x))
        }
    }
}

fun main(args: Array<String>) {
    val startTime1 = System.currentTimeMillis()
    val result1 = f3m(41)(42)(43)
    val time1 = System.currentTimeMillis() - startTime1
    val startTime2 = System.currentTimeMillis()
    val result2 = f3m(41)(42)(43)
    val time2 = System.currentTimeMillis() - startTime2
    println("First call to memoized function: result = " +
            "$result1, time = $time1")
    println("Second call to memoized function: result = " +
            "$result2, time = $time2")
}
```

This program produces the following output:

```
First call to memoized function: result = -40, time = 3003
Second call to memoized function: result = -40, time = 0
```

This output shows that the first access to the memoized function took 6,786 milliseconds, and the second returned immediately.

On the other hand, using a function of a tuple can seem easier after you define the `Tuple` class because you can use a `data class` for which Kotlin will provide `equals` and `hashCode` functions automatically. The following example shows the implementation of `Tuple4` (if you need only `Tuple2` or `Tuple3`, you can use the `Pair` or `Triple` classes):

```
data class Tuple4<T, U, V, W>(val first: T,
                              val second: U,
                              val third: V,
                              val fourth: W)
```

The following listing shows an example of testing a memoized function taking `Tuple4` as its argument.

Listing 4.5   A memoized function of a Tuple4

```
val ft = { (a, b, c, d): Tuple4<Int, Int, Int, Int> ->
    longComputation(a) + longComputation(b)
        - longComputation(c) * longComputation(d) }


val ftm = Memoizer.memoize(ft)


fun main(args: Array<String>) {
    val startTime1 = System.currentTimeMillis()
    val result1 = ftm(Tuple4(40, 41, 42, 43))
    val time1 = System.currentTimeMillis() - startTime1
    val startTime2 = System.currentTimeMillis()
    val result2 = ftm(Tuple4(40, 41, 42, 43))
    val time2 = System.currentTimeMillis() - startTime2
    println("First call to memoized function: result = " +
            "$result1, time = $time1")
    println("Second call to memoized function: result = " +
            "$result2, time = $time2")
}
```

4.5   *Are memoized functions pure?*

Memoizing is about maintaining state between function calls. A memoized function's behavior depends on the current state, but it'll always return the same value for the same argument. Only the time needed to return the value will be different. The memoized function is still a pure function if the original function is pure.

A variation in time can be a problem. A function like the original Fibonacci function needing many years to complete can be called *non-terminating*, so an increase in time can create a problem. On the other hand, making a function faster shouldn't be a real problem. If it is, there's a much bigger problem somewhere else!

Summary

- A recursive function calls itself, using this call to itself as an element for further computation.
- Recursive functions push the current computation state onto the stack before recursively calling themselves.
- The Kotlin default stack size is limited. If the number of recursive steps is too high, you'll get a `StackOverflowException`.
- Tail-recursive functions are functions in which the recursive call is in the last (*tail*) position.
- In Kotlin, tail-recursive functions are optimized using Tail Call Elimination (TCE).
- Lambdas can be made recursive.
- Memoization allows functions to remember their computed result in order to speed up later access.
- Memoization can be made automatic.

Data handling with lists

In this chapter

- Classifying data structures
- Using the ubiquitous singly linked list
- Understanding the importance of immutability
- Handling lists with recursion and functions

Data structures are one of the most important concepts in programming, as well as in everyday life. The world as you see it is a huge data structure composed of simpler data structures, which are in turn composed of simpler structures. Each time you model something, be it objects or facts, you end up with data structures.

Data structures come in many types. In computing, data structures referring to the multiple occurrences of data of a given common type are generally represented as a whole by the term *collections*. A collection is a group of data items that have some relationship to each other. In its simplest form, this relationship is that they belong to the same group.

This chapter covers data structures and how to create your own implementation of the singly linked list. Kotlin has its own lists, both mutable and immutable. But the Kotlin immutable list isn't really immutable, and it doesn't implement data sharing, making operations such as adding and removing elements less efficient. The immutable list you'll develop in this chapter is far more efficient for stack operations, and it's immutable.

5.1   *How to classify data collections*

A data structure is a structured piece of data. Data collections are one specific category of data structures. Data collections can be classified from many different points of view. You can class data collections in linear collections, associative collections, and graph collections:

- *Linear collections are collections in which elements are related along a single dimension.* In such a collection, each element has a relationship to the next element. The most common example of a linear collection is the list.
- *Associative collections are collections that can be viewed as a function.* Given an object o, a function f(o) returns true or false according to whether this object belongs to the collection or not. Unlike linear collections, there's no relationship between the elements of the collection. These collections aren't ordered, although it's possible to define an order on the elements. The most common examples of associative collections are the set and the associative array (which is also called a map or a dictionary). You'll study a functional implementation of maps in chapter 11.
- *Graphs are collections in which each element is related to multiple other elements.* A particular example is the tree and, more specifically, the binary tree, where each element is related to two other elements. You'll learn more about trees in chapter 10.

5.2   *Different types of lists*

In this chapter, I focus on the most common type of linear collection: the list. The list is the most widely used data structure in programming, so it's generally used to teach many data structure-related concepts.

> **IMPORTANT**   What you'll learn in this chapter isn't specific to lists but is shared by many other data structures (which may not be collections).

Lists can be further classified based on several different aspects, including the following:

- *Access*—You can access some lists from one end only and others from both ends. Lists can be written from one end and read from the other end. Finally, with some lists, you can access any element using its position in the list, which is also called its *index*.
- *Type of ordering*—In some lists, the elements are read in the same order in which they were inserted. This kind of structure is said to be FIFO (first in, first out). In others, the order of retrieval is the inverse of the order of insertion (LIFO, or last in, first out). And some lists allow you to retrieve the elements in a completely different order.
- *Implementation*—The concepts of access type and ordering are strongly related to the implementation you choose for your list. If you choose to represent the list by linking each element to the next, you'll get a completely different result from the

access point of view rather than from an implementation based on an indexed array. Or if you choose to link each element to the next as well as to the previous one, you'll get a list that can be accessed from both ends.

Figure 5.1 shows different types of lists offering different kinds of access. This figure shows the principle behind each type of list, but not the way those are implemented.

5.3 *Relative expected list performance*

One important criterion when choosing a type of list is the expected performance for various kinds of operations. Performance is often expressed in Big O notation. This notation is mainly used in mathematics, but when used in computing, it indicates the way the complexity of an algorithm changes when responding to a change of input size. When used to characterize the performance of list operations, this notation shows how the performance varies as a function of the length of the list. For example, consider the following performances:

- $O(1)$—The time needed for an operation is constant. (You can think of it as meaning that the time for one element is multiplied by 1 for n elements.)
- $O(\log(n))$—The time for an operation on n elements is the time for one element multiplied by $\log(n)$.
- $O(n)$—The time for n elements is the time for one element multiplied by n.
- $O(n^2)$—The time for n elements is the time for one element multiplied by n^2.

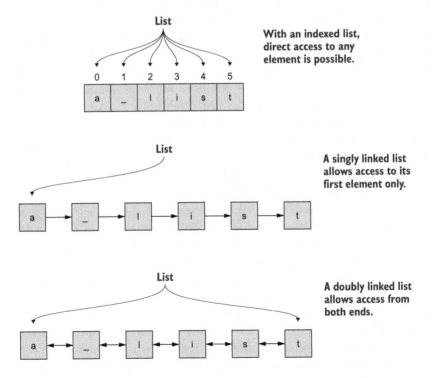

Figure 5.1 Different types of lists offer different types of access to their elements.

It would be ideal to create a data structure with $O(1)$ performance for all types of operations. Unfortunately, this isn't possible yet. Each type of list offers a different performance for different operations. Indexed lists provide $O(1)$ performance for data retrieval and near to $O(1)$ for insertion. Singly linked lists deliver $O(1)$ performance for insertion and retrieval on one end and $O(n)$ for the other end.

Choosing the best structure is a compromise. Most often, you'll seek $O(1)$ performance for the most frequent operations, and you'll have to accept $O(\log(n))$ or even $O(n)$ for some operations that don't occur often.

Be aware that this way of measuring performance has a real meaning for structures that can be scaled infinitely. This isn't the case for the data structures you'll manipulate because these structures are limited in size by the available memory. A structure with $O(n)$ access time might always be faster than another one with $O(1)$ due to this size limitation. If the time for one element is much smaller for the first structure, memory limitation can prevent the second from showing its benefits. It's often better to have $O(n)$ performance with an access time of 1 nanosecond to one element rather than $O(1)$ with an access time of 1 ms. (The latter will be faster than the former only for sizes over 1 million elements.)

5.3.1   *Trading time against memory space and complexity*

You saw that choosing an implementation for a data structure is generally a question of trading time against time. You'll choose an implementation that's faster on some operations but slower on others, based on which operations are the most frequent. But when trading time, there are other decisions to make.

Imagine you want a structure from which elements can be retrieved in a sorted order, the smallest first. You might choose to sort the elements on insertion, or you might prefer to store them as they arrive and search for the smallest on retrieval only. When deciding which to use, one important criterion would be whether the retrieved element is systematically removed from the structure. If not, it might be accessed several times without removal. In this case, it would probably be better to sort the elements at insertion time in order to avoid sorting them several times on retrieval. This use case corresponds to what's called a *priority queue* in which you're waiting for a given element. You might test the queue many times until the expected element is returned. Such a use case requires that elements be sorted at insertion time.

But what if you want to access elements by several different sort orders? For example, you might want to access elements in the same order they were inserted or in the reverse order. The result might correspond to the doubly linked list of figure 5.1. It seems that in such a case, elements should be sorted at retrieval time.

You might favor one order, leading to $O(1)$ access time from one end and $O(n)$ from the other end, or you might invent a different structure, perhaps giving $O(\log(n))$ access time from both ends. Another solution would be to store two lists, one in insertion order and one in reverse order. This way, you'd have a slower insertion time but $O(1)$ retrieval from both ends. One drawback is that this approach would probably use more memory, so you can see that choosing the right structure might also be a question of trading time against memory space.

But you might also invent some structure minimizing both insertion time and retrieval time from both ends. These types of structures have already been invented, and you'd only have to implement them, but such structures are much more complex than the simplest ones, so you'd be trading time against complexity.

5.3.2 Avoiding in-place mutation

Most data structures change over time because elements are inserted and removed. To handle such operations, you can use two approaches. The first one is *update in place*.

Update in place consists of changing the elements of the data structure by mutating the structure itself. This was considered a good idea when all programs were single-threaded (although it wasn't). It's even much worse now that all programs are multithreaded. This doesn't only concern replacing elements. It's the same for adding or removing, sorting, and all operations that mutate the structure. If programs are allowed to mutate data structures, these structures can't be shared without sophisticated protections that are rarely done right the first time, leading to deadlock, livelock, thread starving, stale data, and all sorts of troubles.

> **Update in place**
>
> In a 1981 article titled "The transaction concept: virtues and limitations," Jim Gray wrote:[1]
>
> *Update in place: a poison apple?*
>
> *When bookkeeping was done with clay tablets or paper and ink, accountants developed some clear rules about good accounting practices. One of the cardinal rules is double-entry bookkeeping so that calculations are self-checking, thereby making them fail-fast, meaning that an error is detected as soon as it is committed, instead of possibly appearing long later, when checking the result (or not being apparent at all). A second rule is that one never alters the books; if an error is made, it is annotated and a new compensating entry is made in the books. The books are a complete history of the transactions of the business...*

What's the solution? Use immutable data structures. Many programmers are shocked when they first read this. How can you do useful things with data structures if you can't mutate them? After all, you often start with empty structures and want to add data to them. How can you possibly do this if those are immutable?

The answer is simple. As with double-entry accounting, instead of changing what existed previously, you create new data to represent the new state. Instead of adding an element to an existing list, you create a new list with the added element. The main benefit is that if another thread is manipulating the list at insertion time, it's not affected by the change because it doesn't see it. Generally, this conception immediately raises two protests:

- If the other thread doesn't see the change, it's manipulating stale data.
- If making a new copy of the list with the added element is a time and memory-consuming process, immutable data structures then lead to poor performance.

---

[1] Jim Gray, "The transaction concept: virtues and limitations," Technical Report 81.3 (Tandem Computers, June 1981), http://www.hpl.hp.com/techreports/tandem/TR-81.3.pdf.

Both arguments are fallacious. The thread manipulating the stale data is, in fact, manipulating the data as it was when it started reading it. If inserting an element occurs after the manipulation is finished, there's no concurrency problem. But if the insertion occurs while the manipulation is going on, what would occur with a mutable data structure? Either it wouldn't be protected against concurrent access, and the data might be corrupted or the result false (or both), or some protection mechanism would lock the data, delaying the insertion until after the manipulation by the first thread is complete. In the second case, the end result would be exactly the same as with an immutable structure.

The objection about performance is true if you use data structures implying a whole copy on each modification, which is the case of Kotlin immutable lists. This problem, however, is easy to solve by using special structures implementing data sharing, as you'll learn in this chapter.

5.4   *What kinds of lists are available in Kotlin?*

Kotlin offers two types of lists: mutable and immutable. Both are backed by Java lists but are enhanced with a huge number of functions, thanks to Kotlin's extension functions system.

Mutable lists work like Java lists. You can mutate a list by adding, inserting, or removing an element; in which case, the previous version of the list is lost. On the other hand, immutable lists can't be modified, at least through direct operation. Adding an element to an immutable list creates a copy of the original list with the new element added. This works well, but performance is less than optimal for some operations because these lists aren't persistent by nature. They are made to persist using a well-known technique called *defensive copy*. Although the term defensive copy means making a copy to defend oneself against concurrent mutation from other threads, it can also be applied to defend others from one's own mutations.

Whether you need more efficient immutable lists than what Kotlin offers is arguable. It mostly depends on your use case. If you need a high-performance, immutable LIFO structure like a stack, no doubt you need something more efficient than the Kotlin immutable list. But in any case, even if you don't need a high-performance LIFO list, learning how to create it is fundamental if you want to write safer programs. Every function that you'll create for working on immutable persistent lists enriches your basic knowledge of the subject to such an extent that you can't avoid it.

5.4.1   *Using persistent data structures*

As I said, making a copy of the data structure before inserting an element is a time-costly operation that leads to poor performance. But this isn't the case if you use *data sharing*, which is the technique on which immutable persistent data structures are based. Figure 5.2 shows how elements could be removed and added to create a new immutable singly linked list with optimal performance.

As you can see in the figure, no copying occurs at all. Such a list might be much more efficient for removing and inserting elements than a mutable list. No, functional data structures (immutable and persistent) aren't always slower than mutable ones. They're

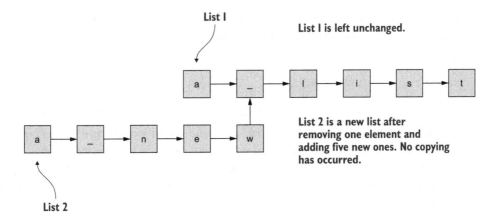

Figure 5.2 Removing and adding elements without mutation or copying

often even faster (although they might be slower in some operations). In any case, they're much safer.

5.4.2 *Implementing immutable, persistent, singly linked lists*

The structure of the singly linked list shown in figures 5.1 and 5.2 is theoretical. The list can't be implemented that way because elements can't be linked to one another. They'd have to be special elements to allow these links, and you want your lists to be able to store any element. The solution is to devise a recursive list structure composed of the following:

- An element that will be the first element of the list, also called the *head*.
- The rest of the list, which is a list by itself and is called the *tail*.

You already encountered a generic element that's composed of two elements of different types: the `Pair`. A singly linked list of elements of type A is in fact a `Pair<A, List<A>>`. The `Pair` class is not open for extension, but you could define your own class:

```
open class Pair<A, B>(val first: A, val second: B)
```

```
class List<A>(val head: A, val tail: List<A>): Pair<A, List<A>>(head, tail)
```

But as I explained in chapter 4, you need a terminal case as you do in every recursive definition. By convention, this terminal case is called `Nil` and corresponds to the empty list. And as `Nil` has no head nor tail, it's not a `Pair`. Your new definition of a list is then either

- An empty list (`Nil`) or
- A pair of an element and a list

Instead of using a `Pair` with properties `first` and `second`, you'll create a specific `List` class with two properties: `head` and `tail`. This simplifies the handling of the `Nil` case. `Nil` could be declared as an `object`, meaning it would be a singleton because there needs to be only one instance of the empty list. In such a case, you'd create it as a List<Nothing> that can be cast into a list of any type. You could define these elements as

```
open class List<A>

object Nil : List<Nothing>()

class Cons<A>(private val head: A, private val tail: List<A>): List<A>()
```

But there would be a major drawback: anyone could extend the List class, which might lead to an inconsistent implementation of lists, and anyone could access the Nil and Cons subclasses, which are implementation details that shouldn't be made public. The solution is to declare the List class sealed and define the Nil and Cons subclasses inside the List class:

```
sealed class List<A> {

    internal object Nil: List<Nothing>()

    internal class Cons<A>(private val head: A,
                           private val tail: List<A>): List<A>()
}
```

Figure 5.3 shows the complete listing of your first list implementation.

For experimenting with your new List, you'll need some functions. Listing 5.1 shows the basic implementation of this list including these functions.

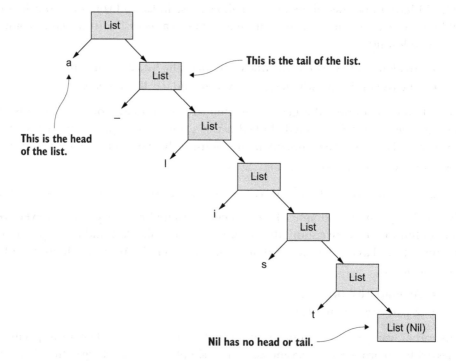

Figure 5.3   The representation of the singly linked list implementation

Listing 5.1   Singly linked lists

The Nil subclass | **Sealed classes are implicitly abstract and** | **The abstract isEmpty function has a different**
represents an empty list. | **their constructor is implicitly private.** | **implementations in each extending class.**

```
sealed class List<A> {          ◄───────────────

    abstract fun isEmpty(): Boolean     ◄──────      Extending classes are defined inside the
                                                     List class and made private.
    private object Nil : List<Nothing>() {    ◄──────

        override fun isEmpty() = true

        override fun toString(): String = "[NIL]"
    }

    private class Cons<A>(                              The Cons subclass
            internal val head: A,                       represents non-empty lists.
            internal val tail: List<A>) : List<A>() {   ◄──────

        override fun isEmpty() = false

        override fun toString(): String = "[${toString("", this)}NIL]"

        tailrec private fun toString(acc: String, list: List<A>): String =
            when (list) {          ◄──────────────────────────────
                is Nil -> acc
                is Cons -> toString("$acc${list.head}, ", list.tail)
            }                                  The toString function is implemented as a
    }                                          corecursive function (as you learned in chapter 4).

    companion object {

        operator
        fun <A> invoke(vararg az: A): List<A> =   //
                az.foldRight(Nil as List<A>) { a: A, list: List<A> ->
                    Cons(a, list)     ◄──────
                }                          The first argument of the foldRight
    }                                      function is where the Nil object is
}                                          explicitly cast into a List<A>.
```

The invoke function declared with the keyword
operator can be called as ClassName().

In the listing, the List class is implemented as a *sealed class.* Sealed classes allow defining *algebraic data types* (ADT), meaning types that have a limited set of subtypes. Sealed classes are implicitly abstract and their constructor is implicitly private. Here the List class is parameterized with the parameter type A, which represents the type of the list elements.

The List class contains two private subclasses to represent the two possible forms a List can take: Nil for an empty list and Cons for a nonempty one. (The name *Cons* means *construct.*) The Cons class takes as parameters an A (the head) and a List<A> (the tail). By convention, the toString function always includes NIL as the last element, so the implementation returns [NIL]. These parameters are declared internal so that they won't be visible from outside the file or the module in which the List class is declared. The subclasses have been made private, so you must construct lists through calls to the companion object invoke function.

The List class also defines the abstract isEmpty() function, which returns true if the list is empty and false otherwise. The invoke function, together with the modifier operator, allows calling the function with a simplified syntax:

```
val List<Int> list = List(1, 2, 3)
```

This isn't a call to the constructor (the List constructor is private), but to the companion object invoke function. The foldRight function in this listing is a standard Kotlin function for arrays and collections. You've already defined such a function in chapter 4, but you'll learn more about it later in this chapter.

5.5   *Data sharing in list operations*

One of the huge benefits of immutable persistent data structures like the singly linked list is the performance boost provided by data sharing. You can already see that accessing the first element of the list is immediate. It's a matter of accessing the head property. Removing the first element is equally fast. All you have to do is return the value of the tail property. Let's now see how to get a new list with an additional element.

EXERCISE 5.1

Implement the function cons, adding an element at the beginning of a list. (Remember *cons* stands for *construct*.)

HINT

This function can have the same implementation for both subclasses, so you can define it as a concrete function in the List class.

SOLUTION

This function creates a new list that uses the current list as the tail and the new element as the head:

```
fun cons(a: A): List<A> = Cons(a, this)
```

EXERCISE 5.2

Implement setHead, a function for replacing the first element of a List with a new value.

HINT

You can't change the head of an empty list, so in such a case, you should throw an exception. (In the next chapter, you'll learn how to safely handle this case.)

SOLUTION

You could implement this function in the List class, taking advantage of the when construct and smart casts:

```
fun setHead(a: A): List<A> = when (this) {
    Nil -> throw IllegalStateException("setHead called on an empty list")
    is Cons -> tail.cons(a)
  }
}
```

As you can see, you don't need to explicitly cast the List into Nil and Cons. This is automatically done by Kotlin. Also note that, thanks to the use of a sealed class, you don't need an else clause. Kotlin sees that all subclasses are processed.

If you're a former Java programmer, you might not like this style of programming. Here, is is the equivalent of using the Java instanceof operator, which is generally considered bad practice. There's nothing inherently wrong in using instanceof in Java, however. It's considered bad practice because it isn't object-oriented.

NOTE Kotlin isn't only an object-oriented programming (OOP) language. It's a multi-paradigm language that favors using the right tool for the job. In the end, it's up to you to choose the technique you prefer.

On the other hand, checking types just because it's not forbidden isn't a good option either. Using the right tool for the job includes using OOP techniques when those might be better. Is this the case here? At first sight, it might seem like it's not. Let's figure out why by creating an abstract setHead function in the parent List class with separate implementations in Nil and Cons:

```
sealed class List<A> {

    abstract fun setHead(a: A): List<A>

    private object Nil: List<Nothing>() {

        override fun setHead(a: Nothing): List<Nothing> =
            throw IllegalStateException("setHead called on an empty list")

        ...

    }

    private class Cons<A>(internal val head: A,
                         internal val tail: List<A>) : List<A>() {

        override fun setHead(a: A): List<A> =  tail.cons(a)
    ...
```

This seems okay, but it isn't. If you try to call setHead on an empty list, you get a Class-CastException instead of the expected IllegalStateException. This is because when an A is received by the setHead function of the Nil class, it's cast into a Nothing because Nothing is the parameter type of the setHead function implementation. This causes a ClassCastException as Nothing isn't a supertype of A. (On the contrary, A is a supertype of Nothing.) You can use the Nothing type to make the code compile, but it can't be instantiated at runtime. As a result, no function taking Nothing as a parameter type can ever be called.

Does this mean there's no way to implement `setHead` as an abstract function in the `List` class? No. A simple solution consists in declaring an abstract `Empty<A>` class and a `Nil<Nothing>` object implementing this class. This would be a better choice if you had many functions to define, each taking an A argument. But for now, `setHead` and `cons` are the only ones. Furthermore, the `cons` function can have the same implementation for both subclasses, so you can keep it like this. In chapter 11, you'll use an abstract class with a singleton object implementation to represent empty trees.

5.6   *More list operations*

You can rely on data sharing to implement various other operations in an efficient way—often much more efficient than what can be done with mutable lists. In the rest of this section, you'll add functionality to the linked list based on data sharing.

EXERCISE 5.3

Returning the `tail` property of a list has the same effect as removing the first element, although no mutation occurs. Write a more general function, `drop`, that removes the first n elements from a list. This function won't remove the elements but returns a new list corresponding to the intended result. This list won't be anything new because you'll use data sharing, so nothing will be created. Figure 5.4 shows how you should proceed.

The signature of the function is this:

```
fun drop(n: Int): List<A>
```

In case n is higher that the length of the list, just return an empty list. (You might prefer to call this function `dropAtMost`.)

HINT

You should use corecursion to implement the `drop` function. You can implement an abstract function in the `List` class with two different implementations in `Nil` and `Cons`. Or is there a better solution?

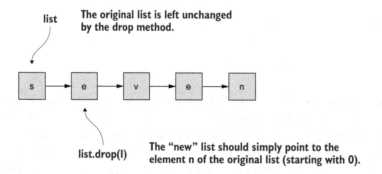

Figure 5.4   Dropping the *n* first elements of a list while not mutating or creating anything

SOLUTION

Implementing an abstract function in the List class seems straightforward. Add the abstract keyword in front of the function signature. The implementation in Nil returns this. A recursive implementation in Cons could be

```
override fun drop(n: Int): List<A> = if (n == 0) this else tail.drop(n - 1)
```

But this blows the stack for n higher than a few thousand (somewhere between 10,000 and 20,000), provided the list is long enough. As you saw in chapter 4, you should change recursion into corecursion by adding an additional parameter. This seems easy, and the following solution may come to mind:

```
override fun drop(n: Int): List<A> {
  tailrec fun drop(n: Int, list: List<A>): List<A> =
                  if (n <= 0) list else drop(n - 1, list.tail())
  return drop(n, this)
}
```

However, this won't work if n is higher than the length of this list. Using corecursion prevents the terminal case from being handed to the Nil implementation. In such a case, you need to explicitly test for Nil and you can't rely on polymorphism. But not relying on polymorphism means you don't have to declare an abstract function in the List class with two different implementations. The following function in the List class will do the job:

```
fun drop(n: Int): List<A> {
    tailrec fun drop(n: Int, list: List<A>): List<A> =
        if (n <= 0) list else when (list) {
            is Cons -> drop(n - 1, list.tail)
            is Nil -> list
        }
    return drop(n, this)
}
```

5.6.1 *Benefiting from object notation*

Putting functions in classes is a choice. You can also define your function outside the class at package level. As I've mentioned, declaring a function inside a class is exactly the same as adding this to its parameters. You could, therefore, define the drop function as

```
class List<A> {
    ...
}

fun <A> drop(aList: List<A>, n: Int): List<A> {
    tailrec fun drop_(list: List<A>, n: Int): List<A> = when (list) {
        List.Nil -> list
        is List.Cons -> if (n <= 0) list else drop_(list.tail, n - 1)
    }
    return drop_(aList, n)
}
```

Then you can see that the helper function is no longer necessary because it has exactly the same signature as the main function:

```
class List<A> {

    ...
}


tailrec fun drop(list: List<A>, n: Int): List<A> = when (list) {
    List.Nil -> list
    is List.Cons -> if (n <= 0) list else drop(list.tail, n - 1)
}
```

One drawback is that you must now declare the `Nil` and `Cons` class `internal` rather than `private` because, unlike Java, the enclosing class has no access to private inner or nested classes. Not a big deal, though. This can be solved by declaring the function in the *class companion object*:

```
companion object {

    tailrec fun <A> drop(list: List<A>, n: Int): List<A> = when (list) {
        Nil -> list
        is Cons -> if (n <= 0) list else drop(list.tail, n - 1)
    }


    ...
}
```

With this solution, you can call the function by prefixing its name with the name of the class, as do Java programmers when calling static functions:

```
fun main(args: Array<String>) {
    val list = List(1, 2, 3)
    println(List.drop(list, 2))
}
```

Alternatively, you can import the function. On the other hand, instance functions are often easier to use than functions defined at the package level or in companion objects. That's because instance functions let you compose function calls using object notation, which is much easier to read. For example, if you want to drop two elements of a list of integers and then replace the first element of the result with a 0, you can use package-level functions:

```
val newList = setHead(drop(list, 2), 0);
```

Each time you add a function to the process, the function name is added to the left, and the additional arguments, besides the list itself, are added to the right, as shown in figure 5.5.

Using object notation makes the code much easier to read:

```
val newList = list.drop(2).setHead(0);
```

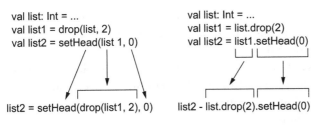

Figure 5.5   Without object notation (left), composed functions can be difficult to read. Using object notation (right) results in much more readable code.

As a library designer, the best option would probably be to offer both possibilities. Given that you put the function in the companion object, adding an instance version is as simple as

```
fun drop(n: Int): List<A> = drop(this, n)
```

Now you have the best of both worlds. You don't need a helper function (or you might consider that the function in the companion object is the helper function), and you don't need a specific implementation in each subclass. If you don't want the function in the companion object to be accessible from the outside, you can make it private. In this case, you can also put it in the list class, and you're back at the starting point.

As for the question of which solution to choose, there isn't a unique answer. It's up to you to choose the solution that fits your needs or your style. A solution with less code is usually preferable, though, because the more code you have, the more you have to maintain. Besides this, try to minimize the visible parts.

EXERCISE 5.4

Implement a `dropWhile` function to remove elements from the head of the `List` as long as a condition holds true. Here's the signature of the function:

```
fun dropWhile(p: (A) -> Boolean): List<A>
```

SOLUTION

Assuming you chose the companion object approach, here's how to implement the helper function:

```
private
tailrec fun <A> dropWhile(list: List<A>,
                          p: (A) -> Boolean): List<A> = when (list) {
    Nil -> list
    is Cons -> if (p(list.head)) dropWhile(list.tail, p) else list
}
```

The following instance function in the `List` class calls the helper function:

```
fun dropWhile(p: (A) -> Boolean): List<A> = dropWhile(this, p)
```

5.6.2   Concatenating lists

A common operation on lists consists in adding one list to another to form a new list containing all elements of both lists. It would be nice to be able to link both lists, but this isn't possible. The solution is to add all elements of one list to the other list. But elements can only be added to the front (head) of the list, so if you want to concatenate list1 to list2, you must start by adding the last element of list1 to the front of list2, as indicated in figure 5.6.

One way to proceed is to first reverse list1, producing a new list, and then add each element to list2, this time starting from the head of the reversed list. But you haven't yet defined a reverse function. Can you still define concat? Yes, you can. Consider how you could define this function:

- If list1 is empty, return list2.
- Else return the addition of the first element (list1.head) of list1 to the concatenation of the rest of list1 (list1.tail) to list2.

This recursive definition can be translated into the following code:

```
fun <A> concat(list1: List<A>, list2: List<A>): List<A> = when (list1) {
    Nil -> list2
    is Cons -> concat(list1.tail, list2).cons(list1.head)
}
```

You can add an instance function in List, calling the companion object version with this as its first argument:

```
fun concat(list: List<A>): List<A> = concat(this, list)
```

The beauty of this solution (for some readers) is that you don't need a figure to expose how it works because it isn't working. It's a mathematical definition translated into code.

The main drawback of this definition (for other readers) is that, for the same reason, it can't easily be represented in a figure. This can sound like humor, but it's not. This

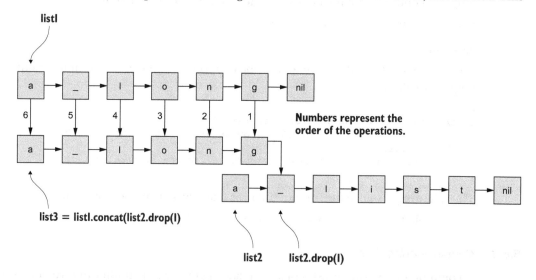

Figure 5.6   Sharing data by concatenation. You can see that both lists are preserved and that list2 is shared by the resulting list. But you can also see that you can't proceed exactly as is indicated in the figure because you'd have to access the last element of list1 first. This isn't possible because of the list's structure.

solution doesn't represent the process of concatenating lists (from which you could draw a flowchart). It expresses the result directly in the form of an expression. And this code doesn't compute the result. It's the result!

> **NOTE** Programming with functions as a replacement for control structures most often involves thinking in terms of what the intended result is rather than how to obtain it. Functional code is a direct translation of a definition into code.

Obviously, this code will overflow the stack if `list1` is too long, although you'll never have a stack problem with the length of `list2`. The consequence is that you won't have to worry if you're careful to only add small lists to the front end of lists of any length.

An important point to note is that what you're doing is adding elements of the first list in reverse order to the front of the second list. This is obviously different from the commonsense understanding of concatenation: adding the second list to the tail of the first one. This is definitely not how it works with the singly linked list.

If you need to concatenate lists of an arbitrary length, you might think you need to apply what you learned in chapter 4 to make the `concat` function stack safe—replace recursion with corecursion. Unfortunately, this isn't possible. As a consequence, this approach is limited by the stack size. You'll later see how you can solve the problem by trading (stack) memory space for time. For now, if you think of what you've done, you might guess that there's more room left for abstraction here. What if the `concat` function were only a specific application of a much more general operation? Maybe you could abstract this operation, make it stack safe, and then reuse it to implement many other operations? Wait and see!

You may have noticed that the complexity of this operation (and hence, the time it'll take to be executed by Kotlin) is proportional to the length of the first list. If you concatenate `list1` and `list2` of length n1 and n2, the complexity is O(n1), which means it's independent from n2. Depending on n1 and n2, this operation can be much more efficient than concatenating two mutable lists in imperative programming.

5.6.3 *Dropping from the end of a list*

It's sometimes necessary to remove elements from the end of a list. Although the singly linked list isn't the ideal data structure for this kind of operation, you must still be able to implement it.

EXERCISE 5.5

Write a function to remove the last element from a list. This function should return the resulting list. Implement it as an instance function with the following signature:

```
fun init(): List<A>
```

You may be wondering why this is called `init` instead of something like `dropLast`. The term comes from Haskell (http://zvon.org/other/haskell/Outputprelude/init_f.html).

HINT

There might be a way to express this function in terms of another one, and one I've already spoken about. Maybe now would be the right time to create the helper function.

SOLUTION

To remove the last element, you need to traverse the list (from front to back) and build up the new list (from back to front) because the last element in a list must be `Nil`. This is a consequence of the way lists are created with `Cons` objects. This results in a list with the elements in reverse order, so the resulting list must be reversed. That means you only have to implement a reverse function:

```
tailrec fun <A> reverse(acc: List<A>, list: List<A>): List<A> =
    when (list) {
        Nil -> acc
        is Cons -> reverse(acc.cons(list.head), list.tail)
    }
```

This code is the implementation in the companion object. And next is the instance function in `List` calling it with `this`:

```
fun reverse(): List<A> = reverse(List.invoke(), this)
```

Note that you can't use the `List()` syntax to call the invoke function without an argument. You must explicitly call it; otherwise, Kotlin thinks you're calling a constructor and throws an exception because the `List` class is abstract. Remember, you can choose a different organization, such as putting the helper function inside the calling function:

```
fun reverse(): List<A> {
    tailrec fun <A> reverse(acc: List<A>,
                            list: List<A>): List<A> = when (list) {
        Nil -> acc
        is Cons -> reverse(acc.cons(list.head), list.tail)
    }
    return reverse(List.invoke(), this)
}
```

With the reverse function, you can implement `init` easily:

```
fun init(): List<A> = reverse().drop(1).reverse()
```

This is the implementations for the `Cons` class. In the `Nil` class, the `init` function throws an exception.

5.6.4 *Using recursion to fold lists with higher-order functions (HOFs)*

In chapter 4, you learned how to fold lists; folding applies to persistent lists as well. But with mutable lists, you can choose to implement these operations through iteration or recursively. With persistent lists, there's no reason to use the iterative approach. Let's consider common folding operations on lists of numbers.

EXERCISE 5.6

Write a function to compute the sum of all elements of a persistent list of integers using recursion. The implementation can be put in the companion object of List or at package level in the same file if you make the subclasses internal instead of private. Putting it at package level might seem more appropriate because it's specific to List<Int>.

SOLUTION

The recursive definition of the sum of all elements of a list is this:

- 0 for an empty list
- head + sum of tail for a nonempty list

The way to express this in Kotlin is as follows:

```
fun sum(ints: List<Int>): Int = when (ints) {
    Nil -> 0
    is Cons -> ints.head + sum(ints.tail)
}
```

But this won't compile because Nil is not a subtype of List<Int>.

5.6.5 *Using variance*

The problem you're having is that although the Nothing type is a child of all types (Int included), you can always upcast a Nothing into any other type, but you can't cast a List<Nothing> into a List<Int>. If you remember what you learned in chapter 2, this is due to the fact that List is invariant in A. To make it work as expected, you must make List covariant in A, which means you have to declare it as List<out A>:

```
sealed class List<out A> {
...
```

If you do this, the List class no longer compiles, displaying the following error message (many similar errors occur in other lines):

```
Error:(7, 17) Kotlin: Type parameter A is declared as 'out'
                        but occurs in 'in' position in type A
```

The error points to the following line:

```
fun cons(a: A): List<A> = Cons(a, this)
```

This means that the List class can't contain functions having a parameter of type A. The parameter is an input for the function, so it's in the in position. Functions can only have an A as their return type (the out position).

UNDERSTANDING VARIANCE

To understand variance, you can think about a basket of apples. You can perform two main kinds of operations regarding this basket:

- Put an apple into the basket
- Take an apple out of the basket

An Apple is a Fruit (a parent class of Apple), and a Gala is an Apple. The inverse isn't true. A Fruit is not an Apple. Although it might sometimes be the case, the predicate A Fruit is an Apple isn't true. In the same way, an Apple isn't a Gala.

You can put a Gala *in* a Basket of Apple, but you can't do so with a Fruit because it might not be an Apple. On the other hand, if you need a Fruit, you can take it *out* of a Basket of Apple. But if you want a Gala, you can't do that because the Basket might contain other varieties of Apple.

But what about an empty Basket? Wouldn't it be useful to be able to say that it's empty of anything you need? If you weren't able to do this, you'd need an empty basket for apples, another one for oranges, and yet another one for each possible type of object.

You could use an empty basket of Any (the Kotlin equivalent of Java Object). But although you'd be able to put anything into the empty basket, you couldn't (usefully) take anything out of it because you'd never know what type of object you'd get. The Kotlin solution for this problem is the Nothing type. Unlike Any, which is the parent type of every other type, Nothing is a child type of all types.

By declaring the A parameter out, you're saying that a List<Gala> is a List<Apple> because a Gala is an Apple. Conversely, a List<Apple> isn't a List<Gala> because an Apple is not a Gala. And this is what allows you to have a single empty list; all you need to do is to declare the empty list as a List<Nothing>. A List<Nothing> is a List<Apple> because a Nothing is an Apple. But a List<Nothing> is also a List<Tiger> because a Nothing is also a Tiger. If you have trouble figuring this out, think of Nothing as being the Absence of. Nothing is an absence of Apple, and it's also an absence of Tiger, as well as the absence of anything else.

GETTING AWAY WITH VARIANCE ABUSE

One of the compiler's jobs is to prevent a programmer's mistakes. If you declare the List parameter type as out A, the compiler won't let you use the A type in the in position, which means you won't be able to put an A into a List<A> using an instance function of List that takes a parameter of type A. You can't do this:

```
sealed class List<out A> {

    fun cons(a: A): List<A> = Cons(a, this) { // Compile error
        ...
    }

    internal class Cons<out A>(internal val head: A,
                              internal val tail: List<A>): List<A>()

    internal object Nil: List<Nothing>()
}
```

This code produces a compilation error with the following message:

```
Type parameter A is declared as 'out' but occurs in 'in' position in type `A`
```

You might think this isn't fair because you know for sure that adding an A to a List<A> is okay. But here you're wrong. It's not okay at all. To demonstrate why, think about what would be the implementation of an abstract cons function in each subclass:

```
sealed class List<out A> {

    abstract fun cons(a: A): List<A>

    internal class Cons<out A>(internal val head: A,
                              internal val tail: List<A>): List<A>() {
        ...
    }

    internal object Nil: List<Nothing>() {

        override fun cons(a: Nothing): List<Nothing> = Cons(a, this) // Error
    }
}
```

If you try this, you'll get an additional error (beside the one noted) in the Nil implementation: the implementation of the cons function is tagged. by the compiler as *non-reachable code*. Why is this? Because this in the Nil class refers to a List<Nothing> and calling Nil.cons(1) would cause 1 to be cast into Nothing. That's not possible because Nothing is a subtype of Int and not the other way around. Now you have two problems to deal with:

- The compiler not allowing you to use A in the in position, although you know it would be valid in some cases
- The casting problem in the Nil class, which you must avoid to eliminate a case where the first problem would arise

To understand what's happening in the Nil class, you must remember that Kotlin is a *strict language*, meaning that function arguments are evaluated whether they are used or not. The problem isn't in the function implementation:

```
Cons(a, this)
```

Before adding the new A to it, this, being a List<Nothing>, can be safely cast in a List<A>. The problem is with the argument of the function:

```
override fun cons(a: Nothing)
```

When the A argument is received by the function, it's immediately cast to the receiver argument type Nothing, which causes an error. This is the consequence of strictness. And this is unfortunate because immediately after, the element would have been added to a List<A> (the result of casting Nil into a List<A>). No downcasting of the argument into Nothing would have been necessary. To solve this problem, you need two tricks:

- Stop the compiler from complaining by taking responsibility for using A in the in position. This can be done using the @UnsafeVariance annotation:

```
fun cons(a: @UnsafeVariance A): List<A>
```

- Remove the downcast of A by putting the implementation in the parent class:

```
sealed class List<out A> {
    fun cons(a: @UnsafeVariance A):List<A> = Cons(a, this)
    ...
```

Here, you're saying to the compiler that it shouldn't worry about a variance problem in the cons function: you're taking responsibility and if something goes wrong, it's on you. Now, you can apply the same technique for functions setHead and concat:

```
sealed class List<out A> {

    fun setHead(a: @UnsafeVariance A): List<A> = when (this) {
        is Cons -> Cons(a, this.tail)
        Nil -> throw IllegalStateException("setHead called on an empty list")
    }

    fun cons(a: @UnsafeVariance A): List<A> = Cons(a, this)

    fun concat(list: List<@UnsafeVariance A>): List<A> = concat(this, list)

    ...
```

You only need to do this for functions taking a parameter of type A, or List<A>. You don't need to do this for functions taking no parameters, nor for the dropWhile function taking a parameter of type (A) -> Boolean. But you also must ensure that when using this trick, no unsafe cast will ever fail. As usual, with greater freedom comes greater responsibility.

Note that there's another possibility that consists in creating an Empty<A> abstract class for representing empty lists and then creating a Nil<Nothing> singleton object. This lets you define abstract functions in the List parent class with specific implementation in Cons or Empty. Here's how the concat function could be defined:

```
sealed class List<A> {

    abstract fun concat(list: List<A>): List<A>

    abstract class Empty<A> : List<A>() {

        override fun concat(list: List<A>): List<A> = list
    }

    private object Nil : Empty<Nothing>()

    private class Cons<A>(private val head: A,
                         private val tail: List<A>) : List<A>() {

        override fun concat(list: List<A>): List<A> =
                Cons(this.head, list.concat(this.tail))
    }
}
```

This solution may be more appealing to former Java programmers because it avoids checking for types as in this example:

```
fun <A> concat(list1: List<A>, list2: List<A>): List<A> = when (list1) {
    Nil -> list2
    is Cons -> Cons(list1.head, concat(list1.tail, list2))
}
```

In any case, thanks to using out variance, your sum function is now perfectly fine!

EXERCISE 5.7

Write a function to compute the product of all elements of a list of doubles using recursion.

SOLUTION

The recursive definition of the product of all elements of a nonempty list is this:

```
head * product of tail
```

But what should it return for an empty list? If you remember your math courses, you'll know the answer. If you don't, you can find the answer in the preceding requirement for a nonempty list.

Consider what will happen when you've applied the recursive formula to all elements. You'll end up with a result that'll have to be multiplied by the product of all elements of an empty list. Because you want to eventually get this result, you have no choice but to say that the product of all elements of an empty list is 1.

This is the same situation as with the sum example, when you use 0 as the sum of all elements of an empty list. 0 is the identity, or neutral element, for the sum operation, and 1 is the identity, or neutral element, for the product. Your product function could be written as follows:

```
fun product(ints: List<Int>): Int = when (ints) {
    List.Nil   -> 1
    is List.Cons -> ints.head * product(ints.tail)
}
```

The product operation is different than the sum operation in one important way: it has an *absorbing element,* which is an element that satisfies the following condition: *a * absorbing element = absorbing element * a = absorbing element.*

The absorbing element for multiplication is 0. By analogy, the absorbing element of any operation (if it exists) is also called the *zero element.* The existence of a zero element lets you escape the computation, also called *short circuiting,* like this:

```
fun product(ints: List<Double>): Double = when (ints) {
    List.Nil   -> 1.0
    is List.Cons -> if (ints.head == 0.0)
                        0.0
                    else
                        ints.head * product(ints.tail)
}
```

But forget about this optimized version and look at the definitions for sum and product. Can you detect a pattern that could be abstracted? Let's look at those functions side-by-side (after having changed the parameter name):

```
fun sum(ints: List<Int>): Int = when (ints) {
    List.Nil   -> 0
    is List.Cons -> ints.head + sum(ints.tail)
}

fun product(ints: List<Double>): Double = when (ints) {
    List.Nil   -> 1.0
    is List.Cons -> ints.head * product(ints.tail)
}
```

Now let's remove the differences and replace them with a common notation:

```
fun sum(list: List<Type>): Type = when (list) {
    List.Nil   -> identity
    is List.Cons -> list.head operator operation(list.tail)
}

fun product(list: List<Type>): Type = when (list) {
    List.Nil   -> identity
    is List.Cons -> ints.head operator operation(list.tail)
}
```

The two functions are the same with some different values for `Type`, `operation`, identity, and `operator`. If you can find a way to abstract these common parts, you'll have to provide the variable information in order to implement both functions without repeating yourself. This common function is what is called a *fold*, which you studied in chapter 4. In that chapter, you learned that there are two kinds of folds: `foldRight` and `foldLeft`, as well as a relationship between these two operations.

Listing 5.2 shows the common parts of the sum and product operations abstracted into a function called `foldRight`, taking as its parameters the list to fold, an identity element, and a HOF (Higher Order Function) representing the operation used to fold the list. The identity element is obviously the identity for the given operation, and the function is in curried form. (See chapter 3 if you don't remember what *curried* means.) The following listing shows the function that represents the operator portion of your code.

> **Listing 5.2   Implementing `foldRight` and using it for sum and product**

A and B represent the types.   **The identity for the folding operation**

```
fun <A, B> foldRight(list: List<A>,
                 identity: B,
                 f: (A) -> (B) -> B): B =
    when (list) {
        List.Nil -> identity
        is List.Cons -> f(list.head)(foldRight(list.tail, identity, f))
    }
```

The function f in curried form, representing the operator

```
fun sum(list: List<Int>): Int =
    foldRight(list, 0) { x -> { y -> x + y } }
```

The names (sum and product) of the operations

```
fun product(list: List<Double>): Double =
    foldRight(list, 1.0) { x -> { y -> x * y } }
```

The Type variable part has been replaced with two types here, A and B. This is because the result of the folding isn't always of the same type as the elements of the list. Here it's abstracted a bit more than what's needed for the sum and product operations, but this will be useful soon. The operation variable part is the names of the two functions.

The fold operation isn't specific to arithmetic computations. You can use a fold to transform a list of characters into a string. In such a case, A and B are two different types: Char and String. But you can also use a fold to transform a list of strings into a single string. Can you see now how you could implement concat?

By the way, foldRight is similar to the singly linked list itself. If you think of the list 1, 2, 3 as

```
Cons(1, Cons(2, Cons(3, Nil)))
```

you can immediately see that it's similar to a right fold:

```
f(1, f(2, f(3, identity)))
```

But perhaps you've already realized that Nil is the identity list concatenation, although you could do without it, provided the list of lists to be concatenated isn't empty. In such a case, it's called a *reduce* rather than a *fold*. This is possible only because the result is of the same type as the elements. It can be put in practice by passing Nil and cons to foldRight as the identity and the function that's used to fold:

```
foldRight(List(1, 2, 3), List()) { x: Int ->
      { y: List<Int> ->
            y.cons(x)
      }
}
```

This produces a new list with the same elements in the same order, as you can see by running the following code:

```
println(foldRight(List(1, 2, 3), List()) { x: Int ->
      { y: List<Int> ->
            y.cons(x)
      }
})
```

This code produces the following output:

```
[1, 2, 3, NIL]
```

Here's a trace of what's happening at each step:

```
foldRight(List(1, 2, 3), List(), x -> y -> y.cons(x));
foldRight(List(1, 2), List(3), x -> y -> y.cons(x));
foldRight(List(1), List(2, 3), x -> y -> y.cons(x));
foldRight(List(), List(1, 2, 3), x -> y -> y.cons(x));
```

You should put the foldRight function in the companion object, and then add an instance function with this as its argument that calls foldRight in the List class:

```
fun <B> foldRight(identity: B, f: (A) -> (B) -> B): B =
            foldRight(this, identity, f)
```

EXERCISE 5.8

Write a function to compute the length of a list. This function will use the `foldRight` function.

SOLUTION

This function can be defined directly in the `List` class:

```
fun length(): Int = foldRight(0) { _ -> { it + 1} }
```

As its first parameter, representing an element of the list, is unused, the convention is to name it `_`. The second parameter is represented by `it`. At each step of the recursion, 1 is added to the count. When a parameter is unused, you can also remove it. The code then becomes this:

```
fun length(): Int = foldRight(0) { { it + 1} }
```

This implementation, besides being recursive (meaning it could overflow the stack for long lists), has poor performance. Even if transformed to corecursive, it's still $0(n)$, meaning the time needed to return the length is proportional to the length of the list. In the next chapters, you'll see how to get the length of a linked list in constant time.

EXERCISE 5.9

The `foldRight` function uses recursion, but it's not tail recursive, so it'll rapidly overflow the stack. How rapidly depends on several factors, the most important of which is the size of the stack. Instead of using `foldRight`, create a `foldLeft` function that's corecursive and stack safe. Here's its signature:

```
public <B> foldLeft(identity: B, f: (B) -> (A) -> B): B
```

HINT

If you don't remember the difference between `foldLeft` and `foldRight`, refer to chapter 4.

SOLUTION

The helper function implementation in the companion object is similar to the `foldRight` function, although the parameter function type is `(B) -> (A) -> B)` instead of `(A) -> (B) -> B`. If the list received as the second parameter is `Nil` (empty list), the `foldLeft` function returns the `acc` accumulator, exactly as the `foldRight` function does. If the list isn't empty (`Cons`), the function calls itself after having applied the parameter function to the accumulator and the head of the list parameter:

```
tailrec fun <A, B> foldLeft(acc: B, list: List<A>, f: (B) -> (A) -> B): B =
    when (list) {
        List.Nil -> acc
        is List.Cons -> foldLeft(f(acc)(list.head), list.tail, f)
    }
```

This helper function is called by the main function in the `List` class:

```
fun <B> foldLeft(identity: B, f: (B) -> (A) -> B): B =
        foldLeft(identity, this, f)
```

EXERCISE 5.10

Use your new `foldLeft` function to create new stack-safe versions of sum, product, and length.

SOLUTION

This is the sum via `foldLeft` function:

```
fun sum(list: List<Int>): Int = list.foldLeft(0, { x -> { y -> x + y } })
```

The product via `foldLeft` function is as follows:

```
fun product(list: List<Double>): Double =
        list.foldLeft(1.0, { x -> { y -> x * y } })
```

And here's the length via `foldLeft` function:

```
fun length(): Int = foldLeft(0) { { _ -> it + 1} }
```

Once again, the second parameter of function `length` (representing each element of the list on each call of the function) is ignored. The first parameter is represented by the it keyword. As a result, you can't remove the underscore parameter without using an explicit name for the first parameter, such as

```
fun length(): Int = foldLeft(0) { i -> { i + 1} }
```

This function is nearly as inefficient as the `foldRight` version and shouldn't be used in production code. Although it won't blow the stack, it's slow because it must count the elements of the list each time it's called.

EXERCISE 5.11

Use `foldLeft` to write a function for reversing a list.

HINT

Be aware of the type of the identity. You'll have to indicate it explicitly.

SOLUTION

Reversing a list via a left fold is simple, starting from an empty list as the accumulator and successively adding each element of the first list to the accumulator through a call to the cons function:

```
fun reverse(): List<A> =
        foldLeft(Nil as List<A>) { acc -> { acc.cons(it) } }
```

As you can see, you need to both specify the parameter type for `Nil` and to cast it into a `List`. Otherwise, Kotlin uses `Nil` as the return type. In the previous version of reverse, you used an helper function taking a `List` as its argument, so the cast occurred implicitly. You can't use `List()` directly because, in the `List` class, this would be the class constructor, which is impossible because the class is abstract. Another solution to work around for this problem is to call the `invoke` function explicitly:

```
fun reverse(): List<A> =
        foldLeft(List.invoke()) { acc -> { acc.cons(it) } }
```

EXERCISE 5.12

Write `foldRight` in terms of `foldLeft`.

HINT

Use the functions you just implemented.

SOLUTION

This implementation can be useful for getting a stack-safe, but slower, version of `foldRight`:

```
fun <B> foldRightViaFoldLeft(identity: B, f: (A) -> (B) -> B): B =
        this.reverse().foldLeft(identity) { x -> { y -> f(y)(x) } }
```

Note that you can also define `foldLeft` in terms of `foldRight`, although it seems much less useful. In fact, the implementation of `foldRight` via `foldLeft` isn't useful either. As you'll see in chapter 9, the main use of `foldRight` is to fold long or infinite lazy collections without evaluating them. Calling `reverse` on a list forces list evaluation, so the magic is tainted.

5.6.6 *Creating a stack-safe recursive version of foldRight*

As I said, the recursive `foldRight` implementation is only for demonstrating these concepts because it's stack-based and shouldn't be used in production. Also note that this is a static implementation. An instance implementation would be much easier to use, allowing you to chain function calls with the object notation.

EXERCISE 5.13

Use what you learned in chapter 4 to write a corecursive version of the `foldRight` function without using `foldLeft` explicitly. Call this function `coFoldRight`.

HINT

Write a helper function in the companion object and a main function in the `List` class. Be aware that there's a trick here, which is why you should make the helper function `private`.

SOLUTION

The trick is that you'll call the helper function with the parameter list reversed. The helper function, by itself, doesn't do the full job. Here's the helper function:

```
private tailrec fun <A, B> cofoldRight(acc: B,
                                       list: List<A>,
                                       identity: B,
                                       f: (A) -> (B) -> B): B =
        when (list) {
            List.Nil -> acc
            is List.Cons ->
                cofoldRight(f(list.head)(acc), list.tail, identity, f)
        }
```

Then write the main function that calls this helper function:

```
fun <B> cofoldRight(identity: B, f: (A) -> (B) -> B): B =
        cofoldRight(identity, this.reverse(), identity, f)
```

Unfortunately, this implementation has the same problem as the one using `foldLeft`: it forces evaluation of the list, which cancels the main benefit of folding right.

EXERCISE 5.14

Implement `concat` in terms of either `foldLeft` or `foldRight`. Put this implementation in the companion object, replacing the previous recursive implementation, and then call this function from an extension function out of the `List` class.

SOLUTION

The `concat` function can be implemented easily using a right fold:

```
fun <A> concatViaFoldRight(list1: List<A>, list2: List<A>): List<A> =
        foldRight(list1, list2) { x -> { y -> Cons(x, y) } }
```

Another solution is to use a left fold. In this case, the implementation will be the same as `reverse` via `foldLeft` applied to the reversed first list, using the second list as the accumulator. In the following implementation, note the use of a function reference (`x::cons`):

```
fun <A> concatViaFoldLeft(list1: List<A>, list2: List<A>): List<A> =
        list1.reverse().foldLeft(list2) { x -> x::cons }
```

If you find that using a function reference make the code less readable, you can use a lambda instead:

```
fun <A> concat(list1: List<A>, list2: List<A>): List<A> =
        list1.reverse().foldLeft(list2) { x -> { y -> x.cons(y) } }
```

You can also use the list constructor directly, as in the implementation based on `foldRight`:

```
fun <A> concat(list1: List<A>, list2: List<A>): List<A> =
        list1.reverse().foldLeft(list2) { x -> { y -> Cons(y, x) } }
```

The implementation based on `foldLeft` is less efficient because it must first reverse the first list. On the other hand, it's stack-safe because it's corecursive rather than recursive.

EXERCISE 5.15

Write a function for flattening a list of lists into a list containing all elements of each contained list.

HINT

This operation consists in a series of concatenations. It's similar to adding all elements of a list of integers, although integers are replaced with lists and addition is replaced with concatenation. Other than this, it's exactly the same as the `sum` function.

SOLUTION

Once again, you can use a function reference instead of a lambda to represent the second part of the function: `{ x -> x::concat }` is equivalent to `{ x -> { y -> x.concat(y) } }`:

```
fun <A> flatten(list: List<List<A>>): List<A> =
        list.foldRight(Nil) { x -> x::concat }
```

To make this function stack-safe, you can use the `coFoldRight` function instead of `foldRight`:

```
fun <A> flatten(list: List<List<A>>): List<A> =
        list.coFoldRight(Nil) { x -> x::concat }
```

5.6.7   *Mapping and filtering lists*

You can define many useful abstractions for working on lists. One abstraction consists in changing all the elements of a list by applying a common function to them.

EXERCISE 5.16

Write a function that takes a list of integers and multiplies each of them by 3.

HINT

Try using the functions you've defined up to now. Don't use (co)recursion explicitly. The goal is to abstract recursion once and for all so you can put it to work without having to reimplement it each time.

SOLUTION

You need to apply `foldRight` with an empty list as the identity value and a function that adds each element multiplied by 3 to a list:

```
fun triple(list: List<Int>): List<Int> =
        List.foldRight(list, List()) { h ->
            { t: List<Int> ->
                t.cons(h * 3)
            }
        }
```

You need to set the type explicitly, either for the identity or for the `t` parameter. This is due to the limited capability of Kotlin regarding type inference. You might also use a left fold, which would make the function stack safe, but would also reverse the list, so you'd need to reverse back the result.

EXERCISE 5.17

Write a function that turns each value in a `List<Double>` into a `String`.

SOLUTION

This operation can be seen as concatenating an empty list of the expected type (`List<String>`) with the original list, with each element being transformed before adding it to the accumulator. As a result, the implementation is similar to what you did with the concat function:

```
fun doubleToString(list: List<Double>): List<String> =
    List.foldRight(list, List())  { h ->
        { t: List<String> ->
            t.cons(h.toString())
        }
    }
```

EXERCISE 5.18

Write a general stack-safe function `map` in the `List` class that lets you modify each element of a list by applying a specified function to it. This time, make it an instance function of `List`. Here's its signature:

```
fun <B> map(f: (A) -> B): List<B>
```

SOLUTION

To make it stack-safe, you can use a left fold and then reverse the result:

```
fun <B> map(f: (A) -> B): List<B> =
    foldLeft(Nil) { acc: List<B> -> { h: A -> Cons(f(h), acc) } }.reverse()
```

Alternatively, you can use the stack-safe `coFoldRight` function that gives the same result (but reversing the list before folding instead of reversing the result of the fold):

```
fun <B> map(f: (A) -> B): List<B> =
    coFoldRight(Nil) { h -> { t: List<B> -> Cons(f(h), t) } }
```

EXERCISE 5.19

Write a `filter` function that removes from a list the elements that don't satisfy a given predicate. Once again, implement this as an instance function with the following signature:

```
fun filter(p: (A) -> Boolean): List<A>
```

SOLUTION

Here's an implementation in the parent `List` class using `coFoldRight`:

```
fun filter(p: (A) -> Boolean): List<A> =
    coFoldRight(Nil) { h -> { t: List<A> -> if (p(h)) Cons(h, t) else t } }
```

EXERCISE 5.20

Write a `flatMap` function that applies to each element of `List<A>`, a function from `A` to `List<B>`, and returns a `List<B>`. Its signature will be this:

```
fun <B> flatMap(f: (A) -> List<B>): List<B> =
```

For example, `List(1,-1,2,-2,3,-3)`.

```
List(1,2,3).flatMap { i -> List(i, -i) }
```

should return

`List(1,-1,2,-2,3,-3)`.

SOLUTION

The `flatMap` function can be seen as a composition of `map`, which uses a function returning a list, and `flatten`, which converts a list of list into a list. The simplest implementation (in the `List` class) is then

```
fun <B> flatMap(f: (A) -> List<B>): List<B> = flatten(map(f))
```

EXERCISE 5.21

Create a new version of `filter` based on `flatMap`.

SOLUTION

Here's a possible implementation:

```
fun filter(p: (A) -> Boolean): List<A> =
   flatMap { a -> if (p(a)) List(a) else Nil }
```

Notice that there's a strong relationship between map, flatten, and flatMap. If you map a function returning a list to a list, you get a list of lists. You can then apply flatten to get a single list containing all the elements of the enclosed lists. You'd get the exact same result by directly applying flatMap.

Summary

- Data structures are one of the most important concepts in programming because they allow handling multiple data as a whole.
- The singly linked list is an efficient data structure for programming with functions. It has the benefit of immutable lists while allowing some modifications, such as the insertion and removal of an element in the first position in constant (and short) time. That's because, unlike with Kotlin's (immutable) lists, these operations don't involve copying elements.
- Using data sharing allows for high performance for some operations, although not for all.
- You can create other data structures to get good performance for specific use cases.
- You can fold lists by recursively applying functions.
- You can use corecursion to fold lists without the risk of overflowing the stack.
- Once you've defined foldRight and foldLeft, you shouldn't need to use (co)recursion again to handle lists. foldRight and foldLeft abstract (co)recursion for you.

Dealing with optional data

Representing optional data has always been a problem in computer programs. The concept of optional data is simple. In everyday life, it's easy to represent the absence of something when this something is stored in a container—whatever it is, it can be represented by an empty container. For example, an absence of apples can be represented by an empty apple basket. The absence of gasoline in a car can be visualized as an empty gas tank. But representing the absence of data in computer programs is a little more difficult.

Most data is represented by a reference pointing to it, so the most obvious way to represent the absence of data is to use a pointer to nothing. That's what we call a *null pointer*. In Kotlin, a *reference* is a pointer to a value.

In most programming languages, references can be changed to point to a new value. For this reason, the term *variable* is often used as a replacement for *reference*. The word *variable* is not much of a problem when all references can be later reassigned to a new value. In such cases, it's normal to use the term *variable* as a replacement for *reference*. But that can be different when you use references that can't be reassigned. In such a case, you end up with two types of variables: those that can vary and those that cannot. It's then safer to use the term *reference*.

Some references can be created null and then changed to point to values. They can even be changed again to point to null if data is removed. In such cases, it's safe to call them *variables*, meaning *variable references*.

Conversely, some references can't be created without making them point to a value, and once this is done, they can't be made to point to a different value. Such references are sometimes called *constants*. In Java, for example, references are generally variables unless declared final, which makes them constants. In Kotlin, variable references are declared with the keyword var, and nonvariable ones, which are also called *immutable references*, are declared as val.

At first, you may think that optional data might only be referenced with var. What would be the point of creating a reference to an absence of data if not to eventually change this to a reference to some data? But how would you represent the absence of data? The most common way is to use what's called a *null reference*. A null reference is a reference not pointing to anything, until some data is assigned to it.

In this chapter, you'll learn how to deal with optional data—absent values that aren't the result of an error. I start by discussing problems with the null pointer. After that, I discuss how Kotlin handles null references and Kotlin's alternatives to null references. For the remainder of the chapter, I describe how to create and use the Option type as a solution for working with optional data. You can use the Option type to compose functions even when the data is absent.

6.1   *Problems with the null pointer*

One of the most frequent bugs in programs that allow null references is the Null-PointerException. This exception is raised when an identifier is de-referenced and found to be pointing to nothing: some data is expected but is found to be missing. Such an identifier is said to be pointing to *null*. In this section, you'll learn about the problems with using null references.

In 1965, when designing ALGOL (an object-oriented language), Tony Hoare invented the null reference. He later came to regret it. Here's what he said about it in 2009:[1]

> *I call it my billion-dollar mistake.... My goal was to ensure that all use of references should be absolutely safe, with checking performed automatically by the compiler. But I couldn't resist the temptation to put in a null reference because it was so easy to implement. This has led to innumerable errors, vulnerabilities, and system crashes, which have probably caused a billion dollars of pain and damage in the last forty years.*

---

[1]   Tony Hoare, "Null References: The Billion Dollar Mistake" (QCon, August 25, 2009), http://www.infoq.com/presentations/Null-References-The-Billion-Dollar-Mistake-Tony-Hoare.

Although by now it should be common knowledge to avoid the null reference, that's far from being the case. The Java standard library, which is also used in Kotlin programs, contains methods and constructors taking optional parameters that must be set to null if the parameters are absent. Take, for example, the java.net.Socket class. This class defines the following constructor:

```
public Socket(String address,
              int port,
              InetAddress localAddr,
              int localPort) throws IOException
```

According to the documentation,[2]

> *"If the specified local address is* null, *it is the equivalent of specifying the address as the local address."*

Here, the null reference is a valid parameter. This is sometimes called a *business null.* This way of handling the absence of data isn't specific to objects. The port can also be absent; but in Java, it can't be null because it's a primitive:

> *A local port number of zero will let the system pick up a free port in the bind operation.*

This kind of value is sometimes called a *sentinel value.* It's not used for the value itself (it doesn't mean port 0), but it's used to specify the absence of a port indication. You can find many other examples of handling the absence of data in the Java standard library.

The use of null to represent absence of data is dangerous because the fact that the local address is null could be unintentional and due to a former error. But this use won't cause an exception. The program will continue working, although not as intended.

There are other cases of business nulls. If you try to retrieve a value from a HashMap using a key that's not in the map, you'll get a null. Is this an error? You don't know. It might be that the key is valid but hasn't been registered in the map, or it might be that the key is supposedly valid and should be in the map, but there was a previous error while computing the key. For example, the key could be null, whether intentionally or due to an error, and this won't raise an exception. It could even return a non-null value because the null key is allowed in a HashMap. This situation is a complete mess. As a professional programmer, you know what to do about this:

- You know that you should never use a reference without checking whether it's null or not. (You do this for each object parameter received by a function, right?)
- You know that you should never get a value from a map without first testing whether the map contains the corresponding key.
- You know that you should never try to get an element from a list without verifying first that the list isn't empty and that it has enough elements if you're accessing the element through its index.

---

2   See https://docs.oracle.com/en/java/javase/11/docs/api/java.base/java/net/Socket.html.

If you do either of these, you never get a `NullPointerException` or an `IndexOutOf-BoundsException`, and you can live with null references without any specific protection. But if you happen to forget and sometimes get these kinds of nasty exceptions, you might want an easier and safer way of dealing with the absence of a value, whether intentional or resulting from an error. In this chapter, you'll learn how to deal with absent values that aren't the result of an error. This kind of data is called *optional data.*

There are always tricks for dealing with optional data. One of the best known and most often used is the list. When a function is supposed to return either a value or nothing, some programmers use the list as the return value. The list can contain 0 or 1 element. Although this works quite well, it has several important drawbacks:

- There's no way to ensure that the list contains at most one element. What should you do if you receive a list of several elements?
- How can you distinguish between a list that's supposed to hold at most one element and a regular list?
- The `List` class defines many functions to deal with the fact that lists can contain several elements. These functions are useless for your use case.
- Lists are complex structures, and you don't need this. A much simpler implementation is sufficient.

6.2   *How Kotlin handles null references*

In chapter 2, you learned how Kotlin handles null references. Normal types in Kotlin can't be null. If a reference is given this kind of type, it can never be null, whether it be a `val` (constant) or a `var` (variable). A null `val` would make little sense. A null `var`, on the other hand, might seem useful. Sometimes you might want to declare a reference of a given type without having any value assigned to it. But you must still declare the reference at some point in order to put it in the right scope. Consider the following example:

```
while(enumeration.hasNext()) {
  result = process(result, enumeration.next())
}
use(result)
```

In this example, elements of an enumeration are combined inside a loop that's executed until there are no more elements. Where would you declare `result` and what initial value would you give it? One solution that comes to mind is to process the first enumeration value outside of the loop:

```
var result = process(enumeration.next())
while(enumeration.hasNext()) {
  result = process(result, enumeration.next())
}
use(result)
```

But this would cause an error if the enumeration has no element. The common solution is to declare the `result` reference as null:

```
var result = null
while(enumeration.hasNext()) {
  result = process(result, enumeration.next())
}
use(result)
```

Now, the `process` function must handle the case when `result` is `null`. (In the former case, it was overloaded with a version taking a single argument.) A `null` result is now a business null, meaning that it's the first iteration. But Kotlin won't let you do this.

Kotlin uses null references, but it forces you to tell the compiler that you know the reference can be null. This won't prevent `NullPointException`, but it forces you to accept the responsibility for doing so. It's like a disclaimer: if you use the `null` reference, you're on your own. Kotlin's compiler can assist you in many ways, which is great for programmers using mutable references. Programmers avoiding mutations, on the other hand, don't use null references. But the way Kotlin represents nullable types is still a great help for safe programming. With Kotlin, programmers can ensure there will never be any null references in their code. (See chapter 2 for a short description of the differences between nullable and non-nullable types in Kotlin.)

As you may remember from chapter 2, references of regular types can't be set to `null`. If you want to be able to set references to `null`, you need to use nullable types. Nullable types are written the same way as regular non-nullable types but with a trailing question mark (?). An `Int` reference can never be set to `null` but an `Int?` reference can. From now on, you'll use only non-nullable types, so you'll never encounter a `Null-PointException` in your code.

6.3 *Alternatives to null references*

Now, you know that there'll never be any `NullPointerException` arising from your code, don't you? Well, it isn't as simple as that because many functions in the Kotlin libraries accept nullable parameters and return values of nullable types. Functions taking nullable arguments aren't a problem thanks to non-nullable types being subtypes of the corresponding nullable ones. `Int` is a subtype of `Int?`, `String` is a subtype of `String?`, and so on, so you can always call a function taking a nullable type with an argument of the corresponding non-nullable type.

Return values are much more of a problem, however. Take the example of a `Map`. The following code won't compile in Kotlin:

```
val map: Map<String, Person> = ...
val person: Person = map["Joe"]
```

The reason is that `map["Joe"]` is syntactic sugar over `map.get("Joe")`, and the `get` function of `Map` must return either a `Person`, if one was found for the key `"Joe"`, or nothing. How could a function return nothing? By returning `null`. Even if you strive to ban null references from your own code, you'll always end up getting some from the libraries you use. You could, however, use no libraries except those you own. This is a solution, but it involves much work. Another solution is to wrap function calls returning `null` in some wrapper function returning something else. But what?

Using libraries isn't the only possible cause of the problem. The following code is an example of a function returning optional data:

```
fun mean(list: List<Int>): Double = when {
    list.isEmpty() -> TODO("What should you return?")
    else -> list.sum().toDouble() / list.size
}
```

The `mean` function is an example of a partial function, as you saw in chapter 3. It's defined for all lists of numbers except the empty list. How should you handle the empty list case? One possibility is to return a sentinel value. What value could you choose? As the type is `Double`, you can use a value that's defined in the `Double` class:

```
fun mean(list: List<Int>): Double = when {
    list.isEmpty() -> Double.NaN
    else -> list.sum().toDouble() / list.size
}
```

This works because `Double.NaN` (not a number) is a `Double` value. So far so good, but you still have three problems:

- What if you need to apply the same principle to a function returning an `Int`? There's no equivalent to the `NaN` value in the `Int` class.
- How can you signal to the user of your function that it could return a sentinel value?
- How can you handle a parametric function, such as the following?

```
fun <T, U> f(list: List<T>): U = when {
    list.isEmpty() -> ???
    else -> ... (some computation producing a U)
}
```

Another solution is to throw an exception:

```
fun mean(list: List<Int>): Double = when {
    list.isEmpty() -> throw IllegalArgumentException("Empty list")
    else -> list.sum().toDouble() / list.size
}
```

But this solution is ugly and creates more trouble than it solves:

- Exceptions are generally used for erroneous results, but here there's no error. There's no result and that's because there's no input data! Or should you consider calling the function with an empty list a bug?
- What exception should you throw? A custom one? Or a standard one?
- The function is no longer a pure function, and it's no longer composable with other functions. In order to compose it, you need to resort to control structures like `try..catch`, which are nothing other than a modern form of `goto`.

You could also return `null` and let the caller deal with it:

```
fun mean(list: List<Int>): Double? = when {
    list.isEmpty() -> null
    else -> list.sum().toDouble() / list.size
}
```

In common languages, returning `null` is the worst possible solution. Look at the consequence in a language like Java:

- It forces (ideally) the caller to test the result for `null` and act accordingly.
- It will crash with a `NullPointerException` if boxing is used because a `null` reference can't be unboxed into a primitive value.
- As with the exception solution, the function is no longer composable.
- It allows the potential problem to be propagated far from its origin. If the caller forgets to test for a `null` result, a `NullPointerException` could be thrown from anywhere in the code.

Kotlin makes things a little better:

- It forces the caller to handle the `null` case by choosing a nullable return type.
- It won't crash on boxing because Kotlin doesn't have primitive types, hence no boxing (at least at the user level).
- It offers operators that allow composing functions returning a nullable type in a safe way. (See chapter 2 for details.)
- Although it doesn't prevent propagation of the problem, it makes the problem less crucial by propagating the obligation to handle it.

As I said earlier, the Kotlin solution is better than the absence of a solution you have to deal with in other languages, but it's still far from ideal. A better solution would be to ask the user to provide a special value that'll be returned if no data is available. For example, the following function computes the maximum value of a list. It uses the `List.max()` function of Kotlin, returning `Int?`, but handles the case of an empty list so that you can make your function return `Int` instead of `Int?`:

```
fun max(list: List<Int>, default: Int): Int = when {
    list.isEmpty() -> default
    else -> list.max()
}
```

But this won't compile because `list.max()` returns type is `Int?`. (It won't ever be null but Kotlin doesn't see that.) You know that the Kotlin idiomatic solution is

```
fun max(list: List<Int>, default: Int): Int = list.max() ?: default
```

But what if you don't have a default value? Sometimes, a default value will be provided later. Or you'll want to apply an effect to the result if there's a value and do nothing otherwise. Look at the following example using the previous `max` function:

```
val max = max(listOf(1, 2, 3), 0)

println("The maximum is $max")
```

If the list is empty, this prints *The Maximum is 0*, which might not be the correct output. After all, the maximum is not 0; there is no maximum. You could write

```
val max = max(listOf(1, 2, 3), 0)

print(if (max != 0) "The maximum is $max\n" else "")
```

But this would be incorrect if the list was to contain only 0(s). You can use the traditional form:

```
val max = listOf(1, 2, 3).max()

if (max != null) println("The maximum is $max")
```

But now you have to deal with null references again. There has to be a better solution!

6.4   Using the Option type

In the remainder of this chapter, you'll create the Option type for dealing with optional data. The Option type you compose will be similar to the List type. You'll implement it as an abstract sealed class, Option, containing two internal subclasses that represent the presence and the absence of data.

We'll call the subclass representing the absence of data None, and the subclass representing the presence of data Some. A Some will contain the corresponding data value. Figure 6.1 shows how the Option type might change the way functions can be composed, and the next listing shows the code for the Option data type.

Listing 6.1   The Option data type

```
sealed class Option<out A> {          ◄──── Option is made covariant in A.

    abstract fun isEmpty(): Boolean

    internal object None: Option<Nothing>() {          ◄──── None is a singleton object that
                                                               will be used for all types.
        override fun isEmpty() = true

        override fun toString(): String = "None"

        override fun equals(other: Any?): Boolean =          All absences of data
                                    other === None          ◄──── are considered equal.

        override fun hashCode(): Int = 0          Instances of Some are considered equal if their values
    }                                             are equal, which is what you obtain by using a data class.

    internal data class Some<out A>(internal val value: A) : Option<A>() {          ◄────

        override fun isEmpty() = false
    }

    companion object {

        operator fun <A> invoke(a: A? = null): Option<A>
The invoke function          = when (a) {
is declared with the             null -> None
operator keyword.                else -> Some(a)
                             }
    }
}
```

Without Option

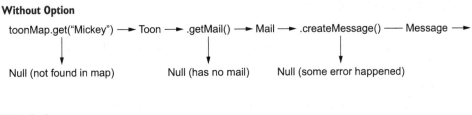

With Option

Figure 6.1 Using an `Option` type for optional data lets you compose functions even when the data is absent. Without the `Option` type, composing functions wouldn't produce a function because the resulting program would potentially throw a `NullPointerException`.

In this listing, you can see how close `Option` is to `List`. They're both abstract classes with two internal implementations. The `None` subclass corresponds to `Nil` and the `Some` subclass to `Cons`. Also note that with the `invoke` function, using `null` for the default value might be seen as a dirty trick. Feel free to overload the function with a version taking no arguments if you prefer. You can now use `Option` for your definition of the `max` function as shown here:

```
fun max(list: List<Int>): Option<Int> = Option(list.max())
```

As it is, the `Option` class isn't useful. All you can do is test whether the result is empty or to print it. You could have added a function for returning the value, but this function would have to throw an exception or return `null` when called on `None`. Returning `null` would defeat the whole purpose of `Option`. Throwing exceptions is bad because it doesn't compose or, at least, it doesn't compose in the same way other results compose. If you know Java, you know that the `Optional` class in Java has a `get` method returning the value if present or throwing an exception otherwise.

Here's what Brian Goetz, Java Language Architect at Oracle, says about it:[3]

Public service announcement: NEVER call Optional.get unless you can prove it will never be null; instead use one of the safe methods like orElse or ifPresent. In retrospect, we should have called get something like getOrElseThrowNoSuchElementException or something that made it far clearer that this was a highly dangerous method that undermined the whole purpose of Optional in the first place. Lesson learned.

Reality is much simpler: there shouldn't be any `get` method in Java `Optional`, and you won't put one in the `Option` class either. Here's the reason: `Option` is a computational context for safely handling optional data. Optional data is potentially unsafe, which is why you need a safe context to put it in. As a consequence, you should *never* take a value out of this context without first making it safe.

---

[3] Brian Goetz's answer to the question "Should Java 8 getters return optional type?" on Stackoverflow (October 12, 2014), https://stackoverflow.com/questions/26328555.

6.4.1 *Getting a value from an Option*

Many functions that you created for List will also be useful for Option. But before you create these functions, let's start with some Option-specific usage. Remember the use of a default value?

EXERCISE 6.1

Implement a getOrElse function that returns either the contained value, if it exists, or a provided default one. Here's how the function signature might look:

```
fun getOrElse(default: A): A
```

SOLUTION

This function is implemented in the Option class and takes a parameter of type A, which isn't compatible with covariance. You should deactivate variance checking by using the @UnsafeVariance annotation as explained in chapter 5:

```
fun getOrElse(default: @UnsafeVariance A): A = when (this) {
    is None -> default
    is Some -> value
}
```

You can now define functions that return options and use the returned value transparently as follows (using the standard Kotlin List class):

```
val max1 = max(listOf(3, 5, 7, 2, 1)).getOrElse(0)
val max2 = max(listOf()).getOrElse(0)
```

Here, max1 is equal to 7 (the maximum value in the list) and max2 is set to 0 (the default value). But you still might have a problem. Look at the following example:

```
fun getDefault(): Int = throw RuntimeException()

fun main(args: Array<String>) {
    val max1 = max(listOf(3, 5, 7, 2, 1)).getOrElse(getDefault())
    println(max1)
    val max2 = max(listOf()).getOrElse(getDefault())
    println(max2)
}
```

This example is a bit contrived. The getDefault function isn't a function at all. But this is only to show you what's happening. What will this example print? If you think it'll print 7 and then throw an exception, take another look at the code.

This example prints nothing and will directly throw an exception because Kotlin is a strict language. Function parameters are evaluated before the function is executed, whether they're needed or not. This means the getOrElse function parameter is evaluated in any case, whether it's called on a Some or a None. The fact that the function parameter isn't needed for a Some is irrelevant. This makes no difference when the parameter is a literal, but it makes a huge difference when it's a function call. The getDefault function will be called in any case, so the first line will throw an exception and nothing will be displayed. This is generally not what you want.

EXERCISE 6.2

Fix the previous problem, adding a new version of the `getOrElse` function with a lazily evaluated parameter.

HINT

Instead of using a literal value, use a function with no argument that returns the value.

SOLUTION

Here's the implementation for this function in the parent `Option` class:

```
fun getOrElse(default: () -> @UnsafeVariance A): A = when (this) {
    is None -> default()
    is Some -> value
}
```

In the absence of a value, the parameter is evaluated through a call to the provided function. The `max` example can now be rewritten as follows:

```
val max1 = max(listOf(3, 5, 7, 2, 1)).getOrElse(::getDefault)
println(max1)
val max2 = max(listOf()).getOrElse(::getDefault)
println(max2)
```

This program prints 7 to the console before throwing an exception.

6.4.2 Applying functions to optional values

One important function in `List` is the `map` function, which allows you to apply a function from A to B to each element of a list of A, producing a list of B. Considering that an `Option` is like a list containing at most one element, you can apply the same principle.

EXERCISE 6.3

Create a `map` function to change an `Option<A>` into an `Option<B>` by applying a function from A to B.

HINT

You can define an abstract function in the `Option` class with one implementation in each subclass. Alternatively, you can implement the function in the `Option` class. In the first case, be aware of the type in the `None` class. The abstract function signature in `Option` will be this:

```
abstract fun <B> map(f: (A) -> B): Option<B>
```

SOLUTION

The `None` implementation is simple. You need to return the `None` singleton. Note that the function to map has to be of type `(Nothing) -> B`:

```
override fun <B> map(f: (Nothing) -> B): Option<B> = None
```

The `Some` implementation isn't much more complex. All you need to do is to get the value, apply the function to it, and wrap the result in a new `Some`:

```
override fun <B> map(f: (A) -> B): Option<B> = Some(f(value))
```

Alternatively, you may prefer to implement the function in the `Option` parent class:

```
fun <B> map(f: (A) -> B): Option<B> = when (this) {
    is None -> None
    is Some -> Some(f(value))
}
```

6.4.3   *Dealing with Option composition*

As you'll soon realize, functions from A to B aren't the most common ones in safe programs. At first, you may have trouble getting acquainted with functions returning optional values. After all, it seems to involve extra work to wrap values in `Some` instances. But with further practice, you'll see that these operations occur only rarely.

When chaining functions to build a complex computation, you'll often start with a value that's returned by some previous computation and pass the result to a new function without seeing the intermediate result. You'll more often use functions from A to `Option<B>` than functions from A to B. Think about the `List` class. Does this ring a bell? Yes, it leads to the `flatMap` function.

EXERCISE 6.4

Create a `flatMap` instance function taking as an argument a function from A to `Option<B>` and returning an `Option<B>`.

HINT

You can define different implementations in both subclasses, but you should try to devise a unique implementation that works for both subclasses and put it in the `Option` class. Its signature will be

```
fun <B> flatMap(f: (A) -> Option<B>): Option<B>
```

Try using some of the functions you've already defined (`map` and `getOrElse`).

SOLUTION

The trivial solution would be to define an abstract function in the `Option` class, returning `None` in the `None` class, and returning `Some(f(value))` in the `Some` class. This is probably the most efficient implementation. But a more elegant solution is to map the `f` function, giving an `Option<Option<B>>`, and then use the `getOrElse` function to extract the value (`Option<B>`), providing `None` as the default value:

```
fun <B> flatMap(f: (A) -> Option<B>): Option<B> = map(f).getOrElse(None)
```

EXERCISE 6.5

Just as you needed a way to map a function that returns an `Option` (leading to `flatMap`), you'll need a version of `getOrElse` for `Option`s default values. Create the `orElse` function with the following signature:

```
fun orElse(default: () -> Option<A>): Option<A>
```

HINT

As you might guess from the name, there's no need to get the value in order to implement this function. This is how Option is mostly used—through Option composition rather than wrapping and getting values. One consequence is that the same implementation works for both subclasses. Don't forget, however, to take care of variance.

SOLUTION

The solution consists in mapping the function _ -> this, which results in an Option <Option<A>>, and then using getOrElse on this result with the provided default value. The _ in the function is used by convention for arguments that aren't used. It stands for the value contained in Option. The value is still used, though, because it's contained in this (if it's present). To allow for variance, you can use the @UnsafeVariance annotation:

```
fun orElse(default: () -> Option<@UnsafeVariance A>): Option<A> =
        map { _ -> this }.getOrElse(default)
```

You could also use a simplified syntax for the function:

```
fun orElse(default: () -> Option<@UnsafeVariance A>): Option<A> =
        map { this }.getOrElse(default)
```

The { x } syntax is the simplest way to write any constant function returning x, whatever argument is used.

EXERCISE 6.6

In chapter 5, you created a filter function to remove from a list all the elements that didn't satisfy a condition expressed in the form of a predicate (meaning a function returning a Boolean). Create the same function for Option. Here's its signature:

```
fun filter(p: (A) -> Boolean): Option<A>
```

HINT

Because an Option is like a List with at most one element, the implementation seems trivial. In the None subclass, you could return None (or this). In the Some class, you could return the original this if the condition holds and None otherwise. But try to devise a smarter implementation that fits in the Option parent class.

SOLUTION

The solution is to flatMap the function used in the Some case:

```
fun filter(p: (A) -> Boolean): Option<A> =
        flatMap { x -> if (p(x)) this else None }
```

Note that it's common practice to use the name p (for *predicate*), which is a function returning a Boolean.

6.4.4 Option use cases

If you already know about the Java Optional class, you may have noticed that Optional contains an isPresent() method that allows you to test whether the Optional contains a value or not. (Optional has a different implementation that's not based on two different subclasses.) You could easily implement such a function in your Kotlin Option class, although you'd call it isSome() because it would test whether the object is a Some or a None. You could also call it isNone(), which might seem more logical, because that would be the equivalent to the List.isEmpty() function.

Although the isSome() function could sometimes be useful, it isn't the best way to use the Option class. If you were to test an Option through an isSome() function before calling some sort of getOrThrow() to get the value, it wouldn't be much different from testing a reference for null before de-referencing it. The only difference would be if you forget to test first: you'd risk seeing an IllegalStateException or NoSuchElementException or whatever exception you chose for the None implementation of getOrThrow(), instead of a NullPointerException.

The best way to use Option is through composition. To do this, you must create all the necessary functions for all use cases. These use cases correspond to what you'd do with the value after testing that it's not null. You could, for example

- Use the value as the input to another function
- Apply an effect to the value
- Use the value if it's not null or use a default value to apply a function or an effect

The first and third use cases have already been made possible through the functions you've already created. Applying an effect can be done in different ways, which you'll learn about in chapter 12.

As an example, look at how you can use the Option class to change the way you'd use a map. In listing 6.2, you'll use an extension function on Map in order to return an Option when querying for a given key. The standard Kotlin implementation of Map .get(key), which you can use as Map[key], returns null if the key isn't found. You'll use the getOption extension function in order to return an Option.

Listing 6.2   Using Option to return a value from a Map

```
import com.fpinkotlin.optionaldata.exercise06.Option
import com.fpinkotlin.optionaldata.exercise06.getOrElse

data class Toon (val firstName: String,
                val lastName: String,
                val email: Option<String> = Option()) {

    companion object {
        operator fun invoke(firstName: String,
                            lastName: String,
                            email: String? = null) =
                Toon(firstName, lastName, Option(email))
    }
}

fun <K, V> Map<K, V>.getOption(key: K) =
                    Option(this[key])
```

Extension function to implement the check-before-use pattern to avoid returning null references

```
fun main(args: Array<String>) {

    val toons: Map<String, Toon>  = mapOf(
            "Mickey" to Toon("Mickey", "Mouse", "mickey@disney.com"),
            "Minnie" to Toon("Minnie", "Mouse"),
            "Donald" to Toon("Donald", "Duck", "donald@disney.com"))

    val mickey =
        toons.getOption("Mickey").flatMap { it.email }
    val minnie = toons.getOption("Minnie").flatMap { it.email }
    val goofy = toons.getOption("Goofy").flatMap { it.email }

    println(mickey.getOrElse { "No data" })
    println(minnie.getOrElse { "No data" })
    println(goofy.getOrElse { "No data" })
}
```

> **Option composition through flatMap**

Note that Option lets you encapsulate into the map implementation the pattern for querying the map with containsKey before calling get.

In this simplified program, you can see how various functions returning Option can be composed. You don't have to test for anything and you don't risk a NullPointer-Exception, although you might be asking for the email of a Toon that doesn't have one, or even for a Toon that doesn't exist in the map. A more idiomatic Kotlin solution, using nullable type operators, is shown in the following listing.

Listing 6.3 Using nullable types in a more idiomatic Kotlin style

```
fun main(args: Array<String>) {

    val toons: Map<String, Toon>  = mapOf(
            "Mickey" to Toon("Mickey", "Mouse", "mickey@disney.com"),
            "Minnie" to Toon("Minnie", "Mouse"),
            "Donald" to Toon("Donald", "Duck", "donald@disney.com"))

    val mickey = toons["Mickey"]?.email ?: "No data"
    val minnie = toons["Minnie"]?.email ?: "No data"
    val goofy = toons["Goofy"]?.email ?: "No data"

    println(mickey)
    println(minnie)
    println(goofy)
}
```

At this stage, you may find the Kotlin style more convenient. But there's a little problem. Both programs display the following result:

```
Some(value=mickey@disney.com)
None
No data
```

The first line is Mickey's email. The second line says "None" because Minnie has no email. The third line says "No data" because Goofy isn't in the map. Clearly, you need a way to distinguish these two cases, but neither using nullable types nor the Option class allows you to distinguish between the two. In chapter 7, you'll see how to solve this problem.

EXERCISE 6.7

Implement the `variance` value function in terms of `flatMap`. The variance of a series of values represents how those values are distributed around the mean. (This isn't related to type variance.) If all values are near the mean, the variance is low. A variance of 0 is obtained when all values are equal to the mean. The variance of a series is the mean of `Math.pow(x - m, 2)` for each element x in the series, where m is the mean of the series. This function is to be implemented at the package level (outside of the `Option` class). Here's its signature:

```
val variance: (List<Double>) -> Option<Double>
```

HINT

To implement this function, you must first create a `mean` function. If you have trouble defining the `mean` function, refer to chapter 5 or use the following:

```
val mean: (List<Double>) -> Option<Double> = { list ->
    when {
        list.isEmpty() -> Option()
        else -> Option(list.sum() / list.size)
    }
}
```

SOLUTION

Once you've defined the `mean` function, the `variance` function is quite simple:

```
val variance: (List<Double>) -> Option<Double> = { list ->
    mean(list).flatMap { m ->
        mean(list.map { x ->
            Math.pow((x - m), 2.0)
        })
    }
}
```

Using value functions isn't mandatory, but you must use value functions if you need to pass them as arguments to HOFs. When you only need to apply them, however, `fun` functions can be simpler to use. If you prefer to use `fun` functions when possible, you might arrive at the following solution:

```
fun mean(list: List<Double>): Option<Double> =
    when {
        list.isEmpty() -> Option()
        else -> Option(list.sum() / list.size)
    }


fun variance(list: List<Double>): Option<Double> =
    mean(list).flatMap { m ->
        mean(list.map { x ->
            Math.pow((x - m), 2.0)
        })
    }
```

As you can see, `fun` functions are simpler to use because the types are simpler. For this reason, you'll use `fun` functions instead of value functions as often as possible. Furthermore, it's easy to switch from one to another. Given this function

```
fun aToBfunction(a: A): B {
  return ...
}
```

you can create an equivalent value function by writing

```
val aToBfunction: (A) -> B = { a -> aToBfunction(a) }
```

Or you can use a function reference:

```
val aToBfunction: (A) -> B = ::aToBfunction
```

Conversely, you can create a `fun` function from the preceding value function:

```
fun aToBfunction(a: A): B = aToBfunction(a)
```

As the implementation of `variance` demonstrates, by using `flatMap` you can construct a computation with multiple stages, any of which can fail. The computation aborts as soon as the first failure is encountered because `None.flatMap(f)` immediately returns `None` without trying to apply `f`.

6.4.5 *Other ways to combine options*

Deciding to use `Option` can seem to have huge consequences. In particular, some developers believe that their legacy code will be made obsolete. What can you do now that you need a function from `Option<A>` to `Option<B>`, and you only have an API with functions for converting an `A` into a `B`? Do you need to rewrite all your libraries? Not at all. You can easily adapt them.

EXERCISE 6.8

Define a `lift` function that takes a function from `A` to `B` as its argument and returns a function from `Option<A>` to `Option<B>`. As usual, use the functions you've already defined. Figure 6.2 shows how the `lift` function works.

HINT

Use the `map` function to create a `fun` function at the package level.

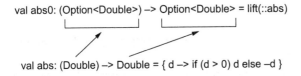

```
val abs0: (Option<Double>) –> Option<Double> = lift(::abs)

val abs: (Double) –> Double = { d –> if (d > 0) d else –d }
```

lift transforms a function from double to double into
a function from Option<Double> to Option<Double>.

```
abs0(None) = None
abs0(Some(d)) = Some(abs(d))
```

Figure 6.2 Lifting a function

SOLUTION

The solution is pretty simple:

```
fun <A, B> lift(f: (A) -> B): (Option<A>) -> Option<B> = { it.map(f) }
```

Most of your existing libraries won't contain value functions; they'll contain only `fun` functions. Converting a `fun` function that takes an `A` as its argument and returns a `B` into a function from `Option<A>` to `Option<B>` is easy. For example, lifting the function `String.toUpperCase` can be done this way:

```
val upperOption: (Option<String>) -> Option<String> =
                        lift { it.toUpperCase() }
```

Or you can use a function reference:

```
val upperOption: (Option<String>) -> Option<String> =
                        lift(String::toUpperCase)
```

EXERCISE 6.9

The previous `lift` function is useless for functions throwing exceptions. Write a version of `lift` that works with functions throwing exceptions.

SOLUTION

For this exercise, you need to wrap the implementation of the function returned by `lift` in a try…catch block, returning `None` if an exception is thrown:

```
fun <A, B> lift(f: (A) -> B): (Option<A>) -> Option<B> = {
    try {
        it.map(f)
    } catch (e: Exception) {
        Option()
    }
}
```

You might also need to transform the function from `A` to `B` into a function from `A` to `Option<B>`. You can apply the same technique:

```
fun <A, B> hLift(f: (A) -> B): (A) -> Option<B> = {
    try {
        Option(it).map(f)
    } catch (e: Exception) {
        Option()
    }
}
```

Note that this approach isn't useful because the exception is lost. In chapter 7, you'll learn how to solve this problem.

What if you want to use a legacy function taking two arguments? Let's say you want to use the Java `Integer.parseInt(String s, int radix)` method with an `Option<String>` and an `Option<Integer>`. How can you do this? The first step is to create a value function from this Java method. That's simple:

```
val parseWithRadix: (Int) -> (String) -> Int =
        { radix -> { string -> Integer.parseInt(string, radix) } }
```

I've inverted the arguments here and created a curried function. This makes sense because inverting the arguments produces (by applying only the first argument) a function that lets you parse *all strings with a given radix*. This can be useful, although not inverting the arguments produces a function that lets you parse *a given string with any radix*. This is generally much less useful, although it depends on your specific use case:

```
val parseHex: (String) -> Int = parseWithRadix(16)
```

The inverse (applying a String first) would make much less sense.

EXERCISE 6.10

Write a function map2 that takes as its arguments an Option<A>, an Option<B>, and a function from (A, B) to C in curried form, and then returns an Option<C>.

HINT

Use the flatMap and possibly the map functions.

SOLUTION

Here's the solution, using flatMap and map. This pattern is important to understand, and you'll come across it often. We'll come back to this in chapter 8:

```
fun <A, B, C> map2(oa: Option<A>,
                   ob: Option<B>,
                   f: (A) -> (B) -> C): Option<C> =
                        oa.flatMap { a -> ob.map { b -> f(a)(b) } }
```

With map2, you can now use any two-argument function as if it had been created for manipulating Option. What about functions with more arguments? Here's an example of a map3 function:

```
fun <A, B, C, D> map3(oa: Option<A>,
                      ob: Option<B>,
                      oc: Option<C>,
                      f: (A) -> (B) -> (C) -> D): Option<D> =
            oa.flatMap { a ->
                ob.flatMap { b ->
                    oc.map { c ->
                        f(a)(b)(c)
                    }
                }
            }
```

Do you see the pattern? (The fact that the last function is map and not flatMap is only due to the fact that f returns a raw value. If it returned an Option, you could still use this pattern by replacing map with flatMap.)

6.4.6 *Composing List with Option*

Composing Option instances isn't all you need. At some point, each new type you define must be composable with any other. In the previous chapter, you defined the List type. To write useful programs, you need to be able to compose List and Option.

The most common operation is converting a List<Option<A>> into an Option<List<A>>. A List<Option<A>> is what you get when mapping a List<B> with a function from B to Option<A>. Usually, what you'll need for the result is a Some<List<A>> if all elements are Some<A>, and a None if at least one element is a None<A>. This is only one possible result. Sometimes, you'll want to ignore the None results and get a list List<A>. This is a completely different use case.

Exercise 6.11

Write a package-level function called sequence that combines a List<Option<A>> into an Option<List<A>>. It'll be a Some<List<A>> if all values in the original list are Some instances, or a None<List<A>> if there is at least one None in the list. Here's its signature:

```
fun <A> sequence(list: List<Option<A>>): Option<List<A>>
```

Note that you must now use the List you defined in chapter 5 and not the Kotlin List.

Hint

To find your way, you can test the list to see whether it's empty, and, if not, make a recursive call to sequence. Then, remembering that foldRight and foldLeft abstract recursion, you could use one of these functions to implement sequence.

Solution

Here's an explicitly recursive version that could be used if you had defined list.head() and list.tail() public functions in List (but it won't compile because you haven't):

```
fun <A> sequence(list: List<Option<A>>): Option<List<A>> {
    return if (list.isEmpty())
        Option(List())
    else
        list.head().flatMap({ hh ->
            sequence(list.tail()).map({ x -> x.cons(hh) }) })
}
```

The functions list.head() and list.tail() shouldn't exist because these functions would possibly throw exceptions when called on an empty list. A solution would be to make these functions return an Option. Fortunately, the sequence function can also be implemented using foldRight and map2:

```
fun <A> sequence(list: List<Option<A>>): Option<List<A>> =
        list.foldRight(Option(List())) { x ->
            { y: Option<List<A>> -> map2(x, y) { a ->
                { b: List<A> -> b.cons(a) } }
            }
        }
```

Note that Kotlin is unfortunately not able to infer types of parameters y and b. (This is where Kotlin isn't as powerful as Java!) Now, consider the following example:

```
val parseWithRadix: (Int) -> (String) -> Int = { radix ->
    { string ->
        Integer.parseInt(string, radix)
    }
}
```

```
val parse16 = hLift(parseWithRadix(16))
val list = List("4", "5", "6", "7", "8", "9", "A", "B")
val result = sequence(list.map(parse16))
println(result)
```

This produces the intended result but is somewhat inefficient because the map function and the sequence function both invoke foldRight.

EXERCISE 6.12

Define a traverse function that produces the same result but invokes foldRight only once. Here's its signature:

```
fun <A, B> traverse(list: List<A> , f: (A) -> Option<B>): Option<List<B>>
```

Then implement sequence in terms of traverse.

HINT

Don't use recursion explicitly. Prefer the foldRight function that abstracts recursion for you.

SOLUTION

First define the traverse function:

```
fun <A, B> traverse(list: List<A> , f: (A) -> Option<B>): Option<List<B>> =
        list.foldRight(Option(List())) { x ->
            { y: Option<List<B>> ->
                map2(f(x), y) { a ->
                    { b: List<B> ->
                        b.cons(a)
                    }
                }
            }
        }
```

Then you can redefine the sequence function in terms of traverse:

```
fun <A> sequence(list: List<Option<A>>): Option<List<A>> =
                    traverse(list) { x -> x }
```

6.4.7   *Using Option and when to do so*

As I said in chapter 2 and in the introduction to this chapter, Kotlin has a different way of handling optional data. You may then wonder what technique you should use—nullable types or Option:

- Nullable types are useful for internal use in some functions, such as generators, when returning null indicates the terminal condition. But such nulls should never leak outside a function; those should be for local use only, and never return null except in local functions.
- Option is fine for truly optional data. But generally, the absence of data is the result of errors that traditional programmers would handle by throwing and catching exceptions. Returning None instead of throwing an exception is like catching an exception and swallowing it silently. It might not be a billion dollar

mistake, but it's still a big one. You'll learn in chapter 7 how to deal with this situation. After that, you'll hardly ever need the Option data type again. But don't worry; all you've learned in this chapter will still be extremely useful.

The Option type is the simplest form of a kind of data type that you'll use again and again. It's a parameterized type, and it comes with a function to make an Option<A> from an A. The Option type also has a flatMap function that can be used to compose Option instances. Although it isn't useful by itself, it has introduced you to a fundamental concept called the *monad*. But List also has the same characteristics. What's important is what these two classes have in common. Don't worry about the term *monad*; there's nothing to be afraid of. Look at it as a design pattern (although it's much more than this).

Summary

- You need a way to represent optional data, which means data that may or may not be present. The Some subtype represents data and the None subtype represents the absence of data.
- Kotlin uses nullable types to represent optional data. These protect you against the NullPointerException when you use non-nullable types, and it forces you to handle null when using nullable types.
- The null pointer is the most impractical and dangerous way to represent the absence of data. Sentinel values and empty lists are other possible ways to represent the absence of data, but they don't compose well.
- The Option data type is a better way to represent optional data.
- You can apply functions to Option using the map and flatMap higher order functions, allowing for easy Option composition. Functions operating on values can be lifted to operate on Option instances.
- List can be composed with Option. A List<Option> can be turned into an Option<List> using the sequence function.
- Option instances can be compared for equality. Instances of subtype Some are equal if their wrapped values are equal. Because there's only one instance of None, all instances of None are equal.
- Although Option can represent the result of a computation producing an exception, all information about the occurring exception is lost.

Handling errors and exceptions

7

In chapter 6, you learned how to deal with optional data without having to manipulate `null` references using the `Option` data type. As you saw, this data type is perfect for dealing with the absence of data when that isn't the result of an error. But it's not an efficient way to handle errors because, although it allows you to cleanly report the absence of data, it swallows the cause of the absence. All missing data is treated the same way, and it's up to the caller to try to figure out what happened. Often, this is impossible.

In this chapter, you'll work through a variety of exercises that teach you how to handle errors and exceptions in Kotlin. One skill you'll learn is how to represent the absence of data due to an error, which the `Option` type doesn't allow. We'll first look at the problems that need solving, and then we'll explore the `Either` type and the `Result` type:

- The `Either` type is useful for functions that can return values of two different types.
- The `Result` type is useful when you need a type that represents either data or an error.

After some discussion and exercises using the `Either` and `Result` types, you'll look at advanced `Result` handling and applying effects, and you'll also see an advanced `Result` composition.

7.1   *The problems with missing data*

Most of the time, the absence of data is the result of an error, either in the input data or in the computation. These are two different cases, but they end with the same result: data is absent and it's meant to be present.

In traditional programming, when a function or a method takes an object parameter, most programmers know that they should test this parameter for `null`. But what they should do if the parameter is `null` is often undefined. Remember the example from listing 6.2 in chapter 6:

```
val goofy = toons.getOption("Goofy").flatMap { it.email }

println(goofy.getOrElse({ "No data" }))
```

In this example, the output of "No data" was obtained because the `Goofy` key wasn't in the map. This could be considered a normal case. But consider this one:

```
    val toon = getName()
            .flatMap(toons::getOption)
            .flatMap(Toon::email)

    println(toon.getOrElse{"No data"})

}

fun getName(): Option<String> = ???
```

If the user enters an empty string, what should you do? An obvious solution would be to validate the input and return an `Option<String>`. In the absence of a valid string, you could return `None`. You also know that such an operation could throw an exception. The program would look like this:

```
    val toon = getName()
            .flatMap(toons::getOption)
            .flatMap(Toon::email)

    println(toon.getOrElse{"No data"})

}

fun getName(): Option<String> = try {
    validate(readLine())
```

```
} catch (e: IOException) {
    Option()
}

fun validate(name: String?): Option<String> = when {
    name?.isNotEmpty() ?: false -> Option(name)
    else -> Option()
}
```

Now think about what could happen when this code is run:

- Everything goes well, and you get an email printed to the console.
- An `IOException` is thrown, and you get No data printed to the console.
- The name entered by the user doesn't validate, and you get No data.
- The name validates but isn't found in the map. You get No data.
- The name is found in the map, but the corresponding toon has no email. You get No data.

What you need is different messages printed to the console to indicate what's happening in each case. If you wanted to use the types you already know, you could use a `Pair<Option<T>, Option<String>>` as the return type of each function, but this is a bit complicated. `Pair` is a product type, which means that the number of elements that can be represented by a `Pair<T, U>` is the number of possible `T` multiplied by the number of possible `U`. You don't need that because every time you have a value for `T`, you'll have `None` for `U`.

In the same way, each time `U` is `Some`, `T` will be `None`. What you need is a *sum type*, which means a type `E<T, U>` that will hold either a `T` or a `U`, but not a `T` and a `U`. The reason why it's called a sum type is that the number of possible different realizations is the sum of the number of possible realizations of `T` and `U`. This is the opposite of a *product type*, such as a `Pair<T, U>`, for which the number of possible realizations is the product of the number of possible `T` by the number of possible `U`.

7.2 The Either type

To handle the case where a function could return values of two different types, such as one representing data and one representing an error, you'll use a special type: the `Either` type. Designing a type that can hold either an `A` or a `B` is easy. You need to slightly modify the `Option` type by changing the `None` type to make it hold a value. You'll also change the names. The two private subclasses of the `Either` type will be called `Left` and `Right` as shown in the following listing.

Listing 7.1　The `Either` type

```
sealed class Either<out A, out B> {

    internal
    class Left<out A, out B>(private val value: A): Either<A, B>() {
        override fun toString(): String = "Left($value)"
    }
```

```
internal
class Right<out A, out B>(private val value: B) : Either<A, B>() {
    override fun toString(): String = "Right($value)"
}

companion object {
    fun <A, B> left(value: A): Either<A, B> = Left(value)
    fun <A, B> right(value: B): Either<A, B> = Right(value)
}
}
```

Now you can easily use `Either` instead of `Option` to represent values that could be absent due to errors. You need to parameterize `Either` with the type of your data and the type of the error.

By convention, you'll use the `Right` subclass to represent success (which is right) and the `Left` subclass to represent error. But you won't call the subclass `Wrong` because the `Either` type can be used to hold data that's represented by one type or another, both being valid.

You have to choose what type will represent the error. You can choose `String` in order to carry an error message, or you can prefer to use some kind of `Exception`. For example, the `max` function returning the maximum value of the list that you defined in chapter 6 could be modified as follows:

```
fun <A: Comparable<A>>  max(list: List<A>): Either<String, A> = when(list) {
    is List.Nil  -> Either.left("max called on an empty list")
    is List.Cons -> Either.right(list.foldLeft(list.head) { x ->  { y ->
            if (x.compareTo(y) == 0) x else y
        }
    })
}
```

In order for the `Either` type to be useful, you need a way to compose it. The simplest composition is with itself. The result of a function returning an `Either` might need to be used as the input of another function returning another `Either`. To compose functions returning `Either`, you need to define the same functions you defined on the `Option` class.

EXERCISE 7.1

Define a map function to change an `Either<E, A>` into an `Either<E, B>`, given a function from A to B. The signature of the map function is as follows:

```
abstract fun <B> map(f: (A) -> B): Either<E, B>
```

HINT

Parameter names `E` and `A` are chosen to make clear which side you should map, `E` standing for error. But it would be possible to define two `map` functions (call them `mapLeft` and `mapRight`) to map one or the other side of an `Either` instance. You're developing a *biased* version of `Either` that will be mappable on one side only.

SOLUTION

The Left implementation is a bit more complex than the None implementation for Option because you need to construct a new Either holding the same (error) value as the original:

```
override fun <B> map(f: (A) -> B): Either<E, B> = Left(value)
```

The Right implementation is exactly like the one in Some:

```
override fun <B> map(f: (A) -> B): Either<E, B> = Right(f(value))
```

EXERCISE 7.2

Define a flatMap function to change an Either<E, A> into an Either<E, B>, given a function from A to Either<E, B>. The signature of the flatMap function is as follows:

```
abstract fun <B> flatMap(f: (A) -> Either<E, B>): Either<E, B>
```

SOLUTION

The Left implementation is exactly the same as for the map function:

```
override fun <B> flatMap(f: (A) -> Either<E, B>): Either<E, B> =
                                                  Left(value)
```

The Right implementation is the same as the Option.flatMap function:

```
override fun <B> flatMap(f: (A) -> Either<E, B>): Either<E, B> = f(value)
```

Note that the E parameter has been made invariant. You won't need to bother with variance because you'll soon get rid of this parameter.

EXERCISE 7.3

Define functions getOrElse and orElse with the following signatures:

```
fun getOrElse(defaultValue: () -> @UnsafeVariance A): A
```

```
fun orElse(defaultValue: () -> Either<E, @UnsafeVariance A>): Either<E, A>
```

HINT

Beware of variance!

SOLUTION

To deactivate variance checking, both functions should have an argument type annotated with @UnsafeVariance. The getOrElse function returns the contained value when this is an instance of Right or the return value of a call to the defaultValue function otherwise. In the Right subclass, you'll need to change access to the value property from private to internal to allow access from the superclass implementation of the get-OrElse function:

```
fun getOrElse(defaultValue: () -> @UnsafeVariance A): A = when (this) {
    is Right -> this.value
    is Left  -> defaultValue()
}
```

The `orElse` function will `map` a constant function returning `this` and call `getOrElse` on the result:

```
fun orElse(defaultValue: () -> Either<E, @UnsafeVariance A>): Either<E, A> =
    map { this }.getOrElse(defaultValue)
```

The `Either` class works fine, but it's far from ideal. The problem is that you don't know what happens if no value is available. Here, you get the default value without knowing if it's the result of a computation or the result of an error. To handle error cases correctly, you'd need a biased version of `Either`, where the left type is known. Rather than using `Either` (which, by the way, has many other interesting use cases), you can create a specialized version using a known fixed type for the `Left` class.

The first question you might ask is, "What type should I use?" Obviously, two different types come to mind: `String` and `RuntimeException`. A string can hold an error message, just as an exception does, but many error situations produce an exception. Using a `String` as the type carried by the `Left` value will force you to ignore the relevant information in the exception and use only the included message. It's better to use `RuntimeException` as the `Left` value. And if you only have a message, you'll wrap it into an exception.

7.3 *The Result type*

What you need is a type representing either data or an error. As this type generally represents the result of a computation that might have failed, you'll call it `Result`. It's similar to the `Option` type, except the subclasses are named `Success` and `Failure` as shown in the following listing. As you can see, this class is much like the `Option` class with the additional stored exception.

Listing 7.2   The `Result` class

Constructors are internal.

The Result class takes only one type parameter corresponding to the success value.

```
import java.io.Serializable

sealed class Result<out A>: Serializable {

    internal
    class Failure<out A>(
        internal val exception: RuntimeException):
                                    Result<A>() {
        override fun toString(): String = "Failure(${exception.message})"
    }

    internal
    class Success<out A>(internal val value: A) :
                                    Result<A>() {
        override fun toString(): String = "Success($value)"
    }

    companion object {
```

The Failure subclass contains a RuntimeException.

```
                    operator fun <A> invoke(a: A? = null): Result<A>
                      = when (a) {
                          null -> Failure(NullPointerException())
                          else -> Success(a)
                      }

                    fun <A> failure(message: String): Result<A> =
                      Failure(IllegalStateException(message))

                    fun <A> failure(exception: RuntimeException): Result<A> =
                      Failure(exception) #H

                    fun <A> failure(exception: Exception): Result<A> =
                      Failure(IllegalStateException(exception))
                  }
              }
```

If a Failure is constructed with a message, it's wrapped into a RuntimeException (more specifically, the IllegalStateException subclass).

If a Result is constructed with a null value, you immediately get a Failure.

If constructed with a RuntimeException, it's stored as is.

If constructed with a checked exception, it's wrapped into a RuntimeException.

To compose `Result`, you'll need the same functions that you defined in the `Option` and `Either` classes, with minor differences.

EXERCISE 7.4

Define `map`, `flatMap`, `getOrElse`, and `orElse` for the `Result` class. For `getOrElse`, you can define two functions: one taking a value as its argument and one taking a function producing the default value. Here are the signatures:

```
fun <B> map(f: (A) -> B): Result<B>
fun <B> flatMap(f: (A) -> Result<B>): Result<B>
fun <A> getOrElse(defaultValue: A): A
fun <A> orElse(defaultValue: () -> Result<A>): Result<A>
```

HINT

Don't forget to process any exception that could be thrown by your implementations and to take care of variance.

SOLUTION

All functions are similar to those of the `Either` class. Here are the implementations of `map` and `flatMap` in the `Success` class:

```
override fun <B> map(f: (A) -> B): Result<B> = try {
    Success(f(value))
} catch (e: RuntimeException) {
    Failure(e)
} catch (e: Exception) {
    Failure(RuntimeException(e))
}

override fun <B> flatMap(f: (A) -> Result<B>): Result<B> = try {
    f(value)
} catch (e: RuntimeException) {
    Failure(e)
```

```
} catch (e: Exception) {
    Failure(RuntimeException(e))
}
```

And here are the implementations for the `Failure` class:

```
override fun <B> map(f: (A) -> B): Result<B> =
    Failure(exception)

override fun <B> flatMap(f: (A) -> Result<B>): Result<B> =
    Failure(exception)
```

The `getOrElse` function is useful when the default value is a literal because it's already evaluated. In that case, you don't need to use lazy evaluation. To avoid variance problems, you must implement this function using the `@UnsafeVariance` annotation:

```
fun getOrElse(defaultValue: @UnsafeVariance A): A = when (this) {
    is Success -> this.value
    is Failure -> defaultValue
}
```

The `orElse` function is used when the default value isn't evaluated. As evaluation could throw an exception, you might want to handle this case as follows:

```
fun orElse(defaultValue: () -> Result<@UnsafeVariance A>): Result<A> =
    when (this) {
        is Success -> this
        is Failure -> try {
            defaultValue()
        } catch (e: RuntimeException) {
            Result.failure<A>(e)
        } catch (e: Exception) {
            Result.failure<A>(RuntimeException(e))
        }
    }
```

Whether you should handle exceptions or not depends on which function implementations you'll use. If you use only your own implementations, you might not need to catch exceptions if you never throw one. But if you want to use functions from the standard library (which is likely), you need to deal with exceptions, applying the safe principle: always catch, never throw. Also note that you could be tempted to define the following function, as you did for `Option`:

```
fun getOrElse(defaultValue: () -> A): A
```

If you want to be sure to never throw an exception, you can't implement this function. What would you return if the constant function () → A throws an exception?

7.4   *Result patterns*

With these added functions, the `Result` class can be used to safely compose functions representing computations that either succeed or fail. This is important because `Result` and similar types are often considered as containers that may or may not contain a value. This description is wrong.

  `Result` is a computational context for a value that may or may not be present. The way to use it is not by retrieving the value, but by composing instances of `Result` using its specific functions. For example, to use this class, you can modify the previous Toon-Mail illustration. First you need to create a special get extension function on Map that returns a Result.Failure if the key is not in the map, as shown in the next listing. You can call this new function getResult.

Listing 7.3 The new `Map.getResult` function returning a `Result`

If the key is contained in the map, return a
Success containing the retrieved object.

Otherwise, return a Failure
containing an error message.

```
fun <K, V> Map<K, V>.getResult(key: K) = when {
    this.containsKey(key) -> Result(this[key])
    else -> Result.failure("Key $key not found in map")
}
```

Then modify the Toon class as shown in the following listing.

Listing 7.4 The modified `Toon` class with the modified email property

Constructor is private.

The email property is now a Result
(which is either a Success or a Failure).

```
data
class Toon private constructor (val firstName: String,
                val lastName: String,
                val email: Result<String>) {

    companion object {
        operator fun invoke(firstName: String,
                            lastName: String) =
            Toon(firstName, lastName,
                Result.failure("$firstName $lastName has no mail"))

        operator fun invoke(firstName: String,
                            lastName: String,
                            email: String) =
            Toon(firstName, lastName, Result(email))
    }
}
```

The invoke function
is overloaded.

If no mail is provided, a
Result.Failure is used as
the default value.

If the object is constructed
with an email, it's wrapped
in a Result.

Now modify the ToonMail program as indicated in the following listing.

Listing 7.5 The modified program using `Result`

```
fun main(args: Array<String>) {

    val toons: Map<String, Toon>  = mapOf(
        "Mickey" to Toon("Mickey", "Mouse", "mickey@disney.com"),
        "Minnie" to Toon("Minnie", "Mouse"),
        "Donald" to Toon("Donald", "Duck", "donald@disney.com"))

    val toon = getName()
        .flatMap(toons::getResult)
        .flatMap(Toon::email)
```

Methods returning Result are
composed through flatMap.

```
        println(toon)

}

fun getName(): Result<String> = try {
    validate(readLine())
} catch (e: IOException) {
    Result.failure(e)
}

fun validate(name: String?): Result<String> = when {
    name?.isNotEmpty() ?: false -> Result(name)
    else -> Result.failure("Invalid name $name")
}
```

The getName function lets you input a name from the keyboard, resulting in a Failure if the name doesn't validate or if an exception is thrown.

You can modify the getName function to represent an exception being thrown by returning a Failure that wraps the exception.

Note how the various operations returning a Result are composed. You don't need to access the value contained in the Result, which may be an exception. The flatMap function is used for such composition. Try to run this program with various input such as these:

```
"Mickey"
"Minnie"
"Goofy"
an empty value (just press the Enter key)
```

Here's what the program prints in each case:

```
Success(mickey@disney.com)
Failure(Minnie Mouse has no mail)
Failure(Key Goofy not found in map)
Failure(Invalid name )
```

This result may seem good, but it isn't. The problem is that Minnie (having no email) and Goofy (not being in the map) are reported as failures. These might be failures, but they might alternatively be normal cases. After all, if having no email was a failure, you wouldn't have allowed a Toon instance to be created without one.

Obviously, this isn't a failure but only optional data. The same is true for the map. It might be an error if a key isn't in the map (assuming it was supposed to be there), but from the map's point of view, it's optional data. You might think this isn't a problem because you already have a type for this (the Option type you developed in chapter 6). But look at the way you've composed your functions:

```
toon = getName()
        .flatMap(toons::getResult)
        .flatMap(Toon::email)
```

This was only possible because getName, Map.getResult, and Toon.email all return a Result. If Map.getResult and Toon.email were to return Option, they'd no longer compose with getName. It's still possible to convert a Result to and from an Option. For example, you could add a toOption function in Result:

```
abstract fun toOption(): Option<A>
```

The Success implementation would be

```
override fun toOption(): Option<A> = Option(value)
```

The Failure implementation would be

```
override fun toOption(): Option<A> = Option()
```

You could then use it as follows:

```
Option<String> result =
    getName().toOption().flatMap(toons::getResult).flatMap(Toon::emmail)
```

But you'd lose all the benefit of using Result! Now if an exception is thrown inside the getName function, it's still wrapped in a Failure but the exception is lost in the toOption function, and the program simply prints

```
none
```

You might think you should go the other way and convert an Option into a Result. This would work (although, in our example, you should call the new toResult function on both Option instances returned by Map.get and Toon.getMail), but it would be tedious. Because you'll usually have to convert Option to Result, a much better way would be to cast this conversion into the Result class. All you have to do is to create a new subclass corresponding to the None case. The Some case doesn't need conversion, apart from changing its name for Success. The next listing shows the new Result class with the new subclass called Empty.

Listing 7.6   The new Result class handling errors and optional data

The getOrElse and orElse functions have been modified to handle the Empty case.

```
sealed class Result<out A>: Serializable {

    abstract fun <B> map(f: (A) -> B): Result<B>

    abstract fun <B> flatMap(f: (A) ->  Result<B>): Result<B>

    fun getOrElse(defaultValue: @UnsafeVariance A): A = when (this) {
        is Result.Success -> this.value
        else -> defaultValue
    }

    fun getOrElse(defaultValue: () -> @UnsafeVariance A): A = when (this) {
        is Result.Success -> this.value
        else -> defaultValue()
    }

    fun orElse(defaultValue: () -> Result<@UnsafeVariance A>): Result<A> =
        when (this) {
            is Success -> this
            else -> try {
                defaultValue()
            } catch (e: RuntimeException) {
```

```
                        Result.failure<A>(e)
                    } catch (e: Exception) {
                        Result.failure<A>(RuntimeException(e))
                    }
            }

    internal object Empty: Result<Nothing>() {

        override fun <B> map(f: (Nothing) -> B): Result<B> = Empty

        override fun <B> flatMap(f: (Nothing) -> Result<B>): Result<B> =
                                                                  Empty

        override fun toString(): String = "Empty"
    }

    internal
    class Failure<out A>(private val exception: RuntimeException):
                                                    Result<A>() {

        override fun <B> map(f: (A) -> B): Result<B> = Failure(exception)

        override fun <B> flatMap(f: (A) -> Result<B>): Result<B> =
                                                  Failure(exception)

        override fun toString(): String = "Failure(${exception.message})"
    }

    internal class Success<out A>(internal val value: A) : Result<A>() {

        override fun <B> map(f: (A) -> B): Result<B> = try {
            Success(f(value))
        } catch (e: RuntimeException) {
            Failure(e)
        } catch (e: Exception) {
            Failure(RuntimeException(e))
        }

        override fun <B> flatMap(f: (A) -> Result<B>): Result<B> = try {
            f(value)
        } catch (e: RuntimeException) {
            Failure(e)
        } catch (e: Exception) {
            Failure(RuntimeException(e))
        }

        override fun toString(): String = "Success($value)"
    }

    companion object {

        operator fun <A> invoke(a: A? = null): Result<A> = when (a) {
            null -> Failure(NullPointerException())
            else -> Success(a)
        }
```

Annotation pointing to `internal object Empty: Result<Nothing>() {`:

Like the None instance in Option, Result contains a singleton instance of Empty, parameterized with Nothing.

```
        operator fun <A> invoke(): Result<A> = Empty

        fun <A> failure(message: String): Result<A> =
                    Failure(IllegalStateException(message))

        fun <A> failure(exception: RuntimeException): Result<A> =
                    Failure(exception)

        fun <A> failure(exception: Exception): Result<A> =
                    Failure(IllegalStateException(exception))
    }
}
```

> **Like Option, the invoke function that takes no parameter returns the Empty singleton.**

Now you can again modify your `ToonMail` application as shown in listings 7.7, 7.8, and 7.9.

Listing 7.7 The `getResult` function

```
fun <K, V> Map<K, V>.getResult(key: K) = when {
    this.containsKey(key) -> Result(this[key])
    else -> Result.Empty
}
```

> **The get function now returns Result. Empty if the key isn't found in the map.**

Listing 7.8 The `Toon` class using `Result.Empty` for optional data

```
data class Toon private constructor (val firstName: String,
                val lastName: String,
                val email: Result<String>) {

    companion object {
        operator fun invoke(firstName: String,
                            lastName: String) =
            Toon(firstName, lastName, Result.Empty)

        operator fun invoke(firstName: String,
                            lastName: String,
                            email: String) =
            Toon(firstName, lastName, Result(email))
    }
}
```

> **If you construct the instance without an email, the property is set to Result.Empty.**

Listing 7.9 The ToonMail application handling optional data correctly

```
fun main(args: Array<String>) {

    val toons: Map<String, Toon> = mapOf(
        "Mickey" to Toon("Mickey", "Mouse", "mickey@disney.com"),
        "Minnie" to Toon("Minnie", "Mouse"),
        "Donald" to Toon("Donald", "Duck", "donald@disney.com"))

    val toon = getName()
        .flatMap(toons::getResult)
        .flatMap(Toon::email)
```

```
        println(toon)

    }

fun getName(): Result<String> = try {
    validate(readLine())
} catch (e: IOException) {
    Result.failure(e)
}

fun validate(name: String?): Result<String> = when {
    name?.isNotEmpty() ?: false -> Result(name)
    else -> Result.failure(IOException())
}
```

The validate function is modified to simulate an IOException when no name is input.

Your program now prints the following results when you enter "Mickey", "Minnie", "Goofy", and an empty string:

```
Success(mickey@disney.com)
Empty
Empty
Failure(java.io.IOException)
```

You may think that something is missing because you can't distinguish between the two different empty cases, but this isn't the case. Error messages aren't needed for optional data. If you think you need a message, the data isn't optional.

7.5   *Advanced Result handling*

So far you've seen a limited use of Result. You should never use Result to directly access the wrapped value (if it exists). The way you used Result in the previous example corresponds to the simpler specific composition use case: get the result of one computation and use it for the input of the next computation.

More specific use cases exist. You could use the value in Result only if it matches some predicate (which means some condition). You could also use the failure case, for which you'd need to map the failure to something else or to transform the failure into a success of exception. You might also need to use several results as the input for a single computation. You'd probably benefit from some helper functions that create Result from computations in order to deal with legacy code. Finally, you'll sometimes need to apply effects to results.

7.5.1   *Applying predicates*

You'll often have to apply a predicate to a Result. (A *predicate* is a function returning a Boolean.) This is something that can easily be abstracted, so that you'll write it only once.

EXERCISE 7.5

Write a function filter taking a condition that's represented by a function from A to Boolean and returning a Result<A>, which will be Success or Failure, depending on whether the condition holds for the wrapped value. The signature will be this:

```
fun filter(p: (A) -> Boolean): Result<A>
```

Create a second function taking a condition as its first argument and a `String` as a second argument, using the string argument for the potential `Failure` case.

HINT

Although it's possible to define abstract functions in the `Result` class and to implement them in subclasses, try not to do so. Instead, use one or more functions you've previously defined to create a single implementation in the `Result` class.

SOLUTION

You need to create a `fun` function that takes the wrapped value as a parameter, applies the argument value function to it, and returns the same `Result` if the condition holds or `Empty` (or `Failure`) otherwise. Then all you have to do is to `flatMap` this function:

```
fun filter(p: (A) -> Boolean): Result<A> = flatMap {
    if (p(it))
        this
    else
        failure("Condition not matched")
}

fun filter(message: String, p: (A) -> Boolean): Result<A> = flatMap {
    if (p(it))
        this
    else
        failure(message)
}
```

EXERCISE 7.6

Define an `exists` `fun` function that takes a value function from `A` to `Boolean` and returns `true` if the wrapped value matches the condition or `false` otherwise. Here's the function signature:

```
fun exists(p: (A) -> Boolean): Boolean
```

HINT

Once again, try not to define an implementation in each subclass. Instead, create a single implementation in the parent class using the functions you have at your disposal.

SOLUTION

The solution is to `map` the function to the `Result<T>`, giving a `Result<Boolean>`, and then to use `getOrElse` with `false` as the default value. You don't need to use a constant function to lazily produce the default value because it's a literal:

```
fun exists(p: (A) -> Boolean): Boolean = map(p).getOrElse(false)
```

Using `exists` as the name of this function may seem questionable. But it's the same function that could be applied to a list, returning `true` if at least one element satisfies the condition. It therefore makes sense to use the same name.

Some might argue that this implementation would also work for a `forAll` function that returns `true` if all elements in the list fulfill the condition. It's up to you to either choose another name or define a `forAll` function in the `Result` class with the same implementation. The important point is understanding what makes `List` and `Result` similar and what makes them different.

7.6   *Mapping failures*

It's sometimes useful to change a `Failure` into a different one. This is like catching an exception and rethrowing something different. The reason could be to replace an error message with a more appropriate one, adding some information that allows the user to determine the cause of the problem. For example, a message such as "Configuration file could not be found" would be much more useful if it included the path that was searched.

EXERCISE 7.7

Define a `mapFailure` function that takes a `String` as its argument and transforms a `Failure` into another `Failure`, using the string as its error message. If the `Result` is `Empty` or `Success`, this function should do nothing.

HINT

Define an abstract function in the parent class.

SOLUTION

Here's the abstract function in the parent class:

```
abstract fun mapFailure(message: String): Result<A>
```

The `Empty` and `Success` implementations return `this`. Here's the implementation in `Empty`:

```
override fun mapFailure(message: String): Result<Nothing> = this
```

And here's the implementation in `Success`:

```
override fun mapFailure(message: String): Result<A> = this
```

The `Failure` implementation wraps the existing exception into a new one created with the given message and returns a new `Failure`:

```
override fun mapFailure(message: String): Result<A> =
        Failure(RuntimeException(message, exception))
```

You can choose `RuntimeException` as the exception type or a more specific custom subtype of a runtime exception. Another useful function would be one that maps an `Empty` to a `Failure`, given a `String` message.

7.7   *Adding factory functions*

You've seen how you can create `Success` and `Failure` from a value. Some other use cases are so frequent that they deserve to be abstracted into supplemental factory functions. To adapt legacy libraries, you'll probably often create `Result` from a value that could possibly be `null`, and you'd want to provide a specific error message for that case. To do this, you could use a function in the companion object with the following signature:

```
operator fun <A> invoke(a: A? = null, message: String): Result<A>
```

A function creating a `Result` from a function from `A` to `Boolean` and an instance of `A` might also be useful:

```
operator fun <A> invoke(a: A? = null, p: (A) -> Boolean): Result<A>
operator fun <A> invoke(a: A? =
                null, message: String, p: (A) -> Boolean): Result<A>
```

EXERCISE 7.8

Implement the previous `invoke` functions.

HINT

You have to make a choice about what to return in each case.

SOLUTION

This exercise presents no difficulties. Here's some possible implementations based on the choice to return `Empty` when no error message is used and a `Failure` otherwise:

```
operator fun <A> invoke(a: A? = null, message: String): Result<A> =
    when (a) {
        null -> Failure(NullPointerException(message))
        else -> Success(a)
    }

operator fun <A> invoke(a: A? = null, p: (A) -> Boolean): Result<A> =
    when (a) {
        null -> Failure(NullPointerException())
        else -> when {
            p(a) -> Success(a)
            else -> Empty
        }
    }

operator fun <A> invoke(a: A? = null,
                        message: String,
                        p: (A) -> Boolean): Result<A> =
    when (a) {
        null -> Failure(NullPointerException())
        else -> when {
            p(a) -> Success(a)
            else -> Failure(IllegalArgumentException(
                "Argument $a does not match condition: $message"))
        }
    }
```

Notice that you don't need to cast argument a to type `A` (instead of `A?`) before applying the predicate. Kotlin knows that it can't be `null` from the previous check in the first `when` clause.

7.8 Applying effects

So far you haven't applied any effects to values wrapped in `Result`, other than by getting this value (through `getOrElse`). This isn't satisfying because it destroys the advantage of using `Result`. On the other hand, you haven't yet learned the necessary techniques to apply effects in a safe way. Effects can be anything that modifies something in the outside world, such as writing to the console, to a file, to a database, or to a field in a mutable component, or sending a message locally or over a network.

> **IMPORTANT**   The technique I'll show you now isn't safe, so it should only be used once all computation is carried out. Effects should be applied in a specifically delimited part of your code, and no further computation should be performed on the values once you apply effects. If you need to apply effects in a safe way and then continue some computation, you'll have to wait until chapter 12 to learn the necessary techniques.

Applying an effect in standard programming would consist of extracting the value (if present) from the `Result` and performing some action with it. For safer programming, you do it the other way round: you pass the effect to the `Result` to have it applied to the contained value (if present).

To represent an effect in Kotlin, you use a function that doesn't return anything and performs the intended effect. This shouldn't be called a function, but that's the way it is in Kotlin. In Java, this would be called a `Consumer`. The return type of such a function in Kotlin is `Unit`.

EXERCISE 7.9

Define a `forEach` function that takes an effect as its parameter and applies it to the wrapped value.

HINT

Define an abstract function in the `Result` class with an implementation in each subclass.

SOLUTION

Here's the abstract function declaration in `Result`:

```
abstract fun forEach(effect: (A) -> Unit)
```

Note that both `forEach` and the `effect` parameter return `Unit`. But for a fun function returning `Unit`, you can omit the return type. The `Failure` implementations do nothing:

```
override fun forEach(effect: (A) -> Unit) {}
```

The `Empty` implementation is similar, but with a slightly different signature:

```
override fun forEach(effect: (Nothing) -> Unit) {}
```

The `Success` implementation is straightforward. You need to apply the effect to the value:

```
override fun forEach(effect: (A) -> Unit) {
    effect(value)
}
```

This `forEach` function would be perfect for the `Option` class you created in chapter 6. But that's not the case for `Result`. Generally, you want to take special actions on a failure.

EXERCISE 7.10

Define the `forEachOrElse` function to handle this use case. It'll have to handle both the `Failure` and the `Empty` cases. Here's its signature in the `Result` class:

```
abstract fun forEachOrElse(onSuccess: (A) -> Unit,
                           onFailure: (RuntimeException) -> Unit,
                           onEmpty: () -> Unit)
```

SOLUTION

All three implementations execute the corresponding function:

```
// Success
override fun forEachOrElse(onSuccess: (A) -> Unit,
                           onFailure: (RuntimeException) -> Unit,
                           onEmpty: () -> Unit) = onSuccess(value)

// Failure
override fun forEachOrElse(onSuccess: (A) -> Unit,
                           onFailure: (RuntimeException) -> Unit,
                           onEmpty: () -> Unit) = onFailure(exception)

// Empty
override fun forEachOrElse(onSuccess: (Nothing) -> Unit,
                           onFailure: (RuntimeException) -> Unit,
                           onEmpty: () -> Unit) = onEmpty()
```

Note that you don't throw any exception. It's the caller's responsibility to deal with the exception. If the programmer wants to throw it, they have to provide `{ throw it }` for the second argument.

EXERCISE 7.11

The `forEachOrElse` function works fine, but it's not optimal. In fact, the `forEach` has the same effect as `forEachOrElse` when using specific arguments so code is duplicated. Can you fix this?

HINT

All arguments should be made optional.

SOLUTION

The solution consists in using default values for the three arguments. Here's the new abstract declaration in the `Result` parent class:

```
abstract fun forEach(onSuccess: (A) -> Unit = {},
                     onFailure: (RuntimeException) -> Unit = {},
                     onEmpty: () -> Unit = {})
```

The new function can be renamed to replace the original `forEach` function. The implementations in the subclasses don't change. Now you can call `forEach` providing an effect for `Success` and `Empty` and ignoring `Failure` (for example) by using named arguments:

```
val result: Result<Int> = if (z % 2 == 0) Result(z) else Result()
result.forEach({ println("$it is even") }, onEmpty =
                         { println("This one is odd") })
```

Note that you only need named arguments after skipping one. Here, you don't need a name for the first argument. You only need to name an argument that isn't at its intended position. The third argument of the function is onEmpty but it comes in second, so it needs to be named.

One frequent use case for the forEach function is as follows. This example uses a hypothetical log function at package level:

```
val result = getComputation()

result.forEach(::println, ::log)
```

Remember that these functions aren't really functions, but are good and simple ways to use Result. More on this in chapter 12.

7.9   *Advanced result composition*

Use cases for Result are more or less the same as for Option. In chapter 6, you defined a lift function for composing Option instances by transforming a function from A to B into a function from Option<A> to Option<B>. You can do the same for Result, which you'll work on in this section through a series of exercises.

EXERCISE 7.12

Write a lift function for Result. Put it at package level with the following signature:

```
fun <A, B> lift(f: (A) -> B): (Result<A>) -> Result<B>
```

SOLUTION

Here's the simple solution:

```
fun <A, B> lift(f: (A) -> B): (Result<A>) -> Result<B> = { it.map(f) }
```

Unlike Option, there's no need to catch exceptions that might be thrown by the f function because those are already handled by map.

EXERCISE 7.13

Define lift2 for lifting a function from A to (B to C), and lift3 for functions from A to (B to (C to D)) with the following signatures:

```
fun <A, B, C> lift2(f: (A) -> (B) -> C):
  (Result<A>) -> (Result<B>) -> Result<C>
fun <A, B, C, D> lift3(f: (A) -> (B) -> (C) -> D):
  (Result<A>) -> (Result<B>) -> (Result<C>) -> Result<D>
```

SOLUTION

Here are the solutions:

```
fun <A, B, C> lift2(f: (A) -> (B) -> C):
  (Result<A>) -> (Result<B>) -> Result<C> =
    { a ->
```

```
        { b ->
            a.map(f).flatMap { b.map(it) }
        }
    }

fun <A, B, C, D> lift3(f: (A) -> (B) -> (C) -> D):
    (Result<A>) -> (Result<B>) -> (Result<C>) -> Result<D> =
    { a ->
        { b ->
            { c ->
                a.map(f).flatMap { b.map(it) }.flatMap { c.map(it) }
            }
        }
    }
}
```

I'm guessing you can see the pattern. You could define `lift` for any number of parameters that way.

EXERCISE 7.14

In chapter 6, you defined a map2 function, taking as its arguments an `Option<A>`, an `Option<B>`, and a function from A to (B to C), and returning an `Option<C>`. Define a map2 function for `Result`.

HINT

Don't use the function you defined for `Option`. Instead, use the `lift2` function you defined in exercise 7.13.

SOLUTION

The solution you defined for `Option` was

```
fun <A, B, C> map2(oa: Option<A>,
                   ob: Option<B>,
                   f: (A) -> (B) -> C): Option<C> =
    oa.flatMap { a -> ob.map { b -> f(a)(b) } }
```

This is the same pattern you used for `lift2`. The map2 function is simply

```
fun <A, B, C> map2(a: Result<A>,
                   b: Result<B>,
                   f: (A) -> (B) -> C): Result<C> = lift2(f)(a)(b)
```

A common use case for such functions is to call functions or constructors with arguments of type `Result` returned by other functions. Take the previous `ToonMail` example. To populate the `Toon` map, you could construct toons by asking the user to input the first name, last name, and mail on the console, using the following functions:

```
fun getFirstName(): Result<String> = Result("Mickey")

fun getLastName(): Result<String> = Result("Mouse")

fun getMail(): Result<String> = Result("mickey@disney.com")
```

The real implementation will be different, but you still have to learn how to safely get input from the console. For now, you'll use these mock implementations. Using these implementations, you could create a `Toon` as follows:

```
var createPerson: (String) -> (String) -> (String) -> Toon =
                          { x -> { y -> { z -> Toon(x, y, z) } } }
```

```
val toon = lift3(createPerson)(getFirstName())(getLastName())(getMail())
```

But you're reaching the limits of abstraction. You might have to call functions or constructors with more than three arguments. In such a case, you could use the following pattern, which is sometimes called *comprehension*:

```
val toon = getFirstName()
    .flatMap { firstName ->
        getLastName()
            .flatMap { lastName ->
                getMail()
                    .map { mail -> Toon(firstName, lastName, mail) }
            }
    }
```

The comprehension pattern has two advantages:

- You can use any number of arguments.
- You don't need to define a function.

Note that you could use `lift3` without defining the function separately, but you'd have to specify the types because of the limited type inference capacity of Kotlin:

```
val toon2 = lift3 { x: String ->
    { y: String ->
        { z: String ->
            Toon(x, y, z)
        }
    }
}(getFirstName())(getLastName())(getMail())
```

Some languages have syntactic sugar for such constructs, roughly equivalent to this:

```
for {
  firstName in getFirstName(),
  lastName in getLastName(),
  mail in getMail()
} return new Toon(firstName, lastName, mail)
```

Kotlin doesn't have this kind of syntactic sugar, but it's easy to do without it. Notice that the calls to `flatMap` or `map` are nested. Start with a call to the first function (or start from a `Result` instance), `flatMap` each new call, and end by mapping the call to the constructor or function you intend to use. For example, to call a function taking five parameters when you only have five `Result` instances, use the following approach:

```
val result1 = Result(1)
val result2 = Result(2)
val result3 = Result(3)
val result4 = Result(4)
val result5 = Result(5)

fun compute(p1: Int, p2: Int, p3: Int, p4: Int, p5: Int) =
    p1 + p2 + p3 + p4 + p5
```

```
val result = result1.flatMap { p1: Int ->
    result2.flatMap { p2 ->
        result3.flatMap { p3 ->
            result4.flatMap { p4 ->
                result5.map { p5 ->
                    compute(p1, p2, p3, p4, p5)
                }
            }
        }
    }
}
```

This example is a bit contrived, but it shows you how the pattern can be extended. Note that it isn't inherent to the pattern that the last call (the most deeply nested) is to map instead of flatMap. That's only because the last function (compute) returns a raw value. If it returned a Result, you'd have to use flatMap instead of map:

```
val result1 = Result(1)
val result2 = Result(2)
val result3 = Result(3)
val result4 = Result(4)
val result5 = Result(5)

fun compute(p1: Int, p2: Int, p3: Int, p4: Int, p5: Int) =
    Result(p1 + p2 + p3 + p4 + p5)

val result = result1.flatMap { p1: Int ->
    result2.flatMap { p2 ->
        result3.flatMap { p3 ->
            result4.flatMap { p4 ->
                result5.flatMap { p5 ->
                    compute(p1, p2, p3, p4, p5)
                }
            }
        }
    }
}
```

But as this last function is often a constructor, and constructors always return raw values, you'll often find yourself using map as the last function call.

Summary

- Representing the absence of data due to an error is necessary. Because the Option type doesn't allow this, you need the Result type. You can also use the Either type to represent data of either one type (Right) or another (Left).
- Either can be mapped or flat-mapped like Option, but it can be on both sides (Right or Left).
- Either can be biased by making one side (Left) always represent the same type (RuntimeException). This biased type is called Result. Success is represented by a Success subtype and failure by a Failure subtype.

- One way to use the `Result` type is to get the wrapped value if it's present or to use a provided default value otherwise. The default value, if not a literal, must be lazily evaluated.

- Composing `Option` (representing optional data) with `Result` (representing data or an error) is tedious. This use case is made easier by adding an `Empty` subtype to `Result`, making the `Option` type useless.

- You can map failures if needed: for example, to make error messages more explicit.

- Several factory functions simplify `Result` creation from various situations like using nullable data or conditional data, which is represented by data and a condition that must be fulfilled.

- You can apply effects to `Result` through the `forEach` function. This function allows applying different effects to `Success`, `Failure`, and `Empty`.

- You can lift functions from A to B (using the `lift` function) to operate from `Result<A>` to `Result<B>`. You can lift functions from A to (B to C) (through the `lift2` function) to a function from `Result<A>` to (`Result<B>` to `Result<C>`).

- You can use the comprehension pattern to compose any number of `Result` data.

Advanced list handling

In chapter 5, you created your first data structure, the singly linked list. At that point, you didn't have all the techniques needed to make this structure a complete tool for data handling. One particularly useful tool you were missing was some way to represent operations producing optional data or operations producing an error.

In chapters 6 and 7, you learned how to represent optional data and errors. In this chapter, you'll learn how to compose operations that produce optional data or errors with lists. You also developed some functions that were far from optimal, such as `length`, and I said that you'd eventually learn more efficient techniques for these operations. In this chapter, you're going to learn how to implement these more efficient techniques. You'll also learn how to automatically parallelize some list operations in order to benefit from the multicore architecture of today's computers.

8.1   *The problem with length*

Folding a list involves starting with a value and composing it successively with each element of the list. This obviously takes an amount of time proportional to the length of the list. Is there any way to make this operation faster? Or, at least, is there a way to make it appear faster? As an example of a fold application, you created a `length` function in `List` in chapter 5 (exercise 5.10) with the following implementation:

```
fun length(): Int = foldLeft(0) { { _ -> it + 1} }
```

In this implementation, the list is folded using an operation that consists of adding 1 to the result for each element of the list. The starting value is 0, and the value of each element is ignored. This is what allows you to use the same definition for all lists. Because the list elements are ignored, the list element's type is irrelevant. You can, however, compare the preceding operation with one that computes the sum of a list of integers:

```
fun sum(list: List<Int>): Int = list.foldRight(0) { x -> { y -> x + y } }
```

The main difference here is that the `sum` function can only work with integers, whereas the `length` function works for any type. Notice that `foldRight` and `foldLeft` are only ways to abstract recursion. The length of a list can be defined as 0 for an empty list and 1 plus the length of the tail for a non-empty list. In the same way, the sum of a list of integers can be defined recursively as 0 for an empty list and the head value plus the sum of the tail for a non-empty one.

There are other operations that can be applied to lists in this way and, among them, several for which the type of the list elements is irrelevant:

- *The hash code of a list can be computed by adding the hash codes of its elements.* As the hash code is an integer (at least for Kotlin objects), this operation doesn't depend on the object's type.
- *The string representation of a list, as returned by the* `toString` *function, can be computed by composing the* `toString` *representation of the list elements.* Once again, the actual type of the elements is irrelevant.

Some operations may depend on some characteristics of the element's type, but not on the specific type itself. For example, a `max` function that returns the maximum element of a list will only need a `Comparator` or the type to be `Comparable`. And a more generic `sum` function could be defined for types implementing a `Summable` interface defining a `plus` function.

8.2   *The performance problem*

All these functions can be implemented using a fold, but such implementations have a major drawback: the time needed to compute the result is proportional to the length of the list. Imagine you have a list of about one million elements and you want to check the length. Counting the elements may seem the only way to go (this is what the fold-based `length` function does). But if you were adding elements to the list until it reaches one million, you surely wouldn't count the elements after adding each one.

In such a situation, you'd keep a count of the elements somewhere and add one to this count each time you added an element to the list. Maybe you'd have to count once if you were starting with a non-empty list, but that's it. You learned this technique, memoization, in chapter 4. The question is, where can you store the memoized value? The answer is obvious: in the list itself.

8.3 The benefits of memoization

Maintaining a count of the elements in the list will take some time, so adding an element to a list will be slightly slower than if you didn't keep the count. It might look like you're trading time against time. If you build a list of one million elements, you'll lose one million times the amount of time needed to add one to the count. In compensation, however, the time needed to get the length of the list will be near 0 (and obviously constant). Maybe the total time lost in incrementing the count will equal the gain when calling `length`. But as soon as you call `length` more than once, the gain is absolutely obvious.

8.3.1 Handling memoization drawbacks

Memoization has a few drawbacks. In this section, I describe those drawbacks and provide some guidance on how to choose whether to use memoization.

Memoization can turn a function that works in $O(n)$ time (time proportional to the number of elements) into $O(1)$ time (constant time). This is a huge benefit, although it has a time cost because it makes the insertion of elements slightly longer. But slowing insertion is generally not a big problem. A much more important problem is the increase in memory space.

Data structures implementing in-place mutation don't have this problem. In a mutable list, nothing keeps us from memoizing the list length as a mutable integer, which takes only 32 bits. But with an immutable list, you need to memoize the length in each element. It's difficult to know the exact increase in size, but if the size of a singly linked list is around 40 bytes per node (for the nodes themselves) plus two 32-bit references for the head and the tail (on a 32-bit JVM), this would result in about 100 bytes per element. In this case, adding the length would cause an increase of slightly over 30%. The result would be the same if the memoized values were references, such as memoizing the maximum or minimum of a list of `Comparable` objects. On a 64-bit JVM, it's even more difficult to calculate due to some optimization in the size of the references, but you get the idea.

> **NOTE** For more information about the size of object references in the JVM, see Oracle's documentation on compressed ordinary object pointers and JVM performance enhancements (https://docs.oracle.com/javase/8/docs/technotes/guides/vm/performance-enhancements-7.html).

It's up to you to decide whether you want to use memoization in your data structures. It can be a valid option for functions that are often called and don't create new objects for their results. For example, the `length` and `hashCode` functions return integers, and the max or min functions return references to already existing objects, so these may be good candidates. On the other hand, the toString function creates new strings that would have to be memoized, so that would probably be a huge waste of memory space. The other factor to take into consideration is how often the function is used. The length function can be used more often than hashCode because using lists as map keys is not a common practice.

EXERCISE 8.1

Create a memoized version of the length function from exercise 3.8. Its signature in the List class is

```
abstract fun lengthMemoized(): Int
```

SOLUTION

The implementation in the Nil class returns 0:

```
override fun lengthMemoized(): Int = 0
```

To implement the Cons version, you must first add the memoizing field to the class:

```
internal class Cons<out A>(internal val head: A,
                          internal val tail: List<A>): List<A>() {

    private val length: Int = tail.lengthMemoized() + 1

    . . .
```

Then you can implement the lengthMemoized function to return the length:

```
override fun lengthMemoized() = length
```

This version will be much faster than the original one. One interesting thing to note is the relationship between the length and isEmpty functions. You might be tempted to think that isEmpty is equivalent to length == 0, but although this is true from the logical point of view, there can be a huge difference in implementation and in performance.

By the way, Kotlin allows for a much more compact solution by using an abstract property. Kotlin automatically generates getters for val properties and allows you to define abstract properties that are implemented in the extending class. The declaration in the List class is

```
abstract val length: Int
```

In the Nil object, the property is set to 0:

```
override val length = 0
```

And in the Cons class, it's initialized exactly like in the previous function implementation:

```
override val length = tail.length + 1
```

Memoizing the maximum or minimum value in a list of Comparable could be done the same way, but it wouldn't help in the case where you want to remove the max or min value from the list. Minimum or maximum elements are often accessed to retrieve elements by priority. In that case, the elements' compareTo function would compare their priorities.

Memoizing priority will let you know immediately which element has the maximum priority, but it wouldn't help much because what you often need is to remove the corresponding element. For such use cases, you'll need a different data structure, which you'll learn to create in chapter 11.

8.3.2 Evaluating performance improvements

As I said, it's up to you to decide if you should memoize some functions of the List class. A few experiments should help you make your decision. Measuring the available memory size before and after the creation of a list of one million integers shows a small increase when using memoization.

Although this measurement technique isn't accurate, the average decrease in available memory is about 22 MB in both cases (with or without memoization), varying between 20 MB and 25 MB. This shows that the theoretical increase of 4 MB (one million * 4 bytes) isn't as significant as you'd expect. On the other hand, the increase in performance is huge. Asking for the length ten times might cost more than 200 ms without memoization. With memoization, the time is 0 (too short a time to be measured in milliseconds). Although adding an element increases the cost (adding one to the tail length and storing the result), removing an element has no cost because the tail length is already memoized.

8.4 List and Result composition

In chapter 7, you saw that Result and List are similar data structures, mainly differing in their cardinality but sharing some of their most important functions, such as map and flatMap. You also saw how lists could be composed with lists, and results with results. Now, you're going to see how results can be composed with lists.

8.4.1 Handling lists returning Result

At this point, you'll probably have noticed that I try to avoid accessing the elements of results and lists directly. Accessing the head or the tail of a list throws an exception if the list is Nil, and throwing an exception is one of the most direct ways to make programs unsafe. But you learned that you could safely access the value in a Result by providing a default value to be used in the case of a failure or empty result. Can you do the same when accessing the head of a list? Not exactly, but you can return a Result.

EXERCISE 8.2

Implement a headSafe function in List<A> that will return a Result<A>.

HINT

Use the following abstract function declaration in List and implement it in each subclass:

```
abstract fun headSafe(): Result<A>
```

SOLUTION

The implementation of the `Nil` class returns an empty `Result`:

```
override fun headSafe(): Result<Nothing> = Result()
```

The `Cons` implementation returns a `Success` holding the head value:

```
override fun headSafe(): Result<A> = Result(head)
```

EXERCISE 8.3

Create a `lastSafe` function returning a `Result` of the last element in the list.

HINT

Don't use explicit recursion, but try to build on the functions you developed in chapter 5. You should be able to define a single function in the `List` class.

SOLUTION

You could solve this in several ways. I'll show a trivial solution first and then discuss its problems. Then I'll show a better solution that avoids those problems. Here's the trivial solution using explicit recursion:

```
fun lastSafe(): Result<A> = when (this) {
    Nil -> Result()
    is Cons -> when (tail) {
        Nil -> Result(head)
        is Cons -> tail.lastSafe()
    }
}
```

This solution has several problems. First, it's recursive, so you should transform it to make it corecursive. This is easy, but you'll have to make it a function taking the list as its argument:

```
tailrec fun <A> lastSafe(list: List<A>): Result<A> = when (list) {
    List.Nil -> Result()
    is List.Cons<A> -> when (list.tail) {
        List.Nil -> Result(list.head)
        is List.Cons -> lastSafe(list.tail)
    }
}
```

A better solution is to use a fold, which abstracts recursion for you. All you need to do is to create the right function for folding. You need to always keep the last value if it exists. This might be the function to use:

```
{ _: Result<A> -> { y: A -> Result(y) } }
```

Then you need to `foldLeft` the list using `Result()` as the identity:

```
fun lastSafe(): Result<A> =
    foldLeft(Result()) { _: Result<A> -> { y: A -> Result(y) } }
```

EXERCISE 8.4

Can you replace the headSafe function with a single implementation using a fold in the List class? What would be the benefits and drawbacks of such an implementation?

SOLUTION

It's possible to create such an implementation:

```
fun headSafe(): Result<A> =
    foldRight(Result()) { x: A -> { _: Result<A> -> Result(x) } }
```

The only benefit is that it's more fun if you like it that way. When devising the lastSafe implementation, you knew you had to traverse the list in order to find the last element. To find the first element, you don't need to traverse the list.

Using foldRight here is exactly the same as reversing the list and then traversing the result to find the last element (which is the first element of the original list). Not very efficient! And by the way, this is exactly what the lastSafe function does to find the last element: reverses the list and takes the first element of the result. Except for the fun, there's no reason to use this implementation. But if you prefer a single implementation in the List class, you can use pattern matching:

```
fun headSafe(): Result<A> = when (this) {
    Nil -> Result()
    is Cons -> Result(head)
}
```

8.4.2 *Converting from List<Result> to Result<List>*

When a list contains the results of some computations, it'll often be a List<Result>. For example, mapping a function from T to Result<U> on a list of T produces a List<Result<U>>. Such values will often have to be composed with functions taking a List<T> as their argument. This means you'll need a way to convert the resulting List<Result<U>> into a List<U>, which is the same kind of flattening involved in the flatMap function. The huge difference is that two different data types are involved: List and Result. You can apply several strategies to this conversion:

- Throw away all failures or empty results and produce a list of U from the remaining list of successes. If there's no success in the list, the result could contain an empty list.
- Throw away all failures or empty results and produce a list of U from the remaining list of successes. If there's no success in the list, the result would be a failure.
- Decide that all elements must be successes for the whole operation to succeed. Construct a list of U with the values if all are successes and return it as a Success<List<U>> or return a Failure<List<U>> otherwise.

The first solution would correspond to a list of results where all results are optional. The second solution means that there should be at least one success in the list for the result to be a success. And the third solution corresponds to the case where all results are mandatory.

EXERCISE 8.5

Write a function called `flattenResult` that takes a `List<Result<A>>` as its argument and returns a `List<A>` containing all the success values in the original list, ignoring the failures and empty values. This will be a package level function with the following signature:

```
fun <A> flattenResult(list: List<Result<A>>): List<A>
```

Try not to use explicit recursion but to compose functions from the `List` and `Result` classes.

HINT

The name chosen for the function is an indication of what you need to do.

SOLUTION

To solve this exercise, you can start by transforming each `Result<A>` element of the list in into either a `List<A>` (if it's a success) or into an empty list (in case of failure) using the following function:

```
{ ra -> ra.map { List(it) }.getOrElse(List()) }
```

The type of this function is `(Result<A>)` → `List<A>`. All you need to do now is to `flatMap` this function to the list of `Result<A>` like this:

```
fun <A> flattenResult(list: List<Result<A>>): List<A> =
        list.flatMap { ra -> ra.map { List(it) }.getOrElse(List()) }
```

EXERCISE 8.6

Write a sequence function that combines a `List<Result<A>>` into a `Result<List<A>>`. It'll be a `Success<List<A>>` if all values in the original list were `Success` instances, or a `Failure<List<A>>` otherwise. Here's its signature:

```
fun <A> sequence(list: List<Result<A>>): Result<List<A>>
```

HINT

Once again, use the `foldRight` function, not explicit recursion. You'll also need the `map2` function you defined in the `Result` class.

SOLUTION

Here's the implementation using `foldRight` and `Result.map2`:

```
import com.fpinkotlin.common.map2

...

fun <A> sequence(list: List<Result<A>>): Result<List<A>> =
    list.foldRight(Result(List())) { x ->
        { y: Result<List<A>> ->
            map2(x, y) { a -> { b: List<A> -> b.cons(a) } }
        }
    }
```

Again, you could prefer a stack-safe implementation based on `foldLeft`, providing you don't forget to reverse the result.

This implementation handles an empty `Result` as if it was a `Failure` and returns the first failing case it encounters, which can be a `Failure` or an `Empty`. This may or may not be what you need.

To stick with the idea that `Empty` means optional data, you'd need to first filter the list to remove the `Empty` elements. But for this, you'd need an `isEmpty` function in the `Result` class returning `true` in the `Empty` subclass and `false` in `Success` and `Failure`:

```
fun <A> sequence2(list: List<Result<A>>): Result<List<A>> =
    list.filter{ !it.isEmpty() }.foldRight(Result(List())) { x ->
        { y: Result<List<A>> ->
            map2(x, y) { a -> { b: List<A> -> b.cons(a) } }
        }
    }
```

EXERCISE 8.7

Define a more generic `traverse` function that traverses a list of `A` while applying a function from `A` to `Result<B>` and producing a `Result<List<B>>`. Here's its signature:

```
fun <A, B> traverse(list: List<A>, f: (A) -> Result<B>): Result<List<B>>
```

Then define a new version of `sequence` in terms of `traverse`.

HINT

Don't use recursion. Prefer the `foldRight` function, which abstracts recursion for you or the `coFoldRight` version if you want to make it stack-safe.

SOLUTION

First define the `traverse` function:

```
fun <A, B> traverse(list: List<A>, f: (A) -> Result<B>): Result<List<B>> =
    list.foldRight(Result(List())) { x ->
        { y: Result<List<B>> ->
            map2(f(x), y) { a -> { b: List<B> -> b.cons(a) } }
        }
    }
```

Then you can redefine the `sequence` function in terms of `traverse`:

```
fun <A> sequence(list: List<Result<A>>): Result<List<A>> =
                            traverse(list, { x: Result<A> -> x })
```

8.5 *Common List abstractions*

Many common use cases for the `List` data type deserve to be abstracted so you don't have to repeat the same code again and again. You'll regularly find yourself discovering new use cases that can be implemented by combining basic functions. You should never hesitate to incorporate these use cases as new functions in the `List` class. The following exercises show several of the most common use cases:

- Zipping and unzipping lists
- Transforming a list of pairs into a pair of lists
- Transforming a list of any type into a pair of lists

8.5.1   *Zipping and unzipping lists*

Zipping is the process of assembling two lists into one by combining the elements having the same index. *Unzipping* is the reverse procedure, consisting of making two lists out of one by deconstructing the elements, such as producing two lists of x and y coordinates from one list of points.

EXERCISE 8.8

Write a `zipWith` function that combines the elements of two lists of different types to produce a new list, given a function argument. Here's the signature:

```
fun <A, B, C> zipWith(list1: List<A>,
                      list2: List<B>,
                      f: (A) -> (B) -> C): List<C>
```

This function takes a `List<A>` and a `List<B>` and produces a `List<C>` with the help of a function from A to B to C.

HINT

The zipping should be limited to the length of the shortest list.

SOLUTION

For this exercise, you must use explicit recursion because recursion must be done on both lists simultaneously. You don't have any abstraction at your disposal for this. Here's a solution:

```
fun <A, B, C> zipWith(list1: List<A>,
                      list2: List<B>,
                      f: (A) -> (B) -> C): List<C> {
    tailrec
    fun zipWith(acc: List<C>,
                list1: List<A>,
                list2: List<B>): List<C> = when (list1) {
        List.Nil -> acc
        is List.Cons -> when (list2) {
            List.Nil -> acc
            is List.Cons ->
                zipWith(acc.cons(f(list1.head)(list2.head)),
                        list1.tail, list2.tail)
        }
    }
    return zipWith(List(), list1, list2).reverse()
}
```

The `zipWith` corecursive helper function is called with an empty list as the starting accumulator. If one of the two argument lists is empty, corecursion is stopped and the current accumulator is returned. Otherwise, a new value is computed by applying the function to the head values of both lists, and the helper function is called recursively with the tails of both argument lists.

EXERCISE 8.9

The previous exercise consisted in creating a list by matching elements of both lists by their indexes. Write a `product` function that produces a list of all possible combinations of elements taken from both lists. Given the two lists `list("a","b", "c")` and

list("d", "e", "f"), and string concatenation, the product of the two lists should be
List("ad", "ae", "af", "bd", "be", "bf", "cd", "ce", "cf").

HINT

For this exercise, you don't need to use explicit recursion.

SOLUTION

The solution is similar to the comprehension pattern you used to compose `Result` in chapter 7. The only difference here is that it produces as many combinations as the product of the number of elements in the lists, although for combining `Result`, the number of combinations was always limited to one:

```
fun <A, B, C> product(list1: List<A>,
                      list2: List<B>,
                      f: (A) -> (B) -> C): List<C> =
    list1.flatMap { a -> list2.map { b -> f(a)(b) } }
```

> **NOTE** It's possible to compose more than two lists this way. The only problem is that the number of combinations will grow exponentially.

One of the common use cases for `product` and `zipWith` is to use a constructor for the combination function. Here's an example using the `Pair` constructor:

```
product(List(1, 2), List(4, 5, 6)) { x -> { y: Int -> Pair(x, y) } }
zipWith(List(1, 2), List(4, 5, 6)) { x -> { y: Int -> Pair(x, y) } }
```

The first expression produces a list of all possible pairs constructed from the elements of both lists:

```
[(1, 4), (1, 5), (1, 6), (2, 4), (2, 5), (2, 6), NIL]
```

The second expression only produces the list of pairs built from elements with the same indexes:

```
[(1, 4), (2, 5), NIL]
```

EXERCISE 8.10

Write an `unzip` function to transform a list of pairs into a pair of lists. Here's its signature:

```
fun <A, B> unzip(list: List<Pair<A, B>>): Pair<List<A>, List<B>>
```

HINT

Don't use explicit recursion. A simple call to `foldRight` should do the job.

SOLUTION

You need to right fold the list using a pair of two empty lists as the identity:

```
fun <A, B> unzip(list: List<Pair<A, B>>): Pair<List<A>, List<B>> =
    list.coFoldRight(Pair(List(), List())) { pair ->
        { listPair: Pair<List<A>, List<B>> ->
            Pair(listPair.first.cons(pair.first),
                 listPair.second.cons(pair.second))
        }
    }
```

EXERCISE 8.11

Generalize the unzip function so it can transform a list of any type into a pair of lists, given a function that takes an object of the list element type as its argument and produces a pair. For example, given a list of Payment instances, you should be able to produce a pair of lists: one containing the credit cards used to make the payments and the other containing payment amounts. Implement this function as an instance function in List with the following signature:

```
fun <A1, A2> unzip(f: (A) -> Pair<A1, A2>): Pair<List<A1>, List<A2>>
```

HINT

The solution is pretty much the same as for exercise 8.10.

SOLUTION

One important thing is that the result of the function is to be used twice. In order not to apply the function twice, you can use a multiline lambda:

```
fun <A1, A2> unzip(f: (A) -> Pair<A1, A2>): Pair<List<A1>, List<A2>> =
    this.coFoldRight(Pair(Nil, Nil)) { a ->
        { listPair: Pair<List<A1>, List<A2>> ->
            val pair = f(a)
            Pair(listPair.first.cons(pair.first),
                listPair.second.cons(pair.second))
        }
    }
```

A smarter solution is to use the let function from the Kotlin standard library:

```
fun <A1, A2> unzip(f: (A) -> Pair<A1, A2>): Pair<List<A1>, List<A2>> =
    this.coFoldRight(Pair(Nil, Nil)) { a ->
        { listPair: Pair<List<A1>, List<A2>> ->
            f(a).let {
                Pair(listPair.first.cons(it.first),
                    listPair.second.cons(it.second))
            }
        }
    }
```

You may wonder why this solution is smarter. There's absolutely no reason except that I like it more. If you don't, feel free to use the multiline version (which, by the way, should be unnoticeably faster). In any case, you can now redefine the version from exercise 8.10 as

```
fun <A, B> unzip(list: List<Pair<A, B>>): Pair<List<A>, List<B>> =
                                            list.unzip { it }
```

8.5.2   *Accessing elements by their index*

In chapter 5, you worked with your first data structure, the singly linked list. The singly linked list isn't the best structure for indexed access to its elements, but sometimes it's necessary to use indexed access. As usual, you should abstract such a process into List functions.

EXERCISE 8.12

Write a `getAt` function that takes an index as its argument and returns the corresponding element. The function shouldn't throw an exception in the case of the index being out of bounds.

HINT

This time, start with an explicitly recursive version. Then try to answer the following questions:

- Is it possible to do it with a fold? Right or left?
- Why is the explicit recursive version better?
- Can you think of a better implementation?

Reminder: you first encountered tail recursion in chapter 4, and chapters 3 and 5 went into folding in depth.

SOLUTION

The explicitly recursive solution is easy:

```
fun getAt(index: Int): Result<A> {
    tailrec fun <A> getAt(list: List<A>, index: Int): Result<A> =
        when (list) {
            Nil -> Result.failure("Dead code. Should never execute.")
            is Cons ->
                if (index == 0)
                    Result(list.head)
                else
                    getAt(list.tail, index - 1)
        }
    return if (index < 0 || index >= length())
        Result.failure("Index out of bound")
    else
        getAt(this, index)
}
```

First, you can check the index to see if it's positive and less than the list length. If it isn't, return a `Failure`. Otherwise, call the helper function to process the list corecursively. This function checks whether the index is 0. If it is, it returns the head of the list it received. Otherwise, it calls itself recursively on the tail of the list with a decremented index.

The `Nil` case in the helper function is dead code. If the list is `Nil`, index will always be either smaller than 0 or greater than or equal to the list length (because it's 0). Consequently, the tail of the argument will never be `Nil`. You might prefer the following version:

```
fun getAt(index: Int): Result<A> {
    tailrec fun <A> getAt(list: Cons<A>, index: Int): Result<A> =
        if (index == 0)
            Result(list.head)
        else
            getAt(list.tail as Cons, index - 1)
```

```
    return if (index < 0 || index >= length())
        Result.failure("Index out of bound")
    else
        getAt(this as Cons, index)
}
```

You could also be tempted to use the `let` function of the standard library:

```
fun getAt(index: Int): Result<A> {
    tailrec fun <A> getAt(list: List<A>, index: Int): Result<A> = // Warning
        (list as Cons).let {
            if (index == 0)
                Result(list.head)
            else
                getAt(list.tail, index - 1)
        }

    return if (index < 0 || index >= length())
        Result.failure("Index out of bound")
    else
        getAt(this, index)
}
```

But this version compiles with a warning because the helper function is no longer tail-recursive. As a consequence, it might overflow the stack.

Using corecursion seems to be the best possible solution. But because folding abstracts recursion, is it possible to use a fold? Yes, it is, and it should be a left fold, but the solution is tricky:

```
fun getAtViaFoldLeft(index: Int): Result<A> =
    Pair(Result.failure<A>("Index out of bound"), index).let {
        if (index < 0 || index >= length())
            it
        else
            foldLeft(it) { ta ->
                { a ->
                    if (ta.second < 0)
                        ta
                    else
                        Pair(Result(a), ta.second - 1)
                }
            }
    }.first
```

First you have to define the identity value. As this value must hold both the result and the index, it'll be a `Pair` holding the `Failure` case. Then you can check the index for validity. If it's found invalid, make the temporary result equal to `it` (the identity). Otherwise, fold to the left with a function returning either the already computed result (`ta`) if the index is less than 0, or a new `Success` otherwise. This solution might seem smarter, but it has two drawbacks:

- You might find it less legible. This is subjective, so it's up to you to decide.
- It's less efficient because it'll continue folding the whole list even after it finds the searched-for value.

EXERCISE 8.13 (HARD)

Find a solution that makes the fold-based version terminate as soon as the result is found.

HINT

You'll need a special version of `foldLeft` for this, as well as a special version of `Pair`.

SOLUTION

First, you need a special version of `foldLeft` in which you can escape the fold when the absorbing element (or zero element) of the folding operation is found. Think of a list of integers that you want to fold by multiplying them. The absorbing element for the multiplication is 0, meaning that multiplying any number by 0 results in 0. Here's the declaration of a *short-circuiting* (or *escaping*) version of `foldLeft` in the `List` class:

```
abstract fun <B> foldLeft(identity: B, zero: B, f: (B) -> (A) -> B): B
```

> ### The zero element
>
> By analogy, the absorbing element of any operation is sometimes called *zero*, but remember that it isn't always equal to 0. The 0 value is only the absorbing element for multiplication. For the addition of positive integers, it would be infinity.

The `Nil` implementation returns the `identity` parameter:

```
override fun <B> foldLeft(identity: B,
                          zero: B, f: (B) -> (Nothing) -> B): B = identity
```

And here's the `Cons` implementation:

```
override fun <B> foldLeft(identity: B, zero: B, f: (B) -> (A) -> B): B {
    fun <B> foldLeft(acc: B,
                     zero: B,
                     list: List<A>, f: (B) -> (A) -> B): B = when (list) {
        Nil -> acc
        is Cons ->
            if (acc == zero)
                acc
            else
                foldLeft(f(acc)(list.head), zero, list.tail, f)
    }
    return foldLeft(identity, zero, this, f)
}
```

As you can see, the only difference is that if the accumulator value is found to be 0, recursion is stopped and the accumulator is returned. Now you need a 0 value for your fold.

The 0 value is a `Pair<Result<A>, Int>` with the `Int` value equal to -1 (the first value smaller than 0). Can you use a standard `Pair` for this? No, you can't, because it must have a special equals function that returns `true` when the integer values are equal, whatever the `Result<A>` is. The complete function is as follows:

```
fun getAt(index: Int): Result<A> {
    data class Pair<out A>(val first: Result<A>, val second: Int) {
```

```
        override fun equals(other: Any?): Boolean = when {
            other == null -> false
            other.javaClass == this.javaClass ->
                            (other as Pair<A>).second == second
            else -> false
        }

        override fun hashCode(): Int =
                first.hashCode() + second.hashCode()
    }

    return Pair<A>(Result.failure("Index out of bound"), index)
        .let { identity ->
            Pair<A>(Result.failure("Index out of bound"), -1).let { zero ->
                if (index < 0 || index >= length())
                    identity
                else
                    foldLeft(identity, zero) { ta: Pair<A> ->
                        { a: A ->
                            if (ta.second < 0)
                                ta
                            else
                                Pair(Result(a), ta.second - 1)
                        }
                    }
            }
        }.first
}
```

Now the fold automatically stops as soon as the searched-for element is found. You can use the new foldLeft function for escaping any computation with a zero element. (Remember: *zero* not 0.) But instead of using a zero element, you can use a predicate and make the function return when this predicate returns true:

```
abstract fun <B> foldLeft(acc: B, p: (B) -> Boolean, f: (B) -> (A) -> B): B
```

The Nil implementation returns identity as previously:

```
override fun <B> foldLeft(identity: B,
                          p: (B) -> Boolean,
                          f: (B) -> (Nothing) -> B): B = identity
```

The Cons implementation is similar to the previous ones, but with a small difference. Instead of testing if acc is equal to zero, you apply the predicate to acc:

```
override fun <B> foldLeft(identity: B,
                          p: (B) -> Boolean,
                          f: (B) -> (A) -> B): B {
    fun <B> foldLeft(acc: B,
                     p: (B) -> Boolean,
                     list: List<A>): B = when (list) {
        Nil -> acc
        is Cons ->
            if (p(acc))
                acc
            else
```

```
                foldLeft(f(acc)(list.head), p, list.tail, f)
    }
    return foldLeft(identity, p, this)
}
```

And here's the `getAt` implementation using this version of `foldLeft`:

```
fun getAt(index: Int): Result<A> {
    val p: (Pair<Result<A>, Int>) -> Boolean = { it.second < 0 }
    return Pair<Result<A>, Int>(Result.failure("Index out of bound"), index)
        .let { identity ->
            if (index < 0 || index >= length())
                identity
            else
                foldLeft(identity, p) { ta: Pair<Result<A>, Int> ->
                    { a: A ->
                        if (p(ta))
                            ta
                        else
                            Pair(Result(a), ta.second - 1)
                    }
                }
        }.first
}
```

8.5.3 *Splitting lists*

Sometimes you'll need to split a list into two parts at a specific position. Although the singly linked list is far from ideal for this kind of operation, it's relatively simple to implement. Splitting a list has several useful applications, among which is processing its parts in parallel using several threads.

EXERCISE 8.14

Write a `splitAt` function that takes an `Int` as its parameter and returns two lists by splitting the list at the given position. There shouldn't be any `IndexOutOfBoundExceptions`. Instead, an index below 0 should be treated as 0, and an index above max should be treated as the maximum value for the index.

HINT

Make the function explicitly recursive.

SOLUTION

An explicitly recursive solution is easy to design:

```
fun splitAt(index: Int): Pair<List<A>, List<A>> {
    tailrec fun splitAt(acc: List<A>,
                        list: List<A>, i: Int): Pair<List<A>, List<A>> =
        when (list) {
            Nil -> Pair(list.reverse(), acc)
            is Cons ->  if (i == 0)
                Pair(list.reverse(), acc)
            else
                splitAt(acc.cons(list.head), list.tail, i - 1)
```

```
        }
    return when {
        index < 0         -> splitAt(0)
        index > length()  -> splitAt(length())
        else              ->
                  splitAt(Nil, this.reverse(), this.length() - index)
    }
}
```

The main function uses recursion to adjust the value of the index, although this function will recurse at most once. The helper function is similar to the getAt function with the difference that the list is first reversed. The function accumulates the elements until the index position is reached, so the accumulated list is in the correct order, but the remaining list has to be reversed back.

EXERCISE 8.15 (NOT SO HARD IF YOU'VE DONE EXERCISE 8.13)

Can you think of an implementation using a fold instead of explicit recursion?

HINT

An implementation traversing the whole list is easy. An implementation traversing the list only until the index is found is much more difficult. It'll need a new special version of foldLeft with escape, returning both the escaped value and the rest of the list.

SOLUTION

A solution traversing the whole list could be as follows:

```
fun splitAt(index: Int): Pair<List<A>, List<A>> {
    val ii = if (index < 0) 0
             else if (index >= length()) length() else index
    val identity = Triple(Nil, Nil, ii)
    val rt = foldLeft(identity) { ta: Triple<List<A>, List<A>, Int> ->
        { a: A ->
            if (ta.third == 0)
                Triple(ta.first, ta.second.cons(a), ta.third)
            else
                Triple(ta.first.cons(a), ta.second, ta.third - 1)
        }
    }
    return Pair(rt.first.reverse(), rt.second.reverse())
}
```

The result of the fold is accumulated in the first list accumulator until the index is reached (after the index value has been adjusted to avoid an index out of bounds condition. Once the index is found, the list traversal continues, but the remaining values are accumulated in the second list accumulator.

One problem with this implementation is that by accumulating the remaining values in the second list accumulator, you're reversing this part of the list. Not only should you not need to traverse the remainder of the list, but it's done twice here: once for accumulating in reverse order and once for eventually reversing the result.

To avoid this problem, modify the special escaping version of `foldLeft` so that it returns not only the escaped result (the absorbing, or zero element), but also the rest of the list, untouched. To achieve this, you must change the signature to return a `Pair`:

```
abstract fun <B> foldLeft(identity: B, zero: B,
                          f: (B) -> (A) -> B): Pair<B, List<A>>
```

Then you need to change the implementation in the `Nil` class:

```
override
fun <B> foldLeft(identity: B, zero: B, f: (B) -> (Nothing) -> B):
                        Pair<B, List<Nothing>> = Pair(identity, Nil)
```

Finally, you must change the `Cons` implementation to return the remainder of the list:

```
override fun <B> foldLeft(identity: B, zero: B, f: (B) -> (A) -> B):
                                        Pair<B, List<A>> {
    fun <B> foldLeft(acc: B, zero: B, list: List<A>, f: (B) -> (A) -> B):
                                        Pair<B, List<A>> =
        when (list) {
            Nil -> Pair(acc, list)
            is Cons -> if (acc == zero)
                Pair(acc, list)
            else
                foldLeft(f(acc)(list.head), zero, list.tail, f)
        }
    return foldLeft(identity, zero, this, f)
}
```

Now you can rewrite the `splitAt` function using this special `foldLeft` function:

```
fun splitAt(index: Int): Pair<List<A>, List<A>> {

    data class Pair<out A>(val first: List<A>, val second: Int) {
        override fun equals(other: Any?): Boolean = when {
            other == null -> false
            other.javaClass == this.javaClass ->
                                (other as Pair<A>).second == second
            else -> false
        }

        override fun hashCode(): Int =
                first.hashCode() + second.hashCode()
    }

    return when {
        index <= 0 -> Pair(Nil, this)
        index >= length -> Pair(this, Nil)
        else -> {
            val identity = Pair(Nil as List<A>, -1)
            val zero = Pair(this, index)
            val (pair, list) = this.foldLeft(identity, zero) { acc ->
                { e -> Pair(acc.first.cons(e), acc.second + 1) }
            }
            Pair(pair.first.reverse(), list)
        }
    }
}
```

Here again, you need a specific `Pair` class with a special `equals` function that returns true when the second elements are equal, not taking into account the first element. Note that the second resulting list doesn't need to be reversed.

> ## When not to use folds
>
> Because it's possible to use a fold doesn't mean you should do so. The preceding exercises are just that: exercises. As a library designer, you need to choose the most efficient implementation.
>
> A good library should have a functional interface and should respect the requirements for safe programming. This means all functions should be true functions with no side effects and all should respect referential transparency. What happens inside the library is irrelevant.
>
> A functional library in an imperative-oriented environment, like the JVM, can be compared to a compiler for a functional-oriented language. The compiled code will always be based on mutating memory areas and registers because this is what the computer understands.
>
> A functional library gives more choices. Some functions can be implemented in a functional style and others in an imperative style; it doesn't matter. Splitting a singly linked list or finding an element by its index is much easier and faster when it's implemented imperatively rather than functionally. That's because the singly linked list isn't adapted for such an operation.
>
> The most functional way to go is probably not to implement functions based on indexes based on folds, but to avoid implementing these functions at all. If you do need structures with these functions, the best thing to do is to create specific structures, as you'll see in chapter 10.

8.5.4   Searching for sublists

One common use case for lists is finding out whether a list is contained in another (longer) list. You want to know whether a list is a sublist of another list.

EXERCISE 8.16

Implement a `hasSubList` function to check whether a list is a sublist of another. For example, the list (3, 4, 5) is a sublist of (1, 2, 3, 4, 5) but not of (1, 2, 4, 5, 6). Implement this function with the following signature:

```
fun hasSubList(sub: List<@UnsafeVariance A>): Boolean
```

HINT

You'll first have to implement a `startsWith` function to determine whether a list starts with a sublist. Once this is done, you'll test this function recursively, starting from each element of the list.

SOLUTION

An explicitly recursive startsWith function can be implemented in the List class, not forgetting to disable variance check in the parameter:

```
fun startsWith(sub: List<@UnsafeVariance A>): Boolean {
    tailrec fun startsWith(list: List<A>, sub: List<A>): Boolean =
            when (sub) {
                Nil  -> true
                is Cons -> when (list) {
                    Nil  -> false
                    is Cons -> if (list.head == sub.head)
                        startsWith(list.tail, sub.tail)
                    else
                        false
                }
            }
    return startsWith(this, sub)
}
```

From there, implementing hasSubList is straightforward:

```
fun hasSubList(sub: List<@UnsafeVariance A>): Boolean {
    tailrec
    fun <A> hasSubList(list: List<A>, sub: List<A>): Boolean =
            when (list) {
                Nil -> sub.isEmpty()
                is Cons ->
                    if (list.startsWith(sub))
                        true
                    else
                        hasSubList(list.tail, sub)
            }
    return hasSubList(this, sub)
}
```

8.5.5 Miscellaneous functions for working with lists

You can develop many other useful functions for working with lists. The following exercises give you some practice in this domain. The proposed solutions are certainly not the only ones. Feel free to invent your own.

EXERCISE 8.17

Create a groupBy function with the following characteristics:

- It takes a function from A to B as a parameter.
- It returns a Map, where keys are the result of the function applied to each element of the list, and values are lists of elements corresponding to each key.

For example, given a list of Payment instances such as

```
data class Payment(val name: String, val amount: Int)
```

the following code should create a Map containing (key, value) pairs, where each key is a name and the corresponding value is the list of Payment instances made by the corresponding person:

```
val map: Map<String, List<Payment>> = list.groupBy { x -> x.name }
```

Use a Kotlin immutable Map<B, List<A>>. To add value, you need to check if the corresponding key is already in the map. If it's found, you add the value to the list corresponding to this key. Otherwise, you create a new binding from the key to a singleton list containing the value to add. This can be done easily with the getOrDefault function of the Map class.

SOLUTION

Here's an imperative version. There's not much to say about it as it's traditional imperative code with a local mutable state. If you want the order of elements to be maintained in the sublists, you need to reverse the list first:

```
fun <B> groupBy(f: (A) -> B): Map<B, List<A>> =
    reverse().foldLeft(mapOf()) { mt: Map<B, List<A>> ->
        { t ->
            val key = f(t)
            mt + (key to (mt[key] ?: Nil).cons(t))
        }
    }
```

Here, you can see the Elvis operator (?:) in action because this example uses a Kotlin immutable map which returns a nullable type. Using nullable types internally is perfectly acceptable for safe programming as long as you don't allow these types to leak out of your functions. Here they do.

A better solution would be to use a map returning Result.Empty instead of null when the key isn't found. You could also use the getOrDefault function:

```
fun <B> groupBy(f: (A) -> B): Map<B, List<A>> =
    reverse().foldLeft(mapOf()) { mt: Map<B, List<A>> ->
        { t ->
            val k = f(t)
            mt + (k to (mt.getOrDefault(k, Nil)).cons(t))
        }
    }
```

A more idiomatic solution is to use the let function of the Kotlin standard library:

```
fun <B> groupBy(f: (A) -> B): Map<B, List<A>> =
    reverse().foldLeft(mapOf()) { mt: Map<B, List<A>> ->
        { t ->
            f(t).let {
                mt + (it to (mt.getOrDefault(it, Nil)).cons(t))
            }
        }
    }
```

But this doesn't help because it solves the problem in the function, where it's not needed, and not outside, where the caller can still use normal access returning null. In chapter 11, you'll learn how to create your own immutable Map that solves this problem.

Reversing the list first costs some time, so you may prefer to use use foldRight instead of foldLeft. There's a potential risk of blowing the stack, however. Here's the solution with foldRight:

```
fun <B> groupBy(f: (A) -> B): Map<B, List<A>> =
    foldRight(mapOf()) { t ->
        { mt: Map<B, List<A>> ->
            f(t).let { mt + (it to (mt.getOrDefault(it, Nil)).cons(t)) }
        }
    }
```

EXERCISE 8.18

Write an unfold function that takes a starting element S and a function f from S to Option<Pair<A, S>>, and produces a List<A> by successively applying f to the S value as long as the result is a Some. The following code should produce a list of integers from 0 to 9:

```
unfold(0) { i ->
    if (i < 10)
        Option(Pair(i, i + 1))
    else
        Option()
}
```

SOLUTION

A simple non stack-safe recursive version is easy to implement:

```
fun <A, S> unfold_(z: S, f: (S) -> Option<Pair<A, S>>): List<A> =
    f(z).map({ x ->
                unfold_(x.second, f).cons(x.first)
            }).getOrElse(List.Nil)
```

Unfortunately, although this solution is smart, it'll blow the stack for a little more than 1,000 recursion steps. To solve this problem, you can create a corecursive version:

```
fun <A, S> unfold(z: S, getNext: (S) -> Option<Pair<A, S>>): List<A> {
    tailrec fun unfold(acc: List<A>, z: S): List<A> {
        val next = getNext(z)
        return when (next) {
            Option.None -> acc
            is Option.Some ->
                unfold(acc.cons(next.value.first), next.value.second)
        }
    }
    return unfold(List.Nil, z).reverse()
}
```

The problem with this corecursive version is that you need to reverse the result. This might not be important for small lists, but it can become annoying if the number of elements grows too much.

This implementation requires that the Option class be in the same module as the List class. A module is one of the following:

- An IntelliJ IDEA module
- A Maven project
- A Gradle source set
- A set of files compiled with one invocation of an Ant task

For this exercise, the Option class has been copied from the common module to the advancedlisthandling module. In a real situation, it would be the inverse, the List class being in the common module.

Here's an example of using unfold:

```
fun main(args: Array<String>) {
    val f: (Int) -> Option<Pair<Int, Int>> =
        { it ->
            if (it < 10_000) Option(Pair(it, it + 1)) else Option()
        }
    val result = unfold(0, f)
    println(result)
}
```

Here, the unfold function generates values until the next function returns None. If you need to use a function that might produce an error, you can use the Result class instead of Option:

```
fun <A, S> unfold(z: S,
                  getNext: (S) -> Result<Pair<A, S>>): Result<List<A>> {
    tailrec fun unfold(acc: List<A>, z: S): Result<List<A>> {
        val next = getNext(z)
        return when (next) {
            Result.Empty -> Result(acc)
            is Result.Failure -> Result.failure(next.exception)
            is Result.Success ->
                unfold(acc.cons(next.value.first), next.value.second)
        }
    }
    return unfold(List.Nil, z).map(List<A>::reverse)
}
```

EXERCISE 8.19

Write a range function that takes two integers as its parameters and produces a list of all integers greater than or equal to the first and less than the second.

HINT

You should use functions you've already defined.

SOLUTION

This is simple if you reuse the function from exercise 8.18:

```
fun range(start: Int, end: Int): List<Int> {
    return unfold(start) { i ->
        if (i < end)
            Option(Pair(i, i + 1))
        else
            Option()
    }
}
```

EXERCISE 8.20

Create an `exists` function that takes a function from `A` to `Boolean` representing a condition and that returns `true` if the list contains at least one element satisfying this condition. Don't use explicit recursion; build on the functions you've already defined.

HINT

There's no need to evaluate the condition for all elements of the list. The function should return as soon as the first element satisfying the condition is found.

SOLUTION

A recursive solution could be defined as follows:

```
fun exists(p:(A) -> Boolean): Boolean =
    when (this) {
        Nil -> false
        is Cons ->  p(head) || tail.exists(p)
    }
```

Because the `||` operator evaluates its second argument lazily, the recursive process stops as soon as an element is found that satisfies the condition expressed by the predicate p.

But this is a non-tail-recursive stack-based function, and it'll blow the stack if the list is long and if no satisfying element is found in the first 1,000 or so elements. Incidentally, it'll also throw an exception if the list is empty, so you'd have to define an abstract function in the `List` class with a specific implementation for the `Nil` subclass. A much better solution consists in reusing the `foldLeft` function with a zero parameter:

```
fun exists(p: (A) -> Boolean): Boolean =
        foldLeft(false, true) { x -> { y: A -> x || p(y) } }.first
```

EXERCISE 8.21

Create a `forAll` function that takes a function from `A` to `Boolean` that represents a condition and that returns `true` if all the elements in the list satisfy this condition.

HINT

Don't use explicit recursion. And once again, you don't always need to evaluate the condition for all elements of the list. The `forAll` function will be similar to the `exists` function.

SOLUTION

The solution is close to the `exists` function with two differences—the identity and zero values are inverted and the Boolean operator is `&&` instead of `||`:

```
fun forAll(p: (A) -> Boolean): Boolean =
        foldLeft(true, false) { x -> { y: A -> x && p(y) } }.first
```

Another possibility is to reuse the `exists` function:

```
fun forAll(p: (A) -> Boolean): Boolean = !exists { !p(it) }
```

This function checks whether an element exists that doesn't meet the inverse of the condition.

8.6 *Automatic parallel processing of lists*

Most computations that are applied to lists resort to folds. A *fold* involves applying an operation as many times as there are elements in the list. For long lists and long-lasting operations, a fold can take a considerable amount of time. As most computers are now equipped with multicore processors (if not multiple processors), you might be tempted to find a way to make the computer process a list in parallel.

In order to parallelize a fold, you need only one thing (beside a multicore processor, of course): an additional operation allowing you to recompose the results of all parallel computations.

8.6.1 *Not all computations can be parallelized*

Take the example of a list of integers. You can't directly parallelize finding the mean of all integers. You could break the list into four pieces (if you have a computer with four processors) and compute the mean of each sublist. But you wouldn't be able to compute the mean of the list from the means of the sublists.

On the other hand, computing the mean of a list implies computing the sum of all elements and then dividing it by the number of elements. And computing the sum is something that can easily be parallelized by computing the sums of the sublists, and then computing the sum of the sublist sums.

This is a very particular example, where the operation used for the fold (the addition) is the same as the operation used to assemble the sublist results. This isn't always the case. Take the example of a list of characters that's folded by adding individual characters to a `String`. To assemble the intermediate results, you need a different operation: string concatenation.

8.6.2 *Breaking the list into sublists*

First, you must break the list into sublists, and you must do this automatically. One important question is how many sublists you should obtain. Initially, you might think that one sublist for each available processor would be ideal, but this isn't exactly the case. The number of processors (or, more precisely, the number of logical cores) isn't the most important factor.

There's a much more crucial question: will all sublist computations take the same amount of time? Probably not, but this depends on the type of computation. If you were to divide the list into four sublists because you decided to dedicate four threads to the parallel processing, some threads might finish quickly, although others might have to make a much longer computation. This would ruin the benefit of parallelization because it might result in most of the computing task being handled by a single thread.

A much better solution is to divide the list into a large number of sublists, and then submit each sublist to a pool of threads. This way, as soon as a thread finishes processing a sublist, it's handed a new one to process. Your first task is to create a function that divides a list into sublists.

EXERCISE 8.22

Write a `divide(depth: Int)` function that divides a list into a number of sublists. The list will be divided in two, and each sublist recursively divided in two, with the `depth` parameter representing the number of recursion steps. This function will be implemented in the `List` parent class with the following signature:

```
fun divide(depth: Int): List<List<A>>
```

HINT

You'll first define a new version of the `splitAt` function that returns a list of lists instead of a `Pair<List, List>`. Let's call this function `splitListAt` and give it the following signature:

```
fun splitListAt(index: Int): List<List<A>>
```

SOLUTION

The `splitListAt` function is a slightly modified version of the `splitAt` function:

```
fun splitListAt(index: Int): List<List<A>> {
    tailrec fun splitListAt(acc: List<A>,
                            list: List<A>, i: Int): List<List<A>> =
        when (list) {
            Nil -> List(list.reverse(), acc)
            is Cons -> if (i == 0)
                List(list.reverse(), acc)
            else
                splitListAt(acc.cons(list.head), list.tail, i - 1)
        }
    return when {
        index < 0        -> splitListAt(0)
        index > length() -> splitListAt(length())
        else             ->
                splitListAt(Nil, this.reverse(), this.length() - index)
    }
}
```

This function always returns a list of two lists. Then you can define the `divide` function as follows:

```
fun divide(depth: Int): List<List<A>> {
    tailrec
```

```
fun divide(list: List<List<A>>, depth: Int): List<List<A>> =
    when (list) {
        Nil -> list // dead code
        is Cons ->
            if (list.head.length() < 2 || depth < 1)
                list
            else
                divide(list.flatMap { x ->
                    x.splitListAt(x.length() / 2)
                }, depth - 1)
    }
return if (this.isEmpty())
    List(this)
else
    divide(List(this), depth)
}
```

The `Nil` case of the when expression is dead code because the local function will never be called with `Nil` as its parameter. You could then use an explicit cast to `Cons`. Also note that you don't really need the `tailrec` keyword because the number of recursion steps will only be *log(length)*. You'll never have enough heap memory to hold a list so long that it would cause a stack overflow.

8.6.3   *Processing sublists in parallel*

To process the sublists in parallel, you'll need a special version of the function to execute. This special version will take, as an additional parameter, an `ExecutorService` configured with the number of threads you want to use in parallel.

EXERCISE 8.23

Create a `parFoldLeft` function in `List<A>` that takes the same parameters as `foldLeft` plus an `ExecutorService` and a function from B to B to B and that returns a `Result<B>`. The additional function will be used to assemble the results from the sublists. Here's the function's signature:

```
fun <B> parFoldLeft(es: ExecutorService,
                    identity: B,
                    f: (B) -> (A) -> B,
                    m: (B) -> (B) -> B): Result<B>
```

SOLUTION

First, you must define the number of sublists you want to use and divide the list accordingly:

```
divide(1024)
```

Then you'll map the list of sublists with a function that'll submit a task to the `Executor-Service`. This task consists of folding each sublist and returning a `Future` instance. The list of `Future` instances is mapped to a function calling `get` on each `Future` to produce a list of results (one for each sublist). You must catch the potential exceptions. Eventually, the list of results is folded with the second function, and the result is returned in a `Success`. In the case of an exception, a `Failure` is returned:

```
fun <B> parFoldLeft(es: ExecutorService,
                    identity: B,
                    f: (B) -> (A) -> B,
                    m: (B) -> (B) -> B): Result<B> =
    try {
        val result: List<B> = divide(1024).map { list: List<A> ->
            es.submit<B> { list.foldLeft(identity, f) }
        }.map<B> { fb ->
            try {
                fb.get()
            } catch (e: InterruptedException) {
                throw RuntimeException(e)
            } catch (e: ExecutionException) {
                throw RuntimeException(e)
            }
        }
        Result(result.foldLeft(identity, m))
    } catch (e: Exception) {
        Result.failure(e)
    }
```

You'll find an example benchmark of this function in the accompanying code (https://github.com/pysaumont/fpinkotlin). The benchmark consists of computing ten times the Fibonacci value of 35,000 random numbers between 1 and 30 with a slow algorithm. Here's a typical result obtained on a eight-core computer:

```
Duration serial 1 thread: 140933
Duration parallel 2 threads: 70502
Duration parallel 4 threads: 36337
Duration parallel 8 threads: 20253
```

EXERCISE 8.24

Although mapping can be implemented through a fold (and can benefit from automatic parallelization), it can also be implemented in parallel, without using a fold. This is probably the simplest automatic parallelization that can be implemented on a list.

Create a parMap function that will automatically apply a given function to all elements of a list in parallel. Here's the function's signature:

```
fun <B> parMap(es: ExecutorService, g: (A) -> B): Result<List<B>>
```

HINT

There is nearly nothing to do in this exercise. Submit each function application to the ExecutorService and get the results from each corresponding resulting function.

SOLUTION

Here's the solution:

```
fun <B> parMap(es: ExecutorService, g: (A) -> B): Result<List<B>> =
    try {
        val result = this.map { x ->
            es.submit<B> { g(x) }
        }.map<B> { fb ->
            try {
```

```
            fb.get()
        } catch (e: InterruptedException) {
            throw RuntimeException(e)
        } catch (e: ExecutionException) {
            throw RuntimeException(e)
        }
    }
    Result(result)
} catch (e: Exception) {
    Result.failure(e)
}
```

The benchmark available in the code accompanying this book will allow you to measure any increase in performance. This increase can vary depending on the machine running the program.

This parallel version of map creates a single task for each element of the list. It's more efficient for mapping a short list with a function representing a long computation. With long lists and fast computations, the gain of speed might not be as high—it could even be negative.

Summary

- You can use memoization to speed up list processing.
- You can convert a List of Result instances into a Result of List.
- You can assemble two lists by zipping them. You can also unzip lists to produce a Pair of lists.
- You can implement indexed access to list elements using explicit recursion.
- You can implement a special version of foldLeft to escape the fold when a zero result is obtained.
- You can create lists by unfolding with a function and a terminal condition.
- Lists can be automatically split, which allows automatic processing of sublists in parallel.

Working with laziness

Imagine you're the bartender in a tiny bar that offers two products: espresso and orange juice. A customer enters and sits. You have two options:

1. You prepare an espresso, press an orange juice, bring the two to the customer, and let them choose.
2. You ask the customer what they'd like to have, prepare it, and serve it.

In programming terms, in the second case, you're being *lazy*, whereas in the first case, you're being *strict*. Choosing the best strategy is up to you. This chapter isn't about morals, but about efficiency.

In this case, there are other options. You could eagerly prepare an espresso and an orange juice before any customer enters. Once a customer comes in, ask the person to pick what they want, serve what's requested, and immediately make a beverage in preparation for the next customer. Seems crazy? Not so.

Imagine you're also offering apple pies and strawberry pies. Would you wait for a customer to enter and choose one kind of pie to prepare it? Or would you eagerly prepare one of each kind? If you choose to be lazy, you would wait for the customer to choose, let's say apple pie. Then you'd prepare an apple pie, cut a slice, and bring it to the customer. This would be the lazy approach, although you'd have at the same time prepared the other apple pie slices.

Programming languages work the same. And as in the example, the normal way is generally so obvious that no one even thinks about it, unless a problem arises. In the first part of this chapter, I compare strictness and laziness. While Kotlin is a strict language, you can still use laziness. For the rest of the chapter, I'll teach various laziness-related skills in Kotlin: how to implement laziness, how to compose with laziness, how to create a lazy list data structure, and finally, how to handle infinite streams.

9.7   *Strictness versus laziness*

Some languages are said to be lazy; others are strict. Generally, this is about how languages evaluate function or method arguments. But in reality, all languages are lazy because laziness is the true essence of programming.

Programming consists of composing program instructions that'll be evaluated when the program is eventually run. If full strictness were enforced, each single instruction you write would be executed as soon as you pressed the Enter key, which is, in fact, what happens when you use a REPL (Read, Eval, Print Loop).

Setting apart the fact that a program is basically a lazy construct, are programs written in strict languages like Kotlin or Java a composition of strict elements? Certainly not. Strict languages are strict regarding method/function argument evaluation, but most other constructs are lazy. Take the example of an `if...else` structure:

```
val result = if (testCondition())
      getIfTrue()
    else
      getIfFalse()
```

Obviously, the `testCondition` function will always be evaluated. But only one of the `getIfTrue` and `getIfFalse` functions will be called, depending on the value returned by `testCondition`. Although the `if...else` structure is strict regarding the condition, it's lazy regarding the two branches. If `getIfTrue` and `getIfFalse` were effects, you couldn't do anything useful with a totally strict `if...else` because both effects would be executed in any case. On the contrary, if these were functions, it wouldn't change the outcome of the program. Both values would be computed, but only the one corresponding to the condition would be returned. This would be a waste of processing time, but it would still be usable.

Strictness and laziness apply not only to control structures and function arguments, but to everything in programming. For example, consider the following declaration:

```
val x: Int = 2 + 3
```

Here, x is immediately evaluated to 5. Because Kotlin is a strict language, it performs the addition immediately. Let's look at another example:

```
val x: Int = getValue()
```

In Kotlin, as soon as the x reference is declared, the getValue function is called to provide the corresponding value. On the other hand, with a lazy language, the getValue function would only be called if and when the value referenced by x were to be used. This can make a huge difference. For example, look at the following program:

```
fun main(args: Array<String>) {
    val x = getValue()
}

fun getValue(): Int {
    println("Returning 5")
    return 5
}
```

This program prints Returning 5 to the console because the getValue function will be called, although the returned value will never be used. In a lazy language, nothing would be evaluated, so nothing would be printed to the console.

9.8 Kotlin and strictness

Kotlin is supposed to be a strict language. Everything is evaluated immediately. Function arguments are said to be *passed by value*, which means they're first evaluated and then the evaluated value is passed. On the other hand, in lazy languages, arguments are said to be *passed by name*, which means unevaluated. Don't be confused by the fact that function arguments in Kotlin are often references. References are addresses, and these addresses are passed by value.

Some languages are strict (like Kotlin and Java), and others are lazy; some are strict by default and are optionally lazy, and others are lazy by default and are optionally strict. Kotlin, however, isn't always strict. These are some of Kotlin's lazy constructs:

- Boolean operators || and &&
- if ... else
- for loop
- while loop

Kotlin also offers lazy constructs such as Sequence, as well as the means to make property evaluation lazy, as you'll soon see.

Consider the Kotlin Boolean operators || and &&. These operators won't evaluate their operands if it isn't necessary for computing the result. If the first operand of || is true, the result is true, whatever the second operand, so there's no need to evaluate it. In the same way, if the first operand of the && operator is false, the result is false, whatever the second operand. Again, there's no need to evaluate it.

Does this remind you of something? In chapter 8, you created a special version of the foldLeft function that could escape the computation when an *absorbing element* (also called *zero element*) was encountered. Here, false is an absorbing element for the && operation and true is an absorbing element for the || operation.

Imagine that you want to simulate Boolean operators with functions. The following listing shows what you could do.

Listing 9.1 The and and or logical functions

```
fun main(args: Array<String>) {
    println(or(true, true))
    println(or(true, false))
    println(or(false, true))
    println(or(false, false))

    println(and(true, true))
    println(and(true, false))
    println(and(false, true))
    println(and(false, false))
}

fun or(a: Boolean, b: Boolean): Boolean = if (a) true else b

fun and(a: Boolean, b: Boolean): Boolean = if (a) b else false
```

Using the Boolean operators provides a simpler way to do this, but your goal here is to avoid these operators. Are you done? Running this program displays the following result on the console:

```
true
true
true
false
true
false
false
false
```

So far, so good. But now try running the program shown in the following listing.

Listing 9.2 The problem with strictness

```
fun main(args: Array<String>) {
    println(getFirst() || getSecond())
    println(or(getFirst(), getSecond()))
}

fun getFirst(): Boolean = true

fun getSecond(): Boolean = throw IllegalStateException()

fun or(a: Boolean, b: Boolean): Boolean = if (a) true else b

fun and(a: Boolean, b: Boolean): Boolean = if (a) b else false
```

This programs prints the following:

```
true
Exception in thread "main" java.lang.IllegalStateException
```

Obviously, the or function isn't equivalent to the || operator. The difference is that || evaluates its operand lazily, which means the second operand isn't evaluated if the first one is `true` because it's unnecessary for computing the result. But the `or` function evaluates its arguments strictly, which means that the second argument is evaluated even if its value isn't needed, so the `IllegalStateException` is always thrown. In chapters 6 and 7, you encountered this problem with the `getOrElse` function because its argument was always evaluated, even if the computation was successful.

9.9 *Kotlin and laziness*

Laziness is necessary on many occasions. Kotlin does, in fact, use laziness for constructs like `if...then`, loops, and `try...catch` blocks. Without this, a `catch` block, for example, would be evaluated even in the absence of an exception.

Implementing laziness is a must when it comes to providing behavior for errors, as well as when you need to manipulate infinite data structures. Kotlin provides a way to implement laziness through the use of a delegate. Here's how it works

```
val first: Boolean by Delegate()
```

where `Delegate` is a class implementing the following function:

```
operator fun getValue(thisRef: Any?, property: KProperty<*>): Boolean
```

Note two important things:

1 The `Delegate` class, which can have any name you choose, doesn't need to implement any interface. It must declare and implement the previous function, which will be called through reflection.

2 If you were declaring a `var` instead of a `val`, the `Delegate` class should also implement the corresponding function to set the `value:operator fun setValue(thisRef: Any?, property: KProperty<*>, value: Boolean)`.

Kotlin also supplies standard delegates, among which `Lazy` can be used to implement laziness:

```
val first: Boolean by lazy { ... }
```

This is a shorthand for using something like

```
class Lazy {
    operator fun getValue(thisRef: Any?,
                          property: KProperty<*>): Boolean = ...
}

val first: Boolean by Lazy()
```

The standard Kotlin `Lazy` interface is, however, slightly more sophisticated. Using this technique, the example that uses functions to implement the Boolean `or` operator becomes this:

```
fun main(args: Array<String>) {
    val first: Boolean by lazy { true }
    val second: Boolean by lazy { throw IllegalStateException() }
    println(first || second)
    println(or(first, second))
}

fun or(a: Boolean, b: Boolean): Boolean = if (a) true else b
```

Unfortunately, this isn't true laziness, as you can see by running this program:

```
true
Exception in thread "main" java.lang.IllegalStateException
```

What's happening here is that the functions used to initialize first and second aren't called when these references are declared; this is normal laziness. But the functions are called when the or function receives the arguments first and second instead of when those are actually needed, which would cause second to never be called because it would never be needed. This isn't laziness at all!

9.10 *Laziness implementations*

Implementing laziness in Kotlin in the same way as it's implemented in lazy languages isn't fully possible. But you can reach the same goal by using the right types. Think about what you did in chapters 5, 6, and 7. In chapter 7, you learned to abstract lists into two related concepts—the elements' type and something else, which was represented by the List type. This "something else" was a compound concept covering cardinality (there can be any number of elements including 0, 1, or more), as well as the fact that those elements were ordered. You could have pushed abstraction further by distinguishing cardinality and order. But let's think about the concept of List as a whole. The result was the parameterized type List<A>.

In chapter 6, you learned to abstract the concept of optionality into two related concepts: the type of the data (let's call it A) and the Option type. And in chapter 7, you learned to abstract the possibility of error into another compound type, Result<A>. As you can see, there's a pattern. On one side, you've a simple type A, and on the other side, you've a kind of modality applied to this simple type. Laziness can be considered another modality, so you can certainly implement it as a type. Let's call it Lazy<A>.

You could object that laziness can be represented in a much simpler way by using a constant function. As you know, because you've already used this concept in the previous chapters, a constant function is a function taking any argument of any type and always returning the same value. Such a function might have the following type:

```
() -> Int
```

Here the function returns an Int. To create a lazy integer value, you can write

```
val x: () -> Int = { 5 }
```

This is silly because 5 is a literal, and it makes no sense to lazily initialize a reference to a literal value. But if you switch back to our previous example using lazy Booleans, you get this:

```
fun main(args: Array<String>) {
    val first = { true }
    val second = { throw IllegalStateException() }
    println(first() || second())
    println(or(first, second))
}

fun or(a: () -> Boolean, b: () -> Boolean): Boolean = if (a()) true else b()
```

This works as expected, producing

```
true
true
```

One difference with laziness as it is implemented in lazy languages is that you've changed the types. A lazy A is not an A, so the or function had to be modified to conform to the new types.

But there's a much more important difference with true laziness: if you use the value twice, the function is called twice. Computing the value is a time-consuming operation. This wastes processor time. It's what's called a *call by name* evaluation, which means that the value isn't evaluated before being needed, but it's evaluated each time it's needed! You could get the same result by using a fun function, but you'd have to provide the return type for the function throwing an exception because Kotlin can't infer it:

```
fun main(args: Array<String>) {
    fun first() = true
    fun second(): Boolean = throw IllegalStateException()
    println(first() || second())
    println(or(::first, ::second))
}

fun or(a: () -> Boolean, b: () -> Boolean): Boolean = if (a()) true else b()
```

Can you think of a solution to solve this problem and only call the function the first time it's needed? This type of evaluation is called *call by need*. If you remember what you learned in chapter 4, you know the answer is memoization.

EXERCISE 9.1

Implement a Lazy<A> type that works like a memoized function () → A. It should be usable in the following example:

```
fun main(args: Array<String>) {
    val first = Lazy {
        println("Evaluating first")
        true
    }
    val second = Lazy {
        println("Evaluating second")
        throw IllegalStateException()
    }
    println(first() || second())
    println(first() || second())
    println(or(first, second))
}

fun or(a: Lazy<Boolean>, b: Lazy<Boolean>): Boolean = if (a()) true else b()
```

And this should produce the following result:

```
Evaluating first
true
true
true
```

HINT

If you make the Lazy type extend the function () → A, it should work fine. This isn't mandatory, but it'll simplify using the type. Use the by lazy construct for memoization and avoid explicit state mutation.

SOLUTION

Here's the solution based on the by lazy construct:

```
class Lazy<out A>(function: () -> A): () -> A {

    private val value: A by lazy(function)

    operator override fun invoke(): A = value
}
```

As you can see, this implementation makes no use of state mutation. State mutation is abstracted into the by lazy construct provided by Kotlin. In chapter 14, you'll learn how to use the same technique to abstract sharing mutable state.

9.10.1 *Composing lazy values*

In the previous example, you composed lazy Boolean values using the or function:

```
fun or(a: Lazy<Boolean>, b: Lazy<Boolean>): Boolean = if (a()) true else b()
```

But this was cheating because you were relying on the laziness of the if...else expression to avoid evaluating the second argument. Imagine a function composing two strings:

```
fun constructMessage(greetings: String,
                     name: String): String = "$greetings, $name!"
```

Now imagine that acquiring each parameter is a resource-consuming task, and you want to provide the result of the constructMessage in a lazy way, so that it might be used or not depending on an external condition. If this condition isn't met, the name and greetings strings should *not* be acquired. For the example, let's say that the condition is that a random integer should be even. Here's how it should work:

```
val greetings = Lazy {
    println("Evaluating greetings")
    "Hello"
}
val name: Lazy<String> = Lazy {
    println("computing name")
    "Mickey"
}

val message = constructMessage(greetings, name)
val condition = Random(System.currentTimeMillis()).nextInt() % 2 == 0
println(if (condition) <compose and print the message>
        else "No greetings when time is odd")
```

Now you have to refactor the constructMessage function so that it uses lazily evaluated arguments. You could use the following:

```
fun constructMessage(greetings: Lazy<String>,
                     name: Lazy<String>): String =
                            "${greetings()}, ${name()}!"
```

There would be no real benefit in using lazy values here because those would be evaluated before being concatenated when calling the constructMessage function, even if the condition wasn't met. What would be useful is a constructMessage function that would return a nonevaluated result, meaning a Lazy<String> without evaluating any of the parameters.

EXERCISE 9.2

Write a lazily evaluated version of the constructMessage function.

HINT

Verify that each part of the message is only evaluated once, whatever the number of calls to the function.

SOLUTION

Here's a function performing a lazy concatenation of the two arguments, along with the test for multiple evaluations:

```
fun constructMessage(greetings: Lazy<String>,
                     name: Lazy<String>): Lazy<String> =
                                  Lazy { "${greetings()}, ${name()}!" }

fun main(args: Array<String>) {
    val greetings = Lazy {
        println("Evaluating greetings")
        "Hello"
    }
    val name1: Lazy<String> = Lazy {
        println("Evaluating name")
        "Mickey"
    }
    val name2: Lazy<String> = Lazy {
        println("Evaluating name")
        "Donald"
    }
    val defaultMessage = Lazy {
        println("Evaluating default message")
        "No greetings when time is odd"
    }
    val message1 = constructMessage(greetings, name1)
    val message2 = constructMessage(greetings, name2)
    val condition = Random(System.currentTimeMillis()).nextInt() % 2 == 0
    println(if (condition) message1() else defaultMessage())
    println(if (condition) message1() else defaultMessage())
    println(if (condition) message2() else defaultMessage())
}
```

You should run the test several times. When the condition is met, you get

```
Evaluating greetings
Evaluating name
Hello, Mickey!
Hello, Mickey!
Evaluating name
Hello, Donald!
```

As you can see, the greeting argument is evaluated only once, and the name argument is evaluated twice (with two different values), even if the function is called three times.

NOTE   This isn't absolutely exact. From the function point of view, the arguments are evaluated each time the function is called as instances of Lazy, but only the first time causes the Lazy instances to be further evaluated.

When the condition isn't met, you get the following:

```
Evaluating default message
No greetings when time is odd
No greetings when time is odd
No greetings when time is odd
```

As you can see, only the default message is evaluated.

The condition has to be *external*, meaning it doesn't involve lazy data. Otherwise, the data would have to be evaluated in order to test the condition. It's also possible to define lazy val curried functions. You learned about curried functions in chapter 3.

EXERCISE 9.3

Write a lazy val curried version of the constructMessage function.

SOLUTION

No real difficulties here:

```
val constructMessage: (Lazy<String>) ->  (Lazy<String>) -> Lazy<String> =
       { greetings ->
           { name ->
               Lazy { "${greetings()}, ${name()}!" }
           }
       }

fun main(args: Array<String>) {
    val greetings = Lazy {
        println("Evaluating greetings")
        "Hello"
    }
    val name1: Lazy<String> = Lazy {
        println("Evaluating name")
        "Mickey"
    }
    val name2: Lazy<String> = Lazy {
        println("Evaluating name")
        "Donald"
    }
    val message1 = constructMessage(greetings)(name1)
    val message2 = constructMessage(greetings)(name2)
    val condition = Random(System.currentTimeMillis()).nextInt() % 2 == 0
    println(if (condition) message1() else defaultMessage())
    println(if (condition) message2() else defaultMessage())
}
```

The result is exactly the same, but the syntax for calling the function had to be adapted. This is a good example of the use of curried functions. You might need to greet many persons with the same message but with a different name. This could then be implemented as

```
val constructMessage: (Lazy<String>) ->  (Lazy<String>) -> Lazy<String> =
       { greetings ->
```

```
            { name ->
                Lazy { "${greetings()}, ${name()}!" }
            }
        }

fun main(args: Array<String>) {
    val greetings = Lazy {
        println("Evaluating greetings")
        "Hello"
    }
    val name1: Lazy<String> = Lazy {
        println("Evaluating name1")
        "Mickey"
    }
    val name2: Lazy<String> = Lazy {
        println("Evaluating name2")
        "Donald"
    }
    val defaultMessage = Lazy {
        println("Evaluating default message")
        "No greetings when time is odd"
    }
    val greetingString = constructMessage(greetings)
    val message1 = greetingString(name1)
    val message2 = greetingString(name2)
    val condition = Random(System.currentTimeMillis()).nextInt() % 2 == 0
    println(if (condition) message1() else defaultMessage())
    println(if (condition) message2() else defaultMessage())
}
```

9.10.2 Lifting functions

Often, you'll have a function working on some evaluated values and you'll want to use this function with unevaluated ones without causing evaluation. After all, this is the essence of programming.

EXERCISE 9.4

Create a function that takes as its argument a curried function of two evaluated arguments and returns the corresponding function for an unevaluated argument that produces the same, but nonevaluated result. Given the function

```
val consMessage: (String) -> (String) -> String =
    { greetings ->
        { name ->
            "$greetings, $name!"
        }
    }
```

write a function named lift2 that produces the following function (without evaluating any argument):

```
(Lazy<String>) -> (Lazy<String>) -> Lazy<String>
```

HINT

Put this function in the `Lazy` companion object in order to prevent clashing with another implementation of `lift2`. Alternatively, you can declare this function at package level and change its name, for example, to `liftLazy2`.

SOLUTION

First, write the signature of the function. The `lift2` function takes as its argument a function of type `(String)` → `(String)` → `String`. This argument type should be put between parentheses and followed by an arrow as shown here:

```
((String) -> (String) -> String) ->
```

Then write the return type of this function:

```
((String) -> (String) -> String) -> (Lazy<String>) ->   (Lazy<String>)
                                                       -> Lazy<String>
```

Add the `val lift2:` to the left of this expression and the equals sign to the right:

```
val lift2: ((String) -> (String) -> String) -> (Lazy<String>) ->
                               (Lazy<String>) -> Lazy<String> =
```

Now write the implementation. As it should produce a function of type

`(Lazy<String>)` → `(Lazy<String>)` → `Lazy<String>`,

you can start with

`{ f → { ls1 → { ls2 → TODO() } } },`

where f is of type `(String)` → `(String)` → `String)` (the function to lift) and `ls1` and `ls2` are of type `Lazy<String>`:

```
val lift2: ((String) -> (String) -> String) -> (Lazy<String>) ->
    (Lazy<String>) -> Lazy<String> =
        { f ->
            { ls1 ->
                { ls2 ->
                    TODO()
                }
            }
        }
```

The rest is now simple. You have a curried function of two `String` arguments and two instances of `Lazy<String>`. Get the values and apply the function. Because you want to get a `Lazy<String>`, create a `Lazy` instance of the result:

```
val lift2: ((String) -> (String) -> String) -> (Lazy<String>) ->
    (Lazy<String>) -> Lazy<String> =
        { f ->
            { ls1 ->
                { ls2 ->
                    Lazy { f(ls1())(ls2()) }
                }
            }
        }
```

Exercise 9.5

Generalize this function to work with any type. This time, write a fun function at package level.

Solution

Start with the signature. Because the function should work with any type, it should be parameterized with A, B, C, and the (unique) parameter is a function of type (A) → (B) → C. The return type is a function of type (Lazy<A>) → (Lazy<B>) → Lazy<C>:

```
fun <A, B, C> lift2(f: (A) -> (B) -> C): (Lazy<A>) -> (Lazy<B>) -> Lazy<C>
```

The implementation is similar to the one from exercise 4, except that the first parameter (the function) is no longer specified because it's the parameter of the fun function and the types are different:

```
fun <A, B, C> lift2(f: (A) -> (B) -> C):
              (Lazy<A>) -> (Lazy<B>) -> Lazy<C> =
        { ls1 ->
           { ls2 ->
              Lazy { f(ls1())(ls2()) }
           }
        }
```

9.10.3 Mapping and flatMapping Lazy

I'm sure you now understand that Lazy is another computational context like List, Option, and Result (and many others that you'll discover later), and you're tempted to map and flatMap it!

Exercise 9.6

Write a map function to apply a function (A) → B to a Lazy<A>, returning a Lazy<B>.

Hint

Define it as an instance function in the Lazy class.

Solution

All you have to do is apply the mapping function to the lazy value. In order not to trigger evaluation, wrap it in a new Lazy:

```
fun <B> map(f: (A) -> B): Lazy<B> = Lazy{ f(value) }
```

This can be tested with the following program:

```
fun main(args: Array<String>) {

    val greets: (String) -> String = { "Hello, $it!" }

    val name: Lazy<String> = Lazy {
        println("Evaluating name")
        "Mickey"
    }
    val defaultMessage = Lazy {
        println("Evaluating default message")
        "No greetings when time is odd"
    }
```

```
    val message = name.map(greets)
    val condition = Random(System.currentTimeMillis()).nextInt() % 2 == 0
    println(if (condition) message() else defaultMessage())
    println(if (condition) message() else defaultMessage())
}
```

If the condition holds, this program prints the following, showing that data is evaluated only once even if it's used twice:

```
Evaluating name
Hello, Mickey!
Hello, Mickey!
```

If the condition doesn't hold, the program output shows that the default message is evaluated only once:

```
Evaluating default message
No greetings when time is odd
No greetings when time is odd
```

EXERCISE 9.7

Write a flatMap function to apply a function (A) → Lazy<B> to a Lazy<A>, returning a Lazy<B>.

HINT

Define it as an instance function in the Lazy class.

SOLUTION

All you have to do is apply the mapping function to the lazy value and trigger evaluation. But as you don't want this to happen until needed, wrap the whole thing a new Lazy:

```
fun <B> flatMap(f: (A) -> Lazy<B>): Lazy<B> = Lazy { f(value)() }
```

This can be tested with the following program:

```
fun main(args: Array<String>) {

    // Imagine getGreetings is a costly function with the side effect
    // of printing "Evaluating greetings" to the console
    val greetings: Lazy<String> = Lazy { getGreetings(Locale.US) }

    val flatGreets: (String) -> Lazy<String> =
                        { name -> greetings.map { "$it, $name!"} }

    val name: Lazy<String> = Lazy {
        println("computing name")
        "Mickey"
    }
    val defaultMessage = Lazy {
        println("Evaluating default message")
        "No greetings when time is odd"
    }
    val message = name.flatMap(flatGreets)
    val condition = Random(System.currentTimeMillis()).nextInt() % 2 == 0
    println(if (condition) message() else defaultMessage())
    println(if (condition) message() else defaultMessage())
}
```

If the condition holds, this program prints the following, showing that both the name and the greeting message are evaluated only once, even if they're used twice:

```
Evaluating name
Evaluating greetings
Hello, Mickey!
Hello, Mickey!
```

If the condition doesn't hold, the program output shows that only the default message is evaluated, and only once:

```
Evaluating default message
No greetings when time is odd
No greetings when time is odd
```

9.10.4 *Composing Lazy with List*

The Lazy type can be composed with other types you've developed in previous chapters. One of the most common operations is transforming a List<Lazy<A>> into a Lazy<List<A>>, so that the list might lazily be composed with functions of A. This kind of composition must be done without evaluating the data.

EXERCISE 9.8

Define a sequence function with the following signature:

```
fun <A> sequence(lst: List<Lazy<A>>): Lazy<List<A>>
```

This will be a fun function defined at package level.

SOLUTION

Again, the solution is simple. You need to map the list with a function evaluating the content of each element. But because the sequence function mustn't evaluate anything, wrap this operation in a new Lazy instance:

```
fun <A> sequence(lst: List<Lazy<A>>): Lazy<List<A>> =
                        Lazy { lst.map { it() } }
```

Here's an example program showing the output of this function:

```
fun main(args: Array<String>) {

    val name1: Lazy<String> = Lazy {
        println("Evaluating name1")
        "Mickey"
    }

    val name2: Lazy<String> = Lazy {
        println("Evaluating name2")
        "Donald"
    }

    val name3 = Lazy {
        println("Evaluating name3")
        "Goofy"
    }
    val list = sequence(List(name1, name2, name3))
    val defaultMessage = "No greetings when time is odd"
    val condition = Random(System.currentTimeMillis()).nextInt() % 2 == 0
```

```
    println(if (condition) list() else defaultMessage)
    println(if (condition) list() else defaultMessage)
}
```

Again, depending on an external condition, the (unevaluated) result or a default message is displayed twice. When the condition holds, the result is printed twice, producing a single evaluation of all elements:

```
Evaluating name1
Evaluating name2
Evaluating name3
[Mickey, Donald, Goofy, NIL]
[Mickey, Donald, Goofy, NIL]
```

When the condition doesn't hold, nothing is evaluated:

```
No greetings when time is odd
No greetings when time is odd
```

9.10.5 *Dealing with exceptions*

When you're working with your own functions, you might not fear exceptions if you're confident that your code will never produce any. When dealing with unevaluated data, however, you're at risk of seeing an exception thrown during evaluation.

Evaluating a single piece of data throwing an exception is nothing special. But evaluating a list of Lazy<A> is more problematic. What should you do if one element throws an exception during evaluation?

EXERCISE 9.9

Write a sequenceResult function with the following signature:

```
fun <A> sequenceResult(lst: List<Lazy<A>>): Lazy<Result<List<A>>>
```

This function should return a Result of List<A> that's not evaluated and that will turn into a Success<List<A>> if all evaluations succeed or a Failure<List<A>> otherwise. Here's an example of a test use case:

```
fun main(args: Array<String>) {

    val name1: Lazy<String> = Lazy {
        println("Evaluating name1")
        "Mickey"
    }

    val name2: Lazy<String> = Lazy {
        println("Evaluating name2")
        "Donald"
    }

    val name3 = Lazy {
        println("Evaluating name3")
        "Goofy"
    }

    val name4 = Lazy {
        println("Evaluating name4")
        throw IllegalStateException("Exception while evaluating name4")
```

```
    }
        val list1 = sequenceResult(List(name1, name2, name3))
        val list2 = sequenceResult(List(name1, name2, name3, name4))
        val defaultMessage = "No greetings when time is odd"
        val condition = Random(System.currentTimeMillis()).nextInt() % 2 == 0
        println(if (condition) list1() else defaultMessage)
        println(if (condition) list1() else defaultMessage)
        println(if (condition) list2() else defaultMessage)
        println(if (condition) list2() else defaultMessage)
}
```

When the condition holds, the program output should be

```
Evaluating name1
Evaluating name2
Evaluating name3
Success([Mickey, Donald, Goofy, NIL])
Success([Mickey, Donald, Goofy, NIL])
Evaluating name4
Failure(Exception while evaluating name4)
Failure(Exception while evaluating name4)
```

And when the condition doesn't hold, you should get

```
No greetings when time is odd
No greetings when time is odd
No greetings when time is odd
No greetings when time is odd
```

SOLUTION

As in the previous exercise, you need to combine instructions to produce the intended result. Once this is done, wrap the implementation into a new Lazy:

```
import com.fpinkotlin.common.sequence

...

fun <A> sequenceResult(lst: List<Lazy<A>>): Lazy<Result<List<A>>> =
        Lazy { sequence(lst.map { Result.of(it) }) }
```

You also need to explicitly import the sequence function. This makes the distinction with the sequence function defined at a package level. Another possibility is to use the traverse function you created in chapter 8:

```
fun <A> sequenceResult2(lst: List<Lazy<A>>): Lazy<Result<List<A>>> =
        Lazy { traverse(lst) { Result.of(it) } }
```

Evaluating the result causes all elements of the list to be evaluated, even if one evaluation results in a Failure. The reason is that the traverse function uses the foldRight function. To make evaluation stop as soon as one element evaluates to a Failure, you'd have to use an escaping fold. The implementation based on traverse is equivalent to

```
fun <A> sequenceResult(lst: List<Lazy<A>>): Lazy<Result<List<A>>> =
    Lazy {
        lst.foldRight(Result(List())) { x: Lazy<A> ->
            { y: Result<List<A>> ->
                map2(Result.of(x), y) { a: A ->
```

```
                                        { b: List<A> ->
                                            b.cons(a)
                                        }
                                    }
```

You don't have an escaping `foldRight`, but you developed an escaping `foldLeft` in chapter 8. You can use it here:

```
fun <A> sequenceResult(list: List<Lazy<A>>): Lazy<Result<List<A>>> =
    Lazy {
        val p = { r: Result<List<A>> -> r.map{false}.getOrElse(true) }
        list.foldLeft(Result(List()), p) { y: Result<List<A>> ->
            { x: Lazy<A> ->
                map2(Result.of(x), y) { a: A ->
                    { b: List<A> ->
                        b.cons(a)
                    }
                }
            }
        }
    }
```

You could define an escaping `traverse` in the list class in order to abstract this process.

9.11 *Further lazy compositions*

As you can see, lazily composing functions is a matter of writing the normal composition and wrapping it into a `Lazy` instance. With this technique, you can compose anything you want in a lazy way. There's no magic here. You can always do the same by wrapping any implementation in a constant function:

```
fun <A> lazyComposition(): Lazy<A> =
        Lazy { <anything producing an A> }
```

Here you are simply writing a program that's executed when and if the `Lazy` instance is invoked.

9.11.1 *Lazily applying effects*

If you used the provided test programs for the previous exercises, you already know how to apply effects to lazy values. You can get the value by invoking Lazy and apply the effect to the result, such as

```
val lazyString: Lazy<String> = ...
...
println(lazyString())
```

But instead of getting the value out of the `Lazy` and applying the effect, you can go the other way round and pass the effect to the `Lazy` to have it applied to the value:

```
fun forEach(ef: (A) -> Unit) = ef(value)
```

But this isn't very useful if you want to conditionally apply an effect such as what you did in the previous tests:

```
if (condition) list1.forEach { println(it) } else println(defaultMessage)
```

What you would need to do is pass the condition an effect to apply if the condition holds and another effect to apply otherwise.

EXERCISE 9.10

Write a forEach function (a method) in the Lazy class, taking as its parameters a condition and two effects and applying the first effect to the contained value if the condition is true and the second effect otherwise.

HINT

To make this function useful, it should allow evaluating the Lazy only if needed. Consequently, you'll need to define three overloaded versions of the function.

SOLUTION

You could be tempted to write something like

```
fun forEach(condition: Boolean, ifTrue: (A) -> Unit, ifFalse: (A) -> Unit) =
    if (condition) ifTrue(value) else ifFalse(value)
```

But this won't work because Kotlin evaluates the arguments of the functions ifTrue and ifFalse as soon as those are received by the forEach function. It makes no difference if both ifTrue and ifFalse use the value. But often, the ifFalse condition won't use it, such as in the following:

```
list1.forEach(condition, ::println, { println(defaultMessage)} )
```

Because the ifFalse handler doesn't use the value, it shouldn't be evaluated. But it could also be the contrary, meaning that the value would be used if the condition doesn't hold. Of course, you could revert (negate) the condition. But you must also take care of the case when both handler would need to evaluate the Lazy. A possible solution is then to write three versions of the function

```
fun forEach(condition: Boolean,
        ifTrue: (A) -> Unit,
        ifFalse: () -> Unit = {}) =
    if (condition)
        ifTrue(value)
    else
        ifFalse()

fun forEach(condition: Boolean,
        ifTrue: () -> Unit = {},
        ifFalse: (A) -> Unit) =
    if (condition)
        ifTrue()
    else
        ifFalse(value)

fun forEach(condition: Boolean,
        ifTrue: (A) -> Unit,
        ifFalse: (A) -> Unit) =
    if (condition)
        ifTrue(value)
    else
        ifFalse(value)
```

Be aware, however, of two problems. To allow Kotlin to select the right function, you'll have to specify explicitly the type of each handler such as in this example:

```
val printMessage: (Any) -> Unit = ::println
val printDefault: () -> Unit = { println(defaultMessage)}
list1.forEach(condition, printMessage, printDefault)
```

The reason for this is that a handler such as {} is valid for arguments of both types (A) → Unit and () → Unit.

If you want to use the default value for the ifTrue: () → Unit argument (meaning doing nothing), you'll have to name the argument on the call site:

```
val printMessage: (Any) -> Unit = ::println
list1.forEach(condition, ifFalse = printMessage)
```

9.11.2 *Things you can't do without laziness*

So far it may seem that the absence of true laziness in evaluating expressions in Kotlin isn't a big deal. After all, why should you bother rewriting Boolean functions when you can use Boolean operators? There are, however, other cases where laziness is really useful. There are even several algorithms that can't be implemented without resorting to laziness. I've already talked about how useless a strict version of if ... else would be. But think about the following algorithm:

1 Take the list of positive integers.
2 Filter the primes.
3 Return the list of the first ten results.

This is an algorithm for finding the first ten primes, but this algorithm can't be implemented without laziness. If you don't believe me, try it. Start with the first line. If you're strict, you'll first evaluate the list of positive integers. You'll never have the opportunity to go to the second line because the list of integers is infinite, and you'll exhaust available memory before reaching the (nonexistent) end.

Clearly, this algorithm can't be implemented without laziness, but you know how to replace it with a different algorithm. The preceding algorithm was functional. If you want to find the result without resorting to laziness, you'll have to replace it with an imperative algorithm, like this one:

1 Take the first integer.
2 Check whether it's a prime.
3 If it is, store it in a list.
4 Check whether the resulting list has ten elements.
5 If it has ten elements, return it as the result.
6 If not, increment the integer by 1.
7 Go to line 2.

Sure, it works. But what a mess! First, it's a bad recipe. Shouldn't you increment the tested integer by 2 rather than by 1 in order to *not* test even numbers? And why test multiples of 3, 5, and so on? But more importantly, it doesn't express the nature of the problem. It's only a recipe for computing the result.

This isn't to say that the implementation details (such as not testing even numbers) aren't important for getting good performance. But these implementation details should be clearly separated from the problem definition. The imperative description isn't a description of the problem. It's a description of another problem giving the same result. A much more elegant solution is to solve this kind of problem with a special structure: the lazy list.

9.11.3 Creating a lazy list data structure

Now that you know how to represent non-evaluated data as instances of `Lazy`, you can easily define a lazy list data structure. You'll call it `Stream`, and it'll be similar to the singly linked list you developed in chapter 5 with some subtle, but important, differences. The following listing shows the starting point of your `Stream` data type.

Listing 9.3　The `Stream` data type

The Lazy class isn't imported here because it's in the same package.

The Stream class is sealed to prevent direct instantiation.

```
import com.fpinkotlin.common.Result


sealed class Stream<out A> {

    abstract fun isEmpty(): Boolean

    abstract fun head(): Result<A>

    abstract fun tail(): Result<Stream<A>>

    private object Empty: Stream<Nothing>() {

        override fun head(): Result<Nothing> = Result()

        override fun tail(): Result<Nothing> = Result()

        override fun isEmpty(): Boolean = true

    }

    private
    class Cons<out A> (internal val hd: Lazy<A>,
                       internal val tl: Lazy<Stream<A>>):
                                       Stream<A>() {

        override fun head(): Result<A> = Result(hd())

        override fun tail(): Result<Stream<A>> = Result(tl())
```

The head function returns a Result<A> so that it can return Empty when called on an empty stream.

For the same reason, the tail function returns a Result<Stream<A>>.

The Empty subclass is exactly the same as the List.Nil subclass.

A non-empty stream represented by the Cons subclass.

The head (called hd) is non-evaluated, taking the form of a Lazy<A>.

Similarly, the tail (tl) is represented by a Lazy<Stream<A>>.

```
        override fun isEmpty(): Boolean = false
    }

    companion object {
```

> **The cons function constructs a Stream by calling the private Cons constructor.**

```
        fun <A> cons(hd: Lazy<A>,
                    tl: Lazy<Stream<A>>): Stream<A> =
                                Cons(hd, tl)

        operator fun <A> invoke(): Stream<A> =
                        Empty
```

> **The invoke operator function returns the Empty singleton object.**

```
        fun from(i: Int): Stream<Int> =
            cons(Lazy { i }, Lazy { from(i + 1) })
    }
}
```

> **The from factory function returns an infinite stream of successive integers starting from the given value.**

Here's an example of how to use this `Stream` type:

```
fun main(args: Array<String>) {
    val stream = Stream.from(1)
    stream.head().forEach({ println(it) })
    stream.tail().flatMap { it.head() }.forEach({ println(it) })
    stream.tail().flatMap {
            it.tail().flatMap { it.head() }
        }.forEach({ println(it) })
}
```

This program prints the following:

```
1
2
3
```

This probably doesn't seem useful. To make `Stream` a valuable tool, you'll need to add some functions to it. But first, you must optimize it slightly.

> **NOTE** It's important to understand the difference between the `Stream` described in this chapter, which is a lazily evaluated list, and what Java calls `Stream`, which are generators. *Generators* are functions that compute the next element from some current state, which might be the previous element or anything else. In particular, this external state can be an already evaluated indexed collection plus an index. This is the case when you use a Java construct such as
>
> ```
> List<A> list = ....
> list.stream()...
> ```

In this Java example, the generator uses the pair (list, index) as the mutable state from which the new value is generated. In such a case, the generator depends on an external mutable state. On the other hand, once the value is evaluated (through a terminal operation), the stream can no longer be used. Kotlin also offers generators such as the `Sequence` construct, although unlike Java, it doesn't handle parallel processing.

This is different from the `Stream` you're defining, in which data is unevaluated but can become partially evaluated while not preventing reusing the stream. In the previous example, you caused evaluation of the first three values of the stream, but this doesn't prevent reusing the stream, as you can see in the following example:

```
fun main(args: Array<String>) {
    val stream = Stream.from(1)
    stream.head().forEach({ println(it) })
    stream.tail().flatMap { it.head() }.forEach({ println(it) })
    stream.tail().flatMap { it.tail()
            .flatMap { it.head() } }.forEach({ println(it) })
    stream.head().forEach({ println(it) })
    stream.tail().flatMap { it.head() }.forEach({ println(it) })
    stream.tail().flatMap { it.tail()
            .flatMap { it.head() } }.forEach({ println(it) })
}
```

This programs displays

```
1
2
3
1
2
3
```

On the other hand, the following Java program would cause an `IllegalStateException` with the message "stream has already been operated upon or closed":

```
public class TestStream {
    public static void main(String... args) {
        Stream<Integer> stream = Stream.iterate(0, i -> i + 1);
        stream.findFirst().ifPresent(System.out::println);
        stream.findFirst().ifPresent(System.out::println);
    }
}
```

Kotlin offers the `Sequence` construct that allows reuse, but it doesn't memoize the generated values, so it's not a lazy list either.

9.12 *Handling streams*

In the rest of this chapter, you'll learn how to create and compose streams while making the most of the fact that the data is unevaluated. But in order to look at the streams, you'll need a function to evaluate them. And to evaluate a stream, you need a function to limit its length. You wouldn't want to evaluate an infinite stream, would you?

EXERCISE 9.11

Create a function `repeat` taking as its argument a function of type `() → A` and returning a stream of A.

SOLUTION

There's no difficulty here. You need to construct (cons) a lazy call to the function argument with a lazy call to the `repeat` function itself:

```
fun <A> repeat(f: () -> A): Stream<A> =
            cons(Lazy { f() }, Lazy { repeat(f) })
```

This function won't cause any stack problem because the call to the `repeat` function is lazy.

EXERCISE 9.12

Create a `takeAtMost` function to limit the length of a stream to at most *n* elements. This function should work on any stream, even if it has fewer than *n* elements. Here's its signature:

```
fun takeAtMost(n: Int): Stream<A>
```

HINT

Declare an abstract function in the `Stream` class and implement it in both subclasses using recursion when needed.

SOLUTION

The `Empty` implementation returns `this`:

```
override fun takeAtMost(n: Int): Stream<Nothing> = this
```

The `Cons` implementation tests whether the argument n is larger that 0. If it is, it returns the head of the stream "consed" with the result of recursively applying the `takeAtMost` function to the tail with argument n - 1. If n is less than or equals 0, it returns the empty stream:

```
override fun takeAtMost(n: Int): Stream<A> = when {
    n > 0 -> cons(hd, Lazy { tl().takeAtMost(n - 1) })
    else -> Empty
}
```

EXERCISE 9.13

Create a `dropAtMost` function to remove at most *n* elements from the stream. This function should work on any stream, even if it has less that *n* elements. Here's its signature:

```
fun dropAtMost(n: Int): Stream<A>
```

HINT

Declare an abstract function in the `Stream` class and implement it in both subclasses using recursion when needed.

SOLUTION

The `Empty` implementation returns this:

```
override fun dropAtMost(n: Int): Stream<Nothing> = this
```

The `Cons` implementation tests whether the argument n is larger than 0. If it is, it returns the result of recursively calling the `dropAtMost` function on the tail of the stream with the argument n - 1. If n is less than or equals to 0, it returns the current stream:

```
override fun dropAtMost(n: Int): Stream<A> =  when {
    n > 0 -> tl().dropAtMost(n - 1)
    else -> this
}
```

EXERCISE 9.14

Think about the two functions takeAtMost and dropAtaMost from the perspective of recursion. What might happen if you call those functions with high value parameters? If you can't figure out the answer, consider the following example:

```
fun main(args: Array<String>) {
    val stream = Stream.repeat(::random).dropAtMost(60000).takeAtMost(60000)
    stream.head().forEach(::println)
}

val rnd = Random()

fun random(): Int {
    val rnd = rnd.nextInt()
    println("evaluating $rnd")
    return rnd
}
```

This test causes a StackOverflowException without evaluating anything! Can you fix this?

SOLUTION

In this example, takeAtMost isn't causing any problem because it's being lazy; nothing will be evaluated past the 60,001st value. On the other hand, the dropAtMost function has to call itself recursively 60,000 times in order for the resulting stream to start with the 60,001st element. This recursion occurs even if no element is evaluated.

The solution is to make dropAtMost corecursive, which usually necessitates using two additional arguments: the stream on which the function is operating and an accumulator for the result. But in this particular case, you don't need an accumulator because the result of each recursive step is ignored. Only the new stream (with one element removed) and the new Int parameter (decreased by one) are needed. Here's the resulting function in the companion object:

```
tailrec fun <A> dropAtMost(n: Int, stream: Stream<A>): Stream<A> =  when {
    n > 0 -> when (stream) {
        is Empty -> stream
        is Cons -> dropAtMost(n - 1, stream.tl())
    }
    else -> stream
}
```

As you can see, if n has reached 0 or if the stream is empty, the stream argument is returned. Otherwise, the function is recursively called on the tail of the stream after decreasing the n parameter. To simplify using this function, the following instance function is added to the Stream class:

```
fun dropAtMost(n: Int): Stream<A> = dropAtMost(n, this)
```

EXERCISE 9.15

In the previous exercise, I said that the takeAtMost function is not creating any stack problem because it's lazy, so nothing is evaluated. You may wonder what happens when the stream is eventually evaluated. To test this case, create a `toList` function turning a stream into a list, evaluating all elements. Use this function to check that the `takeAt-Most` function is harmless by running the following test program:

```
fun main(args: Array<String>) {
    val stream = Stream.from(0).dropAtMost(60000).takeAtMost(60000)
    println(stream.toList())
}
```

HINT

Write a main function in the `Stream` class calling a corecursive helper function in the companion object.

SOLUTION

The function in the companion object will use a corecursive helper function taking a `List<A>` as its accumulator parameter. If the stream is `Empty`, the function returns the accumulator list. Otherwise, it calls itself recursively after having added the head of the stream to the list and using the tail of the stream as its second parameter. The main function calls the helper function with an empty list as the starting accumulator and reverses the resulting list before returning it:

```
fun <A> toList(stream: Stream<A>) : List<A> {
    tailrec
    fun <A> toList(list: List<A>, stream: Stream<A>) : List<A> =
        when (stream) {
            Empty -> list
            is Cons -> toList(list.cons(stream.hd()), stream.tl())
        }
    return toList(List(), stream).reverse()
}
```

An instance function is added to the `Stream` class in order to allow calling it with object notation:

```
fun toList(): List<A> = toList(this)
```

EXERCISE 9.16

Up to now, the only stream you could create was an infinite stream of consecutive integers or a stream of random elements. To make the `Stream` class a bit more useful, create an `iterate` function taking a seed of type A and a function from A to A and returning an infinite stream of A. Then, redefine the `from` function in terms of `iterate`.

SOLUTION

The solution consists in using the `cons` function to create a stream from seed as the head and a lazy recursive call to the `iterate` function using f(seed) as the tail:

```
fun <A> iterate(seed: A, f: (A) -> A): Stream<A> =
            cons(Lazy { seed }, Lazy { iterate(f(seed), f) })
```

Although this function is recursive, it won't blow the stack because the recursive call is lazy. With this function, you can redefine `from` as

```
fun from(i: Int): Stream<Int> = iterate(i) { it + 1 }
```

An interesting use of this function is checking what's evaluated. If you create a function with side effects such as this one

```
fun inc(i: Int): Int = (i + 1).let {
    println("generating $it")
    it
}
```

you can check that the following test program only evaluates values from 0 to 10,010 before printing a list of 10 values from 10,000 to 10,009:

```
fun main(args: Array<String>) {
    fun inc(i: Int): Int = (i + 1).let {
        println("generating $it")
        it
    }
    val list = Stream
                    .iterate(0, ::inc)
                    .takeAtMost(60000)
                    .dropAtMost(10000)
                    .takeAtMost(10)
                    .toList()
    println(list)
}
```

You could also create an `iterate` function taking a Lazy<A> as its seed if you needed to start with an unevaluated seed:

```
fun <A> iterate(seed: Lazy<A>, f: (A) -> A): Stream<A> =
                    cons(seed, Lazy { iterate(f(seed()), f) })
```

EXERCISE 9.17

Write a `takeWhile` function that returns a `Stream` containing all starting elements as long as a condition is matched. Here's the function signature in the `Stream` parent class:

```
abstract fun takeWhile(p: (A) -> Boolean): Stream<A>
```

HINT

Be aware that unlike `takeAtMost` and `dropAtMost`, this function evaluates one element because it'll have to test the first element to verify whether it fulfills the condition expressed by the predicate. You should verify that only the first element of the stream is evaluated.

SOLUTION

This function is similar to the `takeAtMost` function. The main difference is that the terminal condition is no longer n ≤ 0 but the provided function returning `false`:

```
override fun takeWhile(p: (A) -> Boolean): Stream<A> = when {
    p(hd()) -> cons(hd, Lazy { tl().takeWhile(p) })
    else -> Empty
}
```

Once again, you don't need to make the function stack-safe because the recursive call is unevaluated. The `Empty` implementation returns `this`.

EXERCISE 9.18

Write a `dropWhile` function that returns a stream with the front elements removed as long as they satisfy a condition. Here's the signature in the `Stream` parent class:

```
fun dropWhile(p: (A) -> Boolean): Stream<A>
```

HINT

You'll need to write a corecursive version of this function in order to make it stack-safe.

SOLUTION

As in previous recursive functions, the solution will include a function in the `Stream` class calling a stack-safe corecursive helper function in the companion object. Here's the corecursive function in the companion object:

```
tailrec fun <A> dropWhile(stream: Stream<A>,
                          p: (A) -> Boolean): Stream<A> =
        when (stream) {
            is Empty -> stream
            is Cons -> when {
                p(stream.hd()) -> dropWhile(stream.tl(), p)
                else -> stream
            }
        }
```

And here's the main function in the `Stream` parent class:

```
fun dropWhile(p: (A) -> Boolean): Stream<A> = dropWhile(this, p)
```

EXERCISE 9.19

In chapter 8, you created the following `exists` function that was first implemented in the `List` class as

```
fun exists(p:(A) -> Boolean): Boolean =
    when (this) {
        Nil -> false
        is Cons -> p(head) || tail.exists(p)
    }
```

This function traversed the list until an element was found satisfying the predicate p. The rest of the list wasn't examined because the `||` operator is lazy and doesn't evaluate its second argument if the first one evaluates to `true`.

Create an `exists` function for `Stream`. The function should cause elements to be evaluated only until the condition is met. If the condition is never met, all elements will be evaluated.

SOLUTION

A simple solution could be similar to the `exists` function in `List`:

```
fun exists(p: (A) -> Boolean): Boolean = p(hd()) || tl().exists(p)
```

You should make it stack-safe. In order to write a stack-safe implementation, you must make it tail-recursive. Here's a possible implementation in the companion object:

```
tailrec fun <A> exists(stream: Stream<A>, p: (A) -> Boolean): Boolean =
    when (stream) {
        Empty -> false
        is Cons  -> when {
            p(stream.hd()) -> true
            else           -> exists(stream.tl(), p)
        }
    }
```

And here's the main function in the `Stream` class:

```
fun exists(p: (A) -> Boolean): Boolean = exists(this, p)
```

9.12.1 Folding streams

In chapter 5, you saw how to abstract recursion into fold functions, and you learned how to fold lists right or left. Folding streams is a bit different. Although the principle is the same, the main difference is that streams are unevaluated.

A recursive operation could overflow the stack and cause a `StackOverflowException` to be thrown, but a description of a recursive operation won't. The consequence is that in many cases `foldRight`, which can't be made stack-safe in `List`, won't overflow the stack in `Stream`. It will overflow it, however, if it implies evaluating each operation, such as adding the elements of a `Stream<Int>`. It won't if instead of evaluating an operation, it constructs a description of an unevaluated one.

Conversely, the `List` implementation of `foldRight` based on `foldLeft` (which can be made stack-safe) can't be used with streams because it requires reversing the stream. This would cause the evaluation of all elements; it might even be impossible in the case of an infinite stream. And the stack-safe version of `foldLeft` can't be used either because it inverts the direction of the computation.

EXERCISE 9.20

Create a `foldRight` function for streams. This function will be similar to the `List.foldRight` function, but you should take care of laziness.

HINT

Laziness is expressed by the elements being `Lazy<A>` instead of `A`. The signature of the function in the `Stream` parent class will be

```
abstract fun <B> foldRight(z: Lazy<B>,
                           f: (A) -> (Lazy<B>) -> B): B
```

SOLUTION

The implementation in the `Empty` class is obvious:

```
override fun <B> foldRight(z: Lazy<B>,
                           f: (Nothing) -> (Lazy<B>) -> B): B = z()
```

And here's the `Cons` implementation:

```
override fun <B> foldRight(z: Lazy<B>,
                           f: (A) -> (Lazy<B>) -> B): B =
                            f(hd())(Lazy { tl().foldRight(z, f) })
```

This function isn't stack-safe, so it shouldn't be used for such computations as the sum of a list of more than about a thousand integers. You'll see, however, that it has many interesting use cases.

EXERCISE 9.21

Implement the `takeWhile` function in terms of `foldRight`, calling it `takeWhileViaFoldRight`. Verify how it behaves on long lists.

SOLUTION

The starting value is a `Lazy` of an empty stream. The function tests the current element (`p(a)`). If the result is true (meaning that the element fulfills the condition expressed by the predicate p), a stream is returned by "consing" a `Lazy { a }` to the current stream:

```
fun takeWhileViaFoldRight(p: (A) -> Boolean): Stream<A> =
    foldRight(Lazy { Empty }, { a ->
        { b: Lazy<Stream<A>> ->
            if (p(a))
                cons(Lazy { a }, b)
            else
                Empty
        }
    })
```

As you can verify by running the tests provided in the code accompanying this book (https://github.com/pysaumont/fpinkotlin), this function won't overflow the stack, even for streams longer than one million elements. This is because `foldRight` doesn't evaluate the result by itself. Evaluation depends on the function used to make the fold. If this function constructs a new stream (as it does in the case of `takeWhile`), this stream isn't evaluated.

EXERCISE 9.22

Implement `headSafe` using `foldRight`. This function should return either a `Result`.`Success` of the head element or `Result`.`Empty` if the stream is empty.

SOLUTION

The starting element is a non-evaluated empty stream (`Lazy { Empty }`). This'll be the returned value if the stream is empty. The function used to fold the stream ignores the second argument, so the first time it's applied to the hd element, it returns `Result(a)`. This result never changes:

```
fun headSafeViaFoldRight(): Result<A> =
    foldRight(Lazy { Result<A>() }, { a -> { Result(a) } })
```

EXERCISE 9.23

Implement `map` in terms of `foldRight`. Verify that this function doesn't evaluate any of the stream elements.

SOLUTION

Start with a `Lazy` of an empty stream. The function used to make the fold will `cons` a non-evaluated application of the function to the current element with the current result:

```
fun <B> map(f: (A) -> B): Stream<B> =
    foldRight(Lazy { Empty }, { a ->
        { b: Lazy<Stream<B>> ->
            cons(Lazy { f(a) }, b)
        }
    })
```

EXERCISE 9.24

Implement `filter` in terms of `foldRight`. Verify that this function doesn't evaluate more stream elements than needed.

SOLUTION

Again, start with a non-evaluated empty stream. The function used to fold applies the filter to the current argument. If the result is `true`, the element is used to create a new stream by "consing" it with the current stream result. Otherwise, the current stream result is left unchanged (calling `b()` doesn't evaluate any elements):

```
fun filter(p: (A) -> Boolean): Stream<A> =
    foldRight(Lazy { Empty }, { a ->
        { b: Lazy<Stream<A>> ->
            if (p(a)) cons(Lazy { a }, b) else b()
        }
    })
```

This function evaluates the stream elements until the first match is found. See the corresponding tests in the accompanying code for details.

EXERCISE 9.25

Implement `append` in terms of `foldRight`. The append function should be lazy in its argument.

HINT

Beware of variance!

SOLUTION

This function takes a `Lazy<Stream<A>>` as its argument, so `A` is in the `in` position, although the parameter of the `Stream` class is declared `out`. As a result, you must disable variance checking by using the `@UnsafeVariance` annotation.

The starting element is the (non-evaluated) stream you want to append. The folding function creates a new stream by adding the current element to the current result using the cons function:

```
fun append(stream2: Lazy<Stream<@UnsafeVariance A>>): Stream<A> =
        this.foldRight(stream2) { a: A ->
            { b: Lazy<Stream<A>> ->
                Stream.cons(Lazy { a }, b)
            }
        }
```

EXERCISE 9.26

Implement flatMap in terms of foldRight.

SOLUTION

Again, you start with an unevaluated empty stream. The function is applied to the current element, producing a stream to which the current result is appended. This has the effect of flattening the result (transforming a Stream<Stream<B>> into a Stream<B>):

```
fun <B> flatMap(f: (A) -> Stream<B>): Stream<B> =
    foldRight(Lazy { Empty as Stream<B> }, { a ->
        { b: Lazy<Stream<B>> ->
            f(a).append(b)
        }
    })
```

9.12.2 *Tracing evaluation and function application*

It's important to notice the consequence of laziness. With strict collections such as lists, applying a map, a filter, and a new map successively would imply iterating over the list three times as shown here:

```
import com.fpinkotlin.common.List

private val f = { x: Int ->
    println("Mapping " + x)
    x * 3
}

private val p = { x: Int ->
    println("Filtering " + x)
    x % 2 == 0
}

fun main(args: Array<String>) {
    val list = List(1, 2, 3, 4, 5).map(f).filter(p)
    println(list)
}
```

As you can see, functions f and p aren't pure functions because they log to the console. This'll help you understanding what's happening. This program prints the following:

```
Mapping 1
Mapping 2
Mapping 3
Mapping 4
```

```
Mapping 5
Filtering 15
Filtering 12
Filtering 9
Filtering 6
Filtering 3
[6, 12, NIL]
```

This shows that all elements are processed by function f, implying a full traversal of the list. Then all elements are processed by function p, implying a second full traversal of the list that results from the first map. By contrast, look at the following program, which uses a Stream instead of a List:

```
fun main(args: Array<String>) {
    val stream = Stream.from(1).takeAtMost(5).map(f).filter(p)
    println(stream.toList())
}
```

This is the output:

```
Mapping 1
Filtering 3
Mapping 2
Filtering 6
Mapping 3
Filtering 9
Mapping 4
Filtering 12
Mapping 5
Filtering 15
15 [6, 12, NIL]
```

You can see that the stream traversal occurs only once. First the element 1 is mapped with f, giving 3. Then 3 is filtered (and discarded because it's not an even number). Then 2 is mapped with f, giving 6, which is filtered and kept for the result.

As you can see, the laziness of streams lets you compose the descriptions of the computations rather than their results. The evaluation of the elements is reduced to the minimum. The following result is obtained if you use unevaluated values to construct the stream and an evaluating function with logging when removing the printing of the result:

```
generating 1
Mapping 1
Filtering 3
generating 2
Mapping 2
Filtering 6
```

You can see that only the first two elements are evaluated. The rest of the evaluations were the result of the final printing.

EXERCISE 9.27

Write a find function that takes a predicate (a function from A to Boolean) as a parameter and returns a Result<A>. This will be Success if an element is found to match the predicate, or Empty otherwise.

You should have nearly nothing to write. Combine two of the functions you've written in the previous sections.

SOLUTION

Compose the `filter` function with `head`:

```
fun find(p: (A) -> Boolean): Result<A> = filter(p).head()
```

9.12.3 *Applying streams to concrete problems*

In the following exercise, you'll apply streams to concrete problems. By doing so, you'll realize how solving problems with streams is different from the traditional approach.

EXERCISE 9.28

Write a `fibs` function that generates the infinite stream of Fibonacci numbers 1, 1, 2, 3, 5, 8, and so on.

HINT

Consider producing an intermediate stream of pair of integers using the `iterate` function.

SOLUTION

The solution consists in creating a stream of pairs (x, y) with x and y being two successive Fibonacci numbers. Once this stream is produced, you need to `map` it with a function from a pair to its first element:

```
fun fibs(): Stream<Int> =
    Stream.iterate(Pair(1, 1)) { x ->
        Pair(x.second, x.first + x.second)
    }.map({ x -> x.first })
```

This can be simplified using destructuring:

```
fun fibs(): Stream<Int> = Stream.iterate(Pair(1, 1)) {
    (x, y) -> Pair(y, x + y)
}.map { it.first }
```

In this example, `(x, y)` is directly initialized with the first and second element of the `Pair`, transforming the `Pair` into a tuple of its properties. It's the inverse of `Pair(x, y)`, where two values, x and y, are structured into a `Pair`, hence the name *destructuring*.

EXERCISE 9.29

The `iterate` function can be further generalized. Write an `unfold` function that takes as its parameters a starting state of type `S` and a function from `S` to `Result<Pair<A, S>>`, and returns a stream of `A`. Returning a `Result` makes it possible to indicate whether the stream should stop or continue.

Using a state `S` means that the source of data generation doesn't have to be of the same type as the generated data. To apply this new function, write new versions of `fibs` and `from` in terms of the `unfold` function. Here's the `unfold` signature:

```
fun <A, S> unfold(z: S, f: (S) -> Result<Pair<A, S>>): Stream<A>
```

SOLUTION

To start, apply the f function to the initial state z. This produces a Result<Pair<A, S>>. Then map this result with a function from a Pair<A, S>, producing a stream by "consing" the first member of the pair (the A value) with a (non-evaluated) recursive call to unfold and using the second member of the pair as the initial state. The result of this mapping is either Success<Stream<A>> or Empty. Then use getOrElse to return either the contained stream or a default empty stream:

```
fun <A, S> unfold(z: S, f: (S) -> Result<Pair<A, S>>): Stream<A> =
    f(z).map { x ->
              Stream.cons(Lazy { x.first }, Lazy { unfold(x.second, f) })
            }.getOrElse(Stream.Empty)
```

Even simpler, you can use destructuring again:

```
fun <A, S> unfold(z: S, f: (S) -> Result<Pair<A, S>>): Stream<A> =
    f(z).map { (a, s) ->
        Stream.cons(Lazy { a }, Lazy { unfold(s, f) })
    }.getOrElse(Stream.Empty)
```

The new version of from uses the integer seed as the initial state and a function from Int to Pair<Int, Int>. Here the state is of the same type as the value:

```
fun from(n: Int): Stream<Int> = unfold(n) { x -> Result(Pair(x, x + 1)) }
```

The fibs function makes more complete use of the unfold function. The state is a Pair<Int, Int>, and the function produces a Pair<Int, Pair<Int, Int>>:

```
fun fibs(): Stream<Int> =
    Stream.unfold(Pair(1, 1)) { x ->
        Result(Pair(x.first, Pair(x.second, x.first + x.second)))
    }
```

You can see how compact and elegant these function implementations are!

EXERCISE 9.30

Using foldRight to implement various functions is a smart technique. Unfortunately, it doesn't work for filter. If you test this function with a predicate that's not matched by more than 1,000 or 2,000 consecutive elements, it overflows the stack. Write a stack-safe filter function.

HINT

The problem comes from long sequences of elements for which the predicate returns false. Think of a way to get rid of these elements.

SOLUTION

The solution is to remove the long series of elements that return false by using the dropWhile function. To do this, you must reverse the condition (!p(x)) and then test the resulting stream for emptiness. If the stream is empty, return it. (Any empty stream will do because the empty stream is a singleton.) If the stream isn't empty, create a new stream by "consing" the head with the filtered tail.

Because the head function returns a pair, you must use the first element of this pair as the head element of the stream. In theory, you should use the right element of the pair for any further access. Not doing so would cause a new evaluation of the head. But as you don't access the head a second time, only the tail, you can use `stream.getTail()` instead. This allows avoiding the use of a local variable to reference the result of `stream.head()`:

```
fun filter(p: (A) -> Boolean): Stream<A>  =
    dropWhile { x -> !p(x) }.let { stream ->
        when (stream) {
            is Empty -> stream
            is Cons -> cons(stream.hd, Lazy { stream.tl().filter(p)})
        }
    }
```

Another possibility is to use the head function. This function returns a `Result<A>` that can be mapped to produce the new stream through a recursive call. In the end, this produces a `Result<Stream<A>>` that will be empty if no elements satisfy the predicate. All that remains to be done is to call `getOrElse` on this `Result`, passing an empty stream as the default value:

```
fun filter2(p: (A) -> Boolean): Stream<A> =
    dropWhile { x -> !p(x) }.let { stream ->
        when (stream) {
            is Empty -> stream
            is Cons -> stream.head().map({ a ->
                cons(Lazy { a }, Lazy { stream.tl().filter(p) })
            }).getOrElse(Empty)
        }
    }
```

Summary

- Strict evaluation means evaluating values as soon as they're referenced.
- Lazy evaluation means evaluating values only if and when they're needed.
- Some languages are strict and others are lazy. Some are lazy by default and optionally strict, others are strict by default and optionally lazy.
- Kotlin is a strict language. It's strict regarding function arguments.
- Although Kotlin isn't lazy, you can use the by lazy construct combined with a function to implement laziness.
- With laziness, you can manipulate and compose infinite data structures.
- Right folds don't cause stream evaluation; only some functions used for folding do.
- Using folds, you can compose several iterating operations without resulting in multiple iterations.
- You can easily define and compose infinite streams.

More data handling with trees

In chapter 5, you learned about the singly linked list, which is probably the most widely used immutable data structure. Although the list is an efficient data structure for many operations, it has some limitations. The main shortcoming is that the complexity of accessing elements grows proportionally with the number of elements. For example, searching for a particular element may necessitate examining all elements if it happens that the searched-for element is the last in the list. Among other less efficient operations are sorting, accessing elements by their index, and finding the maximal or minimal element. For example, to find the maximal (or minimal) element in a list, one has to traverse the whole list. In this chapter, you'll learn about a new data structure that solves these problems: the binary tree.

This chapter starts with some theory about binary trees. Some readers might think that binary trees are a well-known subject that all programmers would master. If that's you and you've mastered binary trees, you can jump straight to the exercises, which will probably seem easy. For the rest of you, be prepared for exercises that are slightly more difficult than those in the previous chapters. If you can't find the answer to an exercise, you can look at the solution. But I recommend that you return to the exercise later and try again to solve it. Remember, exercises generally build on previous ones, so if you don't understand the solution to one exercise, you'll probably have difficulty solving the succeeding ones.

10.1   *The binary tree*

Data trees are structures in which, unlike in lists, each element is linked to more than one element. In some trees, each element (sometimes called a *node*) can be linked to a variable number of other elements. Most often, though, they're linked to a fixed number of elements. In binary trees, as the name suggests, each element is linked to two elements. Those links are called *branches*. In binary trees, those branches are called the left and right branches. Figure 10.1 shows an example of a binary tree.

The tree represented in the figure isn't common because its elements are of different types. It's a tree of Any. Most often, you'll deal with trees of a more specific type, such as trees of integers.

In figure 10.1, you can see that a tree is a recursive structure. Each branch leads to a new tree (often called a *subtree*). You can also see that some branches lead to a single element. This isn't a problem because this single element is, in fact, a tree with empty branches. Such terminal elements are often called *leaves*. Also note the T element: it has a left branch but no right one. This is because the right branch is empty and is not represented. From this, you can infer the definition of a binary tree. A tree is one of the following:

- A single element such as 56.2, "hi", 42, and -2 in figure 10.1
- An element with one branch (right or left) such as T in figure 10.1
- An element with two branches (right and left), such as a, 1, or $

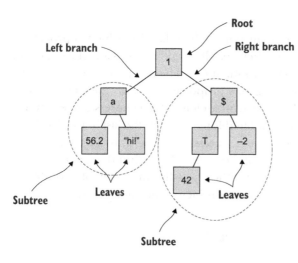

Figure 10.1   **A binary tree is a recursive structure composed of a root and two branches. The left branch is a link to the left subtree, and the right branch is a link to the right subtree. Terminal elements have empty branches (not represented in the figure) and are called leaves.**

Each branch holds a (sub)tree. A tree in which all elements have either two branches or no branches is called a *full* tree. The tree in figure 10.1 isn't full, but the left subtree is.

10.2 Understanding balanced and unbalanced trees

Binary trees can be more or less balanced. A perfectly balanced tree is a tree in which the two branches of all subtrees contain the same number of elements. Figure 10.2 shows three examples of trees with the same elements. The first tree is perfectly balanced and the last tree is totally unbalanced. Perfectly balanced binary trees are sometimes called *perfect* trees.

In this figure, the tree on the right is, in fact, a singly linked list. A singly linked list can be seen as a special case of a totally unbalanced tree.

10.3 Looking at size, height, and depth in trees

A tree can be characterized by the number of elements it contains and the number of levels on which these elements are spread:

- The number of elements is called the *size.*
- The number of levels, not counting the root, is called the *height.*

In figure 10.2, all three trees have a size of 7. The first (perfectly balanced) tree has a height of 2, the second (imperfectly balanced) has a height of 3, and the third (unbalanced) a height of 6.

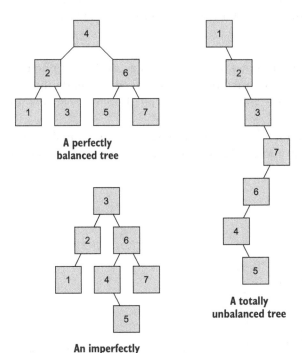

A perfectly balanced tree

An imperfectly balanced tree

A totally unbalanced tree

Figure 10.2 Trees can be more or less balanced. The top tree is perfectly balanced because the two branches of all subtrees contain the same number of elements. The tree on the right is a singly linked list, which is a special case of a totally unbalanced tree.

The word *height* is also used to characterize individual elements. It refers to the length of the longest path from an element to a leaf. The height of the root is the height of the tree, and the height of an element is the height of the subtree having this element as its root.

The *depth* of an element is the length of the path from the root to the element. The first element, also called the *root*, has a depth of 0. In the perfectly balanced tree in figure 10.2, elements 2 and 6 have a depth of 1, and elements 1, 3, 5, and 7 have a depth of 2.

10.4   Empty trees and the recursive definition

In section 10.1, I said that a tree is composed of a root element with zero, one, or two branches. This is a naive definition that doesn't allow for all needed computations. In particular, it doesn't represent empty trees. We can, however, include empty trees by changing the definition slightly. A tree is either

- An empty tree
- A root element with two branches that are themselves trees

According to this new recursive definition, each element that seems to have no branches in figure 10.2 has in fact two empty trees as its left and right branches. Elements that appear as if they had a single branch have, in reality, an empty tree as their second branch. By convention, empty branches are not represented in diagrams. Another more important convention is that the height and depth of an empty tree are equal to –1. You'll see that this is necessary for some operations such as balancing.

10.5   Leafy trees

Binary trees are sometimes represented in a different way, as shown in figure 10.3. In this representation, a tree is represented by branches that don't hold values. Only the terminal nodes hold values. As terminal nodes are called *leaves*, such trees are called *leafy trees*.

The leafy tree representation is sometimes preferred because it makes implementing some functions easier. In this book, however, I'll consider only classic trees, not leafy trees.

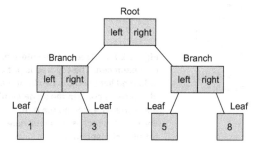

Figure 10.3   A leafy tree holds values only in the terminal nodes, which are called leaves.

10.6 *Ordered binary trees or binary search trees*

An ordered binary tree, also called a *Binary Search Tree*, or simply BST, has the following traits:

- It contains elements that can be ordered.
- All elements in one branch have a lower value than the root element.
- All elements in the other branch have a higher value than the root element.
- The same condition holds for all subtrees.

By convention, elements with lower values than the root are on the left branch, and elements with higher values are on the right branch. Figure 10.4 shows an example of an ordered tree.

NOTE One important consequence of the definition of ordered binary trees is that they can never contain duplicates.

Ordered trees are particularly interesting because they allow for fast retrieval of elements. To find out whether an element is contained in the tree, you

1 Compare the searched-for element with the root. If those are equal, you're done.
2 If the searched-for element has a lower value than the root, proceed recursively with the left branch.
3 If the searched-for element has a higher value than the root, proceed recursively with the right branch.

Compared to a search in a singly linked list, you can see that searching a perfectly balanced ordered binary tree takes an amount of time proportional to the height of the

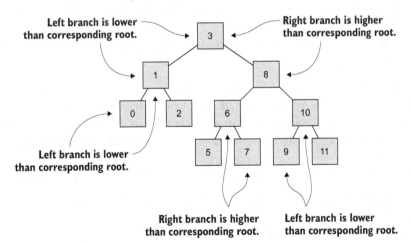

Figure 10.4 An example of an ordered or binary search tree. All elements in one branch (by convention, the left branch) have a lower value than the root element, and all elements in the other branch (by convention, the right branch) have a higher value than the root element. The same traits apply to all subtrees.

tree. This means that a search takes a time proportional to log2(n), with n being the size (number of elements) of the tree. By contrast, the search time in a singly linked list is proportional to the number of elements.

A direct consequence of this is that a recursive search in a perfectly balanced binary tree never overflows the stack. As you saw in chapter 4, the standard stack size allows for 1,000 to 3,000 recursive steps. Because a perfectly balanced binary tree of height 1,000 contains 2^1,000 elements, you'll never have enough main memory for such a tree.

This is good news. But the bad news is that not all binary trees are perfectly balanced. Because the totally unbalanced binary tree is a singly linked list, it has the same performance and the same problem regarding recursion as the list. This means that to get the most from trees, you have to find a way to balance them.

10.7   *Insertion order and the structure of trees*

The structure of a tree (meaning how well balanced it is) depends on the insertion order of its elements. Insertion is done in the same way as searching:

- If the tree is empty, create a new tree with the element as the root and two empty trees as the left and right branches.
- If the tree is not empty, compare the element to be inserted with the root. If those are equal, you're done. There's nothing to insert because you can only insert an element lower or higher than the root.

    Reality is sometimes different. If the objects inserted into the tree can be equal from the tree-ordering point of view but different based on other criteria, you'll probably want to replace the root with the element you're inserting. This is the most frequent case, as you'll soon see:

    - If the element to be inserted is lower than the root, insert it recursively into the left branch.
    - If the element to be inserted is higher than the root, insert it recursively into the right branch.

This process leads to an interesting observation: the balance of the tree depends on the order in which elements are inserted. It's obvious that inserting ordered elements produces a totally unbalanced tree. On the other hand, many insertion orders produce identical trees. Figure 10.5 shows the possible insertion orders that can result in the same tree.

The right part of the figure attempts to represent all possible order of insertions:

- The first element to be inserted is 3. Inserting any other element first results in a different tree.
- The second element must be 1 or 8. Once again, inserting any other element second results in a different tree. If 1 is inserted, the next inserted element must be 0, 2, or 8. If 8 is inserted, the next inserted element must be 6, 10, or 1. Once 6 is inserted, the next element can be 0, 2, 10 (provided those have not yet been inserted), 5, or 7. And so on....

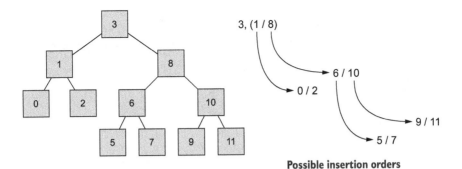

Possible insertion orders

Figure 10.5   Different insertion orders can yield the same tree. A set of ten elements can be inserted into a tree in 3,628,800 distinct orders, but this only produces 16,796 distinct trees. These trees range from perfectly balanced to totally unbalanced. Ordered trees are efficient for storing and retrieving random data, but they're not good at storing and retrieving pre-ordered data.

10.8   *Recursive and non-recursive tree traversal order*

Given a specific tree as represented in figure 10.5, one common use case is to traverse it, visiting all elements one after the other. This is typically the case when mapping or folding trees and, to a lesser extent, when searching the tree for a particular value. When you studied lists in chapter 5, you learned that there are two ways to traverse those: from left to right or from right to left. Trees offer many more approaches and among them we'll make a distinction between recursive and non-recursive ones.

10.8.1   *Traversing recursive trees*

Consider the left branch of the tree in figure 10.5. This branch is itself a tree composed of the root 1, the left branch 0, and the right branch 2. You can traverse this tree in six orders:

- 1, 0, 2
- 1, 2, 0
- 0, 1, 2
- 2, 1, 0
- 0, 2, 1
- 2, 0, 1

You can see that three of these orders are symmetric with the other three: 1, 0, 2 and 1, 2, 0 are symmetric. You start from the root and then visit the two branches, from left to right or from right to left. The same holds for 0, 1, 2 and 2, 1, 0, which differ only in the order of the branches, and again for 0, 2, 1 and 2, 0, 1. Considering only the left to right direction (because the other direction is exactly the same, as if it were seen in a mirror), you're left with three orders, which are named after the position of the root:

- Pre-order (1, 0, 2 or 1, 2, 0)
- In-order (0, 1, 2 or 2, 1, 0)
- Post-order (0, 2, 1 or 2, 0, 1)

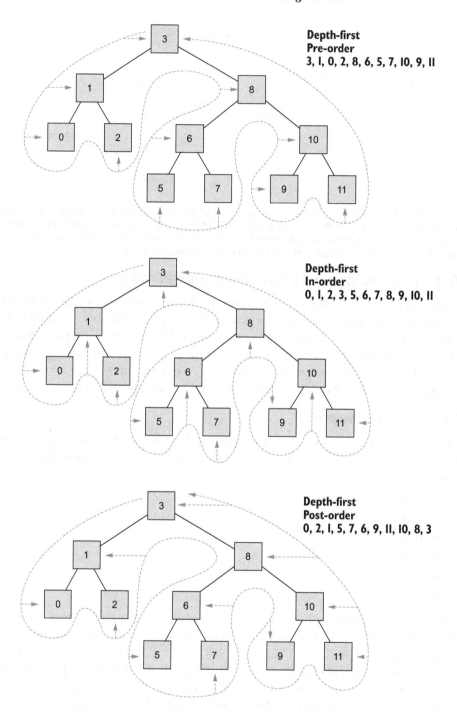

Figure 10.6   Depth-first traversal consists in traversing the tree while giving priority to height. This can be applied with three main orders: pre-order, in-order, and post-order.

These terms are coined after the operator position in an operation. To better see the analogy, imagine the root (1) replaced with a plus (+) sign. This would give you

- Prefix (+, 0, 2 or +, 2, 0)
- Infix (0, +, 2 or 2, +, 0)
- Postfix (0, 2, + or 2, 0, +)

Applied recursively to the whole tree, these orders result in traversing the tree while giving priority to height, leading to the traversal paths shown in figure 10.6. This type of traversal is generally called *depth first* instead of the more logical *height first*. When talking about the whole tree, height and depth refer to the height of the root and depth of the deepest leaf as you learned in section 10.3. These two values are equal.

10.8.2 *Non-recursive traversal orders*

Another way to traverse a tree is to first visit a complete level and then go to the next level. Again, this can be done from left to right or from right to left. This kind of traversal is called *level first*. (When it relates to searching for an element rather than traversing the tree, it is generally called *breadth-first* search.) One example of level-first traversal is shown in figure 10.7.

10.9 *Binary search tree implementation*

You can implement a binary tree in the same way as a singly linked list, with a head (called `value`) and two tails (the branches, called `left` and `right`). In this section, you'll define an abstract `Tree` class with two subclasses named `T` and `Empty`. `T` represents a non-empty tree, whereas `Empty`, unsurprisingly, represents the empty tree.

As with the `List`, the empty tree can be represented by a singleton object, thanks to the fact that Kotlin handles variance. This singleton object will be a `Tree<Nothing>`. Listing 10.1 represents the minimal `Tree` implementation.

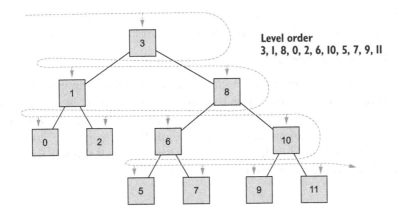

Level order
3, I, 8, 0, 2, 6, I0, 5, 7, 9, II

Figure 10.7 Level-first traversal order consists in visiting all the elements of a given level before going to the next level.

Listing 10.1   The minimal `Tree` implementation

The Tree class is covariant on A, but the Comparable interface is contravariant, so you must deal with that.

The Tree class is parameterized, and the parameter type must extend Comparable.

```
sealed class Tree<out A: Comparable<@UnsafeVariance A>> {

    abstract fun isEmpty(): Boolean

    internal object Empty : Tree<Nothing>() {

        override fun isEmpty(): Boolean = true

        override fun toString(): String = "E"
    }

    internal class T<out A: Comparable<@UnsafeVariance A>>(
                        internal val left: Tree<A>,
                        internal val value: A,
                        internal val right: Tree<A>) : Tree<A>() {

        override fun isEmpty(): Boolean = false

        override fun toString(): String =
                "(T $left $value $right)"
    }

    companion object {

        operator fun <A: Comparable<A>> invoke(): Tree<A> =
                                    Empty
    }
}
```

The empty tree is represented by a singleton object parameterized with Nothing.

All properties are internal so that they can't be accessed directly from other modules.

The T subclass represents a non-empty tree.

The invoke function returns the Empty singleton.

The toString functions are minimal implementations to help see the content of a tree.

This class is quite simple, but it's useless as long as you have no way to construct a real tree. But before adding this, there's a problem you must take into consideration.

10.9.1   *Understanding variance and trees*

In chapter 5, you learned how variance can be applied to lists. Variance also applies to trees. Making a tree covariant on its parameter seems to make sense. After all, a `Tree<Int>` should also be usable where a `Tree<Number>` is expected. This is what you get by making the tree covariant through the use of the `out` keyword. On the other hand, you shouldn't be able to add a `Number` to a `Tree<Int>`. If this was possible, the `Tree` class would be contravariant on its type parameter.

The problem comes from the fact that the `Tree` type parameter must implement the `Comparable` interface. This isn't the Java `Comparable` interface, but a specific Kotlin one:

```
public interface Comparable<in T> {
    public operator fun compareTo(other: T): Int
}
```

As you can see, `Comparable` is contravariant on `T`, meaning that the type parameter `T` occurs only in the `in` position. This would normally make it impossible to make the `Tree` class covariant. You could deal with this, but it would force you to explicitly cast the `Empty` singleton object in a `Tree<T>` each time you needed to use it. You'd still be able to make this cast into a function such as

```
operator fun <A: Comparable<A>> invoke() = Empty as Tree<A>
```

You'd then get a warning from the compiler about the unchecked cast. Which solution to use is up to you, but the use of `@UnsafeVariance` is cleaner and, as it allows making `Tree` covariant, it's also more useful.

Now you need a way to construct trees by adding elements to an existing tree, starting with the empty one.

EXERCISE 10.1

Define a `plus` function to insert a value into a tree. As usual, the `Tree` structure is immutable and persistent, so a new tree with the added value must be constructed, leaving the original tree untouched. Calling this function `plus` lets you use the + operator to add an element to a tree.

HINT

If the element to add is equal to the root, you must return a new tree with the inserted value as the root and leave the two original branches unchanged. Otherwise, a value lower than the root should be added to the left branch, and a value higher than the root should be added to the right branch. You should create a function in the parent `Tree` class with the following signature:

```
operator fun plus(element: @UnsafeVariance A): Tree<A>
```

If you prefer to define an abstract function in the `Tree` parent class and implement it in each subclass, well ... just try.

SOLUTION

The function uses pattern matching to select an implementation based on the type of this tree. If it's `Empty`, it returns a new `T` (the non-empty tree) constructed from the element to add as the value and two empty trees as the branches. If the parameter tree is non-empty, three cases are possible:

- *The element to add is lower than the root.* In this case, a new tree is constructed with the same root and the same right branch, and the new left branch is the result of inserting the element in the original left branch.

- *The element to add is higher than the root.* In this case, a new tree is constructed with the same root and the same left branch, and the new right branch is the result of inserting the element in the original right branch.
- *The element to add is equal to the root.* In this case, the function returns a new tree constructed with the element to add as the root and the two original branches:

```
operator fun plus(element: @UnsafeVariance A): Tree<A> = when (this) {
    Empty -> T(Empty, element, Empty)
    is T -> when {
        element < this.value -> T(left + element, this.value, right)
        element > this.value -> T(left, this.value, right + element)
        else -> T(this.left, element, this.right)
    }
}
```

This is different from what happens in many implementations (the Java `TreeSet`, for example) that are unchanged if you try to insert an element that's equal to an element already in the set. Although this behavior might be acceptable for mutable elements, it's much less acceptable when elements are immutable. You might think it's a waste of time and memory space to construct a new instance of `T` with the same left branch, the same right branch, and a root equal to the current root because you could return `this`. Returning `this` would be equivalent to returning

```
T(this.left, this.value, this.right)
```

If this is what you intended, returning the original tree would be a good optimization. This would work, but it would be tedious to obtain the same result as mutating a tree element. You'd have to remove the element before inserting an equal element with some changed properties. You'll encounter this use case when implementing a map in chapter 11.

10.9.2   What about an abstract function in the Tree class?

Defining an abstract function in the `Tree` parent class with different implementations in each subclass might be seen as a better option by object-oriented programmers. But it won't work. Here's what the implementation in the `Empty` object would look like:

```
override fun <A: Comparable<A>> plus(element: Nothing): Tree<Nothing> =
        T(Empty, element, Empty)
```

This doesn't work because using the `element` parameter of type `Nothing` (in `T(Empty, element, Empty)`) always fails because `Nothing` can't be instantiated. Although you know that `element` isn't of type `Nothing`, you can't specify the type because type parameters aren't allowed for objects. For this reason, you need to define the function in the `Tree` class using pattern matching. In the `Empty` case, the parameter is still of type `A`, and no problem arises.

10.9.3   Overloading operators

Kotlin allows operator overloading. By using the `operator` keyword and naming the function `plus`, you're able to call the operator using the + sign:

```
val tree = Tree<Int>() + 5 + 2 + 8
```

There's no way to avoid specifying the argument type, even if it's indicated on the left of the equal sign. This won't compile:

```
val tree: Tree<Int> = Tree() + 5 + 2 + 8
```

10.9.4 *Recursion in trees*

You may be wondering whether you should implement stack-safe recursion for the helper function because the plus function is recursive. As I said previously, there's no need to do so with a balanced tree because the height (which determines the maximum number of recursion steps) is generally much lower than the size. But you've seen that this isn't always the case, particularly if the elements to be inserted are ordered. This could eventually result in a tree with only one branch, which would have its height equal to its size (minus one) and would overflow the stack.

For now, though, you don't need to deal with this. Rather than implementing stack-safe recursive operations, you'll find a way to automatically balance trees. The simple tree you're working on is only for learning. It'll never be used in production. But balanced trees are more complex to implement, so it's easier to start with the simple unbalanced tree.

EXERCISE 10.2

It's often useful to build a tree from some other type of collection. The two most useful cases are building a tree from a List and building a tree from an array. Implement one function for each of these cases. Use the List type you defined in previous chapters, not the Kotlin List type.

SOLUTION

The solution using a vararg is similar to what you used for List:

```
operator fun <A: Comparable<A>> invoke(vararg az: A): Tree<A> =
    az.foldRight(Empty, { a: A, tree: Tree<A> -> tree.plus(a) })
```

To do the same thing for a Kotlin list, you need to change the type of the argument without changing anything in the implementation:

```
operator fun <A: Comparable<A>> invoke(az: List<A>): Tree<A> =
    az.foldRight(Empty, { a: A, tree: Tree<A> -> tree.plus(a) })
```

The List type you defined in chapters 5 and 8 has, from this point of view, a slight difference: the foldRight function is curried and, furthermore, the List.foldRight function isn't stack-safe. In this case, it's much better to use foldLeft:

```
operator fun <A: Comparable<A>> invoke(list: List<A>): Tree<A> =
    list.foldLeft(Empty as Tree<A>, { tree: Tree<A> ->
        { a: A ->
            tree.plus(a)
        }
    })
```

Using foldLeft and foldRight produces different trees because the order of insertion of the elements won't be the same.

EXERCISE 10.3

One operation often used on trees consists of checking whether a specific element is present in the tree. Implement a `contains` function that performs this check. Here's its signature:

```
fun contains(a: @UnsafeVariance A): Boolean
```

SOLUTION

What you need to do is compare the parameter with the tree `value` (the value at the root of the tree):

- If the parameter is lower, recursively apply the comparison to the left branch.
- If it's higher, recursively apply the comparison to the right branch.
- If the `value` and the parameter are equal, return `true`.

As usual, you'd define this function in the `Tree` class, using the `@UnsafeVariance` annotation on the parameter in order to disable variance checking:

```
fun contains(a: @UnsafeVariance A): Boolean = when (this) {
    is Empty -> false
    is T -> when {
        a < value -> left.contains(a)
        a > value -> right.contains(a)
        else -> value == a
    }
}
```

You might also have solved the exercise with an implementation like this:

```
fun <A: Comparable<@UnsafeVariance A>> contains(a: A): Boolean =
    when (this) {
        is Empty -> false
        is T -> a == value || left.contains(a) || right.contains(a)
    }
```

This is simpler and perfectly correct, although slightly slower if the search implies recursively looking at the right branch. But there's another more important difference: this implementation allows testing for elements of a different type than the element of the tree. This is because the `A` type parameter of this implementation is not the `A` parameter of the `Tree` class. It's shadowing the `Tree` type parameter. This is much clearer if you rename the parameter:

```
fun <B: Comparable<@UnsafeVariance B>> contains(b: B): Boolean =
    when (this) {
        is Empty -> false
        is T -> b == value || left.contains(b) || right.contains(b)
    }
```

With this implementation, you can write something like `Tree(1, 2, 3).contains1("2")` without causing a compile error. Whether this is better or not is up to you.

EXERCISE 10.4

Write two functions to compute the `size` and `height` of a tree. Here are their possible signatures in the `Tree` class:

```
abstract fun size(): Int
abstract fun height(): Int
```

You should try to find a better solution as you did for list length in chapter 8.

SOLUTION

The `Empty` implementation of `size` returns 0. And as I said previously, the `Empty` implementation of the `height` function returns −1. The implementation of the `size` function in the `T` class returns 1 plus the size of each branch. The implementation of the `height` function returns 1 plus the maximum `height` of the two branches:

```
import kotlin.math.max

...

override fun size(): Int = 1 + left.size() + right.size()
override fun height(): Int = 1 + max(left.height(), right.height())
```

Based on this, you can see why the height of an empty tree needs to be equal to −1. If it were 0, the height would be equal to the number of elements in the path instead of the number of segments.

But these functions are inefficient. First of all, the length and the height are computed on each call. These results should be memoized. But the worst thing is that these functions could cause a `StackOverflowException` if the tree is huge and not well balanced. A much better solution is to create two abstract properties in the `Tree` parent class:

```
abstract val size: Int

abstract val height: Int
```

Then you can implement these properties in each subclass:

```
internal object Empty : Tree<Nothing>() {

    override val size: Int = 0

    override val height: Int = -1

    ...

}

internal class T<out A: ...>(override val left: Tree<A>,
                            override val value: A,
                            override val right: Tree<A>) : Tree<A>() {

    override val size: Int = 1 + left.size + right.size

    override val height: Int = 1 + max(left.height, right.height)

    ...

}
```

Remember that creating public properties by default automatically creates accessor functions. The only particularities are that these functions have the same name as the property, and the getter doesn't use parentheses.

EXERCISE 10.5

Write max and min functions to compute the maximum and minimum values contained in a tree.

HINT

Think of what the functions should return in the Empty class.

SOLUTION

In an empty tree, there are no minimum or maximum values. The solution is to return a Result<A> and the Empty implementations should return Result.empty().

The implementation for the T class is a bit tricky. For the max function, the solution is to return the max of the right branch. If the right branch isn't empty, this'll be a recursive call. If the right branch is empty, you'll get a Result.Empty. You then know that the max value is the value of the current tree, so you can call the orElse function on the return value of the right.max() function:

```
override fun max(): Result<A> = right.max().orElse { Result(value) }
```

Recall that the orElse function evaluates its argument lazily, which means it takes a { () → Result<A>> } but the () → part can be omitted. The min function is completely symmetrical:

```
override fun min(): Result<A> = left.min().orElse { Result(value) }
```

10.9.5   *Removing elements from trees*

Unlike singly linked lists, trees allow retrieving a specific element, as you saw when you developed the contains function in exercise 10.3. This should also make it possible to remove a specific element from a tree.

EXERCISE 10.6

Write a remove function that removes an element from a tree. This function will take an element as its parameter. If this element is present in the tree, it'll be removed and the function will return a new tree without this element. This new tree will respect the requirements that all elements on a left branch must be lower than the root, and all elements on the right branch must be higher than the root. If the element isn't in the tree, the function will return the tree unchanged. The function signature will be

```
Tree<A> remove(A a)
```

HINT

You'll need to define a function to merge two trees with the particularity that all elements of one are either greater or smaller than all elements of the other. Be sure to handle variance as needed.

SOLUTION

When the tree is Empty, the function can't remove anything and will return this. Otherwise, here's the algorithm you'll need to implement:

- If a < this.value, remove from left.
- If a > this.value, remove from right.
- Else, merge the left and right branches, discarding the root, and return the result.

The merge is a simplified merge because you know that all elements in the left branch are lower than all elements of the right branch. First you must define the merge function with the following signature:

```
fun removeMerge(ta: Tree<@UnsafeVariance A>): Tree<A>
```

This time, if this tree is empty, the function returns its parameter. Otherwise, the following algorithm is used:

- If ta is empty, return this (this can't be empty).
- If ta.value < this.value, merge ta in the left branch.
- If ta.value > this.value, merge ta in the right branch.

Here's the implementation:

```
fun removeMerge(ta: Tree<@UnsafeVariance A>): Tree<A> = when (this) {
    Empty -> ta
    is T   -> when (ta) {
        Empty -> this
        is T -> when {
            ta.value < value -> T(left.removeMerge(ta), value, right)
            else             -> T(left, value, right.removeMerge(ta))

        }
    }
}
```

Notice that the roots of the two trees can't be equal because the two trees to be merged are supposed to be the left and right branches of the original tree. Now you can write the remove function:

```
fun remove(a: @UnsafeVariance A): Tree<A> = when(this) {
    Empty -> this
    is T   -> when {
        a < value -> T(left.remove(a), value, right)
        a > value -> T(left, value, right.remove(a))
        else -> left.removeMerge(right)
    }
}
```

10.9.6 *Merging arbitrary trees*

In the previous section, you used a restricted merging function that could only merge trees if all values in one tree were lower than all values of the other tree. Merging for trees is the equivalent of concatenation for lists. You need a more general function to handle merging of arbitrary trees.

EXERCISE 10.7 (HARD)

So far you've only merged trees in which all elements in one tree were greater than all elements of the other. Write a `merge` function that merges arbitrary trees. Its signature is

```
abstract fun merge(tree: Tree<@UnsafeVariance A>): Tree<A>
```

SOLUTION

The `Empty` implementation returns its parameter:

```
override fun merge(tree: Tree<Nothing>): Tree<Nothing> = tree
```

The `T` subclass implementation uses the following algorithm, in which "this" means the tree in which the function is defined:

- If the parameter tree is empty, return `this`.
- If the root of the parameter is higher than `this` root, remove the left branch of the parameter tree and merge the result with `this` right branch. Then merge the result with the parameter's left branch.
- If the root of the parameter is lower than `this` root, remove the right branch of the parameter tree and merge the result with `this` left branch. Then merge the result with the parameter's right branch.
- If the root of the parameter is equal to `this` root, merge the left branch of the parameter with `this` left branch and merge the right branch of the parameter with `this` right branch.

Here's the `T` subclass implementation:

```
override fun merge(tree: Tree<@UnsafeVariance A>): Tree<A> = when (tree) {
    Empty -> this
    is T ->   when  {
        tree.value > this.value ->
          T(left, value, right.merge(T(Empty, tree.value, tree.right)))
              .merge(tree.left)
        tree.value < this.value ->
          T(left.merge(T(tree.left, tree.value, Empty)), value, right)
              .merge(tree.right)
        else                    ->
          T(left.merge(tree.left), value, right.merge(tree.right))
    }
}
```

With this implementation, the root of the tree won't be substituted with the root of the parameter tree if both roots are equals. This may or may not correspond to your requirements. If you want the merged root to replace the initial root, change the last line of the implementation to this:

```
T(left.merge(tree.left), tree.value, right.merge(tree.right))
```

This algorithm is illustrated by figures 10.8 through 10.17. In these figures, empty branches are explicitly represented. As a reminder, "`this`" means the tree in which the function is defined.

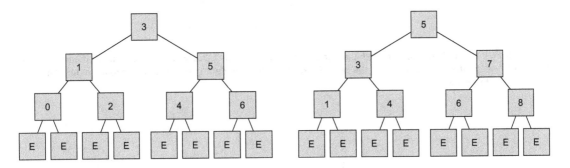

Figure 10.8   The two trees to be merged. On the left is `this` tree and on the right is the parameter tree.

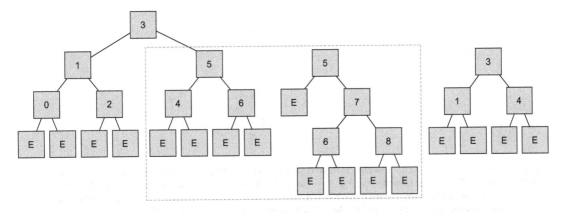

Figure 10.9   The root of the parameter tree is higher than the root of `this` tree. Merge the right branch of `this` tree with the parameter tree with its left branch removed. (The merging operation is represented by the dotted box.)

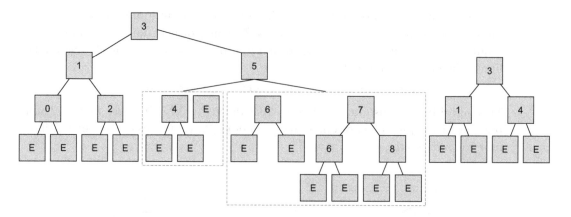

Figure 10.10   The roots of each tree to be merged being equal, you use `this` value for the result of the merge. The left branch will be the result of merging the two left branches, and the right branch will be the result of merging the two right branches.

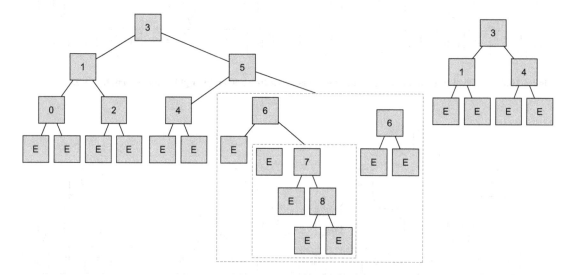

Figure 10.11   For the left branch, merging with an empty tree is trivial and returns the original tree (root 4 and two empty branches). For the right branch, the first tree has empty branches and has 6 as its root, and the second tree has 7 as its root, so you remove the left branch of the 7 rooted tree and use the result to merge with the empty right branch of the 6 rooted tree. The removed left branch will be merged with the result of the previous merge. The 6 rooted tree on the right comes from the 7 rooted tree, where it has been replaced by an empty tree.

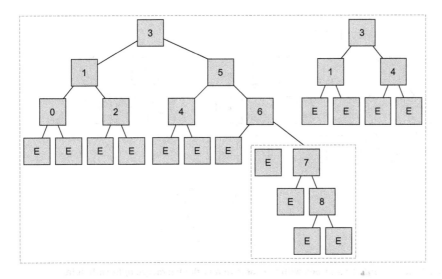

Figure 10.12 The two trees to be merged have equal roots (6) so you merge the branches (left with left and right with right). As the tree to be merged has both branches empty, there is in fact nothing to do.

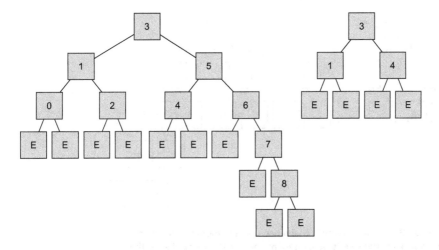

Figure 10.13 Merging an empty tree results in the tree to be merged. Two trees remain with the same root to merge.

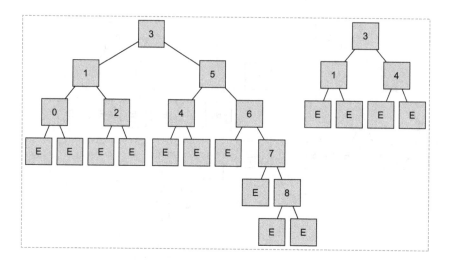

Figure 10.14   Merging two trees with the same root is simple: merge right with right and left with left, and use the results as the new branches.

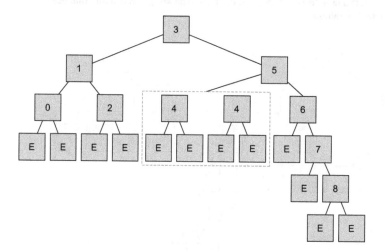

Figure 10.15   The left merge is trivial because the roots are equal and both branches of the tree to be merged are empty. On the right side, the tree to be merged has a lower root (4), so you remove the right branch (E) and merge what remains with the left branch of the original tree.

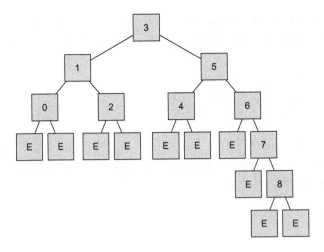

Figure 10.16   Merging two identical trees (doesn't need explanation)

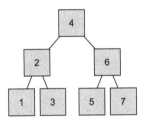

Figure 10.17   The final result after merging the last empty tree

You can see in these figures that merging two trees gives a tree with a size (number of elements) that can be smaller than the sum of the sizes of the original trees because duplicate elements are automatically removed.

On the other hand, the height of the result is higher than you might expect. Merging two trees of height 3 can give a resulting tree of height 5. It's easy to see that the optimal height shouldn't be higher than log2(size). The optimal height is the smallest power of two higher than the resulting size. In this example, the sizes of the two original trees were 7 and their heights were 3. The size of the merged tree is 9, and the optimal height would be 4 instead of 5. In such a small example, this might not be an issue. But when you're merging big trees, you could end up with badly balanced trees, resulting in suboptimal performance, and even possibly a stack overflow when using recursive functions.

10.10 *About folding trees*

Folding a tree is similar to folding a list; it consists of transforming a tree into a single value. For example, in a tree of numerical values, computing the sum of all elements can be represented through a fold. But folding a tree is much more complicated than folding a list.

Computing the sum of the elements in a tree of integers is trivial because the addition is associative in both directions and commutative. The following expressions have the same values:

```
*  (((1 + 3) + 2) + ((5 + 7) + 6)) + 4
*  4 + ((2 + (1 + 3)) + (6 + (5 + 7)))
*  (((7 + 5) + 6) + ((3 + 1) + 2)) + 4
*  4 + ((6 + (7 + 5)) + (2 + (3 + 1)))
*  (1 +(2 + 3)) + (4 + (5 + (6 + (7))))
*  (7 + (6 + 5)) + (4 + (3 + (2 + 1)))
```

Examining these expressions, you can see that they represent some possible results of folding the following tree using addition:

Considering only the order in which the elements are processed, you can recognize the following:

- Post-order left
- Pre-order left
- Post-order right
- Pre-order right
- In-order left
- In-order right

Left and right mean starting from the left and starting from the right, respectively. You can verify this by computing the result for each expression. For example, the first expression can be reduced as follows:

```
(((1 + 3) + 2) + ((5 + 7) + 6)) + 4
((    4    + 2) + ((5 + 7) + 6)) + 4     used: 1, 3
(        6      + ((5 + 7) + 6)) + 4     used: 1, 3, 2
(        6      + (   12   + 6)) + 4     used: 1, 3, 2, 5, 7
(        6      +         18   ) + 4     used: 1, 3, 2, 5, 7, 6
24               + 4                     used: 1, 3, 2, 5, 7, 6
28                                       used: 1, 3, 2, 5, 7, 6, 4
```

Other possibilities exist, but these six are the most interesting. Although these are equivalent for addition, they may not be for other operations, such as adding characters to strings or adding elements to lists.

10.10.1 Folding with two functions

The problem when folding a tree is that the recursive approach will in fact be bi-recursive. You can fold each branch with the given operation, but you need a way to combine the two results into one.

Does this remind you of list-folding parallelization you learned in chapter 8? Yes, you need an additional operation. If the operation needed to fold Tree<A> is a function from B to A to B, you need an additional function from B to B to B to merge the left and right results.

EXERCISE 10.8

Write a `foldLeft` function that folds a tree, given the two functions previously described. Its signature in the `Tree` class is as follows:

```
abstract fun <B> foldLeft(identity: B,
                      f: (B) -> (A) -> B,
                      g: (B) -> (B) -> B): B
```

SOLUTION

The implementation in the `Empty` subclass is straightforward. It returns the `identity` element. The `T` subclass implementation is a bit more difficult. What you need to do is recursively compute the fold for each branch and then combine the results with the root. The problem is that each branch fold returns a B, but the root is an A, and you've no function from A to B at your disposal. The solution to this might be as follows:

- Recursively fold the left branch and the right branch, giving two B values.
- Combine these two B values with the g function, and then combine the result with the root and return the result.

This could be one solution:

```
override
fun <B> foldLeft(identity: B, f: (B) -> (A) -> B, g: (B) -> (B) -> B): B =
        g(right.foldLeft(identity, f, g))(f(left
                                .foldLeft(identity, f, g))(this.value))
```

Simple? Not exactly. The problem is that the g function is a function from B to B to B, so you could easily swap the arguments:

```
override
fun <B> foldLeft(identity: B, f: (B) -> (A) -> B, g: (B) -> (B) -> B): B =
    g(*left*.foldLeft(identity, f, g))(f(*right*
                                .foldLeft(identity, f, g))(this.value))
```

Why is this a problem? If you fold a tree with an operation that's commutative, like addition, the result won't change. But if you use an operation that isn't commutative, you're in trouble. The end result is that the two solutions will give you different results. For example, this function

```
fun main(args: Array<String>) {
    val result = Tree(4, 2, 6, 1, 3, 5, 7)
            .foldLeft(List(),
                        { list: List<Int> -> { a: Int -> list.cons(a) } })
            { x -> { y -> y.concat(x) } }
    println(result)
}
```

produces the following result with the first solution

```
[7, 5, 3, 1, 2, 4, 6, NIL]
```

and the following result with the second solution:

```
[7, 5, 6, 3, 4, 1, 2, NIL]
```

Which is the right result? In fact, both lists, although in different orders, represent the same tree. Figure 10.18 represents the two cases.

This isn't the same difference as `foldLeft` and `foldRight` for the `List` class. Folding from right to left is in fact a left fold of the reversed list. A right fold would look like

```
override
fun <B> foldRight(identity: B, f: (A) -> (B) -> B, g: (B) -> (B) -> B): B =
        g(f(this.value)(left.foldRight(identity, f, g)))(right
                                                .foldRight(identity, f, g))
```

Because there are many traversal orders, there are many possible implementations that give different results with non-commutative operations.

10.10.2 Folding with a single function

It's also possible to fold with a single function taking an additional parameter, which means, for example, a function from B to A to B to B. Once again, there'll be many possible implementations, depending on the traversal order.

EXERCISE 10.9

Write three functions to fold a tree: `foldInOrder`, `foldPreOrder`, and `foldPostOrder`. Applied to the tree in figure 10.18, the elements should be processed as follows:

- In-order: 1 2 3 4 5 6 7
- Pre-order: 4 2 1 3 6 5 7
- Post-order: 1 3 2 5 7 6 4

Here are the function signatures:

```
abstract fun <B> foldInOrder(identity: B, f: (B) -> (A) -> (B) -> B): B
abstract fun <B> foldPreOrder(identity: B, f: (A) -> (B) -> (B) -> B): B
abstract fun <B> foldPostOrder(identity: B, f: (B) -> (B) -> (A) -> B): B
```

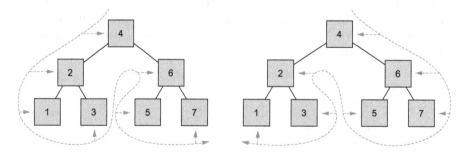

Figure 10.18 Reading the tree from left to right and from right to left. Although both lists are in different orders, they represent the same tree.

SOLUTION

The `Empty` implementations all return `identity`. The implementations in the `T` class are as follows:

```
override fun <B> foldInOrder(identity: B, f: (B) -> (A) -> (B) -> B): B =
    f(left.foldInOrder(identity, f))(value)(right
                            .foldInOrder(identity, f))

override fun <B> foldPreOrder(identity: B, f: (A) -> (B) -> (B) -> B): B =
    f(value)(left.foldPreOrder(identity, f))(right
                            .foldPreOrder(identity, f))

override fun <B> foldPostOrder(identity: B, f: (B) -> (B) -> (A) -> B): B =
    f(left.foldPostOrder(identity, f))(right
                            .foldPostOrder(identity, f))(value)
```

10.10.3 Choosing a fold implementation

You've now written five different fold functions. Which one should you choose? To answer this question, let's consider what properties a fold function should have.

There's a relationship between the way a data structure is folded and the way it's constructed. You can construct a data structure by starting with an empty element and adding elements one by one. This is the reverse of folding. Ideally, you should be able to fold a structure using specific parameters, allowing you to turn the fold into an identity function. For a list, this would be as follows:

```
list.foldRight(List()) { i -> { l -> l.cons(i) } }
```

You could also use `foldLeft`, but the function would be slightly more complex:

```
list.foldLeft(List()) { l -> { i -> l.reverse().cons(i).reverse() } }
```

This isn't surprising, if you look at the `foldRight` implementation. `foldRight` could be implemented using `foldLeft` and reverse.

Can you do the same with tree folding? To achieve this, you'll need a new way to build trees by assembling a left tree, a root, and a right tree. That way, you'll be able to use any of the three folding functions taking only one function parameter.

EXERCISE 10.10 (HARD)

Create a function that combines two trees and a root to create a new tree. Its signature in the companion object will be

```
operator fun <A: Comparable<A>> invoke(left: Tree<A>,
                        a: A, right: Tree<A>): Tree<A>
```

This function should let you reconstruct a tree identical to the original tree using any of these three folding functions: `foldPreOrder`, `foldInOrder`, and `foldPostOrder`.

HINT

You'll have to handle two cases differently. If the trees to be merged are ordered, which means that the maximum value of the first one is lower than the root of the second one, and the minimum value of the second one is higher than the root of the first one, you can assemble the three using the `T` constructor. Otherwise, you should fall back to another way of constructing the result.

You'll also need an additional function (called `mapEmpty`) in `Result`, which returns `Success` if the `Result` is `Empty` and `Failure` otherwise. You'll find this function in the `com.fpinkotlin.common.Result` class.

SOLUTION

You have several ways to implement this function. One is to define a function that tests the two trees to check whether those are ordered. For this, you can first define functions to return the result of the value comparison:

```
fun <A: Comparable<A>> lt(first: A, second: A): Boolean = first < second
```

```
fun <A: Comparable<A>> lt(first: A, second: A, third: A): Boolean =
                       lt(first, second) && lt(second, third)
```

Then you can define the `ordered` function implementing the tree comparison:

```
fun <A: Comparable<A>> ordered(left: Tree<A>,
                               a: A,
                               right: Tree<A>): Boolean =
    (left.max().flatMap { lMax ->
        right.min().map { rMin ->
            lt(lMax, a, rMin)
        }
    }.getOrElse(left.isEmpty() && right.isEmpty()) ||
        left.min()
            .mapEmpty()
            .flatMap {
                        right.min().map { rMin ->
                            lt(a, rMin)
                        }
            }.getOrElse(false) ||
        right.min()
            .mapEmpty()
            .flatMap {
                        left.max().map { lMax ->
                            lt(lMax, a)
                        }
            }.getOrElse(false))
```

The first test (before the first || operator) returns `true` if both trees aren't empty, and the left max, a, and the right min are ordered. The second and third tests handle the cases where the left or the right trees are empty (but not both). The `Result.mapEmpty` function returns `Success<Any>` if the `Result` is `Empty`, and a failure otherwise. Using this function, writing the invoke function is simple:

```
operator
fun <A: Comparable<A>> invoke(left: Tree<A>,
                              a: A, right: Tree<A>): Tree<A> =
    when {
        ordered(left, a, right) -> T(left, a, right)
        ordered(right, a, left) -> T(right, a, left)
        else                    -> Tree(a).merge(left).merge(right)
    }
```

If the trees aren't ordered, you test the inverse order before falling back to the normal insert/merge algorithm. Now you can fold a tree and obtain the same tree as the original one (provided you use the correct function). You'll find the following examples in the test code accompanying this book:

```
tree.foldInOrder(Tree<Int>(),
                    { t1 -> { i -> { t2 -> Tree(t1, i, t2) } } })
tree.foldPostOrder(Tree<Int>(),
                    { t1 -> { t2 -> { i -> Tree(t1, i, t2) } } })
tree.foldPreOrder(Tree<Int>(),
                    { i -> { t1 -> { t2 -> Tree(t1, i, t2) } } })
```

You could also define a fold function taking only one function with two parameters as you did for `List`. The trick is to first transform the tree into a list as shown in this example of `foldLeft`:

```
// abstract in Tree and this implementation in T:

override fun <B> foldLeft(identity: B, f: (B) -> (A) -> B): B =
                    toListPreOrderLeft().foldLeft(identity, f)


// In Tree:
override fun toListPreOrderLeft(): List<A> =
    left.toListPreOrderLeft().concat(right.toListPreOrderLeft()).cons(value)
```

This might not be the fastest implementation, but it could still be useful.

10.11 *About mapping trees*

Like lists, trees can be mapped, but mapping functions to trees is a bit more complicated than mapping functions to lists. Applying a function to each element of a tree may seem trivial, but it's not. The problem is that not all functions preserve ordering. Adding a given value to all elements of a tree of integers will be fine, but using the function $f(x) = x * x$ will be much more complicated if the tree contains negative values because applying the function in place won't result in a binary search tree.

EXERCISE 10.11

Define a `map` function for trees. Try to preserve the tree structure if possible. For example, mapping a tree of integers by squaring values might produce a tree with a different structure, but mapping by adding a constant shouldn't.

HINT

Using one of the fold functions makes it straightforward.

SOLUTION

You have several possible implementations using the various fold functions. Here's an example that can be defined in the `Tree` class:

```
fun <B: Comparable<B>> map(f: (A) -> B): Tree<B> =
    foldInOrder(Empty) { t1: Tree<B> ->
        { i: A ->
            { t2: Tree<B> ->
                Tree(t1, f(i), t2)
            }
        }
    }
```

10.12 About balancing trees

As I said earlier, trees work well if they're balanced, which means that all paths from the root to a leaf element have nearly the same length. In a perfectly balanced tree, the difference in lengths won't exceed 1, which happens if the deeper level isn't full. (Only perfectly balanced trees of size $2^n + 1$ have all paths from the root to a leaf element of the same length.)

Using unbalanced trees can lead to bad performance because operations could need time proportional to the size of the tree instead of to $\log2(size)$. More dramatically, unbalanced trees can cause a stack overflow when using recursive operations. Here are two ways to avoid this problem:

- Balance the unbalanced trees
- Use self-balancing trees

Once you have a way to balance trees, it's easy to make trees self-balancing by automatically launching the balancing process after each operation that could potentially change the tree structure.

10.12.1 Rotating trees

Before you can balance trees, you need to know how to incrementally change the structure of a tree. The technique used is called *rotating* the tree, and it's illustrated in figures 10.19 and 10.20.

EXERCISE 10.12

Write `rotateRight` and `rotateLeft` functions to rotate a tree in both directions. Be careful to preserve the branch order: left elements must always be lower than the root, and right elements must always be higher than the root. Declare abstract functions in the parent class. Make them protected, as they'll only be used from inside the `Tree` class. Here are the signatures in the parent class:

```
protected abstract fun rotateRight(): Tree<A>
protected abstract fun rotateLeft(): Tree<A>
```

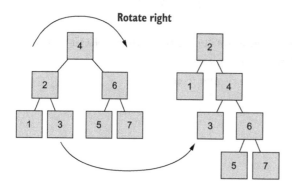

Figure 10.19 Rotating a tree to the right. During the rotation, the line between 2 and 3 is replaced with a line between 2 and 4, so element 3 becomes the left element of 4.

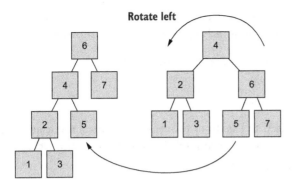

Figure 10.20 Rotating a tree to the left. The left element of 6 becomes 4 (formerly the parent of 6) so element 5 becomes the right element of 4.

SOLUTION

The `Empty` implementations return `this`. In the `T` class, these are the steps for the right rotation:

1 Test the left branch for emptiness.

2 If the left branch is empty, return `this` because rotating right consists in promoting the left element to root. (You can't promote an empty tree.)

3 If the left element isn't empty, it becomes the root, so a new `T` is created with `left.value` as the root. The left branch of the left element becomes the left branch of the new tree. For the right branch, construct a new tree with the original root as the root, the right branch of the original left as the left branch, and the original right as the right branch.

The left rotation is symmetrical:

```
override fun rotateRight(): Tree<A> = when (left) {
    Empty -> this
    is T -> T(left.left, left.value,
                T(left.right, value, right))
}

override fun rotateLeft(): Tree<A> = when (right) {
    Empty -> this
    is T -> T(T(left, value, right.left),
                right.value, right.right)
}
```

The explanation seems complex, but it's simple. Compare the code with the figures 10.19 and 10.20 to see what's happening. If you try to rotate a tree several times, you'll arrive at a point where one branch is empty and the tree can't be rotated any longer in the same direction.

EXERCISE 10.13

To balance the tree, you'll also need functions to transform a tree into an ordered list. Write a function to change a tree into an in-order list from right to left (which means in descending order).

NOTE   If you want to try more exercises, don't hesitate to define a function for in-order left to right, as well as functions for pre-order and post-order.

Here's the signature for the `toListInOrderRight` function:

```
fun toListInOrderRight(): List<A>
```

SOLUTION

This is simple and is more related to lists than to trees. `Empty` implementations return an empty list. You might think of the following implementation (in the `T` class):

```
override fun toListInOrderRight(): List<A> =
        right.toListInOrderRight()
            .concat(List(value))
            .concat(left.toListInOrderRight())
```

Unfortunately, this function overflows the stack if the tree is badly balanced. As you need this function to balance a tree, it'd be sad if it couldn't work with an unbalanced tree.

What you need is a stack-safe corecursive version. This uses a corecursive helper function for balancing the tree, which can be put in the companion object, with the main function in the `Tree` class. Here's the helper function:

```
private tailrec
fun <A: Comparable<A>> unBalanceRight(acc: List<A>,
                                      tree: Tree<A>): List<A> =
    when (tree) {
        Empty -> acc
        is T -> when (tree.left) {
            Empty -> unBalanceRight(acc.cons(tree.value),
                        tree.right)          ◄──────────────── Adds the tree to the
            is T -> unBalanceRight(acc,                        accumulator list.
                        tree.rotateRight())  ◄──
        }                                        Rotates the tree until
    }                                            the left branch is empty
```

And here's the main function in the `Tree` class:

```
fun toListInOrderRight(): List<A> = unBalanceRight(List(), this)
```

The `unBalancedRight` function rotates the tree to the right until the left branch is empty. Then it calls itself recursively to do the same thing to all the right subtrees, after having added the tree value to the accumulator list. Eventually the tree parameter is found empty and the function returns the list accumulator.

10.12.2 Using the Day-Stout-Warren algorithm

The Day-Stout-Warren algorithm is a simple method for efficiently balancing binary search trees:

1 Transform the tree into a totally unbalanced tree.
2 Then apply rotations until the tree is fully balanced.

Transforming the tree into a totally unbalanced one is a simple matter of making an in-order list and creating a new tree from it. As you want to create the tree in ascending order, you'll have to create a list in descending order and then start to rotate the result left. You can choose the symmetric case.

Here's the algorithm for obtaining a fully balanced tree:

1 Rotate the tree left until the result has branches as equal as possible. This means that the branch sizes will be equal if the total size is odd, and will differ by 1 if the total size is even. The result will be a tree with two totally unbalanced branches of near to equal size.

2 Apply the same process recursively to the right branch. Apply the symmetric process (rotating right) to the left branch.

3 Stop when the height of the result is equal to log2(*size*). For this you'll need the following helper function:

```
fun log2nlz(n: Int): Int = when (n) {
    0 -> 0
    else -> 31 - Integer.numberOfLeadingZeros(n)
}
```

Here's what the Javadoc for the `numberOfLeadingZeros` method says:

Returns the number of zero bits preceding the highest-order ("leftmost") one-bit in the two's complement binary representation of the specified int *value. Returns 32 if the specified value has no one-bits in its two's complement representation, in other words if it is equal to zero.*

This method is closely related to the logarithm base 2. For all positive int *values x:*

- *floor(log2(x)) = 31 - numberOfLeadingZeros(x)*
- *ceil(log2(x)) = 32 - numberOfLeadingZeros(x - 1)*

EXERCISE 10.14

Implement the `balance` function to fully balance any tree. This function will be defined in the companion object and will take as its parameter the tree to be balanced.

HINT

This implementation is based on several helper functions: a front function creates the totally unbalanced tree by calling the `toListInOrderRight` function. The resulting list is folded left into a (totally unbalanced) tree, which will then be easier to balance.

You'll also need a function to test whether a tree is fully balanced or not, and one to recursively rotate a tree. Here's how you might want to implement the function for rotating a tree in the companion object:

```
fun <A> unfold(a: A, f: (A) -> Result<A>): A {
  tailrec fun <A> unfold(a: Pair<Result<A>, Result<A>>,
                         f: (A) -> Result<A>): Pair<Result<A>, Result<A>> {
    val x = a.second.flatMap { f(it) }
    return x.map { unfold(Pair(a.second, x), f) }.getOrElse(a)
  }
  return Result(a).let { unfold(Pair(it, it), f).second.getOrElse(a) }
}
```

Unfortunately, this won't work because the helper function isn't tail-recursive. To make it tail-recursive, you need a way to determine whether a Result is a Success. You could determine this in one of two ways:

- By using pattern matching, provided the Result class and the Tree class are in the same module (because Result subclasses are internal)
- By adding an isSuccess function in the Result class

Choose the solution you prefer. I have copied the Result class into this chapter module (along with other necessary classes). A working implementation could be

```
fun <A> unfold(a: A, f: (A) -> Result<A>): A {
  tailrec fun <A> unfold(a: Pair<Result<A>, Result<A>>,
                         f: (A) -> Result<A>): Pair<Result<A>, Result<A>> {
    val x = a.second.flatMap { f(it) }
    return when (x) {
        is Result.Success -> unfold(Pair(a.second, x), f)
        else -> a
    }
  }
  return Result(a).let { unfold(Pair(it, it), f).second.getOrElse(a) }
}
```

This function is called unfold by analogy to List.unfold or Stream.unfold. It does the same job, except that the result type of the function is the same as its input type, but it forgets most of the results, keeping only the two last ones. This makes it faster and it uses less memory. You'll also need to define internal functions to access the value and branches of a tree.

SOLUTION

First, you need to define the utility function that tests whether a tree is unbalanced. For it to be balanced, the difference between the heights of both branches must be 0 if the total size of branches is even, and 1 if the size is odd:

```
fun <A : Comparable<A>> isUnBalanced(tree: Tree<A>): Boolean =
    when (tree) {
        Empty -> false
        is T -> Math.abs(tree.left.height - tree.right.height) >
                                            (tree.size - 1) % 2
    }
```

Then you must create functions to access the value and the branches in a tree. You can do this by using the same technique you used for the height and size. Define abstract properties in the Tree class:

```
internal abstract val value: A
```

```
internal abstract val left: Tree<A>
```

```
internal abstract val right: Tree<A>
```

The `Empty` implementations throws an exception when accessed. That's because you're defining properties and not functions. You can't write

```
override val value: Nothing =
    throw IllegalStateException("No value in Empty")
override val left: Tree<Nothing> =
    throw IllegalStateException("No left in Empty")
override val right: Tree<Nothing> =
    throw IllegalStateException("No right in Empty")
```

Doing so will cause the exception to be thrown as soon as the properties are initialized, meaning as soon as the object is created. If you remember what you've learned in chapter 9, you know you must use lazy initialization:

```
override val value: Nothing by lazy {
    throw IllegalStateException("No value in Empty")
}
override val left: Tree<Nothing> by lazy {
    throw IllegalStateException("No left in Empty")
}
override val right: Tree<Nothing> by lazy {
    throw IllegalStateException("No right in Empty")
}
```

NOTE It's your responsibility to make sure that these functions are never called.

In the `T` class, you need to modify the constructor:

```
internal
class T<out A: Comparable<@UnsafeVariance A>>(override val left: Tree<A>,
                                              override val value: A,
                                              override val right: Tree<A>):
                                                        Tree<A>() {
```

By overriding the properties in the constructor, you're automatically giving them the same visibility (`internal`) as the overridden properties, and not the default (`public`) visibility. Now you can write the main balancing functions:

```
fun <A: Comparable<A>> balance(tree: Tree<A>): Tree<A> =
        balanceHelper(tree.toListInOrderRight().foldLeft(Empty) {
                t: Tree<A> -> { a: A ->
                T(Empty, a, t)
            }
        })

fun <A: Comparable<A>> balanceHelper(tree: Tree<A>): Tree<A> = when {
    !tree.isEmpty() && tree.height > log2nlz(tree.size) -> when {
        Math.abs(tree.left.height - tree.right.height) > 1 ->
                                        balanceHelper(balanceFirstLevel(tree))
        else -> T(balanceHelper(tree.left),
                                        tree.value, balanceHelper(tree.right))
    }
    else -> tree
}
```

```
private fun <A: Comparable<A>> balanceFirstLevel(tree: Tree<A>): Tree<A> =
    unfold(tree) { t: Tree<A> ->
        when {
            isUnBalanced(t) -> when {
                tree.right.height > tree.left.height ->
                                        Result(t.rotateLeft())
                else -> Result(t.rotateRight())
            }
            else -> Result()
        }
    }
}
```

10.12.3 *Automatically balancing trees*

The `balance` function works fine for most trees, but you can't use it with big unbalanced trees because those overflow the stack. You can work around this by using `balance` only on small, fully unbalanced trees or on partially balanced trees of any size. This means that you must balance a tree before it becomes too big. The question is whether you can make the balancing automatic after each modification.

EXERCISE 10.15

Transform the tree you've developed to make it auto-balancing on insertions, merges, and removals.

SOLUTION

The obvious solution is to call `balance` after each operation that modifies the tree as in the following code:

```
operator fun plus(a: @UnsafeVariance A): Tree<A> =
                        balance(plusUnBalanced(a))

private fun plusUnBalanced(a: @UnsafeVariance A): Tree<A> = plus(this, a)
```

This works for small trees (that, in fact, don't need to be balanced), but it won't work for large ones because it's much too slow. One solution is to only partially balance trees. For example, you could run the balancing function only when the height is 100 times the ideal height of a fully balanced tree:

```
operator fun plus(a: @UnsafeVariance A): Tree<A> {

    fun plusUnBalanced(a: @UnsafeVariance A, t: Tree<A>): Tree<A> =
        when (t) {
            Empty -> T(Empty, a, Empty)
            is T -> when {
                a < t.value -> T(plusUnBalanced(a, t.left), t.value, t.right)
                a > t.value -> T(t.left, t.value, plusUnBalanced(a, t.right))
                else        -> T(t.left, a, t.right)
            }
        }

    return plusUnBalanced(a, this).let {
        when {
            it.height > log2nlz(it.size) * 100 -> balance(it)
```

```
        else      -> it
    }
  }
 }
}
```

The performance of the balancing solution may seem far from optimal, but it's a compromise. Creating a tree from an ordered list of 100,000 elements would take 2.5 seconds and produce a perfectly balanced tree of height 16. Replacing the value 100 with 20 in the plusUnBalanced function doubles the time with no benefit, and replacing it with 1,000 multiplies the time by 5.

Summary

- Trees are recursive data structures in which one element is linked to one or several subtrees. In some trees, each node can be linked to a variable number of subtrees. Most often, though, those are linked to a fixed number of subtrees.
- In binary trees, each node is linked to two subtrees. Those links are called *branches*, and those branches are called the left and right branches. Binary search trees allow much faster retrieval of comparable elements.
- Trees can be more or less balanced. Fully balanced trees provide the best performance, whereas totally unbalanced trees have the same performance as lists.
- The size of a tree is the number of elements it contains; its height is the longest path in the tree.
- The tree structure depends on the order of insertion of the tree elements.
- Trees can be traversed in many different orders (pre-order, in-order, post-order), and in both directions (left to right or right to left).
- Trees can be easily merged without traversing them.
- Trees can be mapped or rotated, as well as folded in many ways.
- Trees can be balanced for better performance and to avoid stack overflow in recursive operations.

Solving problems
with advanced trees

11

In the previous chapter, you learned about the binary tree structure and basic tree operations. But you saw that to fully benefit from trees, you must either have specific use cases, such as handling randomly ordered data, or a limited data set in order to avoid any risk of stack overflows. Making trees stack-safe is much more difficult than it was for lists because each computing step involves two recursive calls. That makes it impossible to create tail-recursive versions. In this chapter, you'll learn about two specific trees:

- The red-black tree is a self-balancing, general-purpose tree with high performance. It's suitable for general use and data sets of any size.
- The leftist heap is a specific tree suitable for implementing priority queues.

You'll also learn how to implement maps using trees storing key/values tuples. And you'll see how to create priority queues for noncomparable elements.

11.1 Better performance and stack safety with self-balancing trees

The Day-Stout-Warren balancing algorithm that you used in the previous chapter isn't ideally suited for balancing immutable trees because it's designed for in-place modifications. In order to write safer programs, in-place modifications must be avoided as often as possible.

With immutable data structures, a new structure is created for each change. Consequently, you need to define a balancing process that doesn't involve transforming the tree into a list before reconstructing a totally unbalanced tree and then finally balancing it. Two ways to optimize this process are to

- Directly rotate the original tree (eliminating the list/unbalanced tree process)
- Accept a certain amount of imbalance

You could try to invent a solution, but others have long since done that. One of the most efficient self-balancing tree designs is the red-black tree. This structure was invented in 1978 by Guibas and Sedgewick.[1] In 1999, Chris Okasaki published a functional version of the red-black tree algorithm.[2] The description was illustrated by an implementation in Standard ML and a Haskell implementation was added later. It's this algorithm that you'll implement in Kotlin.

If you're interested in immutable data structures, I strongly encourage you to buy and read Okasaki's book. You can also read his 1996 thesis with the same title. It's much less complete than his book, but it's available as a free download (http://www.cs.cmu .edu/~rwh/theses/okasaki.pdf).

11.1.1 Understanding the basic red-black tree structure

The red-black tree is a binary search tree with some additions to its structure and a modified insertion algorithm that also balances the result. Unfortunately, Okasaki didn't describe removal, which happens to be a far more complex process. But in 2014, authors Germane and Might described this missing method.[3]

In a red-black tree, each tree (including subtrees) has an additional property representing its color. Note that it could be any color or even any property representing a binary choice. Besides this, the structure is exactly the same as the binary tree structure, as shown in the following listing.

---

[1] Leo J. Guibas and Robert Sedgewick, "A dichromatic framework for balanced trees," *Foundations of Computer Science* (1978), http://www.computer.org/csdl/proceedings/focs/1978/5428/00/542800008 -abs.html.

[2] Chris Okasaki, *Purely Functional Data Structures* (Cambridge University Press, 1999).

[3] Kimball Germane and Matthew Might, "Functional Pearl: Deletion, The curse of the red-black tree," *JFP* 24, 4 (2014): 423–433; http://matt.might.net/papers/germane2014deletion.pdf.

Listing 11.1   The red-black tree base structure

```
package com.fpinkotlin.advancedtrees.listing01
```

Colors are imported
to simplify the code.

```
import com.fpinkotlin.advancedtrees.listing01.Tree.Color.B
import com.fpinkotlin.advancedtrees.listing01.Tree.Color.R
import kotlin.math.max

sealed class Tree<out A: Comparable<@UnsafeVariance A>> {

    abstract val size: Int

    abstract val height: Int
```

Abstract properties are
defined in the parent class.

```
    internal abstract val color: Color
```

The isTR and isTB functions test whether
a tree is nonempty and red or nonempty
and black, respectively.

```
    internal abstract val isTB: Boolean

    internal abstract val isTR: Boolean

    internal abstract val right: Tree<A>

    internal abstract val left: Tree<A>
```

Empty, an abstract class, allows
implementing functions in this class
instead of using pattern matching in the
Tree parent class.

```
    internal abstract val value: A

    internal abstract
    class Empty<out A: Comparable<@UnsafeVariance A>>:
                                   Tree<A>() {

        override val isTB: Boolean = false

        override val isTR: Boolean = false
```

Properties that make no
sense in the Empty class are
lazily throwing exceptions.

```
        override val right: Tree<Nothing> by lazy {
            throw IllegalStateException("right called on Empty tree")
        }

        override val left: Tree<Nothing> by lazy {
            throw IllegalStateException("left called on Empty tree")
        }

        override val value: Nothing by lazy {
            throw IllegalStateException("value called on Empty tree")
        }
```

The empty tree is black.

```
        override val color: Color = B

        override val size: Int = 0

        override val height: Int = -1

        override fun toString(): String = "E"
    }
```

```
internal object E: Empty<Nothing>()
```
The empty tree is represented by the E singleton.

```
internal
class T<out A: Comparable<@UnsafeVariance A>>(
                        override val color: Color,
```
Nonempty trees can be black or red.
```
                        override val left: Tree<A>,
                        override val value: A,
                        override val right: Tree<A>) : Tree<A>() {
    override val isTB: Boolean = color == B

    override val isTR: Boolean = color == R

    override val size: Int = left.size + 1 + right.size

    override val height: Int = max(left.height, right.height) + 1

    override fun toString(): String = "(T $color $left $value $right)"
}

companion object {
```
This function returns an empty tree.
```
    operator
    fun <A: Comparable<A>> invoke(): Tree<A> = E

}

sealed class Color {
```
Colors are singleton objects.
```
    // Red
    internal object R: Color() {
        override fun toString(): String = "R"
    }

    // Black
    internal object B: Color() {
        override fun toString(): String = "B"
    }
  }
}
```

The `contains` function hasn't been represented, nor have the other functions such as `fold...`, `map`, and so on, because those aren't different from the standard tree versions. As you'll see, only the `plus` and `minus` functions are different.

11.1.2 *Adding an element to the red-black tree*

The main characteristic of a red-black tree is invariants that must be verified. When modifying the tree, it'll be tested to check whether these invariants are being broken and to restore them through rotations and color changes if necessary. These invariants are as follows:

- An empty tree is black. (This doesn't change, so there's no need to verify it.)

- The left and right subtrees of a red tree are black. It's not possible to find two successive reds when descending the tree.
- Every path from the root to an empty subtree has the same number of blacks.

Adding an element to a red-black tree is then a somewhat complex process that includes checking the invariants after insertion (and rebalancing, if necessary). Here's the corresponding algorithm:

- An empty tree is always black.
- Insertion proper is done exactly as in an ordinary tree but is followed by balancing.
- Inserting an element into an empty tree produces a red tree.
- After balancing, the root is blackened.

Figures 11.1 through 11.7 illustrate insertion of integers 1 through 7 into an initially empty tree. This is the worst possible case, where elements are inserted in order. If using an ordinary binary tree, this would result in a totally unbalanced tree. Figure 11.1 shows the insertion of element 1 into the empty tree. Because you're inserting into an empty tree, the initial color is red. Once the element is inserted, the root is blackened.

Insert 1

Red, because it's inserted into an empty tree

Blacken the root.

Figure 11.1   Step 1: insertion of integer 1 into an initially empty tree

Figure 11.2 shows the insertion of element 2. The inserted element is red, the root is already black, and there's still no need for balancing.

Insert 2

Root is already black

Balance: do nothing

Figure 11.2   Step 2: insertion of integer 2 into an initially empty tree

Figure 11.3 illustrates insertion of element 3. The inserted element is red. The tree is being balanced because it has two successive red elements. As the red element now has two children, they are made black. (Children of a red element must always be black.) Eventually, the root is blackened.

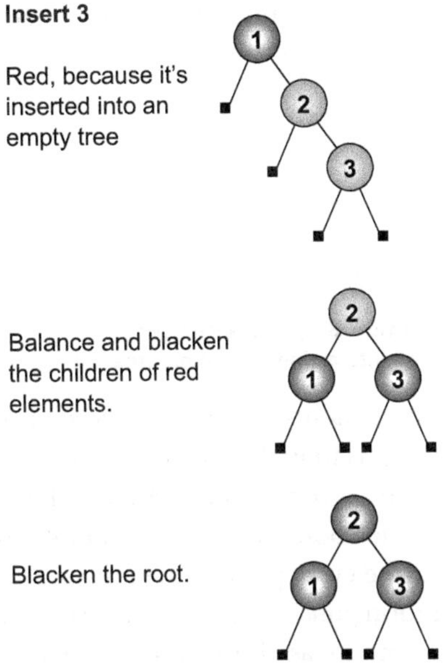

Insert 3

Red, because it's inserted into an empty tree

Balance and blacken the children of red elements.

Blacken the root.

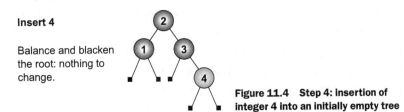

Figure 11.3   Step 3: insertion of integer 3 into an initially empty tree

Figure 11.4 shows the insertion of element 4. No further manipulation is needed.

Insert 4

Balance and blacken the root: nothing to change.

Figure 11.4   Step 4: insertion of integer 4 into an initially empty tree

Figure 11.5 illustrates the insertion of element 5. As you now have two successive red elements, the tree must be balanced by making 3 the left child of 4, and 4 becomes the right child of 2.

Insert 5

Balance

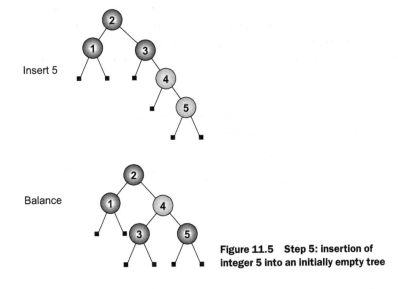

Figure 11.5   Step 5: insertion of integer 5 into an initially empty tree

Figure 11.6 shows the insertion of element 6. No further manipulation is needed.

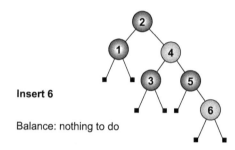

Insert 6

Balance: nothing to do

Figure 11.6   Step 6: insertion of integer 6 into an initially empty tree

In figure 11.7, element 7 is added to the tree. As elements 6 and 7 are two successive red elements, the tree must be balanced. The first step is to make element 5 the left child of 6 and 6 the right child of 4, which again leaves two successive red elements: 4 and 6. The tree is once again balanced, making element 4 the root, 2 the left child of 4, and 3 the right child of 2. The element 6 is blackened because every path to an empty subtree must have the same number of blacks. The last operation consists of blackening the root.

The `balance` function takes the same arguments as the tree constructor: `color`, `left`, `value`, and `right`. These four parameters are tested for various patterns, and the result is constructed accordingly. The `balance` function replaces the tree constructor. You need to modify any process using the constructor to use this function instead. The following list shows how each pattern of arguments is transformed by this function:

- (T B (T R (T R a x b) y c) z d) → (T R (T B a x b) y (T B c z d))
- (T B (T R a x (T R b y c)) z d) → (T R (T B a x b) y (T B c z d))
- (T B a x (T R (T R b y c) z d)) → (T R (T B a x b) y (T B c z d))
- (T B a x (T R b y (T R c z d))) → (T R (T B a x b) y (T B c z d))
- (T color a x b) → (T color a x b)

Each expression in parentheses corresponds to a tree. The letter `T` indicates a non-empty tree, and B and R indicate the black and red colors. Lowercase letters are place-holders for any value that could be valid at the corresponding place. Each left pattern (those to the left of the arrow, →) is applied in descending order, which means that if a match is found, the corresponding right pattern is applied as the resulting tree. This way of presenting things is similar to the `when` expression, with the last line being the default case.

EXERCISE 11.1

Write the `plus`, `balance`, and `blacken` functions for adding an element to the red-black tree. Here are the corresponding signatures:

```
operator fun plus(value: @UnsafeVariance A): Tree<A>
fun balance(color: Color, left: Tree<A>, value: A, right: Tree<A>): Tree<A>
fun <A: Comparable<A>> blacken(): Tree<A>
```

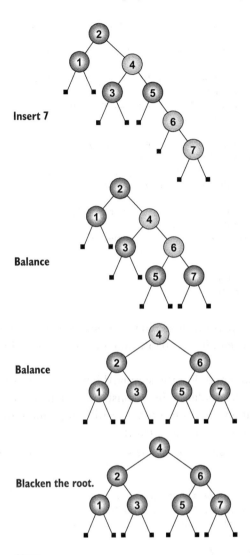

Figure 11.7 Step 7: Insertion of integer 7 into an initially empty tree

HINT

Write an `add` protected function that performs a regular addition of an element and then replaces constructor calls with calls to the `balance` function. Next, write the `blacken` function and, finally, write the `plus` function in the parent class, calling `blacken` on the result of `add`. All these functions should be private or protected, except for the `plus` function, which will be public.

SOLUTION

For the `balance` function, which can be implemented in the `Tree` class, the patterns can be represented with `when` expressions, using the type aliases in order to shorten the code:

```
protected fun balance(color: Color,
                      left: Tree<@UnsafeVariance A>,
                      value: @UnsafeVariance A,
                      right: Tree<@UnsafeVariance A>): Tree<A> = when {
```

```
// balance B (T R (T R a x b) y c) z d = T R (T B a x b) y (T B c z d)
   color == B && left.isTR && left.left.isTR ->
       T(R, left.left.blacken(), left.value, T(B, left.right, value, right))

// balance B (T R a x (T R b y c)) z d = T R (T B a x b) y (T B c z d)
   color == B && left.isTR && left.right.isTR ->
       T(R, T(B, left.left, left.value, left.right.left), left.right.value,
         T(B, left.right.right, value, right))

// balance B a x (T R (T R b y c) z d) = T R (T B a x b) y (T B c z d)
   color == B && right.isTR && right.left.isTR ->
       T(R, T(B, left, value, right.left.left), right.left.value,
         T(B, right.left.right, right.value, right.right))

// balance B a x (T R b y (T R c z d)) = T R (T B a x b) y (T B c z d)
   color == B && right.isTR && right.right.isTR ->
       T(R, T(B, left, value, right.left), right.value, right.right.
   blacken())

// balance color a x b = T color a x b
   else -> T(color, left, value, right)
}
```

Each when case implements one of the patterns listed in the previous section (shown as comments). If you want to compare them, it's probably much easier to do so in a text editor than on the printed page.

The add function is similar to what you did in the standard binary search tree, with the exception that the balance function replaces the T constructor. The add function can be implemented as an abstract function in the Tree class with implementations in Empty and T. Here's the implementation in the Empty class:

```
override fun add(newVal: @UnsafeVariance A): Tree<A> = T(R, E, newVal, E)
```

And here's the T implementation:

```
override fun add(newVal: @UnsafeVariance A): Tree<A> = when {
        newVal < value -> balance(color, left.add(newVal), value, right)
        newVal > value -> balance(color, left, value, right.add(newVal))
        else           -> when (color) {
            B -> T(B, left, newVal, right)
            R -> T(R, left, newVal, right)
        }
    }
}
```

In previous classes, you saw that it wasn't possible to implement some function in the Empty singleton because the A parameter wasn't accessible (the singleton was parameterized with Nothing). Using an abstract Empty class parameterized by A and extending it with the E<Nothing> singleton object, you can implement functions in the Empty class while still having a singleton object for representing empty trees.

The blacken function is also implemented in the Tree class as an abstract function with two implementations. Here's the Empty implementation:

```
override fun blacken(): Tree<A> = E
```

Here's the `T` implementation:

```
override fun blacken(): Tree<A> = T(B, left, value, right)
```

Finally, the `plus` function is defined in the `Tree` class with the `operator` keyword. This lets you use the + operator to call it. It returns the blackened result of add:

```
operator fun plus(value: @UnsafeVariance A): Tree<A> = add(value).blacken()
```

11.1.3 Removing elements from the red-black tree

Removing an element from a red-black tree is discussed by the already familiar authors Germane and Might.[4] The implementation in Kotlin is too long to include in this book, but it's included in the accompanying code (http://github.com/pysaumont /fpinKotlin). It will be used in the next exercise.

11.2 A use case for the red-black tree: *Maps*

Trees of integers aren't often useful (although sometimes they are). One important use of binary search trees is *maps*, also called dictionaries or associative arrays. Maps are collections of key/value pairs that allow insertion, removal, and fast retrieval of each pair.

Maps are familiar to programmers, and Kotlin offers several implementations, among which the most common are the `Map` and the `MutableMap` types. But the `MutableMap` can't be used in a multi-threaded environment without providing some protection mechanisms that are difficult to design correctly and to use. The `Map` type, on the other hand, is protected against these kind of problems. But it isn't efficient because it doesn't rely on data sharing, so a whole new map must be created for each insertion or removal.

11.2.1 Implementing Map

Functional trees like the red-black tree you developed have the advantage of immutability, which lets you use them in multi-threaded environments without bothering about locks and synchronization. This also provides benefits from good performance because most data is shared between the old tree and the new tree when an element is added or removed. Listing 11.3 shows the interface of a `Map` that can be implemented using the red-black tree.

> **Listing 11.3 A functional map**

```
class Map<out K: Comparable<@UnsafeVariance K>, V> {

    operator fun plus(entry: Pair<@UnsafeVariance K, V>): Map<K, V> = TODO()

    operator fun minus(key: @UnsafeVariance K): Map<K, V> = TODO()
```

---

[4] Kimball Germane and Matthew Might, "The missing method: Deleting from Okasaki's red-black trees" (http://matt.might.net/articles/red-black-delete/).

```
fun contains(key: @UnsafeVariance K): Boolean = TODO()

fun get(key: @UnsafeVariance K): Result<MapEntry<@UnsafeVariance K, V>>
                                                          = TODO()

fun isEmpty(): Boolean = TODO()

fun size(): Int = TODO("size")

companion object {
    operator fun invoke(): Map<Nothing, Nothing> = Map()
}
}
```

Exercise 11.2

Complete the `Map` class by implementing all functions.

Hint

You should use a delegate. From this delegate, all functions can be implemented in one line of code. The only problem is choosing how you'll store data in the map. That should be easy. You might have to change the `plus` function argument type, and you might prefer doing the same for the return type of the `get` function. You'll also need to add to the `Tree` class a `get` function to get an element. This function will have the following signature:

```
fun operator get(element: @UnsafeVariance A): Result<A>
```

This function doesn't return its parameter, but a `Result` of the element equal to it if the tree contains such an element or an empty `result` otherwise. Also define an `isEmpty` function in the `Tree` class. Then define a `MapEntry` class to represent the key/value pair and store instances of this component in a tree.

Solution

The `MapEntry` component is similar to a `Pair` with this important difference: it must be comparable and the comparison must be based on the key. The `equals` and `hashCode` functions will also be based on key equality and hash codes. Here's a possible implementation:

```
class MapEntry<K: Comparable<@UnsafeVariance K>, V>

    private constructor(private val key: K, val value: Result<V>):
                                              Comparable<MapEntry<K, V>> {

    override fun compareTo(other: MapEntry<K, V>): Int =
                                  this.key.compareTo(other.key)

    override fun toString(): String = "MapEntry($key, $value)"

    override fun equals(other: Any?): Boolean =
            this === other || when (other) {
                is MapEntry<*, *> -> key == other.key
                else -> false
            }
```

```
    override fun hashCode(): Int = key.hashCode()

    companion object {

        fun <K: Comparable<K>, V> of(key: K, value: V): MapEntry<K, V> =
                MapEntry(key, Result(value))

        operator
        fun <K: Comparable<K>, V> invoke(pair: Pair<K, V>): MapEntry<K, V> =
                MapEntry(pair.first, Result(pair.second))

        operator fun <K: Comparable<K>, V> invoke(key: K): MapEntry<K, V> =
                MapEntry(key, Result())
    }
}
```

Implementing the Map component is now a matter of delegating all operations to a Tree<MapEntry<Key, Value>>. Here's a possible implementation:

```
class Map<out K: Comparable<@UnsafeVariance K>, V>(
            private val delegate: Tree<MapEntry<@UnsafeVariance K, V>> =
                                                        Tree()) {

    operator fun plus(entry: Pair<@UnsafeVariance K, V>): Map<K, V> =
                                    Map(delegate + MapEntry(entry))

    operator fun minus(key: @UnsafeVariance K): Map<K, V> =
                                    Map(delegate - MapEntry(key))

    fun contains(key: @UnsafeVariance K): Boolean =
                                    delegate.contains(MapEntry(key))

    operator fun get(key: @UnsafeVariance K):
                        Result<MapEntry<@UnsafeVariance K, V>> =
                                        delegate[MapEntry(key)]

    fun isEmpty(): Boolean = delegate.isEmpty

    fun size() = delegate.size

    override fun toString() = delegate.toString()

    companion object {

        operator fun <K: Comparable<@UnsafeVariance K>, V> invoke():
                                            Map<K, V> = Map()
    }
}
```

11.2.2 Extending maps

Not all tree operations have been delegated because some operations don't make much sense in the current conditions. You may need additional operations in some special use cases. Implementing these operations is easy: extend the Map class and add delegating functions.

For example, you might need to find the object with the maximal or minimal key. Another possible need is to fold the map, perhaps to get a list of the contained values. Here's an example of a delegating `foldLeft` function:

```
fun <B> foldLeft(identity: B, f: (B) ->
    (MapEntry<@UnsafeVariance K, V>) -> B, g: (B) -> (B) -> B): B =
        delegate.foldLeft(identity, { b ->
            { me: MapEntry<K, V> ->
                f(b)(me)
            }
        }, g)
```

Note that folding maps generally occur in specific use cases that deserve to be abstracted inside the `Map` class.

EXERCISE 11.3

Write a `values` function in the `Map` class that returns a list of the values contained in the map in ascending key order.

HINT

You might have to create a new folding function in the `Tree` class and delegate to it from the `Map` class.

SOLUTION

There are several possible implementations of the `values` function. It would be possible to delegate to the `foldInOrder` function, but this function iterates over the tree values in ascending order. Using this function to construct a list would result in a list in descending order.

You could reverse the result, but this wouldn't be efficient. A much better solution is to add a `foldInReverseOrder` function into the `Tree` class. Recall the `foldInOrder` function:

```
override fun <B> foldInOrder(identity: B, f: (B) -> (A) -> (B) -> B): B =
    f(left.foldInOrder(identity, f))(value)(right.foldInOrder(identity, f))
```

All you have to do is reverse the order:

```
override fun <B> foldInReverseOrder(identity: B,
                        f: (B) -> (A) -> (B) -> B): B =
        f(right.foldInReverseOrder(identity, f))(value)(left
                        .foldInReverseOrder(identity, f))
```

As usual, the `Empty` implementation returns `identity`. Now you can delegate to this function from inside the `Map` class:

```
fun values(): List<V> =
    sequence(delegate.foldInReverseOrder(List<Result<V>>()) { lst1 ->
        { me ->
            { lst2 ->
                lst2.concat(lst1.cons(me.value))
            }
        }
    }).getOrElse(List())
```

11.2.3 *Using Map with noncomparable keys*

The Map class is useful and relatively efficient, but it has a big disadvantage compared to the maps you might be used to: the keys must be comparable. Although the types used for keys are usually comparable, such as integers or strings, what if you need to use a noncomparable type for the keys?

EXERCISE 11.4

Implement a version of Map that works with noncomparable keys.

HINT

You need to modify two things: first, the MapEntry class should be made comparable, although the key isn't. Second, non-equal values might be held in equal map entries, so collisions should be resolved by keeping both colliding entries.

SOLUTION

The first thing to do is to modify the MapEntry class by removing the need for the key to be comparable:

```
class MapEntry<K: Any, V> private constructor(val key: K,
                                              val value: Result<V>):
                                   Comparable<MapEntry<K, V>> {
```

Note that the MapEntry class is still comparable, although the K type isn't.

Second, you must use a different implementation for the compareTo function. One possibility is to compare the map entries based on a key hash-code comparison. Note that you need to slightly change the type parameter of the class, making the key class extend Any. By default, it extends Any?, a nullable type, so you would need to handle nulls in the compareTo implementation. Calling other.hashCode() could otherwise throw a NullPointerException:

```
class MapEntry<K: Any, V> private constructor(val key: K,
                                              val value: Result<V>):
                                   Comparable<MapEntry<K, V>> {

    override fun compareTo(other: MapEntry<K, V>): Int =
                    hashCode().compareTo(other.hashCode())

        ...
```

Then you must handle collisions that happen when two map entries have different keys with the same hash code. In such cases, you should keep both of them. The simplest solution is to store the map entries in a list. To do this, you must modify the Map class. First, the tree delegate (in the constructor) will have a modified type:

```
private val delegate: Tree<MapEntry<Int, List<Pair<K, V>>>> = Tree()
```

Next, you'll need a function to retrieve the list of key/value tuples corresponding to the same key hash code:

```
private fun getAll(key: @UnsafeVariance K): Result<List<Pair<K, V>>> =
    delegate[MapEntry(key.hashCode())]
        .flatMap { x ->
```

```
        x.value.map { lt ->
            lt.map { t -> t }
        }
    }
```

You can then define the `plus`, `contains`, `minus`, and `get` functions in terms of the `getAll` function. Here's the add function:

```
operator fun plus(entry: Pair<@UnsafeVariance K, V>): Map<K, V> {
    val list = getAll(entry.first).map { lt ->
        lt.foldLeft(List(entry)) { lst ->
            { pair ->
                if (pair.first == entry.first) lst else lst.cons(pair)
            }
        }
    }.getOrElse { List(entry) }
    return Map(delegate + MapEntry.of(entry.first.hashCode(), list))
}
```

Here's the minus function:

```
operator fun minus(key: @UnsafeVariance K): Map<K, V> {
    val list = getAll(key).map { lt ->
        lt.foldLeft(List()) { lst: List<Pair<K, V>> ->
            { pair ->
                if (pair.first == key) lst else lst.cons(pair)
            }
        }
    }.getOrElse { List() }
    return when {
        list.isEmpty() -> Map(delegate - MapEntry(key.hashCode()))
        else -> Map(delegate + MapEntry.of(key.hashCode(), list))
    }
}
```

Here's the contains function:

```
fun contains(key: @UnsafeVariance K): Boolean =
        getAll(key).map { list ->
            list.exists { pair ->
                pair.first == key
            }
        }.getOrElse( false)
```

And here's the get function:

```
fun get(key: @UnsafeVariance K): Result<Pair<K, V>> =
        getAll(key).flatMap { list ->
            list.filter { pair ->
                pair.first == key
            }.headSafe()
        }
```

Note that the functions `values` and `foldLeft` no longer compile. You can fix this as an additional exercise. It looks hard but it isn't. Follow the types. If you have trouble, you'll find the solutions in the code available in the GitHub repository (https://github.com/pysaumont/fpinkotlin).

With these modifications, the Map class can be used with noncomparable keys. Using a list for storing the key/value tuples might not be the most efficient implementation, because searching in a list takes time proportional to the number of elements. But in most cases, the list will contain only one element, so the search will return in no time. For the same reason, it isn't useful to optimize the search for the first occurrence matching the key criteria in the get function. If you want to do so, you can use an escaping fold (fold with a "zero" parameter) instead of using filter plus headSafe which would first travel the whole list before taking the first element. If you don't remember how to do so, refer to exercise 8.13.

One thing to note about this implementation is that the minus function tests whether the resulting list of pairs is empty. If it is, it calls the minus function on the delegate. Otherwise, it calls the plus function to re-insert the new list from which the corresponding entry has been deleted. Recall exercise 10.1 from chapter 10. This is possible only because you chose to implement plus in such a way that an element found equal to an element present in the map would be inserted in place of the original one. If you hadn't done that, you'd have to first remove the element and then insert the new one with the modified list.

11.3 *Implementing a functional priority queue*

As you know, a queue is a kind of list with a specific access protocol. Queues can be single-ended, like the singly linked list you've used so often in the previous chapters. In that case, the access protocol is last in, first out (LIFO). A queue can also be double-ended, allowing the first in, first out (FIFO) access protocol. But there are also data structures with more specialized protocols. Among them is the *priority queue.*

11.3.1 *Looking at the priority queue access protocol*

Values can be inserted in a priority queue in any order, but those can only be retrieved in a specific order. All values have a priority level, and only the element with the highest priority is available. *Priority* is represented by an ordering of the elements, which implies that the elements must be comparable in some way.

The priority corresponds to the position of the elements in a theoretical waiting queue. The highest priority belongs to the element with the lowest position (the first element). By convention, the highest priority is represented by the lowest value.

Because a priority queue contains comparable elements, this makes it a good fit for a tree-like structure. But from the user's perspective, the priority queue is seen as a list with a head (the element with the highest priority, meaning the lowest value) and a tail (the rest of the queue).

11.3.2 *Exploring priority queue use cases*

The priority queue has many different use cases. One that comes to mind quickly is sorting. You could insert elements into a priority queue in random order and retrieve them sorted. This isn't the main use case for this structure, but it can be useful for sorting small data sets.

Another common use case is reordering elements after asynchronous parallel processing. Imagine you have a number of pages of data to process. To speed processing, you can distribute the data among several threads that work in parallel. But there's no guarantee that the threads will return their work in the same order that they receive it. To resynchronize the pages, you can put them in a priority queue. The process that's supposed to consume the pages then polls the queue to check if the available element (the head of the queue) is the expected one. For example, if pages 1, 2, 3, 4, 5, 6, 7, and 8 are given to eight threads to be processed in parallel, the consumer polls the queue to see if page 1 is available. If it is, it consumes it. If not, it waits.

In such a scenario, the queue acts both as a buffer and as a way to reorder the elements. This generally implies limited variation in size, because elements are removed from the queue more or less at the same speed they're inserted. This is true if the consumer consumes elements at approximately the same pace as they're produced by the eight threads. If this isn't the case, it might be possible to use several consumers.

As I said earlier, choosing an implementation is generally a matter of trading space against time, or time against time. Here the choice you need to make is between insertion and retrieval times. In the general use case, retrieval time must be optimized over insertion time because the ratio between the numbers of insertion and retrieval operations will generally be largely in favor of retrieval. (The head will be often read without being removed.)

11.3.3   *Looking at implementation requirements*

You could implement a priority queue based on the red-black tree because finding the minimum value is fast. But retrieval doesn't mean removal. If you search for the minimum value and find that it isn't the one you want, you'll have to come back later and search again. One solution to this could be to memoize the lowest value on insertion. The other change you might want to make is in regard to removal. Removing an element is relatively fast, but as you'll always be removing the lowest element, it might be possible to optimize the data structure for this operation.

Another important consideration would be in regard to duplicates. Although the red-black tree doesn't allow duplicates, the priority queue must because it's perfectly possible to have several elements with the same priority. The solution can be the same as for maps—storing lists of elements (instead of single elements) with the same priority. But this probably won't be optimal for performance.

11.3.4   *The leftist heap data structure*

To meet the requirements for a priority queue, you'll use the leftist heap described by Okasaki.[5] Okasaki defines the leftist heap as a heap-ordered tree with an additional leftist property:

---

[5]   Chris Okasaki, *Purely Functional Data Structures* (Cambridge University Press, 1999).

- A heap-ordered tree is a tree in which each branch of an element is greater than or equal to the element itself. This guarantees that the lowest element in the tree is always the root element, making access to the lowest value instantaneous.
- With the leftist property, for each element, the left branch rank is greater than or equal to the right branch rank.
- The *rank* of an element is the length of the right path (also called the right spine) to an empty element. The leftist property guarantees that the shortest path from any element to an empty element is the right path. A consequence of this is that elements are always found in ascending order along any descending path. Figure 11.8 shows an example of a leftist tree.

As you can see, retrieving the highest priority element is possible in constant time because it'll always be the root of the tree. This element is called the *head* of the structure. Removing an element, by analogy with a list, consists in returning the rest of the tree once the root has been removed. This returned value is called the *tail* of the structure.

11.3.5 *Implementing the leftist heap*

The leftist heap main class is called `Heap` and should be a tree implementation. Listing 11.4 shows the basic structure. The main difference from the trees you've developed up to now is that functions such as `right`, `left`, and `head` (equivalent to what was called `value` in previous examples) return a `Result` instead of a raw value. Also note that the rank is computed by the callers of the constructor instead of by the constructor itself. This is an unmotivated design choice to show another way of doing things. As the constructors are private, the difference won't leak outside the `Heap` class.

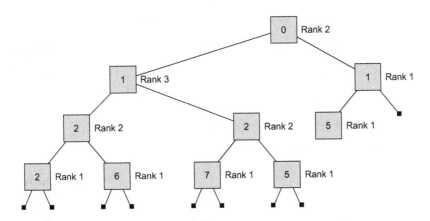

Figure 11.8 A heap-ordered leftist tree, showing that each branch of an element is higher than or equal to the element itself and each left-branch rank is greater than or equal to the corresponding right-branch rank.

Listing 11.4   The leftist heap structures

```
sealed class Heap<out A: Comparable<@UnsafeVariance A>> {

    internal abstract val left: Result<Heap<A>>
    internal abstract val right: Result<Heap<A>>
    internal abstract val head: Result<A>
    protected abstract val rank: Int
    abstract val size: Int
    abstract val isEmpty: Boolean

    abstract class Empty<out A: Comparable<@UnsafeVariance A>>:
                                    Heap<A>() {

        override val isEmpty: Boolean = true

        override val left: Result<Heap<A>> = Result(E)

        override val right: Result<Heap<A>> = Result(E)

        override val head: Result<A> =
            Result.failure("head() called on empty heap")

        override val rank: Int = 0

        override val size: Int = 0
    }

    internal object E: Empty<Nothing>()

    internal class H<out A: Comparable<@UnsafeVariance A>>(
                        override val rank: Int,
                        private val lft: Heap<A>,
                        private val hd: A,
                        private val rght: Heap<A>): Heap<A>()  {

        override val isEmpty: Boolean = false

        override val left: Result<Heap<A>> = Result(lft)

        override val right: Result<Heap<A>> = Result(rght)

        override val head: Result<A> = Result(hd)

        override val size: Int = lft.size + rght.size + 1
    }

    companion object {

        operator fun <A: Comparable<A>> invoke(): Heap<A> = E
    }
}
```

Functions left, right, and head all return a Result.

The size of the tree is the number of elements it contains.

The Empty class is abstract.

The E singleton object represents all empty trees.

The rank property is computed outside of the H subclass and passed to the constructor.

The rank property is computed outside of the H subclass and passed to the constructor.

This function returns an empty tree.

EXERCISE 11.5

The first functionality you'll want to add to your `Heap` implementation is the ability to add an element. Define a `plus` function for this. Make it an instance operator function in the `Heap` class with the following signature:

```
operator fun plus(element: @UnsafeVariance A): Heap<A>
```

The requirement is that if the value is smaller than any element in the heap, it should become the root of the new heap. Otherwise, the root of the heap shouldn't change. Also, the other requirements about rank and length of the right path should be respected.

HINT

Define a function in the companion object to create a `Heap` from an element and another to create a heap by merging two heaps with the following signatures:

```
operator fun <A: Comparable<A>> invoke(element: A): Heap<A>

fun <A: Comparable<A>> merge(first: Heap<A>, second: Heap<A>): Heap<A>
```

Then define the `plus` function in terms of those two.

SOLUTION

The function for creating a heap from a single element is simple. Create a new tree with rank 1, the parameter element as the head, and the two empty heaps as the left and right branches:

```
operator fun <A: Comparable<A>> invoke(element: A): Heap<A> =
        H(1, E, element, E)
```

Creating a heap by merging two heaps is a bit more complicated. For this, you'll need an additional helper function that creates a heap from one element and two heaps:

```
protected
fun <A : Comparable<A>> merge(head: A,
                              first: Heap<A>,
                              second: Heap<A>): Heap<A> =
    when {
        first.rank >= second.rank -> H(second.rank + 1, first, head, second)
        else -> H(first.rank + 1, second, head, first)
    }
```

This code first checks whether the first heap's rank is greater than or equal to the second one. If it is, the new rank is set to the rank of the second heap + 1, and the two heaps are used in first, second order. Otherwise, the new rank is set to the first heap rank + 1, and the two heaps are used in reverse order (second, first). Now the function to merge two heaps can be written as follows:

```
fun <A: Comparable<A>> merge(first: Heap<A>, second: Heap<A>): Heap<A> =
    first.head.flatMap { fh ->
        second.head.flatMap { sh ->
            when {
                fh <= sh -> first.left.flatMap { fl ->
                    first.right.map { fr ->
```

```
                            merge(fh, fl, merge(fr, second))
                    }
            }
            else -> second.left.flatMap { sl ->
                second.right.map { sr ->
                    merge(sh, sl, merge(first, sr))
                }
            }
        }
    }
}.getOrElse(when (first) {
            E -> second
            else -> first
        })
```

If one of the heaps to be merged is empty, you return the other one. Otherwise, you compute the result of the merge. With these functions defined, it's easy to create the plus function:

```
operator fun plus(element: @UnsafeVariance A): Heap<A> =
                        merge(this, Heap(element))
```

11.3.6 *Implementing the queue-like interface*

Although it's implemented as a tree, the heap from the user's perspective is like a priority queue, which means a kind of linked list where the head is always the smallest element. By analogy, the root element of the tree is called the head and what remains after having removed the head is called the tail.

EXERCISE 11.6

Define a `tail` function that returns what's left after removing the head. This function, like the head function, returns a `Result` in order to make it safe when it's called on an empty queue. Here's its signature in the `Heap` parent class:

```
abstract fun tail(): Result<Heap<A>>
```

SOLUTION

The `Empty` implementation is obvious and returns a `Failure`:

```
override fun tail(): Result<Heap<A>> =
    Result.failure(IllegalStateException("tail() called on empty heap"))
```

The H implementation is no more complex, given the functions you defined in the previous exercise. It returns the result of merging the left and right branches:

```
override fun tail(): Result<Heap<A>> = Result(merge(lft, rght))
```

EXERCISE 11.7

Implement a `get` function that takes an `int` parameter and returns the nth element by priority order. This function will return a `Result` to handle the case where no element is found. Here's its signature in the `Heap` parent class:

```
fun get(index: Int): Result<A>
```

SOLUTION

The Empty implementation is obvious and returns a failure:

```
override fun get(index: Int): Result<A> =
        Result.failure(NoSuchElementException("Index out of bounds"))
```

The H implementation is equally simple. It starts by testing the index. If it's 0, it returns Success of the head value. Otherwise, it recursively searches for the element of index *index* - 1 in the tail. Because the tail doesn't exist, but is only the value returned by the tail function (which is a Result), this result is flat-mapped with a recursive call to get:

```
override fun get(index: Int): Result<A> = when (index) {
    0 -> Result(hd)
    else -> tail().flatMap { it.get(index - 1) }
}
```

You might want a more explicit message when no element is found. You can't use the value of the index in the Empty implementation because it's already decremented. To overcome this, there are many possible solutions. Consider this as an additional optional exercise.

11.4 Elements and sorted lists

It will sometimes be useful to transform a Heap into a sorted list. This seems an easy task: simply pop elements out of the heap one at a time and add them to a list. But this is a specific case of a more general fold operation.

EXERCISE 11.8

Create a function pop that pops an element out of the heap, returning an option of a pair containing both the head and the tail of the heap. If the heap is empty, this Option will be None. Then write a function creating a sorted list from a heap.

HINT

Here's the pop function signature:

```
fun pop(): Option<Pair<A, Heap<A>>>
```

SOLUTION

Here's a possible pop implementation. First define an abstract function in the Heap class:

```
abstract fun pop(): Option<Pair<A, Heap<A>>>
```

The implementation in the Empty class returns an empty option:

```
override fun pop(): Option<Pair<A, Heap<A>>> = Option()
```

In the H class, the pop function returns an Option of a pair containing the head and the tail of the heap:

```
override fun pop(): Option<Pair<A, Heap<A>>> =
                Option(Pair(hd, merge(lft, rght)))
```

The return type of the pop function makes it well suited to the unfold function you defined for the List type. Here's how you can implement a toList function in the parent Heap class:

```
fun toList(): List<A> = unfold(this) { it.pop() }
```

EXERCISE 11.9

In the previous exercise, you used the unfold function producing a List<A>. But there's room for abstraction here. This function could be generalized to produce any B type if List<A> was one possible realization of B.

Write an unfold function in Heap producing a B instead of a List<A> and rewrite the toList function in terms of this one. Then write a foldLeft function with the same signature as the List.foldLeft version.

HINT

Start by copying the implementation of the List unfold function into the Heap class and make the necessary changes to replace the List<A> type with a more generic B type. Here's the implementation of the unfold function producing a List:

```
fun <A, S> unfold(z: S, getNext: (S) -> Option<Pair<A, S>>): List<A> {
    tailrec fun unfold(acc: List<A>, z: S): List<A> {
        val next = getNext(z)
        return when (next) {
            is Option.None -> acc
            is Option.Some ->
                unfold(acc.cons(next.value.first), next.value.second)
        }
    }
    return unfold(List.Nil, z).reverse()
}
```

SOLUTION

To make this function generic, you need to replace all references to List<A> with B:

- List.Nil should be replaced with a B identity, which will have to be passed to the function as an additional parameter.
- acc.cons(next.value.first) is the implementation of a function of type (List<A>) → A → (List<A>) that's used to create the list. In a generic version, this function implementation is unknown at compile time, so it'll be passed as an additional parameter.
- The call to reverse before returning the list is specific to List and must be removed:

```
fun <A, S, B> unfold(z: S,
                     getNext: (S) -> Option<Pair<A, S>>,
                     identity: B,
                     f: (B) -> (A) -> B): B {
    tailrec fun unfold(acc: B, z: S): B {
        val next = getNext(z)
        return when (next) {
```

```
                    is Option.None -> acc
                    is Option.Some ->
                        unfold(f(acc)(next.value.first), next.value.second)
            }
        }
        return unfold(identity, z)
}
```

A `foldLeft` function can now be rewritten as

```
fun <B> foldLeft(identity: B, f: (B) -> (A) -> B): B =
            unfold(this, { it.pop() }, identity, f)
```

And you could then rewrite `toList` as

```
fun toList(): List<A> =
    foldLeft(List<A>()) { list -> { a -> list.cons(a) } }.reverse()
```

11.5   A priority queue for noncomparable elements

To insert elements into a priority queue, you must be able to compare their priorities. But priority isn't always a property of elements; not all elements implement the Comparable interface. Elements that don't implement this interface can still be compared using a `Comparator`, so can you do this for the priority queue?

EXERCISE 11.10

Modify the `Heap` class so that it can be used either with `Comparable` elements or with a separate `Comparator`.

SOLUTION

First, you must change the declaration of the `Heap` class replacing

```
sealed class Heap<out A: Comparable<@UnsafeVariance A>>
```

with

```
sealed class Heap<out A>
```

Then you must change the declaration of the subclasses accordingly and add a property to the `Heap` class for holding the `Comparator`. As the comparator is optional, this property will hold a `Result<Comparator>` that's potentially empty. Here's the abstract property in the `Heap` class:

```
internal abstract val comparator: Result<Comparator<@UnsafeVariance A>>
```

The `E` singleton object is removed. The `Empty` class is no longer abstract and is constructed with a `Result<Comparator>` with `Empty` as its default value:

```
internal class Empty<out A>(
    override val comparator: Result<Comparator<@UnsafeVariance A>> =
                                        Result.Empty): Heap<A>() {
```

You'll do the same in the `H` class except you'll use the existing constructor (if there is one) for the default value:

```
internal class H<out A>(override val rank: Int,
        internal val lft: Heap<A>,
```

```
internal val hd: A,
internal val rght: Heap<A>,
override val comparator: Result<Comparator<@UnsafeVariance A>> =
    lft.comparator.orElse { rght.comparator }): Heap<A>()  {
```

The companion object functions for creating an empty `Heap` exist in several versions: one taking no comparator and one taking a `Result<Comparator>`. And to simplify usage, you'll add a version taking a `Comparator`. You also need a specific version of the function creating a `Heap` from a single element:

```
operator fun <A: Comparable<A>> invoke(): Heap<A> = Empty()

operator fun <A> invoke(comparator: Comparator<A>): Heap<A> =
            Empty(Result(comparator))

operator fun <A> invoke(comparator: Result<Comparator<A>>): Heap<A> =
            Empty(comparator)

operator fun <A> invoke(element: A, comparator: Result<Comparator<A>>):
    Heap<A> = H(1, Empty(comparator), element,
            Empty(comparator), comparator)
```

Note that the `invoke()` function without an argument can only be called for a `Comparable` type. As a consequence, it isn't possible to create an empty heap for a noncomparable type without providing a comparator. This is checked by the compiler. The function taking an element as its parameter will be changed to create a comparator or receive one as an additional parameter:

```
operator fun <A: Comparable<A>> invoke(element: A): Heap<A> =
    invoke(element, Comparator { o1: A, o2: A ->  o1.compareTo(o2) })

operator fun <A> invoke(element: A, comparator: Comparator<A>): Heap<A> =
    H(1, Empty(Result(comparator)), element,
        Empty(Result(comparator)), Result(comparator))
```

The merge function, taking an element and two heaps, needs to be modified accordingly, but this time, you'll extract the comparator from the heap arguments:

```
protected fun <A> merge(head: A, first: Heap<A>, second: Heap<A>): Heap<A> =
    first.comparator.orElse { second.comparator }.let {
        when {
            first.rank >= second.rank -> H(second.rank + 1,
                            first, head, second, it)
            else -> H(first.rank + 1, second, head, first, it)
        }
    }
```

For the `merge` function taking two `Heap`s as its arguments, you can use the `Comparator` from either of the two trees to be merged. If none have a `Comparator`, you can use a `Result.Empty`. In order to not extract the comparator from the arguments on each recursive call, you can split the function in two:

```
fun <A> merge(first: Heap<A>, second: Heap<A>,
            comparator: Result<Comparator<A>> =
            first.comparator.orElse { second.comparator }): Heap<A> =
```

```
first.head.flatMap { fh ->
    second.head.flatMap { sh ->
        when {
            compare(fh, sh, comparator) <= 0 ->
                        first.left.flatMap { fl ->
                            first.right.map { fr ->
                    merge(fh, fl, merge(fr, second, comparator))
                }
            }
            else -> second.left.flatMap { sl ->
                second.right.map { sr ->
                    merge(sh, sl, merge(first, sr, comparator))
                }
            }
        }
    }
}.getOrElse(when (first) {
            is Empty -> second
            else -> first
        })
```

The second function uses a helper function called compare:

```
private fun <A> compare(first: A, second: A,
                    comparator: Result<Comparator<A>>): Int =
                    comparator.map { comp ->
    comp.compare(first, second)
}.getOrElse { (first as Comparable<A>).compareTo(second) }
```

This function performs a cast of one of its arguments, but you know there's no risk of a ClassCastException being thrown. That's because you ensured that no heap could be created without a comparator if the type parameter didn't extend Comparable. The plus function must also be modified as follows:

```
operator fun plus(element: @UnsafeVariance A): Heap<A> =
                    merge(this, Heap(element, comparator))
```

Finally, the left and right functions in the Empty class must be changed as follows:

```
override val left: Result<Heap<A>> = Result(this)
override val right: Result<Heap<A>> = Result(this)
```

Summary

- Trees can be balanced for better performance and to avoid stack overflow in recursive operations.
- The red-black tree is a self-balancing tree structure that frees you from worrying about tree balancing.
- Maps can be implemented by delegating to a tree storing key/value tuples.
- Maps with noncomparable keys must handle collisions in order to store elements with the same key representation.
- Priority queues are structures allowing elements to be retrieved by priority order.

- Priority queues can be implemented using a leftist heap, which is a heap-ordered binary tree.
- Priority queues of noncomparable elements can be constructed using an additional comparator.

Functional input/output

So far you've learned how to write safe programs that haven't produced any usable results. You've learned how to compose true functions to build more powerful functions. More interestingly, you've learned how to use nonfunctional operations in a safe, functional way. *Nonfunctional operations* are operations producing side effects such as throwing exceptions, changing the outside world, or depending on the outside world to produce a result. For example, you learned how to take an integer division, which is a potentially unsafe operation, and turn it into a safe one by using it inside a computational context. Here are some examples of computational contexts you've created in previous chapters:

- From chapter 7, the Result type allows using a function that could produce an error in a safe, error-free way.

- From chapter 6, the `Option` type is also a computational context used to safely apply functions that could sometimes (for some arguments) produce no data.
- In chapters 5 and 8, the `List` class you studied is a computational context, but rather than dealing with errors, it allows using functions that work on single elements in the context of a collection of elements. It also deals with the absence of data, represented by an empty list.
- The `Lazy` type from chapter 9 is a computational context for data that might not be initialized until it's needed, and the `Stream` context does the same for collections.

When studying these types, producing a usable result wasn't the objective. In this chapter, you'll learn several techniques for producing practical results from your programs. This includes displaying a result for your users or passing a result to another program.

12.1   *What does effects in context mean?*

Recall what you did to apply a function to the result of an integer operation. Let's say you want to write an `inverse` function that computes the multiplication inverse of an integer value:

```
val inverse: (Int) -> Result<Double> = { x ->
    when {
        x != 0 -> Result(1.toDouble() / x)
        else   -> Result.failure("Division by 0")
    }
}
```

This function can be applied to an integer value, but when composed with other functions, the value will be the output of another function! It'll usually be in context already, often the same type of context. Here's an example:

```
val ri: Result<Int> = ...
val rd: Result<Double> = ri.flatMap(inverse)
```

It's important to note that you don't take the value in `ri` out of context to apply the function. It works the other way round: you pass the function into the context (the `Result` type) so that it can be applied inside it, producing a new context that possibly wraps the resulting value. In the preceding snippet, you're passing the function to the `ri` context, producing the new `rd` context.

   This is neat and safe. No bad things can happen and no exceptions can be thrown. This is the beauty of programming with pure functions: you have a program that always works, whatever data you use as input. But the question is, how can you use this result? Suppose you want to display the result on the console—how can you do this?

12.1.1   *Handling effects*

Pure functions are defined as functions without any observable side effects. An *effect* is anything that can be observed from outside the program. The role of a function is to return a value, and *side effects* are anything besides the returned value that's observable from the outside of the function. It's called a side effect because it comes in addition to the value that's returned. By contrast, an effect is like a side effect, but it's the main (and generally unique) role of a program. Making your programs safe is obtained by writing programs with pure functions (with no side effects) and pure effects (not returning any values) in a functional way.

The question is, what does it mean to handle effects in a functional way? The closest definition I can give at this stage is this: handling effects in a way that doesn't interfere with the principles of functional programming, the most important principle being referential transparency.

There are several ways to approach or reach this goal, but fully attaining it can be complex. Often, simply approaching it is sufficient. It's up to you to decide which technique you want to use. Applying effects inside contexts is the simplest way to make otherwise functional programs produce observable effects.

12.1.2 Implementing effects

As I mentioned, an effect is anything that's observable from outside the program. To be valuable, the effect must generally reflect the result of the program. That being so, you'll generally need to take the result of the program and do something observable with it.

Note that *observable* doesn't always mean observable by a human operator. Often the result is observable by another program, which might then translate this effect into something observable by a human operator, either in a synchronous or an asynchronous way.

Printing to the computer screen can be seen by the operator. This is generally what it's meant to be. Writing to a database, on the other hand, might not always be directly visible to a user. Sometimes the user will look up the result, but usually it'll be read later by another program. In chapter 13, you'll learn how such effects can be used by programs to communicate with other programs.

Because an effect is generally applied to a value, a pure effect can be modeled as a special kind of function, returning no value. This is represented in Kotlin by the following type:

```
(T) -> Unit
```

This type can be instantiated using Any as the type because it's the parent of all types:

```
val display = { x: Any -> println(x) }
```

Or better yet, you can use a function reference:

```
val display: (Any) -> Unit = ::println
```

But most often, effects like functions are used anonymously as in the following example:

```
val ri: Result<Int> = ...
val rd: Result<Double> = ri.flatMap(inverse)
rd.map { it * 1.35 }
```

Here the function { it * 2.35 } has no name. But you could give it a name in order to be able to reuse it:

```
val ri: Result<Int> = ...
val rd: Result<Double> = ri.flatMap(inverse)
val function: (Double) -> Double = { it * 2.35 }
val result = rd.map(function)
```

To apply effects, you'd need something equivalent, such as

```
val ri: Result<Int> = ...
val rd: Result<Double> = ri.flatMap(inverse)
val function: (Double) -> Double = { it * 2.35 }
val result = rd.map(function)
val ef: (Double) -> Unit = ::println
result.map(ef)
```

Guess what? It works! This is possible because ef is a function returning Unit (the equivalent of void in Java, or rather, the equivalent of Void). The previous code is equivalent to

```
val ri: Result<Int> = ...
val rd: Result<Double> = ri.flatMap(inverse)
val function: (Double) -> Double = { it * 2.35 }
val result = rd.map(function)
val ef: (Double) -> Unit = ::println
val x: Result<Unit> = result.map(ef)
```

To apply an effect, you could use this technique, mapping the effect and ignoring the result. But you can do better. As you saw in chapter 7, you wrote a forEach function in the Result class taking an effect and applying it to the underlying value. This function was implemented in the Empty class as follows:

```
override fun forEach(onSuccess: (Nothing) -> Unit,
                     onFailure: (RuntimeException) -> Unit,
                     onEmpty: () -> Unit) {
    onEmpty()
}
```

In the Success class, it was implemented like this:

```
override fun forEach(onSuccess: (A) -> Unit,
                     onFailure: (RuntimeException) -> Unit,
                     onEmpty: () -> Unit) {
    onSuccess(value)
}
```

And in the Failure class, this was the implementation:

```
override fun forEach(onSuccess: (A) -> Unit,
                     onFailure: (RuntimeException) -> Unit,
                     onEmpty: () -> Unit) {
    onFailure(exception)
}
```

The forEach function takes three effects as its parameters: one for Success, one for Failure, and one for Empty. Furthermore, the abstract declaration in the Result parent class declared default values for each effect:

```
abstract fun forEach(onSuccess: (A) -> Unit = {},
                     onFailure: (RuntimeException) -> Unit = {},
                     onEmpty: () -> Unit = {})
```

You can't write unit tests for this function. To verify that it works, you can run the program shown in the following listing and look at the result onscreen. (You can write some tests altering some global or parameter's state and then assert these changes, but this isn't unit testing!)

Listing 12.1 Outputting data

```
fun main(args: Array<String>) {
    val ra = Result(4)
    val rb = Result(0)
    val inverse: (Int) -> Result<Double> = { x ->          Simulates data returned
        when {                                              by functions that could fail
            x != 0 -> Result(1.toDouble() / x)
            else   -> Result.failure("Division by 0")
        }
    }
    val showResult: (Double) -> Unit = ::println
    val showError: (RuntimeException) -> Unit =
                    { println("Error - ${it.message}")}

    val rt1 = ra.flatMap(inverse)
    val rt2 = rb.flatMap(inverse)

    print("Inverse of 4: ")
    rt1.forEach(showResult, showError)        Outputs the resulting value

    System.out.print("Inverse of 0: ")
    rt2.forEach(showResult, showError)        Outputs the error message
}
```

This program produces the following result:

```
Inverse of 4: 0.25
Inverse of 0: Error - Division by 0
```

EXERCISE 12.1

Write a forEach function in the List class that takes an effect and applies it to all the elements of the list. Its signature is this:

```
fun forEach(ef: (A) -> Unit)
```

SOLUTION

You can implement this function in the parent List class or declare it as an abstract function and implement it in both subclasses. Unlike in Result.Empty, there's no reason to evaluate any effect when the list is empty (although you could do so if it suits your use case). The implementation for the `Nil` will be this:

```
override fun forEach(ef: (Nothing) -> Unit) {}
```

The simplest recursive implementation for the `Cons` class would be as follows:

```
override fun forEach(ef: (A) -> Unit) {
    ef(head)
    tail.forEach(ef)
}
```

Unfortunately, this implementation will blow the stack if you've more than a few thousand elements. The solution is to make this function tail-recursive. The easiest way is to define a tail-recursive helper function locally is in the `forEach` function:

```
override fun forEach(ef: (A) -> Unit) {
    tailrec fun forEach(list: List<A>) {
        when (list) {
            Nil -> {}
            is Cons -> {
                ef(list.head)
                forEach(list.tail)
            }
        }
    }
    forEach(this)
}
```

12.2   Reading data

So far we've only dealt with output. Often, outputting data occurs at the end of the program once the result is computed. This allows most of the program to be written without effects with all the benefits of the functional paradigm. Only the output part isn't functional.

We haven't looked at how to input data into programs. Let's do that now. Later you'll look at a more functional way to input data. But first, you'll look at how to do it in a clean (although imperative) way that fits nicely with the functional parts.

12.2.1 Reading data from the console

As an example, you'll read data from the console in a way that, although imperative, allows testing by making your programs deterministic. You'll first develop an example that reads integers and strings. The following listing shows the interface you'll need to implement.

> Listing 12.2   An interface for inputting data

```
interface Input: Closeable {

    fun readString(): Result<Pair<String, Input>>

    fun readInt(): Result<Pair<Int, Input>>
```

Extends the Closeable interface

Inputs an integer and a string, respectively

Passes a message as a parameter

```
fun readString(message: String): Result<Pair<String, Input>> =
                                 readString()

fun readInt(message: String): Result<Pair<Int, Input>> =
                              readInt()
}
```

In the listing, extending the `Closeable` interface will be useful for automatically closing resources that need to be closed. Passing a message as a parameter can be useful for prompting the user.

But here the provided default implementations ignores the message. Note that these functions return `Result<Pair<String, Input>>` and not `Result<String>`, which allows chaining function calls in a referentially transparent manner.

You could write a concrete implementation for this interface, but first you'll write an abstract one (because you might want to read data from some other source, such as a file). You'll put the common code in an abstract class and extend it for each type of input. The following listing shows this implementation.

Listing 12.3 The `AbstractReader` implementation

```
abstract class AbstractReader (                          Builds this class with a
     private val reader: BufferedReader): Input {  ◄───  reader, allowing for
                                                         different sources of input

    override fun readString():
               Result<Pair<String, Input>> = try {   ◄──────────
        reader.readLine().let {
            when {
                it.isEmpty() -> Result()
                else         -> Result(Pair(it, this))
            }
        }                              Reads a line from the reader and returns a
    }                                  Result.Empty if the line is empty, a Result.
    } catch (e: Exception) {           Success if some data is obtained, or a
        Result.failure(e)              Result.Failure if something goes wrong
    }

    override fun readInt(): Result<Pair<Int, Input>> = try {
        reader.readLine().let {
            when {
                it.isEmpty() -> Result()
                else         -> Result(Pair(it.toInt(), this))
            }
        }
    }
    } catch (e: Exception) {
        Result.failure(e)
    }
                                               Delegates to the close function
                                               of the BufferedReader
    override fun close(): Unit = reader.close()  ◄──────
}
```

Now you need to implement the concrete class in order to read from the console, as shown in the next listing. This class is responsible for providing the reader. Additionally, you'll re-implement the two default functions from the interface to display a prompt to the user.

Listing 12.4   The `ConsoleReader` implementation

```
import com.fpinkotlin.common.Result

import java.io.BufferedReader
import java.io.InputStreamReader

class ConsoleReader(reader: BufferedReader): AbstractReader(reader) {

    override fun readString(message: String):
                    Result<Pair<String, Input>> {
        print("$message ")
        return readString()
    }

    override fun readInt(message: String):
                    Result<Pair<Int, Input>> {
        print("$message ")
        return readInt()
    }

    companion object {
        operator fun invoke(): ConsoleReader =
            ConsoleReader(BufferedReader(
                InputStreamReader(System.`in`)))

    }
}
```

The two default functions are reimplemented to display the user prompt.

You must use backticks to reference the in field of a Java System class because in is a reserved word in Kotlin.

Now you can use your `ConsoleReader` class with what you've learned to write a complete program, from input to output. The following listing shows the program.

Listing 12.5   A complete program, from input to output

Calls readString with a user prompt and returns a Result<Tuple<String, Input>>, which is mapped to produce a Result<String>

The business part of the program (what the program is supposed to do from the user's point of view). It can be functionally pure.

```
fun main(args: Array<String>) {

    val input = ConsoleReader()

    val rString = input.readString("Enter your name:")
                            .map { t -> t.first }

    val nameMessage = rString.map { "Hello, $it!" }

    nameMessage.forEach(::println, onFailure =
                        { println(it.message) })
```

Creates the reader

Applies the pattern from the previous section to either the result or an error message

```
val rInt = input.readInt("Enter your age:").map { t -> t.first }

val ageMessage = rInt.map { "You look younger than $it!" }

ageMessage.forEach(::println, onFailure =
    { println("Invalid age. Please enter an integer")})
}
```

**Prints a different message
than the one in the exception**

Note that there is no way to refer to the input value in the ageMessage.forEach effect. For doing so, you would need to use a specific validating context rather than Result.

This program isn't impressive. It's the equivalent of the ubiquitous "Hello" program that's usually the second example (just after "Hello world") in most programming books. Of course, this is only an example. What's interesting is how easy it is to evolve this into something more useful.

EXERCISE 12.2

Write a program that repeatedly asks the user to input an integer ID, a first name, and a last name, and that later displays the list of people on the console. Data input stops as soon as the user enters a blank ID and the list of entered data is then displayed.

HINT

You'll need a class to hold each line of data. Use the Person data class shown here:

```
data class Person (val id: Int, val firstName: String, val lastName: String)
```

Implement the solution in a main function at package level. Use the Stream.unfold function to produce a stream of persons. You might find it easier to create a separate function for inputting the data corresponding to a single person, and to use a function reference as the argument of unfold. This function could have the following signature:

```
fun person(input: Input): Result<Pair<Person, Input>>
```

SOLUTION

The solution is simple. Considering that you have a function for inputting the data for a single person, you can create a stream of persons and print the result as follows (ignoring any error in this case and not taking care of closing resources):

```
import com.fpinkotlin.common.List
import com.fpinkotlin.common.Stream


fun readPersonsFromConsole(): List<Person> =
    Stream.unfold(ConsoleReader(), ::person).toList()

fun main(args: Array<String>) {
    readPersonsFromConsole().forEach(::println)
}
```

All you need now is the `person` function. This function asks for the ID, the first name, and the last name, producing three `Result` instances that can be combined using the comprehension pattern you learned in previous chapters:

```
fun person(input: Input): Result<Pair<Person, Input>> =
    input.readInt("Enter ID:").flatMap { id ->
        id.second.readString("Enter first name:")
            .flatMap { firstName ->
                firstName.second.readString("Enter last name:")
                    .map { lastName ->
                        Pair(Person(id.first,
                                    firstName.first,
                                    lastName.first), lastName.second)
                    }
            }
    }
```

The comprehension pattern is probably one of the most important patterns in functional programming, so you want to master it. Other languages such as Scala or Haskell have syntactic sugar for it, but Kotlin doesn't. This corresponds, in pseudo-code, to something like this:

```
for {
  id in input.readInt("Enter ID:")
  firstName in id.second.readString("Enter first name:")
  lastName in firstName.second.readString("Enter last name:")
} return Pair(Person(id.first, firstName.first, lastName.first), lastName.
    second))
```

You shouldn't miss the syntactic sugar. The `flatMap` idiom is perhaps more difficult to master at first, but it shows what's happening. Many programmers know this pattern as the following:

```
a.flatMap { b ->
    flatMap { c ->
        map { d ->
            getSomething(a, b, c, d)
        }
    }
}
```

They often think it's always a series of `flatMaps` ending with a `map`. This isn't the case. Whether it's `map` or `flatMap` depends solely on the return type. It often happens that the last function (here, `getSomething`) returns a bare value. This is why the pattern ends with a `map`. But if `getSomething` were to return a `Result`, the pattern would be as follows:

```
a.flatMap { b ->
    flatMap { c ->
        flatMap { d ->
            getSomething(a, b, c, d)
        }
    }
}
```

12.2.2 Reading from a file

The way you've designed the program makes it simple to adapt it to reading files. The `FileReader` class is similar to `ConsoleReader`. But one difference is that the companion object invoke function must handle the `Exception` that might be thrown when creating the `BufferedReader`, so it returns a `Result<Input>` instead of a bare value, as shown in the next listing.

Listing 12.6 The `FileReader` implementation

```
class FileReader private constructor(private val reader: BufferedReader) :
                                AbstractReader(reader), AutoCloseable {

    override fun close() {
        reader.close()
    }

    companion object {

        operator fun invoke(path: String): Result<Input> = try {
            Result(FileReader(File(path).bufferedReader()))
        } catch (e: Exception) {
            Result.failure(e)
        }
    }
}
```

EXERCISE 12.3

Write a `ReadFile` program that's similar to `ReadConsole` but that reads from a file containing the entries, each one on a separate line. An example file is provided with the code accompanying this book (http://github.com/pysaumont/fpinkotlin).

HINT

Although it's similar to the `ReadConsole` program, you'll have to deal with the fact that the invoke function returns a `Result`. Try to reuse the same person function. Also note that you should take care of closing the resources. For this, you should use the use function of the Kotlin standard library.

SOLUTION

In the following solution, note how the use function is employed in order to ensure that the file is correctly closed in any case:

```
fun readPersonsFromFile(path: String): Result<List<Person>> =
        FileReader(path).map {
            it.use {
                Stream.unfold(it, ::person).toList()
            }
        }

fun main(args: Array<String>) {
    val path = "<path>/data.txt"
    readPersonsFromFile(path).forEach({ list: List<Person> ->
```

```
        list.forEach(::println)
    }, onFailure = ::println)
}
```

The it reference is used twice in the readPersonsFromFile function, each time representing the parameter of the current lambda expression. If you find this confusing, you can use specific names such as

```
fun readPersonsFromFile(path: String): Result<List<Person>> =
        FileReader(path).map { input1 ->
            input1.use { input2 ->
                Stream.unfold(input2, ::person).toList()
            }
        }
```

But in this specific case, both names represent the same object.

12.3   *Testing with input*

One of the benefits of the approach shown is that the program is easily testable. It would be possible to test your programs by providing files instead of user input at the console, but it's just as easy to interface your program with another program that produces a script of the input commands. The following listing shows an example ScriptReader that you could use for testing.

> **Listing 12.7   A** ScriptReader **that allows you to use a list of input commands**

```
class ScriptReader : Input {

    constructor(commands: List<String>) : super() {
        this.commands = commands
    }

    constructor(vararg commands: String) : super() {
        this.commands = List(*commands)
    }

    private val commands: List<String>


    override fun close() {
    }

    override fun readString(): Result<Pair<String, Input>> = when {
        commands.isEmpty() ->
            Result.failure("Not enough entries in script")
        else -> Result(Pair(commands.headSafe().getOrElse(""),
                ScriptReader(commands.drop(1))))
    }

    override fun readInt(): Result<Pair<Int, Input>> = try {
        when {
            commands.isEmpty() ->
                Result.failure("Not enough entries in script")
            Integer.parseInt(commands.headSafe().getOrElse("")) >= 0 ->
```

The ScriptReader can be created with a list of commands...

...or with a vararg argument

```
                    Result(Pair(Integer.parseInt(
                        commands.headSafe().getOrElse("")),
                        ScriptReader(commands.drop(1))))
            else -> Result()
        }
    } catch (e: Exception) {
        Result.failure(e)
    }
}
```

The next listing shows an example of using the `ScriptReader` class. In the code accompanying this book, you'll find examples of unit testing.

Listing 12.8 Using the `ScriptReader` to enter data

```
fun readPersonsFromScript(vararg commands: String): List<Person> =
        Stream.unfold(ScriptReader(*commands), ::person).toList()

fun main(args: Array<String>) {
    readPersonsFromScript("1", "Mickey", "Mouse",
                          "2", "Minnie", "Mouse",
                          "3", "Donald", "Duck").forEach(::println)
}
```

12.4 *Fully functional input/output*

What you've learned so far is sufficient for most Kotlin programmers. Separating the functional part of the program from the nonfunctional parts is essential and also sufficient. But it's interesting to see how Kotlin programs can be made even more functional.

Whether you want to use the following techniques in Kotlin programs in production is up to you. It might not be worth the additional complexity, but it is useful to learn these techniques so you can make an educated choice.

12.4.1 *Making input/output fully functional*

There are several answers to the question of how can you make input/output (I/O) fully functional. The shortest answer is that you can't. According to the definition of a functional program, which is a program that has no other observable effect than returning a value, there's no way to do any input or output.

But many programs don't need to do any input or output. Some libraries fall into this category. Libraries are programs designed to be used by other programs. They receive argument values and return values resulting from computations based on the arguments. In the first two sections of this chapter, you separated your programs into three parts: one doing the input, one doing the output, and one, the third part, acting as a library and being fully functional.

Another way to handle the problem is to write this library part and produce as the final return value another (nonfunctional) program that handles all the input and output. This is similar in concept to laziness. You can handle I/O as something that happens later in a separate program will be the returned value of our purely functional program.

12.4.2 *Implementing purely functional I/O*

In this section, you'll see how to implement purely functional I/O. Let's start with output. Imagine that you want to display a welcome message to the console. Instead of writing this

```
fun sayHello(name: String) = println("Hello, $name!")
```

you could make the sayHello function return a program that, once run, will have the same effect:

```
fun sayHello(name: String): () -> Unit = { println("Hello, $name!") }
```

You can use this function as follows:

```
fun main(args: Array<String>) {
    val program = sayHello("Georges")
}
```

This code is purely functional. You could argue that it doesn't do anything visible, and this is true. It produces a program that can be run to produce the desired effect. This program can be run by evaluating its result. This result is a program that isn't functional, but we don't care. The main program is functional.

As I've said several times, the best way to make programs safe is to clearly separate functional parts from effects. The technique shown here, if not the easiest to implement, is clearly the ultimate solution when it comes to separating functions from effects.

Is this cheating? No. Think of a program written in any functional language. In the end, it's compiled into an executable program that's absolutely nonfunctional and that can be run on your computer. You're doing exactly the same thing here, except that the program you're producing might seem to be written in Kotlin. In fact, it's not. It's written in some kind of DSL (Domain-Specific Language) that your program is constructing. To execute this program, you can write

```
program()
```

In this example, the program produced is of type () → Unit. This works, but it'd be interesting to do more with this result than simply to evaluate it. For example, you might want to combine several of these kinds of results in many useful ways. For this, you need something much more powerful, so you'll create a new type named IO. You'll start with a single invoke function. At this stage, it's not much different from () → Unit:

```
class IO(private val f: () -> Unit) {

    operator fun invoke() = f()
}
```

Suppose you've the three following functions:

```
fun show(message: String): IO = IO { println(message) }

fun <A> toString(rd: Result<A>): String =
        rd.map { it.toString() }.getOrElse { rd.toString() }
```

```
fun inverse(i: Int): Result<Double> = when (i) {
    0 -> Result.failure("Div by 0")
    else -> Result(1.0 / i)
}
```

You might write the following purely functional program:

```
val computation: IO = show(toString(inverse(3)))
```

This program produces another program that can later be executed:

```
computation()
```

12.4.3 Combining I/O

With your new IO interface, you can potentially build any program, but as a single unit. It'd be interesting to be able to combine such programs. The simplest combination you could use consists of grouping two programs into one. This is what you'll do in the following exercise.

EXERCISE 12.4

Create a function in the IO class that lets you group two IO instances into one. This function will be called plus and it'll have a default implementation. Here's the signature:

```
operator fun plus(io: IO): IO
```

SOLUTION

The solution is to return a new IO with a run implementation that first executes the current IO and then the argument IO:

```
operator fun plus(io: IO): IO = IO {
        f()
        io.f()
    }
```

You'll later need a "do nothing" IO to serve as a neutral element for some IO combinations. You can easily create this in the IO companion object as follows:

```
companion object {
    val empty: IO = IO {}
}
```

Using these new functions, you can create more sophisticated programs by combining IO instances:

```
fun getName() = "Mickey"

val instruction1 = IO { print("Hello, ") }
val instruction2 = IO { print(getName()) }
val instruction3 = IO { print("!\n") }

val script: IO = instruction1
                    + instruction2
                    + instruction3
script()
```

These three lines don't print anything. They are like instructions of the DSL.

Combines the three instructions to create a program

Executes the program

If you prefer, you can use function calls instead of operators:

```
instruction1.plus(instruction2).plus(instruction3)()
```

You can also create a program from a list of instructions:

```
val script = List(
        IO { print("Hello, ") },
        IO { print(getName()) },
        IO { print("!\n") }
)
```

Does this look like an imperative program? In fact, it is. In order to be able to execute it, you must first compile it into a single IO. You can do this with a right fold:

```
val program: IO = script.foldRight(IO.empty) { io -> { io + it } }
```

Or a left fold:

```
val program: IO = script.foldLeft(IO.empty) { acc -> { acc + it } }
```

You can see why you needed a do nothing implementation. Finally, you can run the program as usual:

```
program()
```

Be aware that using a left fold causes the identity IO to be placed in first position, as opposed to a right fold in which the identity IO is placed in last position. Using IO.empty for the identity makes no difference. But if you use another IO (for example, some initialization task), it'll probably have to be executed first, so you'll have to use a left fold. Use a right fold if you want to use some finalizing task as the identity.

12.4.4   *Handling input with IO*

At this point, your IO type only handles output. To make it handle input, one necessary change is to parameterize it with the type of the input value so that it can be used to handle this value. Here's the new parameterized IO type:

```
class IO<out A>(private val f: () -> A) {

    operator fun invoke() = f()

    companion object {

        val empty: IO<Unit> = IO { }

        operator fun <A> invoke(a: A): IO<A> = IO { a }
    }
}
```

The IO class is parameterized and the function it is built with returns an instance of the class parameter type.

The empty instance is parameterized with Unit and created with a function returning nothing. (Be aware that this is different from returning Nothing.)

The invoke function of the companion object takes a bare value and returns it in the IO context.

As you can see, the `IO` interface creates a context for computations in the same way `Option`, `Result`, `List`, `Stream`, `Lazy`, and the like do. It similarly has a function returning an empty instance, as well as a function that puts a bare value in context.

In order to perform computations on `IO` values, you now need functions like `map` and `flatMap` to bind functions to the `IO` context. But in order to be able to test these functions, you'll first define an object for representing the computer console.

EXERCISE 12.5

Define a `Console` object with the three following functions:

```
object Console {

    fun readln(): IO<String> = TODO("")

    fun println(o: Any): IO<Unit> = TODO("")

    fun print(o: Any): IO<Unit> = TODO("")
}
```

SOLUTION

The `print` and `println` functions call the Kotlin equivalent functions on their argument like this:

```
fun println(o: Any): IO<Unit> = IO {
    kotlin.io.println(o.toString())
}

fun print(o: Any): IO<Unit> = IO {
    kotlin.io.print(o.toString())
}
```

You must use the fully qualified function names to avoid the functions calling themselves. You might, however, call your functions by any other name.

The `readln` function calls the `realLine` function of a `BufferedReader` wrapping `System.in`. Remember you must use backticks because *in* is a reserved word in Kotlin:

```
private val br = BufferedReader(InputStreamReader(System.`in`))

fun readln(): IO<String> = IO {
    try {
        br.readLine()
    } catch (e: IOException) {
        throw IllegalStateException(e)
    }
}
```

For the sake of simplicity, you can throw an exception if something goes wrong. Feel free to handle the problem in a more functional way if you prefer.

The `Console` object, at this stage, brings only additional complexity with no benefit. In order to be able to compose `IO` instances, you'll need a `map` function.

EXERCISE 12.6

Define a map function in IO<A> that takes as its argument a function from A to B and returns an IO<B>.

SOLUTION

Here's the implementation that applies the function to the value of this and returns the result in a new IO context:

```
fun <B> map (g: (A) -> B): IO<B> = IO {
    g(this())
}
```

Here's how you can use this function:

```
fun main(args: Array<String>) {
    val script = sayHello()
    script()
}

private fun sayHello(): IO<Unit> = Console.print("Enter your name: ")
        .map { Console.readln()() }
        .map { buildMessage(it) }
        .map { Console.println(it)() }

private fun buildMessage(name: String): String = "Hello, $name!"
```

EXERCISE 12.7

Invoking the IO repeatedly as in Console.readln()() and Console.println(it)() is cumbersome. This is necessary because functions readln and println return IO instances and not raw values. Write a flatMap function to abstract this process. This function takes a function from A to IO<B> as its argument and returns an IO<B>.

SOLUTION

The solution is obvious. All you need to do is to invoke the IO<IO<B>> that the map function returns in order to flatten it to an IO<B>:

```
fun <B> flatMap (g: (A) -> IO<B>): IO<B> = IO {
    g(this())()
}
```

As you can see, this is kind of recursive. It won't be a problem at first because there's only one recursion step, but it could become a problem if you were to chain a huge number of flatMap calls. Now you can compose I/O in a functional way:

```
fun main(args: Array<String>) {
    val script = sayHello()
    script()
}

private fun sayHello(): IO<Unit> = Console.print("Enter your name: ")
        .flatMap { Console.readln() }
        .map { buildMessage(it) }
        .flatMap { Console.println(it) }

private fun buildMessage(name: String): String = "Hello, $name!"
```

The `sayHello` function is totally safe. It never throws an `IOException` because it doesn't perform any I/O operation. It only returns a program that performs these operations once executed, which is done by invoking the returned value (`script()`). Only this invocation can throw an exception.

12.4.5 *Extending the IO type*

By using the `IO` type, you can create impure programs (programs with effects) in a purely functional way. But at this stage, these programs only allow you to read from and print to an element such as your `Console` class. You can extend your DSL by adding instructions to create control structures, such as loops and conditionals.

First, you'll implement a loop similar to the `for` indexed loop. This will take the form of a `repeat` function that takes the number of iterations and the `IO` to repeat as its parameters.

EXERCISE 12.8

Implement the `repeat` function in the `IO` companion object with the following signature:

```
fun <A> repeat(n: Int, io: IO<A> ): IO<List<A>>
```

HINT

To simplify coding in the `IO` class, you might need an additional `fill` function in the `Stream` companion object. This function creates a stream of n non evaluated elements:

```
fun <A> fill(n: Int, elem: Lazy<A>): Stream<A> {
    tailrec
    fun <A> fill(acc: Stream<A>, n: Int, elem: Lazy<A>): Stream<A> =
        when {
            n <= 0 -> acc
            else -> fill(Cons(elem, Lazy { acc }), n - 1, elem)
        }
    return fill(Empty, n, elem)
}
```

You should create a collection of `IO`, representing each iteration, and then fold this collection by combining `IO` instances. To do this, you'll need something more powerful than the `plus` function. Start by implementing a `map2` function with the following signature:

```
fun <A, B, C> map2(ioa: IO<A>, iob: IO<B>, f: (A) ->  (B) -> C): IO<C>
```

SOLUTION

The `map2` function can be implemented as follows:

```
fun <A, B, C> map2(ioa: IO<A>, iob: IO<B>, f: (A) ->  (B) -> C): IO<C> =
    ioa.flatMap { a ->
        iob.map { b ->
            f(a)(b)
        }
    }
```

This is a simple application of the ubiquitous comprehension pattern. With this function at hand, you can easily implement repeat as follows:

```
fun <A> repeat(n: Int, io: IO<A> ): IO<List<A>> =
                Stream.fill(n, Lazy { io })
                        .foldRight( Lazy { IO { List<A>() } }) { ioa ->
                            { sioLa ->
                                map2(ioa, sioLa()) { a ->
                                    { la: List<A> -> cons(a, la) }
                                }
                            }
                        }
```

This may look a bit complex, but that's partly because of the line being wrapped for printing, and partly because it's written as a one-liner for optimization. It's equivalent to this:

```
fun <A> repeat(n: Int, io: IO<A> ): IO<List<A>> {
    val stream: Stream<IO<A>> = Stream.fill(n, Lazy { io })
    val f: (A) -> (List<A>) -> List<A>  =
        { a ->
            { la: List<A> -> cons(a, la) }
        }
    val g: (IO<A>) -> (Lazy<IO<List<A>>>) -> IO<List<A>> =
        { ioa ->
            { sioLa ->
                map2(ioa, sioLa(), f)
            }
        }
    val z: Lazy<IO<List<A>>> = Lazy { IO { List<A>() } }
    return stream.foldRight(z, g)
}
```

TIP If you're using an IDE, it's relatively easy to find the types. For example, in IntelliJ, you need to put the mouse pointer on a reference while holding down the Ctrl key to display the type.

With these functions, you can now write the following:

```
val program = IO.repeat(3, sayHello())
```

This gives you a program that's equivalent to calling the following function as sayHello(3):

```
fun sayHello(n: Int) {

    val br = BufferedReader(InputStreamReader(System.`in`))

    for (i in 0 until n) {
        print("Enter your name: ")
        val name = br.readLine()
        println(buildMessage(name))
    }
}
```

The important difference, however, is that calling sayHello(3) executes the effect three times eagerly, whereas IO.repeat(3, sayHello()) returns a (non evaluated) program that does the same only when its invoke function is called.

It's possible to define many other control structures. You'll find examples in the accompanying code that can be downloaded from http://github.com/pysaumont/ fpinkotlin.

The following listing shows an example of using condition and doWhile functions that do exactly the same thing as if and while in most usual languages.

Listing 12.9 Using IO to wrap imperative programming

```
private val buildMessage = { name: String ->
    IO.condition(name.isNotEmpty(), Lazy {
        IO("Hello, $name!").flatMap { Console.println(it) }
    })
}

fun program(f: (String) -> IO<Boolean>, title: String): IO<Unit> {
    return IO.sequence(Console.println(title),
            IO.doWhile(Console.readln(), f),
            Console.println("bye!")
    )
}

fun main(args: Array<String>) {
    val program = program(buildMessage,
                    "Enter the names of the persons to welcome: ")
    program()
}
```

This example isn't meant to suggest that you should program like this. It's certainly better to use the IO type only for I/O, doing all the computations in functional programming. Implementing an imperative DSL in functional code might not be the most efficient solution, whatever the problem. But it's important to do it as an exercise to understand how it works.

12.4.6 Making the IO type stack-safe

In the previous exercises, you might not have noticed that some of the IO functions used the stack in the same way recursive functions do. The repeat function, for example, overflows the stack if the number of repetitions is too high. How much is too high depends on the stack size and how full it is when the program returned by the function runs. (By now, I expect you understand that calling the repeat function won't blow the stack. Only running the program it returns might do so.)

EXERCISE 12.9

In order to experiment with blowing the stack, create a forever function that takes an IO as its argument and returns a new IO executing the argument in an endless loop. Here's the corresponding signature in the IO companion object:

```
fun <A, B> forever(ioa: IO<A>): IO<B>
```

SOLUTION

This is as simple to implement as it is useless! All you have to do is to make the constructed program infinitely recursive. Be aware that the `forever` function itself shouldn't be recursive. Only the returned program should be.

The solution is to use a helper function of type `()` → `IO`, and to `flatMap` the `IO` argument of the `forever` function with a function invoking this helper function:

```
fun <A, B> forever(ioa: IO<A>): IO<B> {
    val t: () -> IO<B> = { forever(ioa) }
    return ioa.flatMap { t() }
}
```

This function can be used as follows:

```
fun main(args: Array<String>) {
    val program = IO.forever<String, String>(IO { "Hi again!" })
        .flatMap { Console.println(it) }
    program()
}
```

Note that this program blows the stack after a few thousand iterations. This is equivalent to the following:

```
IO.forever<Unit, String>(Console.println("Hi again!"))()
```

If you don't see why it blows the stack, consider the following pseudo-code (which won't compile!) where the t variable in the `forever` function implementation is replaced by the corresponding expression:

```
fun <A, B> forever(ioa: IO<A>): IO<B> {
    return ioa.flatMap { { forever(ioa) }() }
}
```

Now let's replace the recursive call with the corresponding code from the `forever` function implementation:

```
fun <A, B> forever(ioa: IO<A>): IO<B> {
    return ioa.flatMap { { ioa.flatMap { { forever<A, B>(ioa) }() } }() }
}
```

You could continue forever recursively. What you might notice is that the calls to `flatMap` would be nested, resulting in the current state being pushed onto the stack with each call. That would indeed blow the stack after a few thousand steps. Unlike in imperative code, where you execute one instruction after the other, you're calling the `flatMap` function recursively.

To make `IO` stack-safe, you can use a technique called *trampolining*. First, you'll need to represent three states of your program:

- Return represents a computation that's finished, meaning that you need to return the result.

- Suspend represents a suspended computation when some effect has to be applied before resuming the current computation.
- Continue represents a state where the program has to first apply a sub-computation before continuing with the next one.

These states are represented by the three classes shown in the next listing.

NOTE Listings 12.9 through 12.11 are parts of a whole. They aren't supposed to be used with the previous code, but together.

Listing 12.10 The three classes needed to make IO stack-safe

IO is now a sealed class in order to prevent instantiation from the outside the class.

This function taking no argument applies a (side) effect and returns a value.

```
sealed class IO<out A> {

    internal
    class Return<out A>(val value: A): IO<A>()

    internal
    class Suspend<out A>(val resume: () -> A): IO<A>()

    internal
    class Continue<A, out B>(val sub: IO<A>,
                            val f: (A) -> IO<B>): IO<A>()
```

This value will be returned by the computation.

The computation continues by applying this function to the returned value.

This IO is executed first, producing a value.

Some modifications must be made to the enclosing IO class, as shown in listings 12.11 and 12.12.

Listing 12.11 Changes in the stack-safe version of IO

The IO type is now a sealed class.

The invoke function now calls the helper function invoke(this).

```
sealed class IO<out A> {

    operator fun invoke(): A = invoke(this)

    operator fun invoke(io: IO<@UnsafeVariance A>): A {
        tailrec fun invokeHelper(io: IO<A>): A =
            when (io) {
                ...
            }
        return invokeHelper(io)
    }
}
```

The invokeHelper function is shown in listing 12.12.

The invoke(this) function, in turn, calls the invokeHelper function that's made tail-recursive.

```
fun <B> map(f: (A) -> B): IO<B> =
             flatMap { Return(f(it)) }
```

The map function is now defined in terms of applying flatMap to the composition of f and the Return constructor.

```
fun <B> flatMap(f: (A) -> IO<B>): IO<B> =
             Continue(this, f) as IO<B>
```

The flatMap function returns a Continue that's cast into an IO<B>.

```
class IORef<A>(private var value: A) {

    fun set(a: A): IO<A> {
        value = a
        return unit(a)
    }

    fun get(): IO<A> = unit(value)

    fun modify(f: (A) -> A): IO<A> = get().flatMap({ a -> set(f(a)) })
}

internal class Return<out A>(val value: A): IO<A>()

internal class Suspend<out A>(val resume: () -> A): IO<A>()

internal class Continue<A, out B>(val sub: IO<A>,
                            val f: (A) ->  IO<B>): IO<A>()

companion object {

    val empty: IO<Unit> = IO.Suspend { Unit }
```

The empty IO is now a Suspend.

```
    internal fun <A> unit(a: A): IO<A> =
                    IO.Suspend { a }
```

The unit function returns a Suspend.

```
    // rest of the class omitted
    }
}
```

Listing 12.12   The stack-safe `invokeHelper` function

If the received IO is a Return, the computation is over.

If the received IO is a Suspend, the contained effect is executed before returning the resume value.

```
tailrec fun invokeHelper(io: IO<A>): A = when (io) {
    is Return  -> io.value
    is Suspend -> io.resume()
    else       -> {
        val ct = io as Continue<A, A>
        val sub = ct.sub
        val f = ct.f
        when (sub) {
            is Return  -> invokeHelper(f(sub.value))
            is Suspend -> invokeHelper(f(sub.resume()))
            else       -> {
```

If the received IO is a Continue, the contained sub IO is read.

If sub is a Return, the function is called recursively with the result of applying the enclosed function to it.

If sub is a Suspend, the enclosed function is applied to it, possibly producing the corresponding effect.

```
                    val ct2 = sub as Continue<A, A>
                    val sub2 = ct2.sub
                    val f2 = ct2.f
                    invokeHelper(sub2.flatMap { f2(it).flatMap(f) })
                }
            }
        }
    }
```

If sub is a Continue, the IO it contains is extracted (sub2) and flatMapped with sub, which creates the chaining.

The following listing shows how you can use the new stack-safe version.

Listing 12.13 The new stack-safe version of `Console` class

```
object Console {

    private val br = BufferedReader(InputStreamReader(System.`in`))

    /**
     * A possible implementation of readLine as a val function
     */
    val readLine2: () -> IO<String> = {
        IO.Suspend {
            try {
                br.readLine()
            } catch (e: IOException) {
                throw IllegalStateException(e)
            }
        }
    }

    /**
     * A simpler implementation of readLine. A function reference is not
     * possible due to the name clash. Use different names for fun and val
     * functions if you want to use function references
     */
    val readLine = { readLine() }

    /**
     * A fun version of readLine
     */
    fun readLine(): IO<String> = IO.Suspend {
            try {
                br.readLine()
            } catch (e: IOException) {
                throw IllegalStateException(e)
            }
        }

    /**
     * A vall version of printLine
     */
    val printLine: (String) -> IO<Unit> = { s: Any ->
        IO.Suspend {
            println(s)
```

```
        }
    }

    /**
     * A fun version of printLine
     */
    fun printLine(s: Any): IO<Unit> = IO.Suspend { println(s) }

    /**
     * A print function. Note the fully qualified call to kotlin.io.print.
     */
    fun print(s: Any): IO<Unit> = IO.Suspend { kotlin.io.print(s) }
}
```

Now you can use `forever` or `doWhile` without the risk of overflowing the stack. You can also rewrite `repeat` to make it stack-safe. I won't show the new implementation here, but you'll find it in the accompanying code (http://github.com/pysaumont/fpinkotlin).

Keep in mind that this isn't the recommended way to write functional programs. Take it as an example of what can be ultimately done, rather than as good practice. Also note that "ultimately," here, applies to Kotlin programming. With a more functional friendly language, you can craft much more powerful programs.

Summary

- Effects can be passed into `List`, `Result`, and other contexts to be safely applied to values rather than extracting values from these contexts and applying the effects outside, which might produce errors if there are no values.
- Handling two different effects for success and failure can be abstracted inside the `Result` type.
- Reading from files is done in exactly the same way as reading from the console or from memory through the `Reader` abstraction.
- More functional input/output can be obtained through the `IO` type.
- The `IO` type can be extended to a more generic type that makes it possible to perform any imperative task in a functional way by building a program that's executed later.
- The `IO` type can be made stack-safe by using a technique known as "trampolining."

Sharing mutable states
with actors

In the previous chapters, you learned many techniques to help you write safer programs. Most of these techniques come from functional programming. One of these techniques consist in using immutable data to avoid state mutations. Programs without mutable states are safer, more reliable, and easier to design and scale.

You learned how mutable states can be handled in a functional way by passing the state along as an argument to functions. You saw several examples of this technique. You learned to generate streams of data by passing the state of a generator together with each new value. (If you don't remember this, review exercise 9.29 where you implemented the `unfold` function by passing along each generated value together with the new state of the generator.) In chapter 12, you also learned how to pass the console as a parameter to send output to the screen and receive input from the keyboard. These techniques can be widely applied to many domains. But this is often understood to mean that functional programming techniques help to safely share mutable state. This is completely wrong.

Using immutable data structures, for example, doesn't help with sharing mutable state. It prevents unintentional sharing of a mutable state by removing state mutation. Passing the state as part of a function parameter and returning a new (immutable) state as part of the result (in the form of a pair containing both the result and the new state) is perfectly fine when dealing with a single thread. But as long as you need to share state mutation between threads, which is pretty much always the case in modern applications, immutable data structures don't help. To share this kind of data, one needs a mutable reference to it so that the new immutable data can replace the previous one.

Imagine you want to count how many times a function is called. In a single-threaded application, you might do this by adding the counter to the function argument and returning the incremented counter as part of the result. But most imperative programmers would rather increment the counter as a side effect. This would work seamlessly because there's only a single thread, so no locking is necessary to prevent potential concurrent access. This is the same as living on a desert island. If you're the only inhabitant, there's no need for locks on your doors. But in a multithreaded program, how can you increment the counter in a safe way, avoiding concurrent access? The answer is generally to use locks or to make operations atomic, or both.

In functional programming, sharing resources has to be done as an effect, which means, more or less, that each time you access a shared resource, you have to leave functional safety and treat this access as you did for input/output (I/O) in chapter 12. Does this mean that you must then manage locks and synchronization each time you need to share a mutable state? Not at all.

As you learned in the previous chapters, functional programming is also about pushing abstraction to the limit. Sharing a mutable state can be abstracted in such a way that you can use it without bothering about the details. One way to achieve this is to use an actor framework.

In this chapter, you're not going to develop a real, complete actor framework. Creating a complete actor framework is such a tremendous job that you should rather use an existing one. Here you'll develop a minimal actor framework that gives you the feeling of what an actor framework brings to functional programming.

13.1   *The actor model*

In the actor model, a multithreaded application is divided into single-threaded components, called *actors*. If each actor is single-threaded, it doesn't need to share data using locks or synchronization.

Actors communicate with other actors by way of effects, as if such communication were the I/O of messages. This means that actors rely on a mechanism for serializing the messages they receive. (Here, *serialization* means handling one message after the other. This isn't to be confused with object serialization.) Due to this mechanism, actors can process messages one at a time without having to bother about concurrent access to their internal resources. As a result, an actor system can be seen as a series of functional programs communicating with each other through effects. Each actor can be single-threaded, so there's no concurrent access to resources inside. Concurrency is abstracted inside the framework.

13.1.1 Understanding asynchronous messaging

As part of the message processing, actors can send messages to other actors. Messages are sent *asynchronously*, which means an actor doesn't need to wait for an answer—there isn't one. As soon as a message is sent, the sender can continue its job, which mostly consists of processing one at a time a queue of messages it receives. Handling the message queue means that there needs to be some concurrent accesses to the queue. But this management is abstracted in the actor framework so you, the programmer, don't need to worry about this.

Answers to messages might be needed in some cases. Suppose an actor is responsible for a long computation. The client can take advantage of asynchronous communication by continuing its own job while the computation is handled for it. But once the computation is done, there must be a way for the client to receive the result. This is done by making the actor responsible for the computation callback its client and send it the result, once again in an asynchronous way. Note that the client can be the original sender, though that need not always be the case.

13.1.2 Handling parallelization

The actor model allows tasks to be parallelized by using a manager actor that's responsible for breaking the task into subtasks and distributing them to a number of worker actors. Each time a worker actor returns a result to the manager, it's given a new subtask. This model offers an advantage over other parallelization models in that no worker actor is ever idle until the list of subtasks is empty. The downside is that the manager actor doesn't participate in the computation. But in a real application, this generally makes no noticeable difference.

For some tasks, the results of the subtasks may need to be reordered when they're received. In such a case, the manager actor will probably send the results to a specific actor responsible for this job. You'll see an example of this in section 13.3. In small programs, the manager itself can handle this task. In figure 13.1, this actor is called the Receiver actor.

13.1.3 Handling actor state mutation

Actors can be stateless (immutable) or stateful, meaning they're supposed to change their state according to the messages they receive. For example, a synchronizer actor can receive the results of computations that have to be reordered before being used.

Imagine, for example, that you have a list of data that must go through heavy computation in order to provide a list of results. In short, this is a mapping. It could be parallelized by breaking the list into several sublists and giving these sublists to worker actors for processing. But there's no guarantee that the worker actors will finish their jobs in the same order that those jobs were given to them.

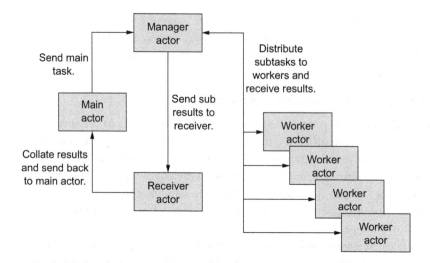

Figure 13.1   The main actor produces the main task and sends it to the manager, which splits it into subtasks that are processed in parallel by several worker actors. Subresults are sent back to the manager, which passes them to the receiver. After collating the subresults, the receiver sends the final result to the main actor.

One solution for resynchronizing the results is to number the tasks. When a worker sends back the result, it adds the corresponding task number so that the receiver can put the results in a priority queue. Not only does this allow automatic sorting, but it also makes it possible to process the results as an asynchronous stream. Each time the receiver receives a result, it compares the task number to the expected number. If there's a match, it passes the result to the client and then looks into the priority queue to see if the first available result corresponds to the new expected task number. If there's a match, the dequeuing process continues until there's no longer a match. If the received result doesn't match the expected result number, it's added to the priority queue.

In such a design, the receiving actor has to handle two mutable pieces of data: the priority queue and the expected result number. Does this mean the actor has to use mutable properties? This wouldn't be a big deal but, because actors are single-threaded, it's not necessary. As you'll see, the handling of property mutations can be included and abstracted into a general state-mutation process, allowing the programmer to use only immutable data.

13.2   *An actor framework implementation*

In this section, you'll learn how to build a minimal but fully functional actor framework. While building this framework, you'll learn how an actor framework allows for safe sharing of mutable state, easy and secure parallelization and reserialization, and modular architecture of applications. At the end of this chapter, you'll see some general things you can do with actor frameworks.

Your actor framework will be made of these four components:

- The `Actor` interface determines the behavior of an actor.
- The `AbstractActor` class contains all the stuff that's common to all actors. This class will be extended by business actors.
- The `ActorContext` acts as a way to access actors. In your implementation, this component will be minimalist and will be used primarily to access the actor state.

    This component isn't necessary in such a small implementation, but most serious implementations use such a component. This context allows, for example, searching for available actors.
- The `MessageProcessor` interface will be the interface you'll implement for any component that has to handle a received message.

13.2.1 Understanding the limitations

As I said, the implementation you'll create here is minimalist; consider it a way to understand and practice using the actor model. You'll be missing many of the functions of a real actor system, particularly those related to the actor context. One other simplification is that each actor is mapped to a single thread. In a real actor system, actors are mapped to pools of threads, allowing thousands or even millions of actors to run on a few dozen threads.

Another limitation of your implementation will be regarding remote actors. Most actor frameworks allow remote actors to be handled in a transparent way, meaning that you can use actors that are running on different machines without having to care about communication. This makes actor frameworks an ideal way to build scalable applications. I won't deal with this aspect in this book.

13.2.2 Designing the actor framework interfaces

First you need to define the interfaces that will constitute your actor framework. The most important is the `Actor` interface that defines several functions. Here's the main function of this interface:

```
fun tell(message: T, sender: Result<Actor<T>>)
```

This function is used to send a message to `this` actor (meaning the actor holding the function). This means that to send a message to an actor, you must have a reference to it. (This is different from real actor frameworks in which messages aren't sent to actors but to actor references, proxies, or some other substitute. Without this enhancement, it wouldn't be possible to send messages to remote actors.) This function (which is actually an effect) takes a `Result<Actor>` as the second parameter. It's supposed to represent the sender, but it's sometimes set to nobody (the empty result) or to a different actor.

Other functions are used to manage the actor lifecycle to ease the use of actors, shown in listing 13.1. This code isn't intended to use the results of the exercises from previous chapters but, rather, the `fpinkotlin-common` module that's available in the code accompanying this book (https://github.com/pysaumont/fpinkotlin). This is mostly the same code as the solutions to the exercises, but with some additional functions.

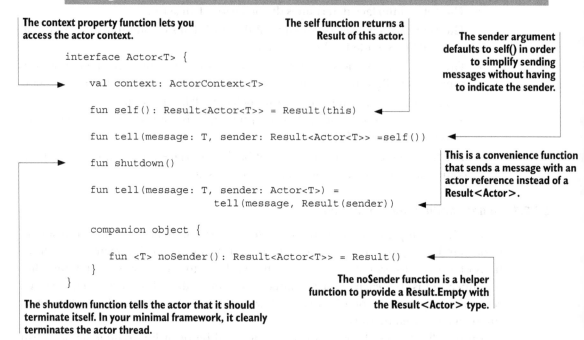

Listing 13.1   The `Actor` interface

The context property function lets you access the actor context.

The self function returns a Result of this actor.

The sender argument defaults to self() in order to simplify sending messages without having to indicate the sender.

```
interface Actor<T> {

    val context: ActorContext<T>

    fun self(): Result<Actor<T>> = Result(this)

    fun tell(message: T, sender: Result<Actor<T>> =self())

    fun shutdown()

    fun tell(message: T, sender: Actor<T>) =
                      tell(message, Result(sender))

    companion object {

        fun <T> noSender(): Result<Actor<T>> = Result()
    }
}
```

This is a convenience function that sends a message with an actor reference instead of a Result<Actor>.

The noSender function is a helper function to provide a Result.Empty with the Result<Actor> type.

The shutdown function tells the actor that it should terminate itself. In your minimal framework, it cleanly terminates the actor thread.

The following listing shows the two other necessary interfaces: `ActorContext` and `MessageProcessor`.

Listing 13.2   The `ActorContext` and `MessageProcessor` interfaces

Allows access to the actor's behavior

```
interface ActorContext<T> {

    fun behavior(): MessageProcessor<T>

    fun become(behavior: MessageProcessor<T>)
}

interface MessageProcessor<T> {

    fun process(message: T,
                sender: Result<Actor<T>>)
}
```

Allows an actor to change its behavior by registering a new MessageProcessor

The MessageProcessor interface has only one function, which represents the processing of one message.

The most important element here is the `ActorContext` interface. The `become` function allows an actor to change its behavior, meaning the way it processes messages. As you can see, the behavior of an actor looks like an effect, taking as its argument a pair composed of the message to process and the sender.

During the life of the application, the behavior of each actor is allowed to change. Generally this change of behavior is caused by a modification to the state of the actor, replacing the original behavior with a new one. This will be clearer once you see the implementation.

13.3 The AbstractActor implementation

The `AbstractActor` implementation represents the part of an actor implementation that's common to all actors. All the message management operations are common and are provided by the actor framework, so that you'll only have to implement the business part. The following listing shows the `AbstractActor` implementation.

Listing 13.3 The `AbstractActor` implementation

```
abstract class AbstractActor<T>(protected val id: String) : Actor<T> {

    override val context: ActorContext<T> =
                        object: ActorContext<T> {

        var behavior: MessageProcessor<T> =
                    object: MessageProcessor<T> {

            override fun process(message: T, sender: Result<Actor<T>>) {
                onReceive(message, sender)
            }
        }

        @Synchronized
        override
        fun become(behavior: MessageProcessor<T>) {
            this.behavior = behavior
        }

        override fun behavior() = behavior
    }

    private val executor: ExecutorService =
            Executors.newSingleThreadExecutor(DaemonThreadFactory())

    abstract fun onReceive(message: T,
                        sender: Result<Actor<T>>)

    override fun self(): Result<Actor<T>> {
        return Result(this)
    }

    override fun shutdown() {
        this.executor.shutdown()
    }

    @Synchronized
    override fun tell(message: T,
                    sender: Result<Actor<T>>) {
```

Initializes the context property to a new ActorContext

Delegates the default behavior to the onReceived function

To change its behavior, the ActorContext registers the new behavior. This is where the mutation occurs, but it's hidden by the framework.

Initializes the underlying ExecutorService

Holds the business processing, implemented by the user of the API

The tell function is how an actor receives a message. It's synchronized to ensure that messages are processed one at a time.

```
executor.execute {
    try {
        context.behavior()
                .process(message, sender)
    } catch (e: RejectedExecutionException) {
        /*
         * This is probably normal and means all pending tasks
         * were canceled because the actor was stopped.
         */
    } catch (e: Exception) {
        throw RuntimeException(e)
    }
}
}
}
```

> When a message is received, it's processed by the current behavior returned by the actor context.

The `ExecutorService` is initialized with a single-thread executor using a daemon thread factory to allow automatic shutdown when the main thread terminates. Also note that when the `ExecutorService` is initialized, the `DaemonThreadFactory` creates daemon threads so that actors don't prevent the application from stopping when the main thread stops. (You'll find the corresponding code in the repository for this book.)

Your actor framework is now complete, though as I mentioned before, this isn't production code. This is a minimal example to show you how an actor framework might work.

13.4   *Putting actors to work*

Now that you've an actor framework at your disposal, it's time to apply it to some concrete problems. Actors are useful when multiple threads are supposed to share some mutable state, as when a thread produces the result of a computation, and this result must be passed to another thread for further processing.

Usually, such mutable state sharing is done by storing values in shared mutable properties, which implies locking and synchronization. You'll first try a minimal actor example, which can be considered as the "`Hello, World!`" of actors. You'll then build a more complete application where an actor is used to distribute tasks to other actors working in parallel.

The first example is the traditional example that's used to test actors. It consists of two ping-pong players and a referee. The game starts when the ball, represented by an integer, is given to one player. Each player then sends the ball to the other until this happens ten times, at which point, the ball is given back to the referee.

13.4.1 *Implementing the Ping Pong example*

First you'll implement the referee. All you need to do is to create an actor, implementing its `onReceive` function. In this function, you'll display a message as shown in the next listing.

Listing 13.4 Creating the `referee` object

```
val referee = object : AbstractActor<Int>("Referee") {
    override fun onReceive(message: Int, sender: Result<Actor<Int>>) {
        println("Game ended after $message shots")
    }
}
```

Next you'll create the two players. As there are two instances, you have two options. The object approach is to create `Player` class as shown in the following listing.

Listing 13.5 The `Player` class

The class is private because it's defined at package level. You could also define it as a local class, inside the main function of the program.

Each player is created with a reference to the referee so that a player can give the ball back to the referee when the game is over. This wouldn't be necessary if the Player class was defined locally in the same function as the referee (for example, in the main function).

The Sound string is a message that's displayed by the players when they receive the ball (either Ping or Pong).

This is the business part of the actor, meaning the part that does what the user expects to see.

If the game is over, gives the ball back to the referee.

Otherwise, sends it back to the other player if present.

If the other player isn't present, registers an issue with the referee.

```
private class Player(id: String,
            private val sound: String,
            private val referee: Actor<Int>):
                    AbstractActor<Int>(id) {

    override fun onReceive(message: Int, sender: Result<Actor<Int>>) {
        println("$sound - $message")
        if (message >= 10) {
            referee.tell(message, sender)
        } else {
            sender.forEach(
                { actor: Actor<Int> ->
                    actor.tell(message + 1, self())
                },
                { referee.tell(message, sender) }
            )
        }
    }
}
```

If you prefer the functional way, you can create a function returning an `Actor` as shown in the following listing.

Listing 13.6 The `player` function

The Sound string is a message that's displayed by the players when they receive the ball (either Ping or Pong).

Creates each player with a reference to the referee so that a player can give the ball back to the referee when the game is over

If the game is over, gives the ball back to the referee

This is the business part of the actor.

```
fun player(id: String,
        sound: String,
        referee: Actor<Int>) =
            object : AbstractActor<Int>("id") {

    override fun onReceive(message: Int, sender: Result<Actor<Int>>) {
        println("$sound - $message")
        if (message >= 10) {
            referee.tell(message, sender)
        } else {
```

```
                          sender.forEach(
Otherwise, send it            { actor: Actor<Int> ->
back to the other                 actor.tell(message + 1, self())
player if present.            },
                              { referee.tell(message, sender) }
                                  )
            }                         If the other player isn't present,
        }                             registers an issue with the referee
    }
```

As you can see, these two solution are nearly identical, showing that objects are indeed functions.

With the player function created (or the Player class), you can finalize your program. But you need a way to keep the application running until the game is over. Without this, the main application thread terminates as soon as the game is started, and the players won't be given the opportunity to play their game. This can be achieved through the use of a semaphore, as shown in the next listing.

Listing 13.7 The Ping Pong example

A semaphore is created with one permit.

When the game is over, the semaphore is released, making one new permit available that allows the main thread to resume.

```
private val semaphore = Semaphore(1)

fun main(args: Array<String>) {
    val referee = object : AbstractActor<Int>("Referee") {

        override fun onReceive(message: Int, sender: Result<Actor<Int>>) {
            println("Game ended after $message shots")
            semaphore.release()
        }
    }
```

If you preferred to define a Player class, the only difference will be the capitalized Player instead of player.

```
    val player1 =
        player("Player1", "Ping", referee)
    val player2 = player("Player2", "Pong", referee)
```

The single available permit is acquired by the current thread and the game is started.

```
    semaphore.acquire()
    player1.tell(1, Result(player2))
    semaphore.acquire()
    // main thread terminates
}
```

When resuming, the main thread terminates. All actor threads are daemons, so they also stop automatically.

The main thread tries to acquire a new permit. As none are available, it blocks until the semaphore is released.

This program displays the following output:

```
Ping - 1
Pong - 2
Ping - 3
Pong - 4
Ping - 5
```

```
Pong - 6
Ping - 7
Pong - 8
Ping - 9
Pong - 10
Game ended after 10 shots
```

13.4.2 Running a computation in parallel

It's now time to look at a more serious example of the actor model in action: running a computation in parallel. To simulate a long-running computation, you'll choose a list of random numbers between 0 and 30, and compute the corresponding Fibonacci value using a slow algorithm.

The application is composed of three kinds of actors: a Manager, in charge of creating a given number of worker actors and distributing the tasks to them; several instances of workers; and a client, which is implemented in the main program class as an anonymous actor. The following listing shows the simplest of these classes, the Worker actor.

> **Listing 13.8 The Worker actor in charge of running parts of the computation**

```
class Worker(id: String) : AbstractActor<Int>(id) {

    override fun onReceive(message: Int, sender: Result<Actor<Int>>) {
        sender.forEach (onSuccess = { a: Actor<Int> ->
                a.tell(slowFibonacci(message), self())       ◀──  When the Worker
            })                                                    receives a number, it
    }                                                             reacts by computing the
                                                                  corresponding Fibonacci
    private fun slowFibonacci(number: Int): Int {                value and sending it back
        return when (number) {                                   to the caller.
            0    -> 1
            1    -> 1
            else -> slowFibonacci(number - 1)   │  An inefficient algorithm is used on
                + slowFibonacci(number - 2)   ◀─┘  purpose to create long-lasting tasks.
        }
    }
}
```

As you can see, this actor is stateless. It computes the result and sends it back to the sender to which it has received a reference. This might be a different actor than the caller.

As the numbers are chosen randomly between 0 and 35, the time needed to compute the result is variable. This listing simulates tasks that take variable amounts of time to execute. Unlike the example of automatic parallelization in chapter 8, all threads/actors are kept busy until the whole computation is finished.

The Manager class is a bit more complicated. The following listing shows the constructor of the class and the properties that are initialized.

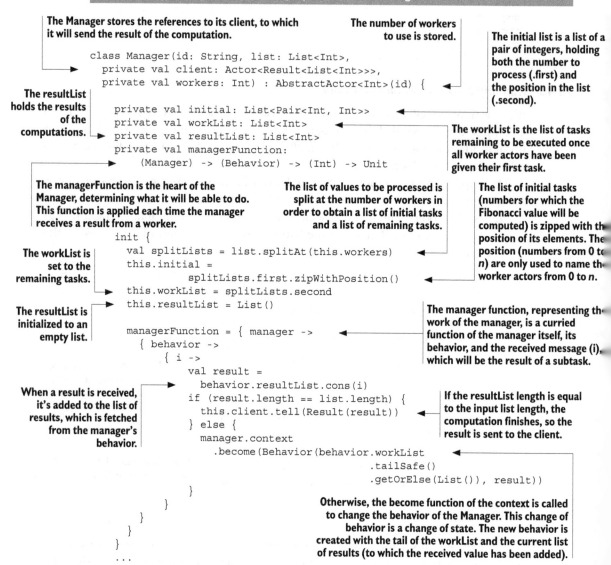

Listing 13.9   The constructor and properties of the `Manager` class

The Manager stores the references to its client, to which it will send the result of the computation.

The number of workers to use is stored.

The initial list is a list of a pair of integers, holding both the number to process (.first) and the position in the list (.second).

```
class Manager(id: String, list: List<Int>,
    private val client: Actor<Result<List<Int>>>,
    private val workers: Int) : AbstractActor<Int>(id) {

    private val initial: List<Pair<Int, Int>>
    private val workList: List<Int>
    private val resultList: List<Int>
    private val managerFunction:
        (Manager) -> (Behavior) -> (Int) -> Unit
```

The resultList holds the results of the computations.

The workList is the list of tasks remaining to be executed once all worker actors have been given their first task.

The managerFunction is the heart of the Manager, determining what it will be able to do. This function is applied each time the manager receives a result from a worker.

The list of values to be processed is split at the number of workers in order to obtain a list of initial tasks and a list of remaining tasks.

The list of initial tasks (numbers for which the Fibonacci value will be computed) is zipped with the position of its elements. The position (numbers from 0 to n) are only used to name the worker actors from 0 to n.

The workList is set to the remaining tasks.

The resultList is initialized to an empty list.

```
init {
    val splitLists = list.splitAt(this.workers)
    this.initial =
            splitLists.first.zipWithPosition()
    this.workList = splitLists.second
    this.resultList = List()

    managerFunction = { manager ->
        { behavior ->
            { i ->
                val result =
                    behavior.resultList.cons(i)
                if (result.length == list.length) {
                    this.client.tell(Result(result))
                } else {
                    manager.context
                        .become(Behavior(behavior.workList
                            .tailSafe()
                            .getOrElse(List()), result))
                }
            }
        }
    }
}
...
```

The manager function, representing the work of the manager, is a curried function of the manager itself, its behavior, and the received message (i), which will be the result of a subtask.

When a result is received, it's added to the list of results, which is fetched from the manager's behavior.

If the resultList length is equal to the input list length, the computation finishes, so the result is sent to the client.

Otherwise, the become function of the context is called to change the behavior of the Manager. This change of behavior is a change of state. The new behavior is created with the tail of the workList and the current list of results (to which the received value has been added).

As you can see, if the computation is finished, the result is added to the result list and sent to the client. Otherwise, the result is added to the current result list. In traditional programming, this would be done by mutating the list of results that would be held by the Manager. This is exactly what happens here, except for two differences:

- The list of results is stored in the behavior.
- Neither the behavior nor the list are mutated. Instead, a new behavior is created and the context is mutated to hold the new behavior as a replacement for

the old one. But you don't have to deal with this mutation. As far as you're concerned, everything is immutable because the mutation is abstracted by the actor framework.

The following listing shows the `Behavior` class implemented as an inner class. The `Behavior` inner class allows you to abstract the actor mutation.

Listing 13.10   The `Behavior` inner class

The Behavior is constructed with the workList (from which the head has been removed prior to calling the constructor) and the resultList (to which a result has been added).

The process function, which is called on reception of a message, first applies the managerFunction to the received message. Then it sends the next task (the head of the workList) to the sender (a Worker actor that will process it) or, if the workList is empty, it instructs the worker actor to shut down.

```
internal inner class Behavior
    internal constructor(
        internal val workList: List<Int>,
        internal val resultList: List<Int>) : MessageProcessor<Int> {

    override fun process(message: Int,
                         sender: Result<Actor<Int>>) {
        managerFunction(this@Manager)(this@Behavior)(message)
        sender.forEach(onSuccess = { a: Actor<Int> ->
            workList.headSafe()
                .forEach({ a.tell(it, self()) }) { a.shutdown() }
        })
    }
}
```

That covers the main parts of the `Manager`. The rest is composed of utility functions that are mainly used for starting the work. The next listing shows these functions.

Listing 13.11   The utility functions of the `Manager`

```
class Manager(id: String, list: List<Int>, . . .

    . . .

    fun start() {
        onReceive(0, self())
        sequence(initial.map { this.initWorker(it) })
            .forEach(onSuccess = { this.initWorkers(it) },
                     onFailure =
                        { this.tellClientEmptyResult(
                            it.message ?: "Unknown error") })
    }

    private fun initWorker(t: Pair<Int, Int>):
                    Result<() -> Unit> =
        Result({ Worker("Worker " + t.second).tell(t.first, self()) })

    private fun initWorkers(lst: List<() -> Unit>) {
        lst.forEach { it() }
    }
```

In order to start, the Manager sends a message to itself. What the message is makes no difference, because the behavior has yet to be initialized.

The workers are then created and initialized.

This function creates a function of type () -> Unit creating a worker actor.

This function executes the actor creation.

```
private
fun tellClientEmptyResult(string: String) {        ◄────────
    client.tell(Result.failure("$string caused by empty input list."))
}


override fun onReceive(message: Int,
               sender: Result<Actor<Int>>) {        ◄──────────
    context.become(Behavior(workList, resultList))
}

. . .
}
```

If there was an error, the client is informed.

This is the initial behavior of the Manager. As part of its initialization, it switches behavior, starting with the workList containing the remaining tasks and the empty resultList.

It's important to understand that the onReceive function represents what the actor will do when it receives its first message. This function won't be called when the workers send their results to the manager.

The last part of the program is shown in listing 13.12. This represents the client code for the application. But unlike the Manager and the Worker, it's not an actor. Instead, the main function *uses* an actor. This is an implementation choice. There's no specific reason for choosing one solution or the other. But a client actor is necessary in order to receive the result.

Listing 13.12   The client application

```
import com.fpinkotlin.common.List
import com.fpinkotlin.common.Result
import com.fpinkotlin.common.range
import java.util.concurrent.Semaphore


private val semaphore = Semaphore(1)        ◄────────
private const val listLength = 20_000       ◄────────
private const val workers = 8   ◄────────
private val rnd = java.util.Random(0)
private val testList =
    range(0, listLength).map { rnd.nextInt(35) }

fun main(args: Array<String>) {
    semaphore.acquire()        ◄─────────────
    val startTime = System.currentTimeMillis()
    val client =    ◄─────────
        object: AbstractActor<Result<List<Int>>>("Client") {
            override fun onReceive(message: Result<List<Int>>,
                    sender: Result<Actor<Result<List<Int>>>>) {
                message.forEach({ processSuccess(it) },
                    { processFailure(it.message ?: "Unknown error") })
                println("Total time: "
                    + (System.currentTimeMillis() - startTime))
                semaphore.release()
            }
        }
}
```

A semaphore is created to allow the main thread to wait for the actors to complete their work.

The number of tasks is initialized.

The number of worker actors is set here.

The list of tasks is created by randomly generating numbers between 0 and 35.

The semaphore is acquired when the program starts.

A client actor is created as anonymous singelton obje

The client releases the semaphore when it receives the result.

The only responsibility of the client is to process the result or any occurring error.

```
    val manager =
        Manager("Manager", testList, client, workers)
    manager.start()
    semaphore.acquire()
}
```

The manager is instantiated and started.

The semaphore is acquired again to wait for the job to finish.

```
private fun processFailure(message: String) {
    println(message)
}

fun processSuccess(lst: List<Int>) {
    println("Input: ${testList.splitAt(40).first}")
    println("Result: ${lst.splitAt(40).first}")
}
```

You can run this program with various lengths for the list of tasks and various numbers of worker actors. On my eight-core Linux box, running with a task length of 20,000 gives the following results:

- One worker actor: 73 sec
- Two worker actors: 37 sec
- Four worker actors: 19 sec
- Eight worker actors: 12 sec
- Sixteen worker actors: 12 sec

These figures aren't precise, but they show that using a number of threads higher than the number of available cores is useless. The result displayed by the program is as follows (only the first 11 results are displayed):

```
Input:  [5, 23, 4, 2, 25, 28, 16, 1, 34, 9, 22, ..., NIL]
Result: [8, 5, 2, 1597, 46368, 121393, 2, 55, 28657, 1, 2, ..., NIL]
Total time: 12558
```

As you can see, there's a problem!

13.4.3 *Reordering the results*

As you may have noticed, the result isn't correct. This is obvious when looking at the second random value (23) and at the corresponding result (5). You can also compare the following values and results. If you run the program on your computer, you'll obtain different results for each run.

What's happening here is that not all tasks take the same amount of time to execute. I deliberately set the computation to perform this way, so that some tasks (computations for low argument values) return quickly, while others (computations for higher values) take much longer. As a result, the returned values aren't in the correct order.

To fix this problem, you need to sort the results in the same order as their corresponding arguments. One solution is to use the Heap data type you developed in chapter 11. You can number each task and use this number as the priority in a priority queue.

The first thing you need to change is the type of the worker actors. Instead of working on integers, they'll need to work on tuples of integers: one integer representing the argument of the computation and one representing the number of the task. The following listing shows the corresponding changes in the Worker class.

> **Listing 13.13   The Worker actor keeping track of the task number**

```
class Worker(id: String) :
   AbstractActor<Pair<Int, Int>>(id) {

       override fun onReceive(message: Pair<Int, Int>,
             sender: Result<Actor<Pair<Int, Int>>>) {
          sender.forEach(onSuccess =
             { a: Actor<Pair<Int, Int>> ->
                a.tell(Pair(slowFibonacci(message.first),
                      message.second) , self())
             })
       }
       ...
}
```

The type parameter is changed from Int to Pair < Int, Int >.

The return message is changed to include the task number.

The signature of the onReceive function is changed to reflect the new actor type.

The task number is the second element of the tuple. This isn't easy to read, given that the task number and the argument of the computation are of the same type (Int). In real life, this shouldn't happen because you should be using a specific type for the task. But if you prefer, you can also use a specific type instead of Pair to wrap both the task and the task number, such as a Task type with a number property.

Changes in the Manager class are more numerous. You need to change the type of the class and the types of the workList and result properties:

```
class Manager(id: String, list: List<Int>,
         private val client: Actor<Result<List<Int>>>,
         private val workers: Int) : AbstractActor<Pair<Int, Int>>(id) {

    private val initial: List<Pair<Int, Int>>
    private val workList: List<Pair<Int, Int>>
    private val resultHeap: Heap<Pair<Int, Int>>
    private val managerFunction: (Manager) -> (Behavior) -> (Int) -> Unit
```

These properties are initialized in the constructor as follows:

```
init {
    val splitLists = list.zipWithPosition().splitAt(this.workers)
    this.initial = splitLists.first
    this.workList = splitLists.second
    this.resultHeap = Heap(Comparator {
         p1: Pair<Int, Int>, p2: Pair<Int, Int> ->
                                p1.second.compareTo(p2.second)
    })
```

The workList now contains pairs (as was the case for the initial list in the former example), and the result is a priority queue (Heap) of pairs. This Heap is initialized with a Comparator based on the comparison of the second element of the pairs.

Using a Task type that wraps both the task and the task number would have allowed you to make this type Comparable, so that a Comparator would have been useless. (I leave this optimization as an exercise for you.) The managerFunction is different too:

```
private val managerFunction:
            (Manager) -> (Behavior) -> (Pair<Int, Int>) -> Unit
```

It's initialized in the constructor like this:

```
managerFunction = { manager ->              The received result is now
    { behavior ->                            inserted into the Heap.
        { p ->
            val result = behavior.resultHeap + p   ◄───
            if (result.size == list.length) {
                this.client.tell(Result(result.toList()
                            .map { it.first }))   ◄─────────
            } else {
                ...                  Once the computation is complete,
            }                         the Heap is converted into a list
        }                            before being returned to the client.
    }
}
```

The Behavior inner class must be changed to reflect the actor type change:

The type of the workList is now
List<Pair<Int, Int>>.

The type of the result is now
Heap<Pair<Int, Int>>.

```
    internal inner class Behavior
        internal
        constructor(internal
                    val workList: List<Pair<Int, Int>>,
            internal val resultHeap: Heap<Pair<Int, Int>>):   ◄────
                    MessageProcessor<Pair<Int, Int>> {   ◄────
                                                             The type parameter of
        override                                             the Behavior class is
        fun process(message: Pair<Int, Int>,                 now Pair<Int, Int>.
                sender: Result<Actor<Pair<Int, Int>>>) {   ◄────
            managerFunction(this@Manager)(this@Behavior)(message)
            sender.forEach(onSuccess = { a: Actor<Pair<Int, Int>> ->
                workList.headSafe()
                        .forEach({ a.tell(it, self()) }) { a.shutdown() }
            })
        }                  The signature of the process function is modified to
    }                                reflect the change of parameter type.
}
```

You still need to apply some minor changes to the rest of the Manager class. The start function must be modified:

The type of the start message must match the
type parameter of the Manager actor.

```
fun start() {
    onReceive(Pair(0, 0), self())   ◄────
    sequence(initial.map { this.initWorker(it) })
        .forEach({ this.initWorkers(it) },
                 { this.tellClientEmptyResult(
                            it.message ?: "Unknown error") })
}
```

The Worker initialization process is slightly different too:

```
private fun initWorker(t: Pair<Int, Int>): Result<() -> Unit> =
    Result({ Worker("Worker " + t.second)
                    .tell(Pair(t.first, t.second), self()) })
```

Last, the onReceive function is modified:

```
override fun onReceive(message: Pair<Int, Int>,
                       sender: Result<Actor<Pair<Int, Int>>>) {
    context.become(Behavior(workList, resultHeap))
}
```

Now the results are displayed in the correct order.

13.4.4 *Optimizing performance*

Although it works fine, this example is far from optimal. The main reason is that all results are put in the resulting priority queue in order to have them sorted. As I said in chapter 11, this isn't the right use case for a priority queue.

A priority queue is designed for putting elements that must be processed in a given order (according to their priority). Elements are supposed to be consumed as they are produced, insuring that the queue never holds more than a few elements at a time. In the present case, elements should be stored only as long as higher-priority elements exist that haven't yet been processed. This isn't the only use case of a priority queue, but it's a perfect one.

To see the problem in practice, try replacing the slowFibonnacci function in the Worker class with an efficient one, such as

```
private fun fibonacci(number: Int): Int {
    tailrec fun fibonacci(acc1: Int, acc2: Int, x: Int): Int = when (x) {
        0 -> 1
        1 -> acc1 + acc2
        else -> fibonacci(acc2, acc1 + acc2, x - 1)
    }
    return fibonacci(0, 1, number)
}
```

In the client program, set listLength to 500,000, and then try the program with 1, 2, 4, or 8 actors (if your computer has enough cores). Here's an example of the results I get:

```
1 actor: 40567 ms 2 actors: 24399 ms 4 actors: 22394 ms 8 actors: 22389 ms
```

You might notice an interesting thing here: when the tasks are short, the benefit of having several concurrent actors is much lower. Typically, there's a gain when going from one to two actors. Putting in more actors doesn't bring more performance. It might not be obvious because these figures are dependent on the computer used, but they're quite slow. As a comparison, you can use the following code, reusing the testList from the WorkersExample program:

```
println(testList.map { fibonacci(it) }.splitAt(40).first)
```

This executes in 700 ms, which is about 30 times faster than the actor version using 2, 4, or 8 actors. One reason for this is the bottleneck caused by the Heap. The Heap data structure isn't meant for sorting. It provides good performance as long as the number of elements is kept low, but here we're inserting all 200,000 results into the heap, sorting the full data set on each insertion. This isn't efficient.

Obviously, this inefficiency isn't an implementation problem, but a problem with using the wrong tool for the job. You'd get much better performance by storing all results and sorting them once when the computation is over, though you'd need to use the right tool for sorting.

Another option is to change the design of the program. One of the problems with the current design is that not only does insertion into the Heap take a long time, but it's done by the Manager thread. Instead of distributing tasks to the worker actors as soon as they've finished a computation, the Manager makes them wait until it has finished the insertion into the heap. One possible solution would be to use a separate actor for inserting into the Heap.

But sometimes a better way to go is to use the right job for the tool. The fact that you're consuming the result synchronously might not be a requirement. If it isn't, you're adding an implicit requirement that makes the problem harder to solve. One possibility would be to pass the results individually to the client. This way, the Heap would be used only when the results are out of order, preventing it from becoming too big.

This kind of use is how a priority queue is intended to be used. To take this into account, you can add a Receiver actor to your program. The Receiver actor is shown in the following listing.

Listing 13.14 The `Receiver` actor in charge of receiving the results asynchronously

```
import com.fpinkotlin.common.List
import com.fpinkotlin.common.Result

class Receiver(id: String,
               private val client: Actor<List<Int>>):
                      AbstractActor<Int>(id) {

    private val receiverFunction: (Receiver) -> (Behavior) -> (Int) -> Unit

    init {
        receiverFunction = { receiver ->
            { behavior ->
                { i ->
                    if (i == -1) {
                        this.client.tell(behavior.resultList.reverse())
                        shutdown()
                    } else {
                        receiver.context
                            .become(Behavior(behavior.resultList.cons(i)))
                    }
                }
            }
        }
    }

    override fun onReceive(i: Int, sender: Result<Actor<Int>>) {
```

The Receiver class is an actor parameterized by the type of data it's meant to receive: Int.

The Receiver client is an actor parameterized by the type List<Int>.

Otherwise, it changes its behavior by adding the result to the result list.

The Receiver function receives an Int. If it's −1, meaning the computation is complete, it sends the result to its client and shuts itself down.

```
        context.become(Behavior(List(i)))
    }

    internal inner class Behavior internal constructor(
        internal val resultList: List<Int>) :
                        MessageProcessor<Int> {

        override fun process(i: Int, sender: Result<Actor<Int>>) {
            receiverFunction(this@Receiver)(this@Behavior)(i)
        }
    }
}
```

The initial onReceive implementation consists of replacing the actor behavior with one that uses a new list containing the first result.

The behavior holds the current list of results.

The main program (WorkersExample.kt) isn't much different from the previous example. The only difference is the addition of the Receiver:

```
fun main(args: Array<String>) {
    semaphore.acquire()
    val startTime = System.currentTimeMillis()
    val client =
        object: AbstractActor<List<Int>>("Client") {
            override fun onReceive(message: List<Int>,
                          sender: Result<Actor<List<Int>>>) {
                println("Total time: "
                        + (System.currentTimeMillis() - startTime))
                println("Input: ${testList.splitAt(40).first}")
                println("Result: ${message.splitAt(40).first}")
                semaphore.release()
            }
        }
    val receiver = Receiver("Receiver", client)
    val manager =
        Manager("Manager", testList, receiver, workers)
    manager.start()
    semaphore.acquire()
}
```

The Receiver is created with the main actor as its client.

The Manager is now created with the Receiver as its client

The Worker actor is exactly the same as in the previous example. This leaves us with the Manager class holding the most important changes. The first change is that the Manager will have a client of type Actor<Int> and will keep track of the length of the list of tasks:

```
class Manager(
            id: String, list: List<Int>,
            private val client: Actor<Int>,
            private val workers: Int) : AbstractActor<Pair<Int, Int>>(id) {
    private val initial: List<Pair<Int, Int>>
    private val workList: List<Pair<Int, Int>>
    private val resultHeap: Heap<Pair<Int, Int>>
```

The Manager has a client of type Actor<Int>.

```
private val managerFunction: (Manager) -> (Behavior) -> (Pair<Int, Int>)
  -> Unit
private val limit: Int
```

The manager keeps track of the length of the list of tasks.

The `Receiver` client now receives results asynchronously, one by one. The manager-Function is different:

```
managerFunction = { manager ->
    { behavior ->
        { p ->
            val result =
                streamResult(behavior.resultHeap + p,
                             behavior.expected, List())
            result.third.forEach { client.tell(it) }
            if (result.second > limit) {
                this.client.tell(-1)
            } else {
                manager.context
                    .become(Behavior(behavior.workList
                        .tailSafe()
                        .getOrElse(List()), result.first, result.second))
            }
        }
    }
}
```

Calling the streamResult function

Sending the termination code

This function now calls the `streamResult` function, returning a `Triple`. The first element is the `Heap` of results to which the received result has been added. The second element is the next expected result number, and the third element is a list of results that are in expected order. If all the tasks have been executed, the client is sent a special termination code. As you can see, most of the work is done in the `streamResult` function:

```
private fun streamResult(result: Heap<Pair<Int, Int>>,
                         expected: Int, list: List<Int>):
            Triple<Heap<Pair<Int, Int>>, Int, List<Int>> {
    val triple = Triple(result, expected, list)
    val temp = result.head
        .flatMap { head ->
            result.tail().map { tail ->
                if (head.second == expected)
                    streamResult(tail, expected + 1, list.cons(head.first))
                else
                    triple
            }
        }
    return temp.getOrElse(triple)
}
```

The `streamResult` function takes as its argument the `Heap` of results, the next expected task number, and a list of integers that's initially empty:

- If the head of the result heap is different from the expected task result number, nothing needs to be done, and the three parameters are returned as a `Triple`.
- If the head of the result heap matches the expected task result number, it's removed from the heap and added to the list. Then the function is called recursively until the head no longer matches, constructing a list of the results in expected order, leaving the others in the heap.

By processing this way, the heap is always kept small. For example, when computing 200,000 tasks, the maximal size of the heap was found to be 121. It was over 100 on 12 occasions, and more than 95% of the time it was less than 2. Figure 13.2 shows the overall process of receiving the results from the `Managers` point of view.

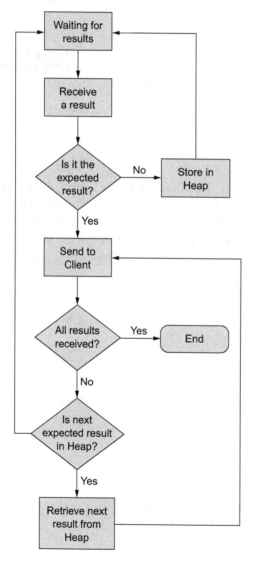

Figure 13.2   The `Manager` receives a result and either stores it in the `Heap` (if it doesn't correspond to the expected number) or sends it to the client. In the latter case, it then looks at the `Heap` to see if the next expected result has already been received.

The onReceive function is different because on starting you'd expect result number 0:

```
override fun onReceive(message: Pair<Int, Int>,
                       sender: Result<Actor<Pair<Int, Int>>>) {
    context.become(Behavior(workList, resultHeap, 0))
}
```

The Behavior class must also be modified. It now holds the expected task number:

```
internal inner class Behavior
    internal constructor(internal val workList: List<Pair<Int, Int>>,
                         internal val resultHeap: Heap<Pair<Int, Int>>,
                         internal val expected: Int) :
                                MessageProcessor<Pair<Int, Int>> {

    ...
```

The last change is in the Manager.start function because the client is now an Actor<Int>:

```
fun start() {
    onReceive(Pair(0, 0), self())
    sequence(initial.map { this.initWorker(it) })
        .forEach({ this.initWorkers(it) },
                 { client.tell(-1) })
}
```

With these modifications, the application is much faster. For example, under the same conditions as in the previous example, here are the times needed to process 1,000,000 numbers with one, two, four, and eight worker actors:

```
1 actor: 40567 ms
2 actors: 12251 ms
4 actors: 11055 ms
8 actors: 11043 ms
```

This process is obviously not as fast as mapping the fibonacci function to the list of numbers. But remember that you switched to the fast version of the function. Parallelizing tasks doesn't help with short tasks. But if you switch back to the slow version of the function, the results are quite different (using a list of 200,000 numbers):

```
simple mapping: 12 mn 46 s
1 actor: 12 mn 2 s
2 actors: 6 mn 2 s
4 actors: 3 mn 3 s
8 actors: 1 mn 40 s
```

Now you can see that parallelization using actors can dramatically boost performances as soon as the tasks to run in parallel are long-lasting. This was only an example to show how actors can be used. Solving this kind of problem is much better handled by other means, such as automatic parallelization of lists (as you saw in chapter 8).

The main use of actors isn't for parallelization, but for the abstraction of sharing a mutable state. In these examples, you used lists that were shared between tasks. Without actors, you'd have had to synchronize access to the workList and resultHeap to handle concurrency. Actors allow you to abstract synchronization and mutation in the framework.

If you look at the business code you wrote (apart from the actor framework itself), you'll find no mutable data, no need to care about synchronization, and no risks of thread starvation or deadlocks. Although they're effect-based (as opposed to functional), actors provide a good way to make functional parts of your code work together, sharing mutable state in an abstracted manner.

Your actor framework is minimal and isn't intended to be used in any serious code. For such uses with Kotlin, you can use one of the available actor frameworks for Java, particularly Akka. Although Akka is written in Scala, it can be used in Kotlin programs as well. When using Akka, you'll never see a line of Scala code unless you want to. To learn more about actors, and Akka in particular, refer to Raymond Roestenburg, Rob Bakker, and Rob Williams's book, *Akka in Action* (Manning, 2016).

Summary

- Actors are components that receive messages in an asynchronous way and process them one after the other.
- Sharing mutable state can be abstracted into actors.
- Abstracting mutable state sharing relieves you of synchronization and concurrency problems.
- The actor model is based on asynchronous messaging and is a nice complement to functional programming.
- The actor model offers easy and safe parallelization.
- Actor mutations are abstracted from the programmer by the framework.
- Several actor frameworks are available to Kotlin programmers.
- Akka is one of the most used actor frameworks available to Kotlin programmers.

Solving common problems functionally

You now have many tools that can make your life as a programmer easier by using safe programming techniques coming from the world of functional programming. But knowing the tools isn't enough. To become efficient using functional techniques, you must make them second nature. You need to think functionally. Just as object-oriented (OO) programmers think in patterns, functional programmers do the same with functions.

When OO programmers have a problem to solve, they look for design patterns they can recognize and attempt to reduce the problem to a composition of patterns. Once they've done that, they need to implement the patterns and compose them.

Functional programmers do the same with functions with one difference: when they find that a function could be used to solve a problem, they don't have to reimplement it. They can reuse it, because functions, unlike design patterns, are reusable code.

Functional programmers try to reduce each problem to a composition of previously implemented functions. This isn't always possible, so they sometimes have to implement new functions. But these new functions become part of their toolbox. The main difference here is that functional programmers are always seeking abstraction because abstraction is what makes functions reusable.

All programmers use libraries that offer more or less the same functionality: generalizing problems in a way that allows reusing code instead of reinventing the wheel each time a new problem needs solving. The difference is in the level of abstraction. Premature abstraction is considered a sin in OO programming, whereas it's one of the fundamental tools of functional programming. Abstraction allows the programmer to not only reuse functions, but to better understand the true nature of the problems at hand.

In this chapter, you'll look at some common problems programmers have to solve in everyday professional life. You'll see how you can approach those problems differently using the functional paradigm. In addition to learning how to solve these everyday problems in a functional way, you'll often need to use imperative code. But what's the best approach to using such code with functional programs? We'll start with an imperative program and modify it to make it more efficient and useful.

14.1   *Assertions and data validation*

Assertions are used to check invariants such as preconditions, post-conditions, control-flow conditions, and class conditions. In functional programming, there's generally no control flow, and classes are usually immutable, so the only conditions to check are pre- and post-conditions. These for the same reasons (immutability and absence of control flow) consist in testing the arguments received by methods and functions, and testing their results before returning them. Testing the argument value is necessary in partial functions such as this:

```
fun inverse(x: Int): Double = 1.0 / x
```

This function returns a usable value for any input, except for 0, for which it returns infinity. As you probably can't do anything with this value, you might prefer to handle it in a specific way. In imperative programming, you could write this:

```
fun inverse(x: Int): Double {
    assert(x == 0)
    return 1.0 / x
}
```

This snippet uses standard Java assertions, which are available in Kotlin. But as assertions can be disabled at runtime, you might want to prevent the program from running with assertions disabled by using the following:

```
if (!Thread.currentThread().javaClass.desiredAssertionStatus()) {
    throw RuntimeException("Asserts must be enabled!!!")
}
```

NOTE If you're running your code in some older versions of IntelliJ, assertions might be enabled by default. In such cases, you should explicitly disable assertions by using the -da VM parameter in your configuration in order to simulate normal execution. In this specific case, it's simpler to write:

```
fun inverse(x: Int): Double = when (x) {
    0    -> throw IllegalArgumentException("div. By 0")
    else -> 1.0 / x
}
```

To be safe, the function should be transformed into a total function as follows:

```
fun inverse(x: Int): Result<Double> = when (x) {
    0    -> Result.failure("div. By 0")
    else -> Result(1.0 / x)
}
```

The most generic form of assertion consists of testing an argument against a specific condition, returning a Result.Failure if the condition isn't matched and a Result.Success otherwise. Take the example of an invoke operator function for a Person type:

```
class Person private constructor(val id: Int,
                                 val firstName: String,
                                 val lastName: String) {


    companion object {
        operator
        fun invoke(id: Int?,
                   firstName: String?,
                   lastName: String?): Person =
                Person(id, firstName, lastName)

    }
}
```

This function might be used with data extracted from a database:

```
val person = Person(rs.getInt("personId"),
                    rs.getString("firstName"),
                    rs.getString("lastName"))
```

In such a case, you might want to validate the data before calling the function. For example, you might want to check that the ID is positive, and that the first and last names aren't null or empty and they start with an uppercase letter. In imperative programming, you could check this by testing each condition before calling the function through the use of assertion functions:

```
class Person private constructor(val id: Int,
                                 val firstName: String,
                                 val lastName: String) {

    companion object {
        operator
        fun invoke(id: Int?, firstName: String?, lastName: String?) =
            Person(assertPositive(id, "null or negative id"),
                   assertValidName(firstName, "invalid first name"),
                   assertValidName(lastName, "invalid last name"))
```

```
        private fun assertPositive(i: Int?,
                                    message: String): Int = when (i) {
            null -> throw IllegalStateException(message)
            else -> i
        }

        private fun assertValidName(name: String?,
                                     message: String): String = when {
            name == null
                || name.isEmpty()
                || name[0].toInt() < 65
                || name[0].toInt() > 91 ->
                            throw IllegalStateException(message)
            else -> name
        }
    }
}
```

But if you want your programs to be safe, you shouldn't throw exceptions. Rather, you should use special contexts such as `Result` for error handling. This kind of validation is abstracted into the `Result` type. All you need to do is to write the validating functions, which means you need to write functions and use function references. Generic validation functions can be placed at package level like so:

```
fun isPositive(i: Int?): Boolean = i != null && i > 0

fun isValidName(name: String?): Boolean =
    name != null && name[0].toInt() >= 65 && name[0].toInt() <= 91
```

You can then validate the data:

```
class Person private constructor(val id: Int,
                                  val firstName: String,
                                  val lastName: String) {

  companion object {
    fun of(id: Int, firstName: String, lastName: String) =
      Result.of (::isPositive, id, "Negative id").flatMap { validId ->
          Result.of(::isValidName, firstName, "Invalid first name")
            .flatMap { validFirstName ->
                Result.of(::isValidName, lastName, "Invalid last name")
                  .map { validLastName ->
                      Person(validId, validFirstName, validLastName)
                  }
            }
      }
    }
  }
}
```

But you can also simplify things by abstracting more of the process into more general functions:

```
fun assertPositive(i: Int, message: String): Result<Int> =
        Result.of(::isPositive, i, message)
```

```
fun assertValidName(name: String, message: String): Result<String> =
        Result.of(::isValidName, name, message)
```

You can then create a `Person` as follows:

```
fun of(id: Int, firstName: String, lastName: String) =
  assertPositive(id, "Negative id")
    .flatMap { validId ->
      assertValidName(firstName, "Invalid first name")
        .flatMap { validFirstName ->
          assertValidName(lastName, "Invalid last name")
            .map { validLastName ->
                Person(validId, validFirstName, validLastName)
            }
        }
    }
```

The following listing shows some examples of validating functions.

Listing 14.1   Examples of functional assertions

```
fun <T> assertCondition(value: T, f: (T) -> Boolean): Result<T> =
    assertCondition(value, f,
        "Assertion error: condition should evaluate to true")

fun <T> assertCondition(value: T, f: (T) -> Boolean,
                        message: String): Result<T> =
        if (f(value))
            Result(value)
        else
            Result.failure(IllegalStateException(message))

fun assertTrue(condition: Boolean,
        message: String = "Assertion error: condition should be true"):
            Result<Boolean> =
        assertCondition(condition, { x -> x }, message)

fun assertFalse(condition: Boolean,
        message: String = "Assertion error: condition should be false"):
            Result<Boolean> =
        assertCondition(condition, { x -> !x }, message)

fun <T> assertNotNull(t: T): Result<T> =
        assertNotNull(t, "Assertion error: object should not be null")

fun <T> assertNotNull(t: T, message: String): Result<T> =
        assertCondition(t, { x -> x != null }, message)

fun assertPositive(value: Int,
        message: String = "Assertion error: value $value must be positive"):
            Result<Int> =
        assertCondition(value, { x -> x > 0 }, message)

fun assertInRange(value: Int, min: Int, max: Int): Result<Int> =
        assertCondition(value, { x -> x in min..(max - 1) },
            "Assertion error: value $value should be > $min and < $max")
```

```
fun assertPositiveOrZero(value: Int,
        message: String = "Assertion error: value $value must not be < 0"):
                Result<Int> =
        assertCondition(value, { x -> x >= 0 }, message)

fun <A: Any> assertType(element: A, clazz: Class<*>): Result<A> =
    assertType(element, clazz,
                "Wrong type: ${element.javaClass}, expected: ${clazz.name}")


fun <A: Any> assertType(element: A, clazz: Class<*>,
                    message: String): Result<A> =
        assertCondition(element, { e -> e.javaClass == clazz }, message)
```

14.2 *Retries for functions and effects*

Impure functions and effects must often be retried if they don't succeed on the first call. Not succeeding generally means throwing an exception. But retrying a function when an exception is thrown is tedious and error-prone.

Imagine you're reading a value from some device that might throw an IOException if the device isn't ready. You might want to retry three times with a delay of 100 ms between each retry. The imperative solution is something like

```
fun get(path: String): String =           ◄────┐  Simulates a function that throws an
        Random().nextInt(10).let {               │  exception 80% of the time
            when {
                it < 8 -> throw IOException("Error accessing file $path")
                else -> "content of $path"
            }
        }
                                     ┌─── Used as the parameter of the forEach
                                     │    function; rt@ indicates where you want
var retries = 0                      │    to return from inside the function
var result: String? = null
(0 .. 3).forEach rt@ {     ◄─────────┘   ┌── As indicated by return@rt, return from
    try {                                │   inside the function used as the
        result = get("/my/path")         │   parameter of the forEach function is
        return@rt     ◄──────────────────┘   triggered when the call to get succeeds.
    } catch(e: IOException) {
        if (retries < 3) {          ┌── If get throws an exception and retries is smaller than 3,
            Thread.sleep(100)  ◄────┘   a retry is attempted after waiting for 100 ms.
            retries += 1
        } else {
            throw e   ◄────┐  If an exception is thrown and retries isn't
        }                  │  smaller than 3, the exception is rethrown.
    }
}
println(result)
```

This code is bad for several reasons:

- You're forced to use var references.
- You have to use a nullable type for the result.
- It's absolutely not reusable, although the concept of retrying is something that's used often.

What you need is a `retry` function that takes as its parameters the following:

- The function to retry
- A maximum number of retries
- A delay value between retries

This function shouldn't rethrow any exceptions. Instead, it should return a `Result`. Here's its signature:

```
fun <A, B> retry(f: (A) -> B,
                 times: Int,
                 delay: Long = 10): (A) -> Result<B>
```

Using this function, you can write

```
val functionWithRetry = retry(::get, 10, 100)
functionWithRetry("/my/file.txt")
        .forEach({ println(it) }, { println(it.message) })
```

You can get this result in many different ways. One way would be to use a fold with short circuiting, folding the range 0 to (*max number of retries*) but escaping as soon as one call to the `get` function succeeds. You can do this easily by using a label and the standard Kotlin `fold` function on a Kotlin range such as

```
fun <A, B> retry(f: (A) -> B, times: Int, delay: Long = 10) = rt@ { a: A ->
    (0 .. times).fold("Not executed") { _, n ->
        try {
            print("Try $n: ")
            return@rt "Success $n: ${f(a)}"
        } catch (e: Exception) {
            Thread.sleep(delay)
            "${e.message}"
        }
    }
}
```

On the other hand, this won't work with the `range` function you developed using your `List` class in exercise 8.19. It seems to be due to a bug in Kotlin and, in any case, it won't compile.[1] A way to solve the problem is to use explicit corecursion, as you learned in chapter 4. As usual, this implies defining a helper local function:

```
fun <A, B> retry(f: (A) -> B,
                 times: Int,
                 delay: Long = 10): (A) -> Result<B> {
    fun retry(a: A, result: Result<B>, e: Result<B>, tms: Int): Result<B> =
            result.orElse {
                when (tms) {
                    0 -> e
                    else -> {
                        Thread.sleep(delay)
                        // log the number of retries
                        println("retry ${times - tms}")
```

---

[1] Read about this Kotlin bug, issue KT-24055, "Incorrect use of label with local return cause internal exception in the compiler" at https://youtrack.jetbrains.com/issue/KT-24055.

```
                    retry(a, Result.of { f(a) }, result, tms - 1)
                }
            }
        }
    return { a -> retry(a, Result.of { f(a) }, Result(), times - 1) }
}
```

This implementation uses a local function that calls itself recursively with a decremented number of retries until either this number is 0 or the call to function f succeeds. You can't take advantage of the `tailrec` keyword because Kotlin doesn't see this function as recursive. This isn't a problem, however, because the number of retries will be low. The `println` instruction is included only to allow you to see what happens.

The local function is initially called with `Result.of { f(a) }` as its parameter, which is somewhat unusual. Generally, you call the local function with the same parameters as the main function, plus additional ones. Here, the use case is a bit special because you don't want an initial delay.

With this function, you can transform any function into a function with automatic retry. You can also use this function with pure effects (returning `Unit`) as in the following example:

```
fun show(message: String) =
    Random().nextInt(10).let {
        when {
            it < 8 -> throw IllegalStateException("Failure !!!")
            else -> println(message)
        }
    }

fun main(args: Array<String>) {
    retry(::show, 10, 20)("Hello, World!").forEach(onFailure =
                                        { println(it.message) })
}
```

14.3 *Reading properties from a file*

Most software applications are configured using property files that are read at startup. Properties are key/value pairs, and both keys and values are written as strings. Whatever the chosen property format (key=value, XML, JSON, YAML, and so on), the programmer always has to read strings and transform them into objects. This process is tedious and error-prone.

You can use a specialized library for reading property files, but if something goes wrong, you'll find yourself throwing exceptions. To get more functional behavior, you'll have to write your own library. This library lets you

- Read properties as strings
- Read properties as numerical values of various types
- Read properties as enums or even arbitrary types
- Read properties as collections of the above types

■ Read properties while providing default values and meaningful error messages in case something goes wrong

■ Read properties while never throwing exceptions

14.3.1 Loading the property file

Whichever format you use, the process is exactly the same: reading the file and handling any exception that could arise in that process. The first thing to do is read the property file and return a `Result<Properties>`, as shown in the next listing.

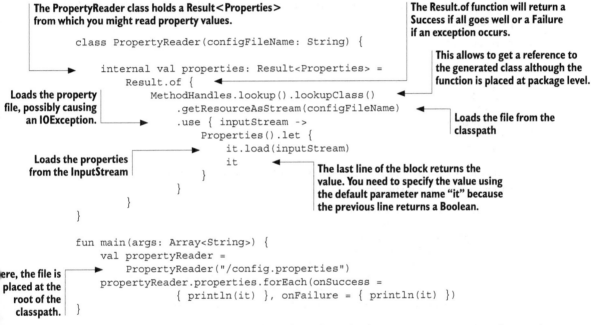

Listing 14.2 Reading a property file

The PropertyReader class holds a Result<Properties> from which you might read property values.

The Result.of function will return a Success if all goes well or a Failure if an exception occurs.

```
class PropertyReader(configFileName: String) {

    internal val properties: Result<Properties> =
        Result.of {
            MethodHandles.lookup().lookupClass()
                .getResourceAsStream(configFileName)
                .use { inputStream ->
                    Properties().let {
                        it.load(inputStream)
                        it
                    }
                }
        }
}
```

Loads the property file, possibly causing an IOException.

This allows to get a reference to the generated class although the function is placed at package level.

Loads the file from the classpath

Loads the properties from the InputStream

The last line of the block returns the value. You need to specify the value using the default parameter name "it" because the previous line returns a Boolean.

```
fun main(args: Array<String>) {
    val propertyReader =
        PropertyReader("/config.properties")
    propertyReader.properties.forEach(onSuccess =
            { println(it) }, onFailure = { println(it) })
}
```

Here, the file is placed at the root of the classpath.

If the file isn't found, the use function doesn't throw an IOException but rather returns a null inputStream, causing a NullPointerException. This function ensures that the stream will be closed in any case.

> **NOTE** In this listing, if you use Intellij, you'll need to rebuild the project before running the example. Running it without rebuilding builds the classes but doesn't copy the resources into the output directory. This is because you load the property file from the classpath. It could, however, be loaded from anywhere on disk or read from a remote URL, or any other source.

14.3.2 Reading properties as strings

When working with property files, the simplest use case consists of reading the properties as strings. This seems straightforward, but be aware that the following won't work:

```
properties.map { it.getProperty("name") }
```

If the property doesn't exist, the getProperty function returns null, which results in a Success("null"). The Properties class can be constructed with a default property list, and the getProperty function can itself be called with a default value. But not all properties have default values. To handle this problem, you need to use the flatMap function together with Result.of:

```
fun readProperty(name: String) =
    properties.flatMap {
        Result.of {
            it.getProperty(name)
        }
    }
```

Now let's say you have a property file in the classpath that contains the following properties:

```
host=acme.org
port=6666
name=
temp=71.3
price=$45
list=34,56,67,89
person=id:3;firstName:Jeanne;lastName:Doe
id=3
type=SERIAL
```

This file is called config.properties and is placed at the root of the classpath. You can access its properties in a safe way with this code:

```
fun main(args: Array<String>) {
    val propertyReader = PropertyReader("/config.properties")
    propertyReader.readProperty("host")
        .forEach(onSuccess = { println(it) }, onFailure = { println(it) })
    propertyReader.readProperty("name")
        .forEach(onSuccess = { println(it) }, onFailure = { println(it) })
    propertyReader.readProperty("year")
        .forEach(onSuccess = { println(it) }, onFailure = { println(it) })
}
```

Given your property file, you'll get the following result:

```
acme.org java.lang.NullPointerException
```

The first line corresponds to the host property, which is correct. The second line corresponds to the name property. It's an empty string, which might or might not be correct—you don't know. That depends on whether the name is optional from the business point of view.

The third line corresponds to the missing year property, but the message isn't informative. It's contained in a Result<String> that could be assigned to a year variable so you'd know which property is missing. But it'd be better to have the name of the property as part of the message. Let's make this error message more useful.

14.3.3 *Producing better error messages*

The problem you're facing here is a good example of what should never happen. Kotlin relies on the Java standard library, so you're confident that things will go as expected. In particular, you expect that if a file isn't found, or if it can't be read, you'll get an IOException. You might even hope to be told the full path of the file, as a missing file is often a file that's not in the right place. A good error message in such a case would be "I am looking for file 'abc' in location 'xyz' but can't find it." Now, look at the code for the getResourceAsStream Java method:

```
public InputStream getResourceAsStream(String name) {
  URL url = getResource(name);
  try {
    return url != null ? url.openStream() : null;
  } catch (IOException e) {
    return null;
  }
}
```

Yes, this is how Java is written. The conclusion is that you should never call a method from the Java standard library without looking at the corresponding code!

The Javadoc says that the method returns "An input stream for reading the resource, or null if the resource could not be found." This means that many things can go wrong. An `IOException might occur if the file isn't found or if there's a problem while reading it. Or the filename could be null. Or the getResource method could throw an exception or return null. (Look at the code for this method to see what I mean.)

The minimum that you should do is provide a different message for each case. And despite the fact that an IOException is unlikely to be thrown, you must still handle this case, as well as the general case of an unexpected exception, as shown in the following listing.

Listing 14.3   Producing specific error messages

```
// properties can now be private
private val properties: Result<Properties> =
  try {
    MethodHandles.lookup().lookupClass()
      .getResourceAsStream(configFileName)
      .use { inputStream ->
        when (inputStream) {
          null ->
            Result.failure("File $configFileName not found in classpath")
          else -> Properties().let {
            it.load(inputStream)
            Result(it)
          }

        }
      }
  } catch (e: IOException) {
    Result.failure("IOException reading classpath resource $configFileName")
```

```
    } catch (e: Exception) {
      Result.failure("Exception: ${e.message} " +
                    " while reading classpath resource $configFileName")
    }
```

If the file isn't found, the message is

```
File /config.properties not found in classpath
```

You also need to deal with property-related error messages. When using code like this

```
val year: Result<String> = propertyReader.readProperty(properties, "year")
```

it's clear that if you get the `NullPointerException` error message, it means the `year` property wasn't found. But in the following example, the message gives no information about which property was missing:

```
data class Person(val id: Int, val firstName: String, val lastName: String)

fun main(args: Array<String>) {
    val propertyReader = PropertyReader("/config.properties")
    val person = propertyReader.readProperty("id")
        .map(String::toInt)
        .flatMap { id ->
            propertyReader.readProperty("firstName")
                .flatMap { firstName ->
                    propertyReader.readProperty("lastName")
                        .map { lastName -> Person(id, firstName, lastName) }
                }
        }
    person.forEach(onSuccess = { println(it) }, onFailure = { println(it) })
}
```

To solve this problem, you have several options at your disposal. The simplest is to map the failure in the `readProperty` helper function of the `PropertyReader` class:

```
fun readProperty(name: String) =
    properties.flatMap {
        Result.of {
            it.getProperty(name)
        }.mapFailure("Property \"$name\" no found")
    }
```

The preceding example produces the following error message, indicating clearly that the `id` property wasn't present in the property file:

```
java.lang.RuntimeException: Property "firstName" not found
```

Another potential source of failure is a parsing error while converting the `id` property string value into an integer. For example, if the property was

```
id=three
```

the error message would be

```
java.lang.NumberFormatException: For input string: "three"
```

This doesn't give you enough information, and that's because it's the standard Java error message for a parsing error. Most standard Java error messages are like this. It's like a `NullPointerException`. It says that a reference was found to be `null`, but it doesn't say which one. What you need is the name of the property that caused the exception—something like this:

```
propertyReader.readProperty("id")
    .map(String::toInt)
    .mapFailure("Invalid format for property \"id\": ???")
```

But you have to write the name of the property twice, and it'd be useful to replace ??? with the value found. (This isn't possible because the value is already lost.) Because you'll have to parse property values for all non-string properties, you should abstract this inside the `PropertyReader` class. To do so, you'll first rename the `readProperty` function:

```
fun readAsString(name: String) =
    properties.flatMap {
        Result.of {
            it.getProperty(name)
        }.mapFailure("Property \"$name\" no found")
    }
```

Then you'll add a `readAsInt` function:

```
fun readAsInt(name: String): Result<Int> =
    readAsString(name).flatMap {
        try {
            Result(it.toInt())
        } catch (e: NumberFormatException) {
            Result.failure<Int>(
                "Invalid value while parsing property '$name' to Int: '$it'")
        }
    }
```

Now you don't need to worry about errors when converting to integers:

```
val person = propertyReader.readAsInt("id")
  .flatMap { id ->
    propertyReader.readAsString("firstName")
      .flatMap { firstName ->
        propertyReader.readAsString("lastName")
          .map { lastName -> Person(id, firstName, lastName) }
      }
  }
person.forEach(onSuccess = { println(it) }, onFailure = { println(it) })
```

If an exception is thrown while parsing the `id` property, you get

```
java.lang.IllegalStateException:
        Invalid value while parsing property 'id' to Int: 'three'")
```

14.3.4 *Reading properties as lists*

You can do the same thing you've done for integers for other numeric types, such as `Long` or `Double`. You can even do much more than this. For example, you can read properties as lists like this:

```
list=34,56,67,89
```

You only need to add a specialized function to handle this case. For that, you can use the following function to read a property as a list of integers:

```
fun readAsIntList(name: String): Result<List<Int>> =
  readAsString(name).flatMap {
    try {
      Result(fromSeparated(it, ",").map(String::toInt))
    } catch (e: NumberFormatException) {
      Result.failure<List<Int>>(
        "Invalid value while parsing property '$name' to List<Int>: '$it'")
    }
  }
```

This code uses the `fromSeparated` function defined in the `List` class that you'll find in module `com.fpinkotlin.common`. That module is available in the code accompanying this book (https://github.com/pysaumont/fpinkotlin). You can change the code to use the Kotlin standard `List` function by changing one line:

```
fun readAsIntList(name: String): Result<List<Int>> =
  readAsString(name).flatMap {
    try {
      // Next line uses Kotlin List
      Result(it.split(",").map(String::toInt))
    } catch (e: NumberFormatException) {
      Result.failure<List<Int>>(
        "Invalid value while parsing property '$name' to List<Int>: $it")
    }
  }
```

But you can do much more! You can read a property as a list of any numerical values by providing the conversion function:

```
fun <T> readAsList(name: String, f: (String) -> T): Result<List<T>> =
  readAsString(name).flatMap {
    try {
      Result(fromSeparated(it, ",").map(f))
    } catch (e: Exception) {
      Result.failure<List<T>>(
        "Invalid value while parsing property '$name' to List: $it")
    }
  }
```

And you can define functions for all sorts of number formats in terms of `readAsList`:

```
fun readAsIntList(name: String): Result<List<Int>> =
                    readAsList(name, String::toInt)

fun readAsDoubleList(name: String): Result<List<Double>> =
                    readAsList(name, String::toDouble)

fun readAsBooleanList(name: String): Result<List<Boolean>> =
                    readAsList(name, String::toBoolean)
```

One frequent use case consists in reading a property as an enum value, which is a particular case of reading a property as any type.

14.3.5 *Reading enum values*

You can first create a function to convert a property to any type T, taking a function from String to Result<T>:

```
fun <T> readAsType(f: (String) -> Result<T>, name: String) =
    readAsString(name).flatMap {
        try {
            f(it)
        } catch (e: Exception) {
            Result.failure<T>(
                "Invalid value while parsing property '$name': '$it'")
        }
    }
```

You can now create a readAsEnum function in terms of readAsType:

```
inline
fun <reified T: Enum<T>> readAsEnum(name: String,
                                    enumClass: Class<T>): Result<T> {
    val f: (String) -> Result<T> = {
        try {
            val value = enumValueOf<T>(it)
            Result(value)
        } catch (e: Exception) {
            Result.failure("Error parsing property '$name': " +
                    "value '$it' can't be parsed to ${enumClass.name}.")
        }
    }
    return readAsType(f, name)
}
```

Note that reified means that type T is to be accessible at runtime. Unlike Java, Kotlin allows accessing type parameters at runtime by using the keyword reified, so that it's not erased. This possibility is only accessible in functions declared with inline, meaning that the compiler is allowed to copy the code of the function at the call site, instead of referencing the original code. This increases the size of the compiled code.

Given the following property

```
type=SERIAL
```

and the following enum

```
enum class Type {SERIAL, PARALLEL}
```

you can now read the property using the following code:

```
val type = propertyReader.readAsEnum("type", Type::class.java)
```

So far you've been reading properties as String, Int, Double, Boolean, lists, or enums. It can also be interesting to read properties as arbitrary objects. For this, you'll have to write the object properties in a kind of serialized form in the property file and then load these properties and deserialize them.

14.3.6 *Reading properties of arbitrary types*

You can use the `getAsType` function to read a property as any type. For example, you could read the following property to get a `Person`:

```
person=id:3,firstName:Jane,lastName:Doe
```

All you need to do is provide a function from `String` to `Result<Person>`. This function should be able to create a `Person` from the string `"id:3,firstName:Jane,last-Name:Doe"`. To simplify its use, you could create a `readAsPerson` function. But as it's type-specific, you shouldn't put it inside the `PropertyReader` class. A better solution is to add a function taking a `PropertyReader` and the property name as its arguments to the `Person` class.

There are several ways to implement this function. One way is to get the property as a list and then split each element, putting the key/value pairs in a map. It would then be easy to create a `Person` from this map. Another way would be to create a second `PropertyReader` that reads from the string after having replaced the commas with newline characters. The following listing shows the `Person` class with two specific functions for constructing instances from a property string.

> Listing 14.4   Methods that read properties as objects or lists of objects

```
data class Person(val id: Int,
                  val firstName: String,
                  val lastName: String) {

  companion object {
    fun readAsPerson(propertyName: String,
                     propertyReader: PropertyReader): Result<Person> {
      val rString = propertyReader.readAsPropertyString(propertyName)
      val rPropReader = rString.map { stringPropertyReader(it) }
      return rPropReader.flatMap { readPerson(it) }
    }

    fun readAsPersonList(propertyName: String,
                         propertyReader: PropertyReader):
                                     Result<List<Person>> =
      propertyReader.readAsList(propertyName, { it }).flatMap { list ->
          sequence(list.map { s ->
            readPerson(PropertyReader
              .stringPropertyReader(PropertyReader.toPropertyString(s)))
          })
      }

    private fun readPerson(propReader: PropertyReader): Result<Person> =
      propReader.readAsInt("id")
        .flatMap { id ->
          propReader.readAsString("firstName")
            .flatMap { firstName ->
                propReader.readAsString("lastName")
                  .map { lastName -> Person(id, firstName, lastName) }
            }
        }
```

```
        }
}
```

With the `readAsPersonList` function, you can read vector properties written as follows:

```
employees=\
 id:3;firstName:Jane;lastName:Doe,\
 id:5;firstName:Paul;lastName:Smith,\
 id:8;firstName:Mary;lastName:Winston
```

These functions necessitate some changes in the `PropertyReader` class, as shown in the next listing.

Listing 14.5 Functions added to the `PropertyReader` class

```
class PropertyReader(
    private val properties: Result<Properties>,        ◄──── Constructs the PropertyReader
    private val source: String) {                             with a Result<Properties>

    ...

    fun readAsPropertyString(propertyName: String):
                        Result<String> =          ◄────
        readAsString(propertyName).map { toPropertyString(it) }

    companion object {                           Converts a single property value into a
                                                 property string that can be used as input
        fun toPropertyString(s: String): String =       for a nested PropertyReader
                        s.replace(";", "\n")    ◄────
                                                 Reads a property and converts
        private                                  the value into a property string
        fun readPropertiesFromFile(configFileName: String):
                        Result<Properties> =     ◄────
            try {                                       The original implementation
                MethodHandles.lookup().lookupClass()    for reading a property file
                    .getResourceAsStream(configFileName)
                    .use { inputStream ->
                        when (inputStream) {
                            null -> Result.failure(
                                "File $configFileName not found in classpath")
                            else -> Properties().let {
                                it.load(inputStream)
                                Result(it)
                            }


                        }
                    }
            } catch (e: IOException) {
                Result.failure(
                    "IOException reading classpath resource $configFileName")
            } catch (e: Exception) {
                Result.failure("Exception: ${e.message}reading classpath"
                                    + " resource $configFileName")
            }

        private fun readPropertiesFromString(propString: String):
```

Registers the source in order to be used in error messages

```
                        Result<Properties> =
            try {
                StringReader(propString).use { reader ->
                    val properties = Properties()
                    properties.load(reader)
                    Result(properties)            A new function to read properties
                }                                      from a property string
            } catch (e: Exception) {
                Result.failure("Exception reading property string " +
                                        "$propString: ${e.message}")
            }

        fun filePropertyReader(fileName: String):        Creates a PropertyReader
                        PropertyReader =                 from a filename
            PropertyReader(readPropertiesFromFile(fileName),
                                        "File: $fileName")

        fun stringPropertyReader(propString: String):
                        PropertyReader =
            PropertyReader(readPropertiesFromString(propString),
                                        "String: $propString")
        }
    }
```

Creates a PropertyReader from a property string →

You can do the same thing for XML property files or for other formats such as JSON or YAML.

14.4   *Converting an imperative program: The XML reader*

Writing new functional programs for any task you have to accomplish is exciting, but most developers generally don't have time for this. Often you'll want to use existing imperative programs in your own code. This is the case each time you want to use an existing library.

You might find it more interesting to start from scratch and build a completely new, 100% functional solution. But you have to be realistic. You generally don't have the time or budget to do this, and you'll have to use existing nonfunctional libraries full of null, exceptions throwing and impure functions mutating their parameters on the outside world.

As you'll soon discover, once you're comfortable with functional techniques, it's a pain to go back to the old imperative coding style. The solution is generally to build a thin functional wrapper around these imperative libraries. As an example, let's examine a common library for reading XML files, JDOM 2.0.6. This is the most commonly used Java library for this task, and it's perfectly usable with Kotlin.

14.4.1   *Step 1: The imperative solution*

Let's start with the example program in listing 14.6. This program comes from one of the numerous sites proposing tutorials about how to use JDOM (http://www.mkyong.com/java/how-to-read-xml-file-in-java-jdom-example/). I've chosen this example because it's minimal and fits easily in the book. This is a Java program using a Java library.

Listing 14.6   Reading XML data with JDOM: Java version

```java
import org.jdom2.Document;
import org.jdom2.Element;
import org.jdom2.JDOMException;
import org.jdom2.input.SAXBuilder;
import java.io.File;
import java.io.IOException;
import java.util.List;

public class ReadXmlFile {

  public static void main(String[] args) {
    SAXBuilder builder = new SAXBuilder();
    File xmlFile = new File("path_to_file");
    try {
      Document document = (Document) builder.build(xmlFile);
      Element rootNode = document.getRootElement();
      List list = rootNode.getChildren("staff");
      for (int i = 0; i < list.size(); i++) {
        Element node = (Element) list.get(i);
        System.out.println("First Name : " +
                                node.getChildText("firstname"));
        System.out.println("\tLast Name : " +
                                node.getChildText("lastname"));
        System.out.println("\tNick Name : " +
                                node.getChildText("email"));
        System.out.println("\tSalary : " + node.getChildText("salary"));
      }
    } catch (IOException io) {
      System.out.println(io.getMessage());
    } catch (JDOMException jdomex) {
      System.out.println(jdomex.getMessage());
    }
  }
}
```

This Java program can easily be rewritten in imperative Kotlin, as you can see in the next listing.

Listing 14.7   Reading XML data with JDOM: Imperative Kotlin version

```kotlin
import org.jdom2.JDOMException
import org.jdom2.input.SAXBuilder
import java.io.File
import java.io.IOException


/**
 * Not testable, throws exceptions.
 */
fun main(args: Array<String>) {

    val builder = SAXBuilder()
```

```
val xmlFile = File("/path/to/file.xml") // Fix the path

try {
    val document = builder.build(xmlFile)
    val rootNode = document.rootElement
    val list = rootNode.getChildren("staff")

    list.forEach {
        println("First Name: ${it.getChildText("firstName")}")
        println("\tLast Name: ${it.getChildText("lastName")}")
        println("\tEmail: ${it.getChildText("email")}")
        println("\tSalary: ${it.getChildText("salary")}")
    }
} catch (io: IOException) {
    println(io.message)
} catch (e: JDOMException) {
    println(e.message)
}
}
```

The data file used with this example is shown in the following listing.

Listing 14.8 The XML file to read

```
<?xml version="1.0"?>
<company>
    <staff>
        <firstName>Paul</firstName>
        <lastName>Smith</lastName>
        <email>paul.smith@acme.com</email>
        <salary>100000</salary>
    </staff>
    <staff>
        <firstName>Mary</firstName>
        <lastName>Colson</lastName>
        <email>mary.colson@acme.com</email>
        <salary>200000</salary>
    </staff>
</company>
```

Let's look at the benefits you get from rewriting this example in a functional way. The first problem you might encounter is that no part of the program can be reused. It's only an example, but even as an example, it should be written in a reusable way so that it's at least testable. Here, the only way to test the program is to look at the console, which will display either the expected result or an error message. As you'll see, it might even display an erroneous result.

14.4.2 Step 2: Making an imperative program more functional

To determine the necessary functions and to make this program more functional, you start by

- Listing the fundamental functions you need

- Writing those functions as autonomous, reusable, and testable units
- Coding the example by composing these functions

The main functions you'll need will do the following:

- Read a file and return the content as an XML string
- Convert the XML string into a list of elements
- Convert a list of elements into a list of string representations of these elements

You'll also need an effect for displaying the list of strings to the computer screen.

NOTE This description is only suitable for a small file that can be loaded entirely in memory.

The first function you'll need, which reads a file and returns the contents as an XML string, can be implemented as the following:

```
fun readFile2String(path: String): Result<String>
```

This function doesn't throw any exceptions; it returns a `Result<String>`.

The second function converts an XML string into a list of elements, so it needs to know the name of the root XML element. It has the following signature:

```
fun readDocument(rootElementName: String,
                 stringDoc: String): Result<List<Element>>
```

The third function receives a list of elements as its argument and returns a list of string representations of those elements. This is implemented by a function with the following signature:

```
fun toStringList(list: List<Element>, format: String): List<String>
```

Eventually you'll need to apply an effect to the data, so you'll have to define it with the following signature:

```
fun <A> processList(list: List<A>)
```

This decomposition in functions doesn't look much different from what you could do in imperative programming. After all, it's good practice to decompose imperative programs into functions with a single responsibility each. But it's more different than it might look.

Note that the `readDocument` function takes as its first parameter a string that's returned by a function that could (in the imperative world) throw an exception. You'll need to deal with the additional function:

```
fun getRootElementName(): Result<String>
```

In the same way, the file path could be returned by the same kind of function:

```
fun getXmlFilePath(): Result<String>
```

The important thing to note is that the argument types and return types of these functions don't match! This is the explicit translation of the fact that the imperative versions of these functions would be partial, which means they'd possibly throw exceptions.

Functions throwing exceptions don't compose well. In contrast, your functions compose perfectly.

COMPOSING THE FUNCTIONS AND APPLYING AN EFFECT

Although the argument and return types don't match, you can compose these functions easily using a comprehension pattern like this:

```
const val format = "First Name : %s\n" +
        "\tLast Name : %s\n" +
        "\tEmail : %s\n" +
        "\tSalary : %s"

fun main(args: Array<String>) {
    val path = getXmlFilePath()
    val rDoc = path.flatMap(::readFile2String)
    val rRoot = getRootElementName()
    val result = rDoc.flatMap { doc ->
        rRoot.flatMap { rootElementName ->
            readDocument(rootElementName, doc)
        }.map { list ->
            toStringList(list, format)
        }
    }
    ...
}
```

To display the result, apply the corresponding effect:

```
result.forEach(onSuccess =
    { processList(it) }, onFailure = { it.printStackTrace() })
```

This functional version of the program is much cleaner, and it's fully testable. Or, at least, it will be when you've implemented all the necessary functions.

IMPLEMENTING THE FUNCTIONS

Your program is relatively elegant, but you still have to implement the functions and effects you're using in order to make it work. The good news is that each function is simple and can be easily tested.

First, you'll implement the getXmlFilePath and getRootElementName functions. In our example, these are constants that would be replaced with a specific implementation in a real application:

```
fun getRootElementName(): Result<String> =
    Result.of { "staff" } // Simulating a computation that may fail.

fun getXmlFilePath(): Result<String> =
    Result.of { "file.xml" } // <- adjust path
```

Then you need to implement the readFile2String function. Here's one of the many possible implementations:

```
fun readFile2String(path: String): Result<String> =
                            Result.of { File(path).readText() }
```

Next, you need to implement the `readDocument` function. This function takes as its parameters an XML string containing the XML data and the name of the root element:

```
fun readDocument(rootElementName: String,
                 stringDoc: String): Result<List<Element>> =
  SAXBuilder().let { builder ->
    try {
      val document =
        builder.build(StringReader(stringDoc))       Can throw a NullPointerException
      val rootElement = document.rootElement          Can throw an IllegalStateException
      Result(List(*rootElement.getChildren(rootElementName)
                          .toTypedArray()))
    } catch (io: IOException) {
      Result.failure("Invalid root element name '$rootElementName' "
                          + "or XML data $stringDoc: ${io.message}")
    } catch (jde: JDOMException) {
      Result.failure("Invalid root element name '$rootElementName' "
                          + "or XML data $stringDoc: ${jde.message}")
    } catch (e: Exception) {
      Result.failure("Unexpected error while reading XML data "
                          + "$stringDoc: ${e.message}")
    }
  }
```

The * at the start of the expression indicates that the resulting array should be used as a vararg and not as a single object.

You first catch `IOException` (which is unlikely to be thrown because you're reading from a string) and `JDOMException`, both of which are checked exceptions, and return a failure with the corresponding error message. But by looking at the JDOM code (remember that no one should call a library method without first looking at how it's implemented), you see that the code might throw an `IllegalStateException` or a `NullPointerException`. Once again, you have to catch `Exception`. The `toStringList` function maps the list to a function responsible for the conversion:

```
fun toStringList(list: List<Element>, format: String): List<String> =
        list.map { e -> processElement(e, format) }


fun processElement(element: Element, format: String): String =
        String.format(format, element.getChildText("firstName"),
                element.getChildText("lastName"),
                element.getChildText("email"),
                element.getChildText("salary"))
```

Finally, you need to implement the effect that will be applied to the result:

```
fun <A> processList(list: List<A>) = list.forEach(::println)
```

14.4.3 *Step 3: Making the program even more functional*

Your program is now much more modular and more testable, and its parts are reusable. But you can still do better. You're still using four nonfunctional elements:

- The file path
- The name of the root element

- The format used to convert the elements to string
- The effect that's applied to the result

By nonfunctional, I mean that these elements are accessed directly from the implementation of your functions, making them nonreferentially transparent. To make your program fully functional, you should make these elements parameters of your program.

The `processElement` function also used specific data in the form of the element names, which correspond to the parameters of the format string used to display them. You can replace the format parameter with a `Pair` (the format string and a list of parameters). This way, the `processElement` function becomes the following:

```
fun toStringList(list: List<Element>,
                 format: Pair<String, List<String>>): List<String> =
        list.map { e -> processElement(e, format) }

fun processElement(element: Element,
                   format: Pair<String, List<String>>): String {
    val formatString = format.first
    val parameters = format.second.map { element.getChildText(it) }
    return String.format(formatString, *parameters.toArrayList().toArray())
}
```

Now your program can be a pure function, taking four arguments and returning a new (nonfunctional) executable program as its result. This version of the program is represented in the following listing.

Listing 14.9 **The fully functional XML reader program**

```
import com.fpinkotlin.common.List
import com.fpinkotlin.common.Result
import org.jdom2.Element
import org.jdom2.JDOMException
import org.jdom2.input.SAXBuilder
import java.io.File
import java.io.FileInputStream
import java.io.IOException
import java.io.StringReader

fun readXmlFile(
        sPath: () -> Result<String>,
        sRootName: () -> Result<String>,
        format: Pair<String, List<String>>,
        effect: (List<String>) -> Unit): () -> Unit {
    val path = sPath()
    val rDoc = path.flatMap(::readFile2String)
    val rRoot = sRootName()
    val result = rDoc.flatMap { doc ->
        rRoot.flatMap { rootElementName ->
            readDocument(rootElementName, doc) }
                .map { list -> toStringList(list, format) }
    }
```

The path and root element name are now received as constant functions. The format includes the parameter names, and the function takes an effect of type (List<String>) -> Unit as an additional parameter.

Evaluates the functions to get the parameter values

Parameterizes the effect to be applied

```
        return {
            result.forEach(onSuccess = { effect(it) },
                    onFailure = { it.printStackTrace() })
        }
}
```

> **The function returns a program, meaning a function of type () -> Unit, applying the effect received as a parameter to the result. This function throws exceptions. There's nothing better to do, because it's an effect and can't return a value.**

```
fun readFile2String(path: String): Result<String> =
                                Result.of { File(path).readText() }


fun readDocument(rootElementName: String,
                stringDoc: String): Result<List<Element>> =
    SAXBuilder().let { builder ->
        try {
            val document = builder.build(StringReader(stringDoc))
            val rootElement = document.rootElement
            Result(List(*rootElement.getChildren(rootElementName)
                                            .toTypedArray()))
        } catch (io: IOException) {
            Result.failure("Invalid root element name '$rootElementName' "
                    + "or XML data $stringDoc: ${io.message}")
        } catch (jde: JDOMException) {
            Result.failure("Invalid root element name '$rootElementName' "
                    + "or XML data $stringDoc: ${jde.message}")
        } catch (e: Exception) {
            Result.failure("Unexpected error while reading XML data "
                    + "$stringDoc: ${e.message}")
        }
    }


fun toStringList(list: List<Element>,
                format: Pair<String, List<String>>): List<String> =
        list.map { e -> processElement(e, format) }

fun processElement(element: Element,
                format: Pair<String, List<String>>):
                                        String {
    val formatString = format.first
    val parameters = format.second.map { element.getChildText(it) }
    return String.format(formatString, *parameters.toArrayList().toArray())
}
```

> **The processElement function is no longer specific.**

At this point, you can test this program with the client code shown in the following listing.

Listing 14.10 The client program to test the XML reader

```
import com.fpinkotlin.common.List
import com.fpinkotlin.common.Result

fun <A> processList(list: List<A>) = list.forEach(::println)

fun getRootElementName(): Result<String> =
```

```
        Result.of { "staff" } // Simulating a computation that may fail.

fun getXmlFilePath(): Result<String> =
        Result.of { "/path/to/file.xml" } // <- adjust path

private val format = Pair("First Name : %s\n" +
        "\tLast Name : %s\n" +
        "\tEmail : %s\n" +
        "\tSalary : %s", List("firstName", "lastName", "email", "salary"))

fun main(args: Array<String>) {
    val program = readXmlFile( { getXmlFilePath() },
                               { getRootElementName() },
                               format, { processList(it) })
    program()
}
```

This program isn't ideal because you haven't handled the potential error that could arise from invalid element names. For example, if you use a wrong element name as in

```
<company>
    <staff>
        <firstname></firstname>
        <lastName>Smith</lastName>
        <email>paul.smith@acme.com</email>
        <salary>100000</salary>
    </staff>
    <staff>
        <firstname>Mary</firstname>
        <lastName>Colson</lastName>
        <email>mary.colson@acme.com</email>
        <salary>200000</salary>
    </staff>
</company>
```

you'll get the following result:

```
First Name : null
  Last Name : Smith
  email : paul.smith@acme.com
  Salary : 100000
First Name : null
  Last Name : Colson
  email : mary.colson@acme.com
  Salary : 200000
```

You can guess what the error is by seeing that all the first names are null. It'd be better to replace the word *null* with an explicit message containing the erroneous element name. A more important problem is that if you forget one of the element names in the list, you'll get an exception from the String.format function because of the following code:

```
val parameters = format.second.map { element.getChildText(it) }
return String.format(formatString, *parameters.toArrayList().toArray())
```

In this code, the array of parameters will have only three elements instead of the expected four. But it will be difficult to locate the source of the error from the exception trace. In fact, the real cause of the problem is that you've taken all the specific data out of the readXmlFile function, such as the root element name, the file path, and the effect to apply, but the processElement function is still specific to the client business use case. The readXmlFile function only allows you to read all elements that are direct children of the root element, gathering some of their direct child elements' values (those whose names are passed along with the format).

A third problem is that the readXmlFile function takes two arguments of the same type. This is a source of error if arguments are swapped, which won't be detected by the compiler. You can easily fix this problem, so let's tackle that next. After that, you'll fix the first two problems.

14.4.4 *Step 4: Fixing the argument type problem*

The third problem is easy to fix by using the value types technique described in chapter 3. Instead of using Result<String> arguments, you can use Result<FilePath> and Result<ElementName>. FilePath and ElementName are value classes for string values as shown here:

```
data class FilePath private constructor(val value: Result<String>) {

    companion object {

        operator fun invoke(value: String): FilePath =
            FilePath(Result.of({ isValidPath(it) }, value,
                                  "Invalid file path: $value"))

        // Replace with validation code
        private fun isValidPath(path: String): Boolean = true
    }
}
```

The ElementName class is similar, but you need to add the validation code if you want some validation to happen. The simplest way is to check the value against a regular expression. To use these new types, the readXmlFile function can be modified as follows:

```
fun readXmlFile(sPath: () -> FilePath,
                sRootName: () -> ElementName,
                format: Pair<String, List<String>>,
                effect: (List<String>) -> Unit): () -> Unit {
    val path = sPath().value
    val rDoc = path.flatMap(::readFile2String)
    val rRoot = sRootName().value
```

As you see, the changes are minimal. The client class must also be modified:

```
fun getRootElementName(): ElementName =
        ElementName("staff") // Simulating a computation that may fail.

fun getXmlFilePath(): FilePath =
        FilePath("/path/to/file.xml") // <- adjust path
```

With these changes, it's now impossible to switch the order of the arguments without being warned by the compiler.

14.4.5 *Step 5: Making the element-processing function a parameter*

The two remaining problems can be solved with a single change: passing the element-processing function as a parameter to the `readXmlFile` method. This way, this function has a single task: it reads the list of first-level elements in the file, applies a configurable function to this list, and returns the result. The main difference is that the function will no longer produce a list of strings and apply a string effect. You'll need to make the function generic. This means only the following changes:

```
fun <T> readXmlFile(
        sPath: () -> FilePath,         ◄─────
        sRootName: () -> ElementName,          │ The function is made generic.
        function: (Element) -> T,       ◄──────
        effect: (List<T>) -> Unit): () -> Unit {
    val path = sPath().value
    val rDoc = path.flatMap(::readFile2String)
    val rRoot = sRootName().value
    val result = rDoc.flatMap { doc ->
        rRoot.flatMap { rootElementName ->
            readDocument(rootElementName, doc) }
                .map { list -> list.map(function) }   ◄───
    }
    return {
        result.forEach(onSuccess = { effect(it) },
                onFailure = { throw it })
    }
}
```

The effect to be applied is now parameterized by List<T>.

The Pair<String, List<String>> format argument has disappeared, and new function argument replaces it. This is the function that will be applied to convert the list of elements to a list of T.

The toStringList and processElement functions have been removed. They're replaced with an application of the received function

The client program can now be modified accordingly. This relieves you from using the `Pair` trick to pass both the format string and the list of parameter names:

```
const val format = "First Name : %s\n" +      ◄─────
        "\tLast Name : %s\n" +                        │ The format is now again set as a simple string
        "\tEmail : %s\n" +
        "\tSalary : %s"

private val elementNames =      ◄───── The list of element names is also set separately.
    List("firstName", "lastName", "email", "salary")

private fun processElement(element: Element): String =      ◄──── The processElement function is now implemented by the client
    String.format(format, *elementNames.map { element.getChildText(it) }
        .toArrayList()
        .toArray())

fun main(args: Array<String>) {
    val program = readXmlFile(::getXmlFilePath,
                              ::getRootElementName,
                              ::processElement,   ◄──── The processElement function is passed as an argument.
                              ::processList)
    ...
```

The `processList` effect hasn't changed. Now it's up to the client to provide a function to convert one element and an effect to apply to this element.

14.4.6 *Step 6: Handling errors on element names*

Now you're left with the problem of errors happening when reading the elements. The function that's passed to the readXmlFile function returns a raw type, meaning that it should be a total function but it's not. It was a total function in the initial example because an error produced the null string. Now that you're using a function from Element to T, you could use Result<String> as the realization of T, but this wouldn't be practical because you'd end up with a List<Result<T>> and you'd have to transform it into a Result<List<T>>. Not a big deal, but this should definitely be abstracted.

The solution is to use a function from Element to Result<T> and to use the sequence function to transform the result into a Result<List<T>>. Here's the new function:

```
fun <T> readXmlFile(sPath: () -> FilePath,
                sRootName: () -> ElementName,
                function: (Element) -> Result<T>,
                effect: (List<T>) -> Unit): () -> Unit {
    val path = sPath().value
    val rDoc = path.flatMap(::readFile2String)
    val rRoot = sRootName().value
    val result = rDoc.flatMap { doc ->
        rRoot.flatMap { rootElementName ->
            readDocument(rootElementName, doc) }
                .flatMap { list ->
                    sequence(list.map(function)) }
    }
    return {
        result.forEach(onSuccess = { effect(it) },
                onFailure = { throw it })
    }
}
    ...
```

> ◀ **The function received as an argument is now a function from Element to Result<T>.**

> ◀ **The result is sequenced, producing a Result<List<T>>. The map function has to be replaced with flatMap.**

The only additional change to be made is to handle the error that might occur in the processElement function. The best approach is once again to examine the code of the getChildText method from JDOM. This method is implemented as follows:

```
/**
 * Returns the textual content of the named child element, or null if
 * there's no such child. This method is a convenience because calling
 * <code>getChild().getText()</code> can throw a NullPointerException.
 *
 * @param cname the name of the child
 * @return text    content for the named child, or null if no such child
 */
public String getChildText(final String cname) {
  final Element child = getChild(cname);
  if (child == null) {
    return null;
  }
  return child.getText();
}
```

As you continue examining the code for the `getChild` method, you can see this method won't throw any exceptions, but it will return `null` if the element doesn't exist. You can modify your `processElement` function like this:

```
fun processElement(element: Element): Result<String> =
    try {
        Result(String.format(format, *elementNames.map {
                                  getChildText(element, it) }
            .toArrayList()
            .toArray())))
    } catch (e: Exception) {
        Result.failure(
            "Exception while formatting element. " +
            "Probable cause is a missing element name in element " +
            "list $elementNames")
    }

fun getChildText(element: Element,
                 name: String): String =
    element.getChildText(name) ?:
        "Element $name is not a child of ${element.name}"
```

The function now returns a Result<String>.

In case of an exception formatting the result, an explicit error message is built.

If the returned value is null, it's replaced with an explicit error message.

Now most potential errors are handled in a functional way, but not all errors can be handled functionally. As I said earlier, exceptions that are thrown by the effect passed to the `readXmlFile` method can't be handled this way. These are exceptions thrown by the program that's returned by the function. When the function returns the program, it hasn't yet been executed. These exceptions must be caught while executing the resulting program, for example:

```
fun main(args: Array<String>) {
    val program = readXmlFile(::getXmlFilePath,
                              ::getRootElementName,
                              ::processElement,
                              ::processList)
    try {
        program()
    } catch (e: Exception) {
        println("An exception occurred: ${e.message}")
    }
}
```

You'll find the complete example in the code accompanying this book at http://github.com/pysaumont/fpinkotlin.

14.4.7 *Step 7: Additional improvements to the formerly imperative code*

One might object that the `processElement` function closes over the `format` and `elementNames` references, which might not seem functional. (If you don't remember what closure means, see chapter 3.) In fact, this isn't a real problem in the example because those are constants. But in real life, they probably wouldn't be constants.

The solution to this problem is easy. These closures are additional implicit arguments of the `processElement` function. The indication of the problem is that unlike the definition of the function, these two values should be part of the client program, meaning the `main` function.

You could put the `processElement` function in the `main` function too (as a local function), but this would make it nonreusable. The solution is to use explicit argument with a curried `val` function as explained in chapter 3:

```
val processElement: (List<String>) -> (String) -> (Element) ->
                               Result<String> = { elementNames ->
    { format ->
        { element ->
            try {
                Result(String.format(format,
                    *elementNames.map { getChildText(element, it) }
                        .toArrayList()
                        .toArray()))
            } catch (e: Exception) {
                Result.failure("Exception while formatting element. " +
                        "Probable cause is a missing element name in" +
                        " element list $elementNames")
            }
        }
    }
}
```

Now, you can call the `readXmlFile` function with a partially applied version of the `processElement` function. The two values `format` and `elementNames` are specific to your client implementation, although the `processElement` function is still generic and no longer closes over these values. You can put the `processElement` and `getChildText` generic functions into the `ReadXmlFile.kt` file, and you can define the `processList`, `getRootElementName`, and `getXmlFilePath` as local to the `main` function:

```
fun main(args: Array<String>) {

    fun <A> processList(list: List<A>) = list.forEach(::println)

    // Simulating a computation that may fail.
    fun getRootElementName(): ElementName = ElementName("staff")

    fun getXmlFilePath(): FilePath =
                    FilePath("/path/to/file.xml") // <- adjust path

    val format = "First Name : %s\n" +
            "\tLast Name : %s\n" +
            "\tEmail : %s\n" +
            "\tSalary : %s"

    val elementNames =
            List("firstName", "lastName", "email", "salary")

    val program = readXmlFile(::getXmlFilePath,
                            ::getRootElementName,
                            processElement(elementNames)(format),
                            ::processList)
    try {
```

```
        program()
   } catch (e: Exception) {
        println("An exception occurred: ${e.message}")
   }
}
```

You can apply the same process to all your programming tasks. By abstracting every possible subtask into a function, you'll make your programs more testable and, as a consequence, more reliable. You'll also be able to reuse these functions in other programs without having to test them again. Appendix B shows you how to apply abstraction to testing.

Summary

- Putting values in the Result context is the functional equivalent of assertions.
- Property files can be read in a safe manner using the Result context.
- Functional property reading relieves you of handling conversion errors.
- Properties can be read as any type, enum, or collection in an abstracted way.
- Automatic retries can be abstracted into functions.
- Functional wrappers can be built around legacy imperative libraries.

appendix A
Mixing Kotlin with Java

Kotlin was first created as a language running on the Java Virtual Machine (JVM). JetBrains then introduced Kotlin JS, a version of the language running on the Java-Script VM, as well as Kotlin/Native, a version compiling to native binaries that runs without any VM. The vast majority of Kotlin programs are, however, designed to run in the JVM environment.

Such programs take advantage of the Java standard library, meaning that you can call any method of this library from a Kotlin program. There's no limit to this, although you should probably not call any of these methods without first verifying whether Kotlin offers a better solution. On the other hand, Java programs can use libraries developed in Kotlin, although not as easily. Kotlin offers much more than Java, and those features unavailable in Java must be handled with extra care. Not all libraries are available to Java programs.

The two solutions for programmers consist in calling Java compiled libraries from Kotlin source code or calling Kotlin compiled libraries from Java source code. But you can also mix Kotlin and Java source code in the same project, with some limitations. In this appendix, I show you

- How to create and manage mixed Kotlin projects using Gradle
- How to call Java from Kotlin
- How to call Kotlin from Java
- Specific problems with mixed Kotlin/Java projects

NOTE The example code from this appendix is available at https://github .com/pysaumont/fpinkotlin in the `examples` directory.

A.1   Creating and managing mixed projects

The most efficient way to create and manage Kotlin projects is to use Gradle, which is the de facto standard for building Kotlin programs. Gradle is also one of the best tools for managing Java projects, so you won't be surprised to learn that Gradle is the way to go for mixed Java/Kotlin projects. With mixed projects, you can use the best of both worlds, including the huge mass of Java code that's available in open source and usable in your Kotlin programs.

If you're already using Gradle to build Java programs, you can build and manage Kotlin or mixed Kotlin/Java projects as you already do for pure Java projects. Otherwise, now might be the right time to switch to a modern build tool. But even if you already are a Gradle user, you might benefit in learning how to write Gradle scripts using Kotlin.

In May 2016, the Gradle team announced that Kotlin would become the language of choice for writing Gradle scripts. Prior to that, the Groovy language was used for this purpose. This announcement didn't imply that support for Groovy was deprecated in Gradle. You can still write Gradle scripts using Groovy, but Kotlin is so much more practical that I recommend you give it a try. And if you're new to Gradle, I recommend you go directly for Kotlin.

Kotlin offers many benefits when writing Gradle scripts for Kotlin or mixed Java/Kotlin projects. The most evident is that you don't have to learn yet another language. But a more important benefit is that you'll get much better support for Kotlin Gradle scripts in your IDE (at least when using IntelliJ). IntelliJ offers the same level of support for Kotlin Gradle scripts as for Kotlin programs, including syntax checking, auto completion, and refactoring.

A.1.1   Creating a simple project with Gradle

Creating a simple Gradle Kotlin/Java project couldn't be easier. Here's an example:

```
plugins {
    application
    kotlin("jvm") version "1.3.21"
    // Change version according to your needs
}

application {
    mainClassName = "com.mydomain.mysimpleproject.MainKt"
}

repositories {
    jcenter()
}

dependencies {
    compile(kotlin("stdlib"))
}
```

Save this script under the name build.gradle.kts in a directory by the name of your project; for example, MySimpleProject. In this directory, add a subdirectory structure such as the following:

```
MySimpleProject
    src
        main
            java
            kotlin
        test
            java
            kotlin
```

You're done! You can now add Kotlin and Java files to your project and manage your project using the various Gradle commands. To create a Kotlin program with a Java dependency, add the following files to your project:

- `MySimpleProject/src/main/java/com/mydomain/mysimpleproject/MyClass.java`
- `MySimpleProject/src/main/kotlin/com/mydomain/mysimpleproject/Main.kt`

Here's the content of MyClass.java:

```java
package com.mydomain.mysimpleproject;

public class MyClass {

    public static String getMessage(Lang language) {
        switch (language) {
            case ENGLISH:
                return "Hello";
            case FRENCH:
                return "Bonjour";
            case GERMAN:
                return "Hallo";
            case SPANISH:
                return "Hola";
            default:
                return "Saluton";
        }

    }
}
```

And here's the content of Main.kt:

```kotlin
package com.mydomain.mysimpleproject

fun main(args: Array<String>) {
    println(MyClass.getMessage(Lang.GERMAN))
}

enum class Lang { GERMAN, FRENCH, ENGLISH, SPANISH }
```

You can now run your project using the following Gradle command in the project directory (MySimpleProject):

```
<path_to_Gradle>/bin/gradle run
```

If you want to build and assemble your project into a ZIP or TAR file, use the following Gradle command in the project directory (MySimpleProject):

```
<path_to_Gradle>/bin/gradle assembleDist
```

This should create the two following files:

- `MySimpleProject/build/distributions/MySimpleProject.tar`
- `MySimpleProject/build/distributions/MySimpleProject.zip`

You can then extract one of these archives somewhere and use the included shell script to launch it.

A.1.2   *Importing your Gradle project into IntelliJ*

Importing your Gradle project into IntelliJ is straightforward:

- Select *File > New > Project from Existing Sources*, select your project directory, and click *OK*.
- Select *Import Project from External Model, then Gradle*, and click *Next*.
- Select *Use Default Gradle Wrapper*, and then click *Finish*.

Alternatively, you can select a local distribution of Gradle. You can also select a minimum JDK version, such as JDK 6 (the version used by Android). And for creating a empty project for which you have created the build script only, you can select the *Create Directories for Empty Content Roots Automatically* option. This automatically creates the necessary directory structure, including Java and Kotlin `main` and `test` directories, as well as a `resource` directory. If some of these already exist, they'll be preserved. Now you can continue developing your project, adding Kotlin and Java files at will.

A.1.3   *Adding dependencies to your project*

To add dependencies to your project, you need to use the standard Gradle syntax:

```
val kotlintestVersion = "3.1.10"
val logbackVersion = "1.2.3"
val slf4jVersion = "1.7.25"

plugins {
    application
    kotlin("jvm") version "1.3.21" // Change version according to your needs
}

application {
    mainClassName = "com.mydomain.mysimpleproject.MainKt"
}

repositories {
    jcenter()
}
```

```
dependencies {
    compile(kotlin("stdlib"))
    testCompile("io.kotlintest:kotlintest-runner-junit5:$kotlintestVersion")
    testRuntime("org.slf4j:slf4j-nop:$slf4jVersion")
}
```

In the plugins block, you can't use a variable for the version. Only literals are allowed, so you might have to indicate the version twice in your file if you need to access the Kotlin version number somewhere else. This is a known limitation that should be removed in next versions of Gradle.

A.1.4 Creating multi-module projects

No serious project is composed of a single module. To create a multi-module project, you'll need two files in the project repository: settings.gradle.kts and build.gradle .kts. The settings.gradle.kts file contains the list of modules such as

```
include("server", "client", "common")
```

The build.gradle.kts file contains the general configuration:

```
ext["kotlintestVersion"] = "3.1.10"
ext["logbackVersion"] = "1.2.3"
ext["slf4jVersion"] = "1.7.25"

plugins {
    base
    kotlin("jvm") version "1.3.21" // Change version according to your needs
}

allprojects {

    group = "com.mydomain.mymultipleproject"

    version = "1.0-SNAPSHOT"

    repositories {
        jcenter()
        mavenCentral()
    }
}
```

In the project directory, you'll create one subdirectory for each subproject, each with its own build.gradle.kts file. Here's the file for the server module:

```
plugins {
    application
    kotlin("jvm")
}

application {
    mainClassName = "com.mydomain.mymultipleproject.server.main.Server"
}

dependencies {
    compile(kotlin("stdlib"))
    compile(project(":common"))
}
```

NOTE   You must not specify the version for the Kotlin plugin. Gradle automatically picks the version from the parent project.

The `server` project depends on the `common` project, and this project module dependency is specified by prefixing the name with a colon. The `application` configuration indicates the name of the main class for the project, but not all subprojects have a main class. The whole structure of the multi-module project is as follows:

```
MyMultipleProject
    settings.gradle.kts
    build.gradle.kts
    client
        build.gradle.kts
    common
        build.gradle.kts
    server
        build.gradle.kts
```

That's all you need. You can now create a new project in IntelliJ as indicated in the previous section. All the necessary subdirectories for Java sources (`main` and `test`), Kotlin sources (`main` and `test`) and `resources` are created.

A.1.5   Adding dependencies to a multiple module project

In each module, you can add dependencies exactly as for a single-module project. Additionally, you might want to declare the version number in a single place to make maintenance easier. That way, when you need to update a version, you only have to do it once in the parent module instead of in each module. For this, you need to use a special object called `ext` that can be set in the parent build script and used in the subprojects. In the parent build script, add the following line:

```
ext["slf4jVersion"] = "1.7.25"
```

Then you can use this value in each subproject:

```
dependencies {
    compile(kotlin("stdlib"))
    testRuntime("org.slf4j:slf4j-nop:${project.rootProject.
     ext["slf4jVersion"]}")
}
```

A.2   Java library methods and Kotlin code

Calling Java library methods from Kotlin code is the most common interaction between the two languages. In fact, no Kotlin program running on a JVM can avoid calling Java methods, whether explicitly or implicitly. This is because most Kotlin standard library functions call Java standard library methods.

Calling Java methods from Kotlin code would be simple if Kotlin and Java types were the same, but they aren't. This is fortunate because Kotlin types are much more powerful than Java types, but it means you have to be careful how you handle the differences and the conversions.

A.2.1 Using Java primitives

The most visible difference is probably the absence of primitives in Kotlin. In Java, `int` and `Integer` are the primitive and object representations of an integer value, respectively. Kotlin only uses `Int`, which is sometimes called a *value type*, meaning that it can be handled like an object but performs like a primitive. But Java may well have value types in the near future.[1]

Although an `Int` is an object in Kotlin, computation is done under the hood as if it were a primitive. The same is true for other Java primitives that have value type equivalents in Kotlin (such as `byte`, `short`, `long`, `float`, `double`, and `boolean`; all have a corresponding value type in Kotlin). The only difference, besides that they must be handled as objects, is that in Kotlin, the first letter is a capital letter.

Kotlin automatically does the conversion between Java primitives and Kotlin value types. You can still use the `Integer` Java type in Kotlin, but you won't gain any of the benefits of using value types. In Kotlin, you can also use the other numeric Java object types, but as the names are the same, you'll have to use the fully qualified name, such as `java.lang.Long`. You'll then get the following compile warning:

```
Warning:(...) Kotlin: This class shouldn't be used in Kotlin. Use kotlin.Long
    instead.
```

You should almost always avoid using Java numerical object types because Kotlin does a serious job of handling the conversion. Consider the following:

```
val a: java.lang.Long = java.lang.Long.valueOf(3L)
```

This won't compile and you'll get the following error message:

```
Error:(...) Kotlin: Type mismatch: inferred type is kotlin.Long! but java.
    lang.Long was expected
```

Kotlin automatically converts the result of the call to the `java.lang.Long.valueOf()` method to `kotlin.Long`, so this code doesn't compile. You can, however, write

```
val a: java.lang.Long = java.lang.Long(3)
```

But why would you want to do so? Java primitives are converted to non-nullable types (for example, Java `int` is converted to `Int`), but the object numerical types are converted to nullable types (for example, Java `Integer` is converted to `Int?`).

A.2.2 Using Java numerical object types

Java also provides numerical types with no primitive equivalent, such as `BigInteger` and `BigDecimal`. These types can be used in Kotlin with the additional benefit that Kotlin simplifies their handling. For example, you can write

```
val a = BigInteger.valueOf(3)

val b = BigInteger.valueOf(5)

println(a + b == BigInteger.valueOf(8))
```

---

[1] See http://cr.openjdk.java.net/~jrose/values/values-0.html for a description of value types in the Project Valhalla.

This prints

```
true
```

Not only can you use the + operator with `BigInteger`, but you can compare it with `==` for equality. This is because Kotlin converts + into a call to the `add` method and `==` into a call to the `equals` method. (In Kotlin, comparing for identity is made with the `===` operator.)

A.2.3   *Failing fast on null values*

Java object types are always nullable, but primitive types aren't. Kotlin makes a distinction between nullable and non-nullable types. For example, the inferred type for `BigInteger.valueOf()` is Kotlin `BigInteger?`. Kotlin also offers the `BigInteger` type, which is a subtype of `BigInteger?` and isn't nullable. If you were to write the types explicitly, you'd get

```
val a: BigInteger? = BigInteger.valueOf(3)
```

But in this case, you wouldn't be able to use the + operator because this would result in a possible `NullPointerException`. The de-referencing operator . can't be used, either. Here's what you'd have to do instead:

```
val a: BigInteger? = BigInteger.valueOf(3)

val b: BigInteger? = BigInteger.valueOf(5)

println(a?.add(b) == BigInteger.valueOf(8))
```

Here you're using the `?.` safe de-referencing operator, which returns `null` if the value it's used on is `null`. If you let Kotlin infer the type, Kotlin does something like this:

```
val a: BigInteger! = BigInteger.valueOf(3)
```

This code won't compile, but it shows what Kotlin does. `BigInteger!` is what is called a *non denotable* type, meaning a type that you can't write in your program but one that the Kotlin compiler uses internally. (IntelliJ will show these types where they are inferred.) What you write is this:

```
val a: BigInteger = BigInteger.valueOf(3)
```

Kotlin will throw a `NullPointerException` if the value returned by the Java method is `null`. This of course will never occur with `BigInteger.valueOf`, but with Java methods that could return `null` (there are many of them in the Java standard library), it insures your program will fail as fast as possible, preventing the `null` to leak inside your code.

If you prefer, you can still declare the type explicitly as nullable, such as `BigInteger?`. See chapter 2 for more information about nullable types in Kotlin.

A.2.4   *Using Kotlin and Java string types*

Kotlin uses a special string type called `kotlin.String`, whereas Java uses the `java.lang.String` type. Once again, the Kotlin type is much more powerful. To show a simple example, look at what you have to do to remove the last character of a string in Java:

```java
String string = "abcde";
String string2 = string.substring(0, string.length() - 1);
```

The equivalent code in Kotlin is this:

```kotlin
val s: String = "abcde".dropLast(1)
```

The kotlin.String class offers dozens of useful functions like this one. Besides this, conversion from and to java.lang.String is fully automated and transparent to the programmer.

A.2.5 *Implementing other type conversions*

Collections and arrays provide the main other type conversions that occur when calling Java methods. Arrays of primitives are converted to special types: ByteArray, IntArray, LongArray, and so on. Arrays of objects of type T are converted to Array<T>, which are invariant (like Java arrays). But you can use variant arrays if you specify those; for example, Array<out T>.

By default, collections are converted into mutable collections of non-nullable types. For example, a java.util.List<String> is converted to a kotlin.collections. MutableList<String>.

Although Kotlin converts Java collections to Kotlin non nullable collections of non nullable types, it will only verify that the collection is not null, but it will not check whether the collection contains null elements. This could be a huge problem because you might assume it would do this check at runtime. Let's say you have the following Java code:

```java
package test;

import java.util.Arrays;
import java.util.List;

public class Test {

    public static List<Integer> getIntegerList() {
        return Arrays.asList(1, 2, 3, null);
    }
}
```

You might want to call the getIntegerList method from Kotlin as

```kotlin
val list: MutableList<Int> = test.Test.getIntegerList()

println(list)
```

This causes no error and prints

```
[1, 2, 3, null]
```

But if you do the following in Kotlin

```kotlin
val list: MutableList<Int> = test.Test.getIntegerList()

list.forEach { println(it + 1) }
```

you'll get a NullPointerException when Kotlin tries to call the add function on null.

A.2.6   *Using Java varargs*

When calling a Java method taking a `vararg` as its argument from Kotlin, Kotlin lets you use an array prefixed with the spread operator, `*`. Consider the following example of a Java method:

```
public static void show(String... strings) {
    for (String string : strings) {
        System.out.println(string);
    }
}
```

This method can be called from Kotlin using an array:

```
val stringArray = arrayOf("Mickey", "Donald", "Pluto")
MyClass.show(*stringArray)
```

A.2.7   *Specifying nullability in Java*

As I said earlier, all non primitive Java types are always nullable. On the other hand, they can be annotated, and many tools use such annotations to indicate that references of certain types should never be null. Although there's a standard specification for this (JSR-305 `javax.annotation`), many tools prefer their own set of annotations:

- IntelliJ uses the `@Nullable` and `@NotNull` from the `org.jetbrains.annotations` package to specify nullability in Java.
- Eclipse uses the `org.eclipse.jdt.annotation` package.
- Android has the `com.android.annotations` and `android.support.annotations` packages.
- FindBugs uses the `edu.umd.cs.findbugs.annotations`.

When used to specify nullability, Kotlin understands all these annotations (and more). For example, a Java property can be annotated with

```
@NotNull
public static List<@NotNull Integer> getIntegerList() {
    return null;
}
```

IntelliJ flags the `null` element with a message saying "Passing 'null' argument to parameter annotated with @NotNull," but this doesn't prevent the Java code from compiling. When calling this method from Kotlin, the inferred type is `(Mutable)List<Int>` instead of `(Mutable)List<Int!>!` and the compiler will issue an exception:

```
java.lang.IllegalStateException: @NotNull method test/MyClass.getIntegerList
    must not return null
```

Unfortunately, this won't work for the type parameter. Consider the following Java method:

```
@NotNull
public static List<@NotNull Integer> getIntegerList() {
    return Arrays.asList(1, 2, 3, null);
}
```

You'll get a warning about the `null` value in Java, but nothing in Kotlin until you try using the `null` value, which causes a `NullPointerException`. Using `@NotNull` on a type parameter isn't different than specifying a non-null parameter type on the Kotlin side or even not specifying any type. That's because Kotlin infers `List<Int!>` (nondenotable type), giving the exact same result. If, however, you want to use parameter type annotations, you'll have to use at least version 1.5.0 of the `org.jetbrains.annotation` library and have your compilation target level set to at least Java 8.

> **NOTE** Kotlin supports the JSR-305 specification, so if you need more Java annotation support, refer to https://kotlinlang.org/docs/reference/java-interop.html.

A.2.8 *Calling getters and setters*

Java getters and setters can be called as standard methods from Kotlin code. Kotlin also allows (and recommends) calling them with the Kotlin property syntax. Let's say you have the following Java class:

```
public class MyClass {

    private int value;

    public int getValue() {
        return value;
    }

    public void setValue(int value) {
        this.value = value;
    }
}
```

You can access the `value` property using either the method syntax or the property syntax:

```
val myClass = MyClass()
myClass.value = 1
println(myClass.value)

myClass.setValue(2)
println(myClass.getValue())
```

The former is highly recommended. The property syntax can be used to read the Java field when there's no setter, which is the case if the field is initialized in the constructor. It'll work even if there's no field at all, such as

```
public class MyClass {

    public int getValue() {
        return 0;
    }
}
```

But it won't work for setting a property with no getter. For Boolean properties with a Java getter starting with `is`, the Kotlin property name is prefixed with `is`. Consider the following Java class:

```
public class MyClass {

    boolean started = true;
    boolean working = false;

    public boolean isStarted() {
        return started;
    }

    public boolean getWorking() {
        return working;
    }
}
```

These properties can be read in Kotlin using the following syntax:

```
val myClass = MyClass()

myClass.started = true
myClass.working = false
println(myClass.started)
println(myClass.isStarted)
println(myClass.working)
```

This avoids the clash that would occur if a Java class has both `isSomething` and `get-Something` methods. Setters in Java are actually methods returning `void`. If such methods are called from Kotlin with the method/function syntax, they return `Unit`, which is a singleton object:

```
val result: Unit = myClass.setWorking(false)
```

A.2.9   Accessing Java properties with reserved names

Sometimes, you might need to access from Kotlin a Java property that has a name that clashes with a reserved word in Kotlin, such as `in` and `is` that are used as short names for `input` or `inputStream`. If you're writing both the Java or the Kotlin code, the best thing to do is to avoid such names. But if you're using a library you don't control, you can use backticks to escape the property name. Here's an example.

Java class:

```
public class MyClass {

    private InputStream in;

    public void setIn(InputStream in) {
        this.in = in;
    }

    public InputStream getIn() {
        return in;
    }
}
```

Kotlin code:

```
val input = myClass.`in`
```

A.2.10 *Calling checked exceptions*

In Kotlin, all exceptions are unchecked. As a consequence, Kotlin lets you call a Java method throwing a checked exception without using a `try...catch` block.

Java:

```
try {
    Thread.sleep(10);
} catch (InterruptedException e) {
    // handle exception
}
```

Kotlin:

```
Thread.sleep(10)
```

Unlike what's often done in Java, this doesn't work as a wrapper. If you use a `try...catch` block and an exception is thrown, it'll still be the original exception and not an unchecked wrapper exception.

A.3 *SAM interfaces*

Unlike Kotlin, Java doesn't have function types; functions are handled by converting lambdas into something that's equivalent to a Single Abstract Method (or SAM) interface implementation. (It isn't an implementation of the interface, but it acts as if it's one.)

Kotlin, on the other hand, has true function types, so no such conversion is needed. But when calling Java methods taking SAM interfaces as their parameters, Kotlin functions are automatically converted. For example, you can write the following Kotlin code:

```
val executor = Executors.newSingleThreadExecutor()
executor.submit { println("Hello, World!") }
```

The `submit` Java method takes a `Runnable` as its parameter. In Java, the same program would be written as follows:

```
ExecutorService executor = Executors.newSingleThreadExecutor();
executor.submit(() -> System.out.println("Hello, World!"));
```

Note that you can explicitly create a `java.lang.Runnable` in Kotlin using the following syntax:

```
val runnable = Runnable { println("Hello, World!") }
```

But this isn't the way to go. One should rather create a Kotlin function and have it converted automatically into a `Runnable` when calling a Java method:

```
val executor = Executors.newSingleThreadExecutor()
val runnable: () -> Unit = { println("Hello, World!") }
executor.submit(runnable)
```

A.4   Kotlin functions and Java code

Calling a Kotlin function from Java code isn't more difficult than the other way round. But because Kotlin is more feature-rich than Java, you'll often lose some functionality.

A.4.1   Converting Kotlin properties

Properties in Java consist in coding conventions. In Kotlin, properties are a language feature. Although Kotlin programs are compiled into Java bytecode, the compiler takes care of the conversion. Kotlin properties are converted into the standard set of Java field and accessors:

- A private field with the same name as the property
- A getter with the name of the property with a capital initial and prefixed with `get`
- A setter with the name of the property with a capital initial and prefixed with `set`

The only exception is that if the Kotlin property name starts with `is`. This name is used for the getter, and the setter name is obtained by replacing `is` with `set`.

A.4.2   Using Kotlin public fields

Kotlin public fields are exposed as Java properties (meaning with getters and setters). If you want to use them as Java fields, you have to annotate them in the Kotlin code like this:

```
@JvmField
val age = 25
```

In this case, you can no longer access the Kotlin property from Java using accessors. Also note that Kotlin properties declared with `lateinit` can be accessed both as fields or with getters. They can't be annotated with `@JvmField`.

A.4.3   Static fields

Kotlin has no explicitly static fields, but some Kotlin fields can be seen as static. This is the case of fields declared in objects, including companion objects, as well as fields declared at package level. All these fields can be accessed from Java code in the same way as properties, although with some differences. Fields declared in companion objects can be accessed with getters and setters using the following syntax:

```
int weight = MyClass.Companion.getWeight();
```

But if the field is declared with `const`, you have to access it as a static field of the enclosing class:

```
int weight = MyClass.weight;
```

The same result can be obtained if the field is annotated with `@JvmField`. For fields declared in standalone objects, use the following syntax:

```
String firstName = MyObject.INSTANCE.getFirstName();
```

Once again, if the field is declared with `const` or annotated with `@JvmField`, it must be accessed like a static field:

```
String firstName = MyObject.firstName;
```

Fields declared at package level can be accessed as if they were static fields of a class with the name of the enclosing file without the .kt extension, but postfixed with Kt. Imagine the following code in MyFile.kt:

```
const val length = 12

val width = 3
```

These fields can be accessed from Java as:

```
int length = MyFileKt.length;
int width = MyFileKt.getWidth();
```

But note that package-level fields can't be annotated with @JvmField.

A.4.4 *Calling Kotlin functions as Java methods*

Functions declared with fun in classes can be accessed from Java as methods. Functions declared in objects or at package level can be accessed as if they were static methods. Consider the following MyFile.kt program file:

```
fun method1() = "method 1"

class MyClass {

    companion object {
        fun method2() = "method 2"

        @JvmStatic
        fun method3() = "method 3"
    }
}

object MyObject {
    fun method4() = "method 4"

    @JvmStatic
    fun method5() = "method 5"
}
```

These functions can be called from Java in various ways:

```
String s1 = MyFileKt.method1();
String s2 = MyClass.Companion.method2();
String s3a = MyClass.method3();
String s3b = MyClass.Companion.method3();
String s4 = MyObject.INSTANCE.method4();
String s5a = MyObject.method5();
String s5b = MyObject.INSTANCE.method5();
```

Note that MyObject.INSTANCE.method5() produces the warning message "Static member accessed via instance reference" as if you were calling a Java static method on a class instance.

CALLING EXTENSION FUNCTIONS FROM JAVA

Extension functions in Kotlin are compiled to static functions with the receiver as an additional parameter. You can call them from Java in the form to which those are compiled. Consider the following extension function defined in a file named `MyFile.kt`:

```
fun List<String>.concat(): String = this.fold("") { acc, s -> "$acc$s" }
```

Although this function is used in Kotlin as if it were an instance function on a list of strings, you have to call it as a static method in Java:

```
String s = MyFileKt.concat(Arrays.asList("a", "b", "c"));
```

CALLING A FUNCTION WITH A DIFFERENT NAME

You can change the name by which a Kotlin function can be called from Java code. For this, you need to use the `@JvmName("newName")` annotation on the Kotlin function. From the Java point of view, there are a few reasons to do this, and you might be forced to do this even if you never call the function from Java code. Consider the two following functions:

```
fun List<String>.concat(): String = this.fold("") { acc, s -> "$acc$s" }
fun List<Int>.concat(): String = this.fold("") { acc, i -> "$acc$i" }
```

This won't compile because

- Kotlin functions are compiled to Java bytecode.
- Type erasure causes the type parameters to be removed on compilation.

As a result, these two functions are equivalent to the following Java methods:

```
MyFileKt.concat(List<String> list)
MyFileKt.concat(List<Integer> list)
```

These two methods can't coexist in the same class (`MyFileKt`) because they compile to

```
MyFileKt.concat(List list)
MyFileKt.concat(List list)
```

Even if you never call these functions from Java, you need to either put them in separate files or change the compiled name of at least one of them using an annotation:

```
fun List<String>.concat(): String = this.fold("") { acc, s -> "$acc$s" }

@JvmName("concatIntegers")
fun List<Int>.concat(): String = this.fold("") { acc, i -> "$acc$i" }
```

Names of generated Java getters and setters for Kotlin properties can be changed in the same way:

```
@get:JvmName("retrieveName")
@set:JvmName("storeName")
var name: String?
```

DEALING WITH DEFAULT VALUES AND PARAMETERS

In Kotlin, functions parameters can have default values. Such functions can be called from Java code but all parameters must be specified, even those with a default value.

The Java way for dealing with a default value is through overloading. To make the function available as overloaded Java methods, use the `@JvmOverloads` annotation:

```
@JvmOverloads
fun computePrice(price: Double,
                 tax: Double = 0.20) = price * (1.0 + tax)
```

The `computePrice` Kotlin function will be available in Java as

```
Double computePrice(Double price,)
Double computePrice(Double price, Double tax)
```

If several parameters have default values, you won't get all possibilities:

```
@JvmOverloads
fun computePrice(price: Double,
                 tax: Double = 0.20,
                 shipping: Double = 8.75) = price * (1.0 + tax) + shipping
```

In this case, the following Java methods are available:

```
Double computePrice(Double price,)
Double computePrice(Double price, Double tax)
Double computePrice(Double price, Double tax, Double shipping)
```

As you can see, there's no way to pass only `price` and `shipping` and use the default value for `tax`. Additionally, the `@JvmOverloads` annotation can also be used on constructors:

```
class MyClass @JvmOverloads constructor(name: String, age: Int = 18)
```

DEALING WITH FUNCTIONS THROWING EXCEPTIONS

All exceptions are unchecked in Kotlin. As a consequence, if you try to catch the exception in the Java code calling a Kotlin function throwing exceptions, you'll get a compile error. Consider the following Kotlin function:

```
fun readFile(filename: String): String = File(filename).readText()
```

You might want to call this function from Java in a `try...catch` block, such as

```
try {
  System.out.println(MyFileKt.readFile("myFile"));
} catch (IOException e) {
  e.printStackTrace();
}
```

But this will not compile and you'll get the following error:

```
Error: exception java.io.IOException is never thrown in body of corresponding
    try statement
```

To prevent this, you need to indicate explicitly what exception is thrown, using the `@Throws` annotation:

```
@Throws(IOException::class)
fun readFile(filename: String): String = File(filename).readText()
```

Note that the `@Throws` annotation is not repeatable. If your function throws several exceptions that are checked in Java, use the following syntax:

```
@Throws(IOException::class, IndexOutOfBoundsException::class)
fun readFile(filename: String): String = File(filename).readText()
```

You don't need to indicate explicitly unchecked exception because Java lets you catch them freely.

A.4.5   *Converting types from Kotlin to Java*

Kotlin makes a difference between nullable and non-nullable types; Java does not. The difference is lost in the conversion.

Numerical types are converted either to primitives or to object types following what's declared on the Java side. Immutable collections are converted to Java collections. For example, a list created with `listOf` in Kotlin is converted into a Java `Arrays.ArrayList` in Java. Java `Arrays.ArrayList` is a private class in `Arrays` that extends `AbstractList` without implementing the add method. As a consequence, if you try to add an element, you'll get an `UnsupportedOperationException`, which might make you think that the list is unmodifiable. You can't add or remove an element, but you can change an element by calling the `set` method, passing it the index of the element to replace the new element. The immutable lists in Kotlin are far less immutable when converted to Java.

Kotlin also has specific types that don't exist in Java:

- `Unit` is converted to `void`, although it doesn't mean exactly the same thing. (In Kotlin, `Unit` is a singleton object.) By nature, it might look closer to `Void` (if you've ever encountered this type in Java), but by its functions, it's more equivalent to `void`.
- `Any` is converted to `Object`.
- `Nothing` isn't converted because nothing exists in Java corresponding to this type. When used as a type parameter, such as `Set<Nothing>`, the conversion produces a raw type (`Set`).

Functions of 1 to 22 arguments are converted to special Kotlin types `kotlin.jvm`
`.functions.Function1` to `kotlin.jvm.functions.Function22`. These are SAM interfaces, which makes much more sense than the Java function interfaces.

A.4.6   *Function types*

Functions with no arguments are converted to `kotlin.jvm.functions.Function0`, which corresponds to the Java `Supplier` interface.

Kotlin functions of type `()` → `Unit` are converted into instances of `kotlin.jvm`
`.functions.Function0<Unit>`, which corresponds to Java `Runnable`. `Function1<A, Unit>` corresponds to Java `Consumer<A>`, and `Function2<A, B, Unit>` corresponds to Java `BiConsumer<A, B>`. Other Kotlin functions returning `Unit` are sort of multiconsumers with no equivalent in Java.

You can use all the converted functions as you would do in Java, except that they all implement a method called `invoke` instead of the Java `apply`, `test`, `accept`, or `get`. If you need to convert one of these functions into a Java type, it's easy if the corresponding

type exists in Java. For example, consider the following Kotlin function of type
Function1<Int, Boolean>

```
@JvmField
val isEven: (Int) -> Boolean = { it % 2 == 0}
```

you can use this function directly in Java:

```
System.out.println(MyFileKt.isEven.invoke(2));
```

The type of this function in Java is kotlin.jvm.functions.Function1<Integer,
Boolean>. To convert it into an IntPredicate, you need to write

```
IntPredicate p = MyFileKt.isEven::invoke;
```

A.5   *Specific problems with mixed Kotlin/Java projects*

Although mixing Kotlin and Java in the same project is simple (whether using Gradle
or IntelliJ, or both), you should be careful about incremental compiling. *Incremental
compiling* is a technique consisting in compiling only the parts of the program that
need to be compiled. It can go from compiling only the classes that have changed since
the last compilation to compiling line by line while you type code.

Both Gradle and Intellij can do some sort of incremental compiling, but looking for
classes that have changed since last compile isn't enough. If a class hasn't changed but
depends on another one that has changed, both should be recompiled.

This generally works fine with Java or Kotlin projects, but mixed projects are a bit
more troublesome. You might encounter this problem when working on your project
and several modules depend on a module called common. When working on module A,
you might have to modify module common. In that case, when running your code during
development, IntelliJ or Gradle only compiles the necessary classes from module A and
common. If you later modify module B, introducing changes to module common, running
your changes only compiles these two modules (B and common). As a consequence, you
may have broken module A by changing its dependencies on module common, but you
won't see that.

The best way to avoid this problem is to regularly rebuild the whole project. By doing
so, you'll immediately see if something has been broken. Otherwise, you may end up
making many changes and requiring additional work to fix things.

Another problem that you might encounter is getting a different result when running your code with IntelliJ and with Gradle. In a professional environment, it's common to compile and run your code with IntelliJ while programming, although the
project will later be built on a build server using Gradle. Before pushing your changes
to the repository from where the build server will build it, you'll want to test the Gradle
build on your workstation. Doing this, you might be surprised to see compile errors that
didn't occur with IntelliJ.

The reason for this is simple, and it's easy to avoid or fix. But if you don't know how,
you might spend hours trying to understand why, when compiling with Gradle, the
compiler doesn't see in your Java code the new function you added in Kotlin, although

IntelliJ has no problem with that. The reason is that unlike IntelliJ, Gradle might not clean the Kotlin generated bytecode and will instead continue using the older compiled version (without the newly added function).

If you encounter this problem, do an explicit `clean` in Gradle. This erases all compiled code and makes the compile time longer, but it's much safer. And realize you're lucky: you could have run your program using an old version of the function causing no compilation problem but producing an erroneous result. In such a case, you might scratch your head for a long time before finding the reason!

Summary

In this appendix, you've learned how to mix Java and Kotlin in your projects. A Kotlin project is always implicitly dependent on Java code (the Java standard library), so even if you don't need to create explicit mixed projects, you need to master some of the material presented here. The technique presented lets you

- Set up and manage a mixed project (single module or multi-module) with Gradle or IntelliJ, including writing Gradle build scripts in Kotlin. If you want to use Eclipse, you'll have to create a Gradle project and import it. And, although you can build a project directly in IntelliJ, it's much better and easier to do it with Gradle and import the project. The main benefit is that your project descriptor is readable and can be versioned in your code repository.
- Call Java programs from Kotlin code.
- Call Kotlin programs from Java code.

Mixed projects allow using the best of both worlds, including the huge mass of Java code that's available in open source and usable in your Kotlin programs.

appendix B
Property-based testing in Kotlin

Testing is probably one of the most controversial subjects in programming. This controversy concerns all aspects of testing: whether to test, when you should test, what you should test, how much you should test, how often you should test, how can you measure the quality of tests, what the best coverage metrics are, and more. But none of these subjects can be considered alone. And they're nearly all dependent on other questions that are far-less-often debated.

In this appendix, I cover how to write effective tests and how to make your program more testable using property-based testing. You'll learn how to

- Devise a set of properties that the result of your program must fulfill
- Write interfaces, then tests, and lastly implementations so that your tests won't depend on implementation only
- Use abstraction to simplify testing by removing parts that you should trust
- Write generators to generate random values for your tests, along with accompanying data that you can use to check the properties
- Set up tests that use thousands of input data and that run before each build

NOTE The example code for this appendix is available at https://github.com/pysaumont/fpinkotlin in the examples directory.

B.1   *Why property-based testing?*

Nearly every programmer agrees that some sort of unit testing is necessary, although testing is certainly not the ideal way to ensure that programs are correct. Tests can't prove that a program is correct.

Failing tests prove that the program is probably incorrect (only 'probably' because it might be a problem with the test itself!). But successful tests certainly don't prove that the tested program is correct. They only prove that you haven't been smart enough to find the bugs. If you put equal effort into developing your tests as you do into writing your programs, it still wouldn't be enough. And still, you generally invest much less effort in testing than in writing programs.

A better way to go would be to prove that your programs are correct. This is what functional programming tries to do, but it's seldom fully possible. The ideal program is one for which there's only one possible implementation. That may sound crazy, but if you think about it, you'll realize that the risk of bugs is proportional to the number of possible implementations for your programs. You should, therefore, try to minimize the number of possible implementations.

One way to do this is through abstraction. Take the example of a program that finds all elements in a list of integers that are multiples of a given one and takes the maximum of them. In traditional programming, you could do this with an indexed loop as in the following example (bugs are intentional):

```
// example00
fun maxMultiple(multiple: Int, list: List<Int>): Int {
    var result = 0
    for (i in 1 until list.size) {
        if (list[i] / multiple * multiple == list[i] && list[i] > result) {
            result = list[i]
        }
    }
    return result
}
```

How would you test such a program? Of course, you see the bugs, so you'd start by fixing them before writing tests. But if you were the one responsible for these bugs, you wouldn't see them. You'd instead want to test the implementation for limit values. The two parameters being an integer and a list, you'd probably want to test 0 as the int parameter or an empty list. The first condition would cause a java.lang .ArithmeticException: / by zero exception. The second condition would produce a result of 0.

Note that passing 0 and an empty list to this implementation wouldn't cause an exception but would produce 0 as the result.

Another bug in this example is that the first element is ignored. In a majority of cases, this won't cause any problems:

- When the list is empty.
- When the first parameter is 0 (because you fixed the division by 0 problem).
- When the first element isn't a multiple of the first parameter.
- When the first element is a multiple of the first parameter but not the greatest one.

Of course, you now know what to do: write a test with a nonzero first parameter and a list in which the first element is the highest multiple. But wait … if you were smart enough to figure that out, you wouldn't have made this error, so testing, in this case, isn't useful.

Some programmers say that tests should be written prior to the implementations. Although I totally agree with this, how would it help here? You might write a test for 0 and empty lists, but how could you know in advance that you should write a test with a nonzero first parameter and a list in which the first element is the highest multiple? You can only do that when you know the implementation.

Testing when knowing the implementation is not ideal because if you're the one who wrote the implementation, you'll be biased. On the other hand, if you're writing tests for an implementation you didn't write, it can be fun to try to make it fail.

But the real game is trying to break the program without seeing the implementation. And because you write both the test and the implementation, there's no better moment to write this kind of test than before starting to work on the implementation. The process should then be

1 Write the interface.
2 Write the tests.
3 Write the implementation and check if the tests pass.

Let's look at each of these.

B.1.1 *Writing the interface*

Writing the interface is easy. It consists in writing the signature of the function:

```
fun maxMultiple(multiple: Int, list: List<Int>): Int = TODO()
```

B.1.2 *Writing the tests*

Now you have to write the tests. For a traditional test, you might start with

```
// example00 test
import io.kotlintest.shouldBe
import io.kotlintest.specs.StringSpec

internal class MyKotlinLibraryKtTest: StringSpec() {

    init {
        "maxMultiple" {
            val multiple = 2
            val list = listOf(4, 11, 8, 2, 3, 1, 14, 9, 5, 17, 6, 7)
            maxMultiple(multiple, list).shouldBe(14)
        }
    }
}
```

You can write as many tests as you want using specific values. You will, of course, treat all the special values such as 0 and empty list, but what else can you do?

Generally, what programmers do is choose some input values and verify that the corresponding output is correct. In the previous example, you're testing the equality between 14 and the result of passing 2 and [4, 11, 8, 2, 3, 1, 14, 9, 5, 17, 6, 7] to the tested function.

But how did you find 14? By applying to the tuple of arguments the same process that you'll be implementing for the function. It might fail because humans aren't perfect. But most often it will succeed because this test consists of doing the same thing twice: once in your head and once with a computer program. This isn't different from writing the implementation first, then running it with the given parameters, and then writing the test to verify it is the same output.

> **NOTE** You're testing that you wrote what you thought was the correct implementation. You're not testing that this is a correct implementation for the problem. For better testing, you need to check something other than the equality between the result computed by your code and the one computed in your head. This is what property-based testing is all about.

Before you look at how to write an implementation, let's dive a littler deeper into property-based testing.

B.2   *What is property-based testing?*

Property-based testing is testing whether the result verifies some properties in relation to the input data. For example, if you were to write a program to concatenate strings (written as +), the properties to check might be

- (string1 + string2).length == string1.length + string2.length
- string + "" == string
- "" + string == string
- string1.reverse() + string2.reverse() == (string2 + string1). reverse()

Testing these properties would be enough to guarantee that the program is correct. (The first three aren't even needed.) With that, you could check millions of randomly generated strings without bothering about the actual result. The only thing that matters is that the properties are verified.

The first thing you need to do before even starting coding (whether it be the main program or the tests) is to think about the problem in terms of the properties that should be verified when considering the input and the output of the function. You can immediately see that a function with no side effects is much easier to deal with in that case.

Considering your maximum multiple problems, when writing the interface, you realize that it's not always easy to find such properties. Remember that you must find a set of properties that can be verified on all tuples of type ((Int, List<Int>), Int) that will be true if the last Int is the correct result of applying the function to the pair Int, List<Int>. Here's a reminder of the function signature:

```
fun maxMultiple(multiple: Int, list: List<Int>): Int = TODO()
```

Finding some properties might seem easy, but finding significant ones is more difficult. Ideally, you should find the smallest set of properties that guarantees that the result is correct. But you must do that without using the same logic that you'll use for implementing the function. Two ways of finding such properties include

- Finding conditions that should hold
- Finding conditions that shouldn't hold

For example, when iterating over elements in the list, you shouldn't find one that's both a multiple of the first parameter and greater than the result. The problem is that when testing this, you'd probably be using the same algorithm as when implementing the function, so it wouldn't be more relevant than calling the function twice and verifying that you get the same result on each call! The solution here is abstraction.

B.3 *Abstraction and property-based tests*

What you should do is find a way to abstract parts of the problem, write functions to implement each part, and test them individually. You already know how to do this. If you remember what you learned in chapter 5, you can see that the operation is a fold. You can abstract the problem into two functions—the folding function and the function used as the folding function's second parameter:

```
fun maxMultiple(multiple: Int, list: List<Int>): Int =
    list.fold(initialValue) { acc, int -> ... }
```

Here I'm using the standard Kotlin `fold` function working on Kotlin lists. If you prefer to use the `List` you developed in chapter 5, it would be

```
fun maxMultiple(multiple: Int, list: List<Int>): Int =
    list.foldLeft(initialValue) { acc -> { int -> ... } }
```

> **NOTE** In the rest of this appendix, I use standard Kotlin types.

Now you need to test the function used for the fold. As a consequence, you won't be using an anonymous function such as the lambda in the previous example, but rather something like this:

```
fun maxMultiple(multiple: Int, list: List<Int>): Int =
    list.fold(0, ::isMaxMultiple)

fun isMaxMultiple(acc: Int, value: Int) = ...
```

By doing this, you've changed the problem into one that might be easier to test. The reason for this is that you've abstracted the iteration part. And you don't have to test this part. It's supposed to have been tested elsewhere. If you use the Kotlin `fold` function, you simply trust the language. If you use the `foldLeft` function from chapter 5, you've already tested it so you can trust it too.

> **IMPORTANT** You should never test a function from the language or from an external library. If you don't trust it, don't use it.

The problem you need to solve now is a bit tricky. Let's say the value for the `multiple` parameter is 2. The implementation is then straightforward:

```
fun isMaxMultiple(acc: Int, elem: Int): Int =
    if (elem / 2 * 2 == elem && elem > acc) elem else acc
```

What you need to do is replace 2 with the value of the `multiple` parameter. Using a local function would be possible:

```
fun maxMultiple(multiple: Int, list: List<Int>): Int {
    fun isMaxMultiple(acc: Int, elem: Int): Int =
        if (elem / multiple * multiple == elem && elem > acc) elem else acc
    return list.fold(0, ::isMaxMultiple)
}
```

The difficulty with such an implementation is that it doesn't solve your testing problem. Once again, abstraction is the way to go. You can abstract the `multiple` parameter as follows:

```
// example01
fun isMaxMultiple(multiple: Int) =
    { max: Int, value: Int ->
        when {
            value / multiple * multiple == value && value > max -> value
            else                                               -> max
        }
    }
```

Abstraction is something you'll always do. For example, here it's absolutely natural for all programmers to abstract `value / multiple * multiple == value` into a call to the `rem` function, represented in infix notation by the `%` operator:

```
fun isMaxMultiple(multiple: Int) =
    { max: Int, value: Int ->
        when {
            value % multiple == 0 && value > max -> value
            else                                 -> max
        }
    }
```

Now the function can be unit tested. The `isMaxMultiple` function can be used in tests as

```
fun test(value: Int, max:Int, multiple: Int): Boolean {
    val result = isMaxMultiple(multiple)(max, value)

        ... check properties
}
```

You can find several properties to test:

- `result >= max`
- `result % multiple == 0 || result == max`
- `(result % multiple == 0 && result >= value) || result % multiple != 0`

You can also find other properties. Ideally, you should end up with the minimum set of properties that guarantees that the result is correct. In reality, it doesn't matter much if you have some redundancy. Redundant properties are harmless (unless they take a long time to check). Missing properties are more of a problem. But a huge benefit is that you can now test your test!

B.4   *Dependencies for property-based unit testing*

To write unit tests in Kotlin, you can use various test frameworks. Most of them depend in one way or another on well-known Java test frameworks such as JUnit. To implement property-based testing, you'll use Kotlintest. Kotlintest relies on JUnit and adds a DSL (Domain Specific Languages) that lets you choose among many testing styles, including property-based testing. To use Kotlintest in your project, add the following line to the dependencies block of your build.gradle file:

```
dependencies {
    ...

    testCompile("io.kotlintest:kotlintest-runner-junit5:${project
                        .rootProject.ext["kotlintestVersion"]}")
    testRuntime("org.slf4j:slf4j-nop:${project
                        .rootProject.ext["slf4jVersion"]}")
}
```

Note the use of variables for the version numbers. Add these lines in all of your module build scripts. In order to avoid having to update version numbers in all modules, add the following definition to the build script of the parent project:

```
ext["kotlintestVersion"] = "3.1.10"
ext["slf4jVersion"] = "1.7.25"
```

The `testRuntime` dependency on Slf4j isn't mandatory. If you omit it, you'll get a warning message, but the tests will still work.

Kotlintest uses Slf4j for logging and is, by default, verbose. If you don't want logging for tests, use the `slf4j-nop` dependency to suppress logging and logging errors. You can also chose whichever logging implementation you like and provide the corresponding configuration to suit your needs.

B.5   *Writing property based tests*

Tests are created in the same place as standard JUnit tests: in the src/test/kotlin directory of each subproject. If you're using IntelliJ, click the function to test, type Alt+Enter, and select Create Test. In the dialog box, select a version of JUnit. IntelliJ will complain that this version is absent and will propose to fix this. Ignore this error and check that the destination package is in the correct branch (`java` or `kotlin`, in case of a mixed project). Change the proposed name for the class if you want, but don't select any function to test, and then click OK. IntelliJ creates an empty file in the correct package.

Each test class has the following structure:

```
// example01 test
import io.kotlintest.properties.forAll
import io.kotlintest.specs.StringSpec
```

```
class MyClassTest: StringSpec() {

    init {
        "test1" {
            forAll {
                // check properties here
            }
        }
    }
}
```

Alternatively, you can specify the number of tests to run (default is 1,000):

```
import io.kotlintest.properties.forAll
import io.kotlintest.specs.StringSpec

class MyClassTest: StringSpec() {

    init {
        "test1" {
            forAll(3000) {
                // check properties here
            }
        }
    }
}
```

The last parameter of the forAll function is a function that should return true for the test to pass. This function can take several arguments which are automatically generated. For example, you can use

```
// example01 test
class MyKotlinLibraryTest: StringSpec() {

    init {
        "isMaxMultiple" {
            forAll { multiple: Int, max:Int, value: Int ->
                isMaxMultiple(multiple)(max, value).let { result ->
                    result >= value
                        && result % multiple == 0 || result == max
                        && ((result % multiple == 0 && result >= value)
                                            || result % multiple != 0)
                }
            }
        }
    }
}
```

The name of the test is "isMaxMultiple". The name is used to display the result. You can put several of these blocks inside the init block, but they must have different names. The name is found through introspection. Having different names isn't enforced at compile time, but if several tests are found with the same name at runtime, you'll get an IllegalArgumentException with the message "Cannot add test with duplicate name isMaxMultiple" and no tests will be executed.

All parameters of the lambda passed as the argument of the forAll function are generated by the standard generators provided by Kotlintest. This might not be what you need. For integers, the default generator is provided by the `Gen.int()` function. The previous test is then equivalent to

```
class MyKotlinLibraryTest: StringSpec() {

    init {
        "isMaxMultiple" {
            forAll(Gen.int(), Gen.int(), Gen.int())
                { multiple: Int, max:Int, value: Int ->
                    isMaxMultiple(multiple)(max, value).let { result ->
                        result >= value
                            && result % multiple == 0 || result == max
                            && ((result % multiple == 0 && result >= value)
                                            || result % multiple != 0)
                    }
                }
        }
    }
}
```

If you specify one generator explicitly, you need to specify all. The default `Gen.int()` generator generates 0, `Int.MAX_VALUE`, `Int.MIN_VALUE`, and many random `Int` values to make the default 1,000 tests or the number of tests specified. Each generator attempts to generate limit values plus random values. The `String` generator, for example, always generates an empty string. If you run this test, it fails with the following error message:

```
Attempting to shrink failed arg -2147483648
Shrink #1: 0 fail
Shrink result => 0

...

java.lang.AssertionError: Property failed for
Arg 0: 0 (shrunk from -2147483648)
Arg 1: 0 (shrunk from -2147483648)
Arg 2: 0 (shrunk from 2147483647)
after 1 attempts
Caused by: expected: true but was: false
Expected :true
Actual   :false
```

This means the test has failed for some value. In such a case, Kotlintest attempts to shrink the value in order to find the smallest value that makes the test fail.

This is useful for tests that fail when a value is too high. It wouldn't be practical to just report the failure. You'll then need to try the lowest value to find the point of failure. Here you can see that all arguments shrink to 0, without making the test pass. In fact, the test always fails if the first argument is 0 because you can't divide by 0.

What you need here is a generator for non-null integers. The `Gen` interface offers many generators for all kinds of uses. For example, positive integers can be generated with `Gen.positiveIntegers()`:

```
// example02 test
class MyKotlinLibraryTest: StringSpec() {
```

```
init {
    "isMaxMultiple" {
        forAll(Gen.positiveIntegers(), Gen.int(), Gen.int())
            { multiple: Int, max:Int, value: Int ->
                isMaxMultiple(multiple)(max, value).let { result ->
                    result >= value
                        && result % multiple == 0 || result == max
                        && ((result % multiple == 0 && result >= value)
                                            || result % multiple != 0)
                }
            }
    }
}
```

And now the test is a success.

B.5.1 Creating your own custom generators

Kotlintest offers many generators for most standard types (numbers, Boolean, and strings) as well as collections. But sometimes you'll need to create your own generator. The standard case is when you want to generate instances of your own classes. The process is simple. You need to implement the following interface:

```
interface Gen<T> {
    fun constants(): Iterable<T>
    fun random(): Sequence<T>
}
```

The constants function produces the set of limit values (such as Int.MIN_VALUE, 0 and INT.MAX_VALUE for integers). Most often, you'll make it return an empty list. The random function returns a sequence of randomly created instances.

Creating an instance is a recursive process. If the constructor of the class you want to generate instances of only takes parameters for which generators already exist in Gen, just use them. For other types of parameters, use custom generators.

As much as possible, you should avoid creating a generator from scratch. All data objects are compositions of numbers, strings, Boolean enums and, recursively, other objects. In the end, you can generate any object by combining the existing generators. The best way to combine generators is by using one of their bind functions, such as

```
data class Person(val name: String, val age: Int)

val genPerson: Gen<Person> =
    Gen.bind(Gen.string(), Gen.choose(1, 50))
        { name, age -> Person(name, age) }
```

B.5.2 Using custom generators

As a use case, you might want to use a custom generator if one already exists, but you want to avoid some specific values or you want to include a condition on the generated values. A more uncommon but useful case is when you want to be able to maintain some control on the generated values.

For example, if you need to write a program that computes the set of characters used in a string, how would you verify that the result for a randomly generated string is correct? You might devise criteria to test such as

- All characters in the resulting set must exist in the input string.
- All characters in the input string must exist in the resulting set.

This is quite simple. But imagine that instead of a set, your function has to produce a map with each character used in the string as a key in the map and the number of occurrences of that character as the value. For example, imagine you're required to write a program that takes a list of strings and groups those that are composed of the exact same set of characters. You could write it as

```
// example03
fun main(args: Array<String>) {
    val words = listOf("the", "act", "cat", "is", "bats",
                    "tabs", "tac", "aabc", "abbc", "abca")

    val map = getCharUsed(words)

    println(map)
}


fun getCharUsed(words: List<String>) =
        words.groupBy(::getCharMap)

fun getCharMap(s: String): Map<Char, Int> {
    val result = mutableMapOf<Char, Int>()
    for (i in 0 until s.length) {
        val ch = s[i]
        if (result.containsKey(ch)) {
            result.replace(ch, result[ch]!! + 1)
        } else {
            result[ch] = 1
        }
    }
    return result
}
```

This program would return the following (although on a single line):

```
{
    {t=1, h=1, e=1}=[the],
    {a=1, c=1, t=1}=[act, cat, tac],
    {i=1, s=1}=[is],
    {b=1, a=1, t=1, s=1}=[bats, tabs],
    {a=2, b=1, c=1}=[aabc, abca],
    {a=1, b=2, c=1}=[abbc]
}
```

How would you test your program? You can try it on several lists of words, but this wouldn't guarantee it would work on all combinations. You'd better use property-based testing, generating lists of random strings, and then checking some properties. But how to devise a good set of properties? Those properties would be complex.

Rather than devising complex properties, you might create a generator for strings that randomly add characters to the generated string while updating a map. When the generation is done, the generator outputs a `Pair<String, Map<Char, Int>>`. With this generated data, you only have one property to test: the map produced by the tested program must be equal to the generated map. Here's an example of such a generator:

```
// example03 test
val stringGenerator: Gen<List<Pair<String, Map<Char, Int>>>> =
        Gen.list(Gen.list(Gen.choose(97, 122)))
                .map { intListList ->
                    intListList.asSequence().map { intList ->
                        intList.map { n ->
                            n.toChar()
                        }
                    }.map { charList ->
                        Pair(String(charList.toCharArray()),
                                        makeMap(charList))
                    }.toList()
                }

fun makeMap(charList: List<Char>): Map<Char, Int> =
                        charList.fold(mapOf(), ::updateMap)

fun updateMap(map: Map<Char, Int>, char: Char) = when {
    map.containsKey(char) -> map + Pair(char, map[char]!! + 1)
    else -> map + Pair(char, 1)
}
```

This generator produces a sequence of list of pairs of one random string and one map containing all characters in the string as keys and the number of occurrences of each as values. Note that the maps aren't obtained by analyzing the strings. The strings are built from the same data as the maps.

Using this generator, the getCharUsed program can be easily tested because you only have one property to test. This property is still a bit complex to read, but at least you don't need a huge set of properties and you're certain that the test is exhaustive:

```
// example03 test
import io.kotlintest.properties.forAll
import io.kotlintest.specs.StringSpec

class SameLettersStringKtTest: StringSpec() {

    init {
        "getCharUsed" {
            forAll(stringGenerator) {
                list: List<Pair<String, Map<Char, Int>>> ->
                    getCharUsed(list.map { it.first }).keys.toSet() ==
                            list.asSequence().map { it.second }.toSet()
            }
        }
    }
}
```

Note that the lists are transformed into sets before comparing. This is to take into account that the generated list of strings could contain several occurrences of the same string. The generator generates a list of up to 100 strings of up to 100 characters. If you want to parametrize these values, you might be tempted to write a new generator from scratch; for example:

```
// example04 test
class StringGenerator(private val maxList: Int,
                      private val maxString: Int) :
                           Gen<List<Pair<String, Map<Char, Int>>>> {

  override
  fun constants(): Iterable<List<Pair<String, Map<Char, Int>>>> =
                           listOf(listOf(Pair("", mapOf())))

  override
  fun random(): Sequence<List<Pair<String, Map<Char, Int>>>> =
    Random().let { random ->
      generateSequence {
        (0 until random.nextInt(maxList)).map {
          (0 until random.nextInt(maxString))
            .fold(Pair("", mapOf<Char, Int>())) { pair, _ ->
              (random.nextInt(122 - 96) + 96).toChar().let { char ->
              Pair("${pair.first}$char", updateMap(pair.second, char))
            }
          }
        }
      }
    }
}
```

You can do the same for the maximum and minimum values of the characters in the generated strings. But a better way to go is to create a modified list generator:

```
class ListGenerator<T>(private val gen: Gen<T>,
                       private val maxLength: Int) : Gen<List<T>> {

    private val random = Random()

    override fun constants(): Iterable<List<T>> =
                    listOf(gen.constants().toList())

    override fun random(): Sequence<List<T>> = generateSequence {
        val size = random.nextInt(maxLength)
        gen.random().take(size).toList()
    }

    override fun shrinker() = ListShrinker<T>()
}
```

This generator can then be used in the generator for strings:

```
fun stringGenerator(maxList: Int,
            maxString: Int): Gen<List<Pair<String, Map<Char, Int>>>> =
    ListGenerator(ListGenerator(Gen.choose(32, 127), maxString), maxList)
        .map { intListList ->
            intListList.asSequence().map { intList ->
                intList.map { n ->
```

```
                    n.toChar()
            }
    }.map { charList ->
            Pair(String(charList.toCharArray()), makeMap(charList))
    }.toList()
}
```

The length of the generated string could be limited by adding a filter to the outside list generator (generating the list of strings), but this would be totally inefficient because only 1/10,000,000 generated strings would pass the filter, so generation would be slow. And furthermore, this kind of filtering would only allow limiting the length of the generated strings, not the length of the list of strings.

Here's how this generator can be used:

```
class SameLettersStringKtTest: StringSpec() {

    init {
        "getCharUsed" {
            forAll(stringGenerator(100, 100)) {
                list: List<Pair<String, Map<Char, Int>>> ->
                getCharUsed(list.map { it.first }).keys.toSet() ==
                        list.asSequence().map { it.second }.toSet()
            }
        }
    }
}
```

Another way to solve the same testing problem is to push abstraction further as you saw in the beginning of this appendix.

B.5.3 *Simplifying the code through further abstraction*

The getCharUsed function already uses two abstractions: the groupBy function and the getCharMap function. This function can, in fact, be further abstracted:

```
// example05
fun getCharUsed(words: List<String>): Map<Map<Char, Int>, List<String>> =
                                        words.groupBy(::getCharMap)

fun getCharMap(s: String): Map<Char, Int> = s.fold(mapOf(), ::updateMap)

fun updateMap(map: Map<Char, Int>, char: Char): Map<Char, Int> =
    when {
        map.containsKey(char) -> map + Pair(char, map[char]!! + 1)
        else -> map + Pair(char, 1)
    }
```

The getCharMap function uses two abstractions. One is the fold function, which doesn't need to be tested, and the other is the updateMap function, which is the only one that needs to be tested. Finding properties to test is easy:

- For any char and map containing this char as a key, getCharMap(map, char) [char] should be equal to map[char] + 1.
- For any char and map not containing this char as a key, getCharMap(map, char) [char] should be equal 1.

- For any `char` and `map`, the result of removing the `char` key from `getCharMap` `(map, char) [char]` and from `map` should be equal. (This property verifies that no other modification is done to the map.)

For this test, you'll need to generate random maps populated with random data. You can write the following `MapGenerator` (generating chars in the `[a..z]` range:

```
// example05 test
fun mapGenerator(min: Char = 'a', max: Char = 'z'): Gen<Map<Char, Int>> =
    Gen.list(Gen.choose(min.toInt(), max.toInt())
                .map(Int::toChar)).map(::makeMap)
```

And you can use it as in the following test:

```
// example05 test
class UpdateMapTest: StringSpec() {

    private val random = Random()

    private val min = 'a'

    private val max = 'z'

    init {
        "getCharUsed" {
            forAll(mapGenerator()) { map: Map<Char, Int> ->
                (random.nextInt(max.toInt() - min.toInt())
                                    + min.toInt()).toChar().let {
                    if (map.containsKey(it)) {
                        updateMap(map, it)[it] == map[it]!! + 1
                    } else {
                        updateMap(map, it)[it] == 1
                    } && updateMap(map, it) - it == map - it
                }
            }
        }
    }
}
```

Notice that the principle of maximum abstraction also applies to tests. One thing that might be abstracted is the generation of each `Char`. The `Gen` interface doesn't offer a `Char` generator, but you can easily create one. And because you might want to generate only some specific characters, you can also abstract the character selection into a separate function:

```
// example06 test
fun charGenerator(p: (Char) -> Boolean): Gen<Char> =
        Gen.choose(0, 255).map(Int::toChar).filter(p)
```

Now you can rewrite your test in a much cleaner way:

```
class UpdateMapTest: StringSpec() {

    init {
        "getCharUsed" {
            forAll(MapGenerator,
            charGenerator(Char::isLetterOrDigit)) {
```

```
                map: Map<Char, Int>, char ->
                    if (map.containsKey(char)) {
                        updateMap(map, char)[char] == map[char]!! + 1
                    } else {
                        updateMap(map, char)[char] == 1
                    }
                    && updateMap(map, char) - char == map - char
            }
        }
    }
}
```

But you can still simplify the code by using a default value for the map. When you query the map for a character which isn't found, the value should be 0. This makes sense because it's the number of occurrences.

Rather than initializing the map with every possible character bound to 0 occurrence, you need to call the getOrDefault function instead, or the [] syntax (which is equivalent to the get function):

```
// example06 test
class UpdateMapTest: StringSpec() {

    init {
        "getCharUsed" {
            forAll(MapGenerator,
                    charGenerator(Char::isLetterOrDigit)) {
                map: Map<Char, Int>, char ->
                updateMap(map, char)[char] == map.getOrDefault(char, 0) + 1
                    && updateMap(map, char) - char == map - char
            }
        }
    }
}
```

Now you've reduced the part to test to the bare minimum and you have setup a powerful way to test the results. By running the test while generating thousands of values on each build, you soon have tested your program with millions of data cases. Because both the main program and the test use the updateMap function, you should probably put it in a common module.

Summary

In this appendix, you've learned how to write effective tests and make your program more testable using property-base testing. You've learned how to

- Devise a set of properties that the result of your program must fulfill
- Write interfaces, then tests, and lastly implementations, so that your tests won't depend on implementation
- Use abstraction to simplify testing by removing parts that you should trust
- Write generators to generate random values for your test along with accompanying data that can be use to check the properties
- Set up tests using thousands of input data and that run before each build

index

Get the eBook FREE!

(PDF, ePub, Kindle, and liveBook all included)

We believe that once you buy a book from us, you should be able to read it in any format we have available. To get electronic versions of this book at no additional cost to you, purchase and then register this book at the Manning website.

Go to https://www.manning.com/freebook and follow the instructions to complete your pBook registration.

That's it!
Thanks from Manning!